Data Preprocessing, Active Learning, and Cost Perceptive Approaches for Resolving Data Imbalance

Dipti P. Rana
Sardar Vallabhbhai National Institute of Technology, Surat, India

Rupa G. Mehta
Sardar Vallabhbhai National Institute of Technology, Surat, India

A volume in the Advances in Data Mining and
Database Management (ADMDM) Book Series

Published in the United States of America by
IGI Global
Engineering Science Reference (an imprint of IGI Global)
701 E. Chocolate Avenue
Hershey PA, USA 17033
Tel: 717-533-8845
Fax: 717-533-8661
E-mail: cust@igi-global.com
Web site: http://www.igi-global.com

Library of Congress Cataloging-in-Publication Data

Names: Rana, Dipti P., 1976- editor. | Mehta, Rupa G., 1967- editor.
Title: Data preprocessing, active learning, and cost perceptive approaches
  for resolving data imbalance / Dipti P. Rana and Rupa G. Mehta, editors.
Description: Hershey, PA : Engineering Science Reference, [2021] | Includes
  bibliographical references and index. | Summary: "This edited book
  provides a selection of chapters to improve the understanding of the
  impact of imbalanced data and its resolving techniques based on the Data
  Preprocessing, Active Learning, and Cost Perceptive Approaches"--
  Provided by publisher.
Identifiers: LCCN 2021004523 (print) | LCCN 2021004524 (ebook) | ISBN
  9781799873716 (h/c) | ISBN 9781799873723 (s/c) | ISBN 9781799873730
  (eISBN)
Subjects: LCSH: Electronic data processing--Data preparation. |
  Verification (Logic)--Data processing. | Data integrity. | Fake news. |
  Fraud investigation. | Web usage mining.
Classification: LCC QA76.9.D345 D387 2021 (print) | LCC QA76.9.D345
  (ebook) | DDC 005.7--dc23
LC record available at https://lccn.loc.gov/2021004523
LC ebook record available at https://lccn.loc.gov/2021004524

This book is published in the IGI Global book series Advances in Data Mining and Database Management (ADMDM)
(ISSN: 2327-1981; eISSN: 2327-199X)

British Cataloguing in Publication Data
A Cataloguing in Publication record for this book is available from the British Library.

All work contributed to this book is new, previously-unpublished material. The views expressed in this book are those of the authors, but not necessarily of the publisher.

For electronic access to this publication, please contact: eresources@igi-global.com.

Advances in Data Mining and Database Management (ADMDM) Book Series

David Taniar
Monash University, Australia

ISSN:2327-1981
EISSN:2327-199X

MISSION

With the large amounts of information available to organizations in today's digital world, there is a need for continual research surrounding emerging methods and tools for collecting, analyzing, and storing data.

The **Advances in Data Mining & Database Management (ADMDM)** series aims to bring together research in information retrieval, data analysis, data warehousing, and related areas in order to become an ideal resource for those working and studying in these fields. IT professionals, software engineers, academicians and upper-level students will find titles within the ADMDM book series particularly useful for staying up-to-date on emerging research, theories, and applications in the fields of data mining and database management.

COVERAGE

- Data Warehousing
- Customer Analytics
- Predictive Analysis
- Enterprise Systems
- Heterogeneous and Distributed Databases
- Database Testing
- Information Extraction
- Profiling Practices
- Data Analysis
- Data Quality

IGI Global is currently accepting manuscripts for publication within this series. To submit a proposal for a volume in this series, please contact our Acquisition Editors at Acquisitions@igi-global.com or visit: http://www.igi-global.com/publish/.

The Advances in Data Mining and Database Management (ADMDM) Book Series (ISSN 2327-1981) is published by IGI Global, 701 E. Chocolate Avenue, Hershey, PA 17033-1240, USA, www.igi-global.com. This series is composed of titles available for purchase individually; each title is edited to be contextually exclusive from any other title within the series. For pricing and ordering information please visit http://www.igi-global.com/book-series/advances-data-mining-database-management/37146. Postmaster: Send all address changes to above address. Copyright © 2021 IGI Global. All rights, including translation in other languages reserved by the publisher. No part of this series may be reproduced or used in any form or by any means – graphics, electronic, or mechanical, including photocopying, recording, taping, or information and retrieval systems – without written permission from the publisher, except for non commercial, educational use, including classroom teaching purposes. The views expressed in this series are those of the authors, but not necessarily of IGI Global.

Titles in this Series

For a list of additional titles in this series, please visit:
http://www.igi-global.com/book-series/advances-data-mining-database-management/37146

Ranked Set Sampling Models and Methods
Carlos N. Bouza-Herrera (Universidad de La Habana, Cuba)
Engineering Science Reference • © 2021 • 305pp • H/C (ISBN: 9781799875567) • US $195.00

Data Science Advancements in Pandemic and Outbreak Management
Eleana Asimakopoulou (Independent Researcher, Greece) and Nik Bessis (Edge Hill University, UK)
Engineering Science Reference • © 2021 • 255pp • H/C (ISBN: 9781799867364) • US $225.00

Industry Use Cases on Blockchain Technology Applications in IoT and the Financial Sector
Zaigham Mahmood (University of Northampton, UK & Shijiazhuang Tiedao University, China)
Engineering Science Reference • © 2021 • 400pp • H/C (ISBN: 9781799866503) • US $245.00

Analyzing Data Through Probabilistic Modeling in Statistics
Dariusz Jacek Jakóbczak (Koszalin University of Technology, Poland)
Engineering Science Reference • © 2021 • 331pp • H/C (ISBN: 9781799847069) • US $225.00

Applications of Big Data in Large- and Small-Scale Systems
Sam Goundar (British University Vietnam, Vietnam) and Praveen Kumar Rayani (National Institute of Technology, Durgapur, India)
Engineering Science Reference • © 2021 • 377pp • H/C (ISBN: 9781799866732) • US $245.00

Developing a Keyword Extractor and Document Classifier Emerging Research and Opportunities
Dimple Valayil Paul (Department of Computer Science, Dnyanprassarak Mandal's College and Research Centre, Goa University, Goa, India)
Engineering Science Reference • © 2021 • 229pp • H/C (ISBN: 9781799837725) • US $195.00

Intelligent Analytics With Advanced Multi-Industry Applications
Zhaohao Sun (Papua New Guinea University of Technology, Papua New Guinea)
Engineering Science Reference • © 2021 • 392pp • H/C (ISBN: 9781799849636) • US $225.00

Handbook of Research on Automated Feature Engineering and Advanced Applications in Data Science
Mrutyunjaya Panda (Utkal University, India) and Harekrishna Misra (Institute of Rural Management, Anand, India)
Engineering Science Reference • © 2021 • 392pp • H/C (ISBN: 9781799866596) • US $285.00

701 East Chocolate Avenue, Hershey, PA 17033, USA
Tel: 717-533-8845 x100 • Fax: 717-533-8661
E-Mail: cust@igi-global.com • www.igi-global.com

Editorial Advisory Board

Table of Contents

Detailed Table of Contents

Chapter 1

Anjali S. More, Sardar Vallabhbhai National Institute of Technology, Surat, India
Dipti P. Rana, Sardar Vallabhbhai National Institute of Technology, Surat, India

In today's era, multifarious data mining applications deal with leading challenges of handling imbalanced data classification and its impact on performance metrics. There is the presence of skewed data distribution in an ample range of existent time applications which engrossed the attention of researchers. Fraud detection in finance, disease diagnosis in medical applications, oil spill detection, pilfering in electricity, anomaly detection and intrusion detection in security, and other real-time applications constitute uneven data distribution. Data imbalance affects classification performance metrics and upturns the error rate. These leading challenges prompted researchers to investigate imbalanced data applications and related machine learning approaches. The intent of this research work is to review a wide variety of imbalanced data applications of skewed data distribution as binary class data unevenness and multiclass data disproportion, the problem encounters, the variety of approaches to resolve the data imbalance, and possible open research areas.

Chapter 2

D. Himaja, Vignan's Foundation for Science, Technology, and Research (Deemed), Guntur, India
T. Maruthi Padmaja, Vardhaman College of Engineering, Hyderabad, India
P. Radha Krishna, National Institute of Technology, Warangal, India

Learning from data streams with both online class imbalance and concept drift (OCI-CD) is receiving much attention in today's world. Due to this problem, the performance is affected for the current models that learn from both stationary as well as non-stationary environments. In the case of non-stationary environments, due to the imbalance, it is hard to spot the concept drift using conventional drift detection methods that aim at tracking the change detection based on the learner's performance. There is limited work on the combined problem from imbalanced evolving streams both from stationary and non-stationary environments. Here the data may be evolved with complete labels or with only limited labels. This chapter's main emphasis is to provide different methods for the purpose of resolving the issue of class imbalance in emerging streams, which involves changing and unchanging environments with supervised and availability of limited labels.

Chapter 3

Vrps Sastry Yadavilli, National Institute of Technology, Tadepalligudem, India
Karthick Seshadri, National Institute of Technology, Tadepalligudem, India

Aspect-level sentiment analysis gives a detailed view of user opinions expressed towards each feature of a product. Aspect extraction is a challenging task in aspect-level sentiment analysis. Hence, several researchers worked on the problem of aspect extraction during the past decade. The authors begin this chapter with a brief introduction to aspect-level sentimental analysis, which covers the definition of key terms used in this chapter, and the authors also illustrate various subtasks of aspect-level sentiment analysis. The introductory section is followed by an explanation of the various feature learning methods like supervised, unsupervised, semi-supervised, etc. with a discussion regarding their merits and demerits. The authors compare the aspect extraction methods performance with respect to metrics and a detailed discussion on the merits and demerits of the approaches. They conclude the chapter with pointers to the unexplored problems in aspect-level sentiment analysis that may be beneficial to the researchers who wish to pursue work in this challenging and mature domain.

Chapter 4

Debapriya Banik, Jadavpur University, India
Debotosh Bhattacharjee, Jadavpur University, India

Medical images mostly suffer from data imbalance problems, which make the disease classification task very difficult. The imbalanced distribution of the data in medical datasets happens when a proportion of a specific type of disease in a dataset appears in a small section of the entire dataset. So analyzing medical datasets with imbalanced data is a significant challenge for the machine learning and deep learning community. A standard classification learning algorithm might be biased towards the majority class and ignore the importance of the minority class (class of interest), which generally leads to the wrong diagnosis of the patients. So, the data imbalance problem in the medical image dataset is of utmost importance for the early prediction of disease, specifically cancer. This chapter attempts to explore different problems concerning data imbalance in medical diagnosis. The authors have discussed different rebalancing strategies that offer guidelines for choosing appropriate optimal procedures to train the samples by a classifier for an efficient medical diagnosis.

Chapter 5

Vaishali S. Tidake, MVPS's KBT College of Engineering, Nashik, India
Shirish S. Sane, K. K. Wagh Institute of Engineering Education and Research, Nashik, India

Usage of feature similarity is expected when the nearest neighbors are to be explored. Examples in multi-label datasets are associated with multiple labels. Hence, the use of label dissimilarity accompanied by feature similarity may reveal better neighbors. Information extracted from such neighbors is explored by devised MLFLD and MLFLD-MAXP algorithms. Among three distance metrics used for computation of label dissimilarity, Hamming distance has shown the most improved performance and hence used for further evaluation. The performance of implemented algorithms is compared with the state-of-the-art MLkNN algorithm. They showed an improvement for some datasets only. This chapter introduces parameters MLE and skew. MLE, skew, along with outlier parameter help to analyze multi-label and imbalanced nature of datasets. Investigation of datasets for various parameters and experimentation explored the need for data preprocessing for removing outliers. It revealed an improvement in the performance of implemented algorithms for all measures, and effectiveness is empirically validated.

Chapter 6
Praveen Kumar Maduri, Galgotias College of Engineering and Technology, India
Tushar Biswas, Galgotias College of Engineering and Technology, India
Preeti Dhiman, Galgotias College of Engineering and Technology, India
Apurva Soni, Galgotias College of Engineering and Technology, India
Kushagra Singh, Galgotias College of Engineering and Technology, India

Plants play a significant role in everyone's life. They provide us essential elements like food, oxygen, and shelter, so plants must be supervised and nurtured properly. During cultivation, crops are prone to different kinds of diseases which can severely damage the whole yield leading to financial losses for farmers. In last 10 years, researchers have used different machine learning techniques to detect the disease on plants, but either the methods were not efficient enough to be implemented or were not able to cover the wide area in which plant diseases can be detected. So, the author has introduced a method which is efficient enough to easily detect plant disease and can be implemented in large fields. The author has used a combination of CNN and k-means clustering algorithms. By using this method, crops disease is detected by analyzing the leaves, which notifies users for action in the initial stage. Thus, the proposed method prevents whole crops from getting damaged and saves time and energy of farmers as disease will be identified way before a human eye can detect it on a large farm.

Chapter 7
Apurbalal Senapati, Central Institute of Technology, Kokrajhar, India
Soumen Maji, Central Institute of Technology, Kokrajhar, India
Arunendu Mondal, Central Institute of Technology, Kokrajhar, India

To control the spread of COVID-19, around the world, many countries imposed lockdowns. Numerous studies were reported on COVID-19 in different disciplines with various aspects. The doubling time is a mathematical technique to estimate the current rate of spread of the disease. Researchers used the doubling technique to address the COVID-19 pandemic situation. The larger doubling period represents a low spreading rate, whereas the smaller doubling period represents a high spreading rate. In other words, high infection implies the low doubling period and low infection implies the high doubling period. So, there is an inverse relationship between doubling time and the infection rate. But the real-life data does not follow such a rule properly in various domains. The data shows that after a certain time when the infection is high, the doubling period is also high, which misleads our general concept of doubling time. This chapter addressed this issue by investigating the real-time COVID-19 data. To overcome this limitation, a gradient smoothing technique has been proposed.

Chapter 8
Bharat Tidke, Sardar Vallabhbhai National Institute of Technology, Surat, India
Swati Tidke, College of Engineering, Pune, India

In this age of the internet, no person wants to make his decision on his own. Be it for purchasing a product, watching a movie, reading a book, a person looks out for reviews. People are unaware of the fact that these reviews may not always be true. It is the age of paid reviews, where the reviews are not just written to promote one's product but also to demote a competitor's product. But the ones which are turning out to be the most critical are given on brand of a certain product. This chapter proposed a novel approach for brand spam detection using feature correlation to improve state-of-the-art approaches. Correlation-based feature engineering is considered as one of the finest methods for determining the relations among the features. Several features attached with reviews are important, keeping in focus customer and company needs in making strong decisions, user for purchasing, and company for improving sales and services. Due to severe spamming these days, it has become nearly impossible to judge whether the given review is a trusted or a fake review.

Chapter 9
   Isha Y. Agarwal, Sardar Vallabhbhai National Institute of Technology, Surat, India
   Dipti P. Rana, Sardar Vallabhbhai National Institute of Technology, Surat, India
   Devanshi Bhatia, Sardar Vallabhbhai National Institute of Technology, Surat, India
   Jay Rathod, Sardar Vallabhbhai National Institute of Technology, Surat, India
   Kaneesha J. Gandhi, Sardar Vallabhbhai National Institute of Technology, Surat, India
   Harshit Sodagar, Sardar Vallabhbhai National Institute of Technology, Surat, India

Social media has completely transformed the way people communicate. However, every revolution brings with it some negative impacts. Due to its popularity amongst tons of global users, these platforms have a huge volume of data. The ease of access with minimal verification of new users on social media has led to the creation of the bot accounts used to collect private data, spread false and harmful content, and also poses many security threats. A lot of concerns have been raised with the increment in the quantity of bot accounts on different social media platforms. Also there is a high imbalance between bot and non-bot accounts where the imbalance is a result of 'normal behavior' of bot users. The research aims at identifying the artificial bots accounts on Twitter using various machine learning algorithms and content-based classification based on features provided on the platform and recent tweets of users respectively.

Chapter 10
   Isha Y. Agarwal, Sardar Vallabhbhai National Institute of Technology, Surat, India
   Dipti P. Rana, Sardar Vallabhbhai National Institute of Technology, Surat, India
   Kshitij R. Suri, Sardar Vallabhbhai National Institute of Technology, Surat, India
   Punitkumar Jain, Sardar Vallabhbhai National Institute of Technology, Surat, India
   Saumya Awasthi, Sardar Vallabhbhai National Institute of Technology, Surat, India
   Krittika Roy, Sardar Vallabhbhai National Institute of Technology, Surat, India

Mental health is a major issue in our society, and people treat this issue as a subject that should not be spoken about. So, many such individuals utilize social media as a platform to share their thoughts and fears. This emphasizes the researchers to identify sufferers who require treatment. Many approaches have been devised to detect early markers of mental health illness, some of which include learning algorithms based on the heuristic of equally distributed balanced data. However, they yield biased results towards the majority data (i.e., normal behaviour). Thus, new perception is needed to explore the available data. This research deals with the first identification of such users from weblog data, and the similarity-based sampled data is then given to the classifier. The experiment analysis shows the effectiveness of this work and will provide the user's mental state information early to take timely necessary steps.

 Isha Y. Agarwal, Sardar Vallabhbhai National Institute of Technology, Surat, India
 Dipti P. Rana, Sardar Vallabhbhai National Institute of Technology, Surat, India

Fake news has grabbed attention lately. In this chapter, the issue is tackled from the point of view of collection of quality data (i.e., instances of fake and real news articles on a balanced distribution of subjects). It is predicted that in the near future, fake news will supersede true news. In the media ecosystem this will create a natural imbalance of data. Due to the unbounded scale and imbalance existence of data, detection of fake news is challenging. The class imbalance problem in fake news is yet to be explored. The problem of imbalance exists as fake news instances increase in some cases more than real news. The goal of this chapter is to demonstrate the effect of class imbalance of real and fake news instances on detection using classification models. This work aims to assist researchers to better resolve the problem by illustrating the precise existence of the relationship between the imbalance and the resulting impact on the output of the classifier. In particular, the authors determine that data imbalance and accuracy are inversely proportional to each other.

 Shivani Vasantbhai Vora, CGPIT, Uka Tarsadia University, Bardoli, India
 Rupa G. Mehta, Sardar Vallabhbhai National Institute of Technology, Surat, India
 Shreyas Kishorkumar Patel, Sardar Vallabhbhai National Institute of Technology, Surat,
  India

Continuously growing technology enhances creativity and simplifies humans' lives and offers the possibility to anticipate and satisfy their unmet needs. Understanding emotions is a crucial part of human behavior. Machines must deeply understand emotions to be able to predict human needs. Most tweets have sentiments of the user. It inherits the imbalanced class distribution. Most machine learning (ML) algorithms are likely to get biased towards the majority classes. The imbalanced distribution of classes gained extensive attention as it has produced many research challenges. It demands efficient approaches to handle the imbalanced data set. Strategies used for balancing the distribution of classes in the case study are handling redundant data, resampling training data, and data augmentation. Six methods related to these techniques have been examined in a case study. Upon conducting experiments on the Twitter dataset, it is seen that merging minority classes and shuffle sentence methods outperform other techniques.

 Jenish Dhanani, Sardar Vallabhbhai National Institute of Technology, Surat, India
 Rupa G. Mehta, Sardar Vallabhbhai National Institute of Technology, Surat, India
 Dipti P. Rana, Sardar Vallabhbhai National Institute of Technology, Surat, India
 Rahul Lad, Sardar Vallabhbhai National Institute of Technology, Surat, India
 Amogh Agrawal, Sardar Vallabhbhai National Institute of Technology, Surat, India
 Karan Chevli, Sardar Vallabhbhai National Institute of Technology, Surat, India
 Jashwanth Gummula Reddy, Sardar Vallabhbhai National Institute of Technology, Surat, India

Recently, legal information retrieval has emerged as an essential practice for the legal fraternity. In the legal domain, judgment is a specific kind of legal document, which discusses case-related information and the verdict of a court case. In the common law system, the legal professionals exploit relevant judgments to prepare arguments. Hence, an automated system is a vital demand to identify similar judgments effectively. The judgments can be broadly categorized into civil and criminal cases, where judgments with similar case matters can have strong relevance compared to judgments with different case matters. In similar judgment identification, categorized judgments can significantly prune search space by restrictive search within a specific case category. So, this chapter provides a novel methodology that classifies Indian judgments in either of the case matter. Crucial challenges like imbalance and intrinsic characteristics of legal data are also highlighted specific to similarity analysis of Indian judgments, which can be a motivating aspect to the research community.

Chapter 14

Mitali Desai, Sardar Vallabhbhai National Institute of Technology, Surat, India
Rupa G. Mehta, Sardar Vallabhbhai National Institute of Technology, Surat, India
Dipti P. Rana, Sardar Vallabhbhai National Institute of Technology, Surat, India

Data imbalance is a key challenge in the majority of real-world classification problems. It refers to the disparity of data instances corresponding to either of the class labels. Data imbalance is studied in detail with respect to many data domains such as transaction data, medical data, e-commerce data, meteorological data, social media data, and web data. But the scholarly data domain is yet to be analyzed pertaining to data imbalance. In this chapter, the scholarly data domain is explored with a focus to study various forms of data imbalance. A well-known and popular scholarly platform, ResearchGate (RG), is targeted to extract real scholarly data. An extensive experimental analysis is performed on the extracted data in order to identify the existence of both data-level and network-level imbalance. The outcome contributes to the learning of various types of data imbalance that exist in scholarly data. Resolving the existing data imbalance will substantially help in achieving efficient and accurate outcomes in many real-world scholarly literature applications.

Chapter 15

Dipti P. Rana, Sardar Vallabhbhai National Institute of Technology, Surat, India
Navodita Saini, Sardar Vallabhbhai National Institute of Technology, Surat, India

Each gender is having special personality and behavior characteristics that can be naturally reflected in the language used on social media to review, spread information, make relationships, etc. This information is used by different agencies for their profits. The magnified study of this information can reflect the implicit biases of their creators' gender. The ratio of gender is imbalanced across the global world, social media, discussion, etc. Twitter is used to discuss the issues caused by COVID-19 disease like its symptoms, mental health, advice, etc. This fascinating information motivated this research to propose the methodology gender-based tweet analysis (GTA) to study and magnify gender's impact on emotions of tweet data. The analysis of the experiment discovered the biases of gender on emotions of tweet data and highlighted the future real-world applications which may become more productive if gender biases are considered for the safety and benefit of society.

Preface

Data deluges our lives. Data should be decomposed, processed, and transformed into knowledge that is suitable for human use and generate a powerful entity that drives productive activities as well as makes crucial decisions. Machine learning and data mining approaches are based on the heuristic of equally distributed balanced data and provide the biased result towards the majority data class, which is not acceptable considering imbalanced data is omnipresent in real life scenarios of health data, social media, environment, weather, marketing, news, legal domain, scholarly platform, finance, etc. The number of instances for a given problem which follow a different distribution for labels leads to the imbalanced data problem. The major challenge for the imbalanced data classification is the preprocessing and the cost-effective training of the minority class labels into the final model which attracts the researchers' community. Due to the multifaceted and demand of new perception for imbalanced data, there is a need for efficient learners which can learn from imbalanced data for fool proof application model using the novelty at sampling approach of data pre-processing, an active learning approach, and a cost perceptive approach to resolve data imbalance.

Data Preprocessing, Active Learning, and Cost Perceptive Approaches for Resolving Data Imbalance offers new aspects for imbalanced data learning by providing the advancements of the traditional methods, with respect to variety of application domains, through case studies and research from experts in academia and engineering. The chapters provide theoretical frameworks and latest empirical research findings that help to improve the understanding of the impact of imbalanced data and its resolving techniques based on data pre-processing, active learning, and cost perceptive approaches. This book is ideal for data scientists, data analysts, developers, engineers who want to design imbalance learning techniques to solve different real-world problems. Also, this book will be useful for researchers, academicians, and students looking for comprehensive review of solution approaches for learning from imbalanced data.

ORGANIZATION OF THE BOOK

The book is organized into 15 chapters written by researchers, scholars and professors from prestigious educational institutions. A brief description of each of the chapters follows:

Chapter 1 deals with leading challenges of handling imbalanced data classification and its impact on performance metrics of multifarious data mining applications in today's era. There is the presence of skewed data distribution in an ample range of existent time applications which engrossed the attention of researchers. The survey reviewed by authors for a wide variety of imbalanced data applications of skewed data distribution as binary class data unevenness and multiclass data disproportion, the problem encountered, the variety of approaches to resolve the data imbalance and possible open research area.

Chapter 2 draws attention to today's world problem of learning from data streams with both Online Class Imbalance and Concept Drift (OCI-CD). Due to these problems, the performance is affected for the current models that learn from both stationary as well as non-stationary environments. The authors' main emphasis is to provide different methods for the purpose of resolving the issue of class imbalance in emerging streams, which involves changing and unchanging environments with supervised and availability of limited labels.

Chapter 3 attempts to aspect extraction which is an imbalanced classification problem as the distribution of product aspects over all user opinion sentences is not uniform as the users tend to specify few aspects very frequently in review sentences and leaving some infrequent but popular aspects. To extract implicit aspects requires extensive domain knowledge and aspect level sentiment analysis can provide a detailed view of user opinions expressed towards each feature of a product. This challenging task introduced by the authors and also pointed to the unexplored problems in aspect level sentiment analysis to the researchers.

Chapter 4 identifies the difficulty caused in the disease classification task from the medical images which mostly suffer from data imbalance problems as a specific type of disease in a dataset appears in a small section of the entire dataset. So analyzing medical datasets with imbalanced data is a significant challenge for the machine learning and deep learning community to avoid the wrong diagnosis of the patients and the early prediction of disease. The authors discuss different rebalancing strategies that offer guidelines for choosing appropriate optimal procedures to train the samples by a classifier for an efficient medical diagnosis.

Chapter 5 reviews the outliers' existence that affects the performance of existing algorithms for classification of multi-label datasets. The authors worked on label dissimilarity together with feature similarity for better revealing of neighbors for multi-label datasets. Information extracted from such neighbors is further explored by authors by devising MLFLD and MLFLD-MAXP algorithms. Out of three distance metrics found that Hamming distance showed the most improved performance for computation of label dissimilarity and used further. The performance of both algorithms is compared with the state-of-the-art MLkNN algorithm.

Chapter 6 draws attention required to detect imbalance data problems of disease in plants as plants play a significant role in everyone's life. Researchers have used different machine learning techniques to detect the disease on plants but either the methods were not efficient enough to be implemented or were not able to cover the wide area in which plant diseases can be detected. So, the author has introduced a method which is efficient enough to easily detect plant disease in large fields and prevents the whole crop from getting damaged and saves time and energy of farmers as disease will be identified way before a human eye can detect it.

Chapter 7 addresses the pandemic problem of COVID-19 prevalent on the globe. Researchers use the doubling technique to address the spread of disease. High infection implies the low doubling period and low infection implies the high doubling period. So, there is an inverse relationship between doubling time and the infection rate which is not followed by the real-life data of pandemic situation. The data shows that after a certain time when the infection is high the doubling period is also high, which misleads the general concept of doubling time. The authors proposed a gradient smoothing technique to overcome this limitation on the real-time COVID-19 data.

Chapter 8 discusses the spam detection from the product reviews as nowadays the spam review is becoming business to harm the opposite company sales. The spam reviews are less in quantity and it is nearly impossible to judge whether the given review is a trusted or a fake review making it a problem of imbalance data. The chapter proposes a novel approach for brand spam detection using feature correlation to improve state-of-the-art approaches and to improve the purchase of user and sales and service of company.

Chapter 9 aims at identifying the artificial bots accounts on different social media platforms as there is a raise in the quantity of bot accounts. There is a high imbalance between bot and non-bot accounts and the imbalance is a result of 'normal behavior' of bot users. The authors utilized the machine learning algorithms on features provided on the platform and content-based classification on recent tweets of users to identify the bot accounts effectively.

Chapter 10 deals with the mental health a major issue of our society as now individuals having this issue and they utilize social media as a platform to share their thoughts and fear. The social media data shared by the people who are facing mental illness is very imbalance compared to data of normal behaivour people. Thus, according to the authors, new perception is needed to explore the data and proposed the identification of users with suspicious behaviour from log data and then using similarity-based sampling of social media data.

Chapter 11 views the problem of Fake News from the point of view of collection of quality data, i.e. instances of fake and real news articles on a balanced distribution of subjects. The authors aim to resolve the problem by illustrating the precise existence of the relationship of imbalance fake news in the real news and the resulting impact on the classifier result. It determines that data imbalance and accuracy are inversely proportional to each other and the result of classifier can be improvised with the help of sampling the news data.

Chapter 12 highlights that tweets have sentiments of the user and which inherits the imbalanced class distribution of emotions. Thus, the emotion analysis of twitter data demands efficient approaches. The authors used strategies for balancing the distribution of classes by handling redundant data, resampling training data, and data augmentation and experiments depicted that merging minority classes and shuffle sentence methods outperform other state-of-art techniques.

Chapter 13 provides a novel angle to classify the judgments of the Legal domain. Judgment is a specific kind of legal document, which discusses case-related information and the verdict of a court case and broadly categorized into Civil and Criminal cases. The judgments with similar case matters can have strong relevance compared to judgments with different case matters. The legal professionals exploit relevant judgments to prepare arguments. But, there are crucial challenges like imbalance and intrinsic characteristics of Legal data which are highlighted specific to similarity analysis of Indian judgments.

Chapter 14 contributes to the learning of various types of data imbalance that exist in scholarly data. Scholarly data domain is yet to be analyzed pertaining to data imbalance. In this chapter, the scholarly data domain is explored with a focus to study various forms of data imbalance. A well-known and popular scholarly platform ResearchGate (RG) is targeted to extract real scholarly data. An extensive experimental analysis is performed on the extracted data and identified the existence of both data-level and network-level imbalance.

Chapter 15 discusses the presence of different gender participation on social media to opine for the different topics which are utilized by many applications further to make crucial decisions. As the data provider did not provide the data about account holder gender because of privacy and thus bias and discrimination influence the systems in terms of time, money, and often with the people lives. The authors analyzed the tweets for the varying emotions from the gender perspective and provided a new direction to the researchers to think of.

This book can be used as reference or textbook for graduate and higher-level courses in machine learning, data mining, and pattern recognition, to name a few. We are thankful to all contributors who contributed the cutting-edge research for the book. We wish our sincere thanks to all our editorial board members without whom this book cannot be initiated and also to review the chapters from their busy schedule. We are thankful to the reviewers who reviewed and helped to refine the content to prepare the book with concrete context. We are thankful to the members of our research group who contributed in the publicity of the book and attracted the contributors of the book. We are also thankful to our families for their silent support. We also like to thank Jan Travers and Maria Rohde of IGI Global for their timely support, valuable suggestions, and encouragement during the entire development stage of this book.

Dipti P. Rana
Sardar Vallabhbhai National Institute of Technology, Surat, India

Rupa G. Mehta
Sardar Vallabhbhai National Institute of Technology, Surat, India

Chapter 1
Review of Imbalanced Data Classification and Approaches Relating to Real-Time Applications

Anjali S. More

Sardar Vallabhbhai National Institute of Technology, Surat, India

Dipti P. Rana

https://orcid.org/0000-0002-5058-1355

Sardar Vallabhbhai National Institute of Technology, Surat, India

ABSTRACT

In today's era, multifarious data mining applications deal with leading challenges of handling imbalanced data classification and its impact on performance metrics. There is the presence of skewed data distribution in an ample range of existent time applications which engrossed the attention of researchers. Fraud detection in finance, disease diagnosis in medical applications, oil spill detection, pilfering in electricity, anomaly detection and intrusion detection in security, and other real-time applications constitute uneven data distribution. Data imbalance affects classification performance metrics and upturns the error rate. These leading challenges prompted researchers to investigate imbalanced data applications and related machine learning approaches. The intent of this research work is to review a wide variety of imbalanced data applications of skewed data distribution as binary class data unevenness and multiclass data disproportion, the problem encounters, the variety of approaches to resolve the data imbalance, and possible open research areas.

DOI: 10.4018/978-1-7998-7371-6.ch001

INTRODUCTION

Data cataloging into specific classes is one of the foremost techniques in the domain of machine learning and mining with the heuristics of balanced dataset i.e. the data is equally distributed among the classes. This heuristic is not true in the existent world applications and the majority of the related applications are having imbalanced dataset where data is skewed towards one class or more than one classes. The imbalanced nature of data is having their own importance, one cannot neglect them. Thus, many researchers are motivated to deal with imbalanced classification for real-life applications. There is an incessant growth of instances of data availability in many application eras such as finance, health care, computer network system, security, internet of things, etc. where it is very much essential to advance the primary perceptive of knowledge discovery and data analysis to take the critical decision.

Nowadays, though there is existence of data discovery techniques, imbalanced data applications relating to real-life scenarios have shown the great attraction to the researchers to focus on imbalanced applications and review the problems occurred due to data unevenness. The individuals working in industry as well as academia gets attracted towards diverted data applications as review in the survey section by Alberto Fernández et al. (2009).

Several realistic application areas deal with the handling of uneven data representation, the minority instance class gets ignored due to the majority instance class. Unequal data distribution leans performance metrics towards the majority class. The review study in this research focuses on the most important application categories of imbalanced data distribution as binary class imbalance and multiclass data imbalance. To deal with the promising issues arising from class imbalance this study presents a review of imbalanced data applications, imbalanced data categories, problems encountered due to this characteristic, and the methodologies to deal with distorted data relating to real-life applications.

BACKGROUND

Classification is the most popular technique to correctly classify an instance with unknown class. Many real-world data sets show evidence of unequal class distributions in which maximum data samples are belonging to one of the larger class and far fewer data instances are falling into minority class. In case of medical diagnosis example, which consist of the cases that relates to diagnosis for a rare disease. For the referred example, only 2% of the patients are positive diagnosis and 98% diagnosis as negative. Dealing with such imbalanced datasets and related classification generates the need of machine learning algorithms. In current time the data diverted applications are relating to binary as well as multiclass data imbalance. In both category of imbalanced class either of one class having maximum instance and which diverts the performance towards majority class, i.e. performance is leaned towards majority class. The traditional classifiers reveal accurate forecast for the majority instance class and diversify the performance in case of minority data sample class. The cost of misclassification an imbalanced class can be harmful for the real world application like disease diagnostics. Thus, in today's era, Stefan Lessmann (2014) and Rebeen A. H., Masashi K. & Jens L (2020) show imbalanced data applications have received considerable attention from the research community to further boost their performance by numerous machine learning algorithms. Lars W. Jochumsen et al. (2016), Nahit Emanet et al. (2014), explained in the study that there are diverse approaches to tackle the trouble of extremely imbalanced data applications. In particular, the study deals with the description of preprocessing, cost-sensitive learning, Support Vector

Machine (SVM), Artificial Neural Network (ANN), Fuzzy Rule (FR), Decision Tree Classifier (DTC), Ensemble Techniques and the review of other data level and algorithm level techniques. The proposed research work looks at the major aim to resolve data discrepancy and deal with real-life scenarios to provide the detailed survey of last two decades to review the possible open research area.

MAIN FOCUS OF THE CHAPTER

Omni presence of imbalanced data in each and every real time applications, affects the application's result severely, this chapter mainly focuses on the following:

1. The research study aims to review imbalanced data characteristics which create a measurable impact on the performance rate of classification.
2. This study emphasizes key categories of data imbalance to deal with uneven data distribution applications.
3. The imbalance data highlights the problems which may encounter, if not handled properly.
4. The possible categories of approaches according to the level of solution.
5. The subsequent intention of the proposed chapter is to highlight the detailed literature of imbalanced data application in two decades ranging from 2000 to current time 2020 and best suitable conventional classifiers from the variety of classifiers such as Decision Tree (DT), Support Vector Machine (SVM), K Nearest Neighbor (KNN), Random Forest (RF), and other invented hybrid approaches for escalating heftiness of diverted classification.
6. The research provides the open research area direction to resolve data imbalance.

Imbalanced Data Characteristics

Due to the nature of application, there are many imbalanced data characteristics available as described in the following section.

Lack of Data Density

In disproportionate data applications, the classes having less number of instances are considered as a lack of data density classes. Comparatively less number of available data instances and corresponding missing information are ignored and leans towards diminution in accuracy rate.

Unequal Data Distribution among Class/Classes

As listed above there is an extensive variety of real-time imbalanced data applications in this current age. Binary, as well as multiclass imbalanced applications dealing with majority class (maximum instance class) and minority (less instance class); will affect the performance of classification.

Presence of Noise in Dataset

Unwanted data sample generation is referred to as noise in data classification. Noise will create a major upshot on minority class as compare to majority data sample class. While dealing with classification, noisy data samples affect the inherent features of the datasets. Unwanted noisy samples create new properties in datasets. Data segregation boundaries may get affected due to noisy sample generation.

BALALNCED DATA VS DATA IMBALALNCE

Balanced Data

The dataset which deals with equal data instance distribution among classes is referred to as Balanced Dataset (BD). In the case of BD Classification, there are no chances of diversion of performance metrics.

Sample Case Scenario

Consider the distribution of players in the game as an example of BD.

Figure 1. Balanced data classification

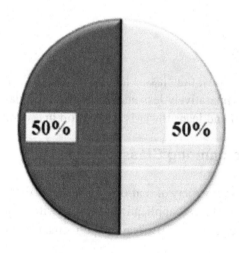

Distribution of Players in Game

⊔ Team A   ▦ Team B

If there are two teams in a game playing one versus another then there is an equal team member in both teams. As depicted in Figure 1 Team A and Team B deal with equal distribution of players.

Imbalanced Data

Data imbalance has two major categories as Binary Imbalanced Data (BImD) and Multiclass Imbalanced Data (MImD).

Sample Case Scenario

While discussing the data imbalanced application, consider the medical diagnosis of patients.

Figure 2. Imbalanced data classification

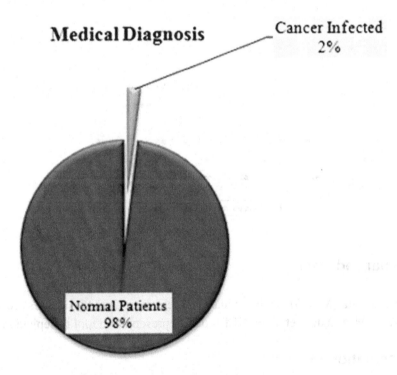

As depicted in Figure 2 only 2% of patients are cancer disease infected and 98% are normal patients. This category of data imbalance is referred to as BImD.

Binary Imbalanced Data

In Binary Imbalanced Data (BImD), one of the class deals with maximum data instances belonging to class category 1 (Majority Class) and another class deals with less number of data instances belonging to class category 2 (Minority Class).

Sample Representation of BImD

Figure 3 indicates Binary Imbalanced Class (BImD) data representation of Haberman dataset using KEEL data representation tool. Here, the x-axis shows the patient age, y-axis shows the year of operation and the class label is positive, if patient is survived and negative, if patient is not survived. As the figure indicates there is an uneven data distribution among the positive and negative classes.

Figure 3. Binary imbalanced class example (Haberman) data representation

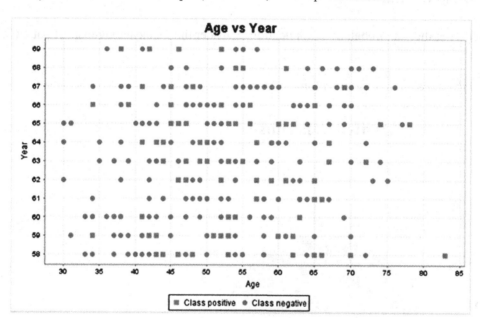

Multiclass Imbalanced Data

Multiclass Imbalanced Data (MImD) is the imbalance where more than two classes are available. Data representation of Wine MImD dataset using KEEL data representation tool is depicted in Figure 4.

Sample Representation of MImD

As the Figure 4 indicates there is an uneven data distribution among multiple classes as indicated Class 1 (Red data samples), Class2 (Blue data samples), and Class3 (Green data samples).

Between Class and Within Class Data Imbalance

Diverted data classification deals with numerous categories of the presence of data imbalance. Two major categories are focused on in this chapter as shown in Figure 5.

Figure 5 part (a) indicates between class data imbalance and Figure 5 part (b) represents between class data imbalance and within-class data imbalance N. Japkowicz (2001).

Figure 4. Multiclass imbalanced example (Wine) data representation

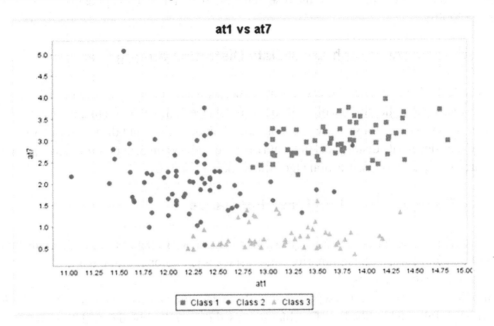

Categorization of Data Imbalance

The real time applications have variety of data for the different and unique purpose. This section defines the variety of data imbalance categories to understand the causal of the data imbalance.

Imbalance Category I: Distorted Construction of Data Samples within Binary Class imbalance

While dealing with the binary data imbalance classification problem, there are two patchy classes as majority (outnumbered data instance class) and minority data instance class. Global construction of majority and minority classes generates challenges in classification. If the classes are overlapping with each other, there is uncertainty in class; outlier and infrequent data classes degrade the performance

Figure 5. Balanced and imbalanced data classification sample example

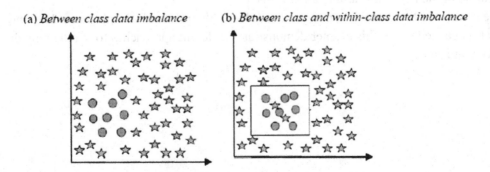

which motivated authors to investigate the research towards imbalanced application (Lars et al. (2016) Sun Y.et al (2009)).

Imbalance Category II: High-Level Data Distortion among Classes

Another key feature that diverts the classification performance is high-level data distortion between classes. Current age applications with high data imbalance ratios are fluctuating from 2:99, 2:998, 2:9998, etc. As an instance, in security applications, fraud detection, and disease diagnosis there is the existence of high-level data distortion. High data diversion effects on data preprocessing and eventually, it will create an impact on classification algorithms Akila et al. (2016).

Imbalance Category III: Within Class Imbalance

While dealing with distorted data applications, there is presence of data imbalance within class. In this category of data imbalance, either minority class instances get ignored or the majority instance class is more focused in many scenarios.

The problems occurred due to the presence of these data imbalance are mentioned in the following section which is followed by the list of problems caused due to the imbalance data nature, the categorization of approaches to deal these and detailed literature review of imbalanced data applications to resolve the data imbalance.

PROBLEMS ENCOUNTERED DUE TO DATA IMBALANCE

The disproportion of data instances among classes diverts the poverty inaccuracy rate. These major challenges fascinated researchers to review imbalance data applications and their related performance improvising machine learning approaches. The focal intent to study is to review the data balancing approaches and other techniques to increase the ease to deal with diverted data instance application and improve the classification performance metrics. Figure 6 highlights major problems encountered due to Data Imbalance. There are numerous challenges due to BImD and MImD as depicted in Figure 6.

Some of them are incorporation of class voting, diversion of performance metrics due to majority class, augmented misclassification rate, generation of novel class, data inequity problem, generation of error code, infinite inhabitants of data and data attribute selections, etc. The researchers are working to resolve these problems through the up-gradation of existing algorithms, data sampling techniques, and hybridization of the machine learning algorithms.

To deal with the listed problem that occurred due to the presence of imbalance data, the literature investigation carried out in this chapter demonstrates different approaches to handle data diversion at three different levels.

LEVEL OF APPROACHES TO RESOLVE DATA IMBALANCE

To resolve the data imbalance, researchers are looking for the solution mostly by changing the distribution of data as part of pre processing or by changing the machine learning approach itself or by combining both data and machine learning approach as per the suitability of the imbalanced data of the applications.

Level 1: Data Level Approaches

Data Level Approaches (DLA) deal with data balancing at the data level. As an instance, it deals with throwing out unwanted data instances from the majority instance class to acquire data balance through the Under Sampling (US) mechanism (Ankilash V. Chawla and Kevin W. Bowyer (2002). Another data level approach is Over Sampling (OS) which increases the data instances through synthetic data instance generation or Random Oversampling (Anjali S. More and Dipti P. Rana (2020)), etc. Advanced data level approaches deal with dynamic US or OS techniques (Lars et al. (2016)).

Figure 6. Problems encountered due to data imbalance

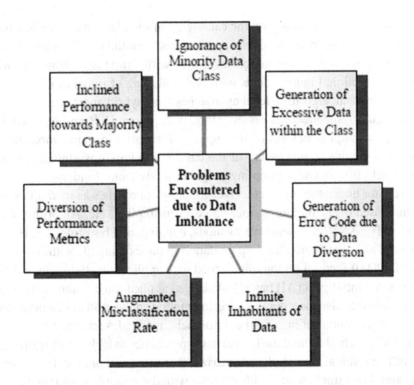

Level 2: Algorithmic Approaches

Algorithmic Approaches (AA) emphasize to propose novel algorithm or to elaborate on the up-gradation of existing algorithms which lighten the biased performance measures and helps to advance the classification precision rate (Nahit et al. (2014)).

Level 3: Hybridization Approaches

A more vibrant and progressive approach belongs to Hybridization Approach (HA) which will work with the collaboration of level 1 (DLA) and level 2 (AA) approaches. First hybrid approach offered by (Estabrooks and Japkowicz) (2001). The hybridization approach dynamically handles skewed data balancing with an upgraded algorithm and it is the choice of researchers to combine the data level approach and algorithm level approach as hybrid approach.

LITERATURE REVIEW OF APPROACHES TO DEAL WITH IMBALANCED DATASET

The research study in this chapter deals with the cataloging of imbalanced dataset handling approaches listed through literature review imbalanced data applications from the last 20 years' time span (2000 to 2020). It indicates there are three broad categories to deal with BImD and MImD of different types as described in the above section. Figure 7 deals with the cataloging of imbalanced dataset handling approach as data level approach, algorithm level approaches, and hybrid approaches.

As indicated in Figure 7, the literature review More, A. S., Rana, D. P. and Agarwal, I., (2018) dealt with numerous data level approaches as down sampling of majority instance imbalanced class and up scaling of minority class with preprocessing of the dataset, random, unsystematic, instructive under-sampling, one-sided selection for under-sampling, neighborhood cleaning under-sampling, the condensed nearest neighbor rule for under-sampling, etc. Oversampling approaches as random oversampling with replacement, radial-based oversampling, kernel-based oversampling, etc. Algorithm level approaches to deal with SVM, DTC, ANN, cost-sensitive methods, bagging, and boosting, etc. Hybrid approaches incorporate data level and algorithmic level up gradation in the existing algorithms.

Japkowicz et al. (2000) focused on the imbalanced data application study which deals with binary and multiclass Artificial Intelligent (AI) based Imbalanced application domain study, significance, and dealing strategies. The study also incorporates experimentation analysis on imbalanced data applications relating to finance, telecommunication, smart environment, medical, security, etc.

Estabrooks et al. (2001) highlighted the hybrid data approaches to tackle highly imbalanced applications in the area of text mining. This study summarizes that data level approaches under sampling and oversampling are simple for implementation but tuning with data sampling approaches is not an effortless job. Estabrooks et al. presented an experimental analysis with a blend of resampling approaches in a combination of experts' framework. This blended approach works superior to tackle uneven data distribution applications. Ankilash V. Chawla et al. (2002) suggested both category BImD and MImD applications in the era of social, finance, telecommunication, smart environment, medical, security, etc. with the incorporation of Artificial Minority Class Oversampling Technique to balance imbalanced datasets and deal with the classification.

Francisco Azuaje et al. (2003) studied and presented the predictive eminence assessment of bi-molecular data classifiers. The experimental study highlighted here deals with the data instance size, related re-sampling techniques and the amount of train-test data experimentation. This study suggested implementing data resampling according to the complexity of the prediction based on conventional and most feasible performance metrics evaluation is obtained by applying numerous methods.

The Authors Andrew Estabrooks et al. (2004), Sotiris Kotsiantis et al. (2005) and Sotiris Kotsiantis et al. (2006) highlighted the real life imbalanced applications belonging to both the categories BImD and MImD. Andrew Estabrooks et al. studied current age imbalanced scenarios dealing with multiple sampling approaches for classification in the era of computational intelligence. Sotiris Kotsiantis et al. focused intrusion detection, security social, finance, telecommunication, smart environment, medical, etc. with the amalgamation of Machine Learning Methodologies (MLM).

Sotiris Kotsiantis et al. (2006) utilized Support Vector Machine (SVM) classification for smart environment, medical, security, etc. diverted data applications. The main motto is to partition the data and apply SVM for classification. Subsequent section of this chapter deals with categorization of machine learning algorithms used for imbalanced data classification. In the year 2007, Eyda Ertekin et al. (2007) used borderline algorithm and oversampling approaches for dealing with finance, healthcare, social, etc. applications.

Maciej A. Mazurowskia et al. (2008) focused on Imbalanced medical decision making applications dealing with implementation of Neural Network Training (NNT) algorithm. The author Mahbod Tavallaee et al. (2009) elaborated the binary class anomaly detection applications in the security and intrusion detection domain with machine learning algorithms.

Dimitrios Gounaridis et al. (2010) diverted data semi-automated classification using Random Forests classification is focused for agriculture related binary class datasets. Highly skewed data applications relating to real life dependent on SVM etc. are focused and by Yang Liu et al. (2011) in the social, finance, telecommunication, etc. domain. Chunkai Zhang et al. (2012) highlighted study of targeted classification related to medical BImD.

The author, Victoria López et al. (2013) described the study related to the experimentation details of medicine, telecommunications, finance, ecology, biology, binary application domains which deals with within data imbalance dataset with characteristics as data intrinsic and data disjoint. Jia Pengfei et al. (2014) focused Marketing model to diagnose the breast cancer infected patients, credit card applications in the security, medical domain with the use of numerous classification algorithms.

The author Feng Hu et al. (2014) explained the implementation of N-Hyper Graph Algorithm for classification for classifying imbalance dataset in social and medical domains. Implementation of machine learning techniques for passive remote sensing applications in the domain of hyper spectral applications is explained by Tomohiro Matsuki et al. (2015).

V. García et al. (2016) explained the Diverted data applications as, diagnosis of uncommon diseases, deceitful telephone calls detection, cataloging of text, information repossession and data extraction tasks. Yijing et al. (2017) explained data imbalanced applications dealing with one verses one and one verses all oversampling approaches to resolve data diversion and improvise classification.

Figure 7 elaborates cataloging of imbalanced dataset handling approaches listed through literature review. It incorporates with approaches at data level, algorithm level and hybridized approaches. Hybrid approaches incorporates data level and algorithmic level up-gradation. Each branch further lists the numerous categories under specified approach as depicted in Figure 7.

Figure 7. Imbalanced dataset handling approaches

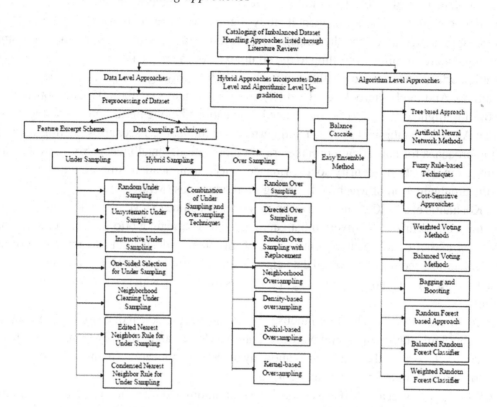

In the year 2020, numerous researchers' attention is attracted by imbalanced real life applications. Hubert Jegierski et al. (2020) explained the work related to Face book and Twitter data analysis in binary social media applications. Eyad Elyan et al. (2020) elaborated imbalanced data handling in health science and security applications which deals with class decomposition and synthetics sample generation by oversampling methods. Jiawen Kong1 et al. (2020) focused BImD applications for anomaly detection.

Data imbalance relating to smart monitoring of energy utilization, assessing resident situation and smart environments and health care applications relating to smart environment, medical and security domain are elaborated by Rebeen Ali et al. (2020). Jaehyung Kim et al. (2020) highlighted major-to-minor translation of imbalanced data and classification related to twitter data analysis in social media domain. The detailed literature review from year 2000 to 2020 carried out in this chapter focused wide variety of real time imbalanced application domain and the dealing approaches as summarized in Table 1.

As explained in detailed literature review in above section, Figure 8 represents machine learning algorithms used for imbalanced data classification at data level, algorithmic level and hybrid approaches. A. S. More et al. (2017) explained in the literature study that the approaches used are Naïve Bayes Classifier (NBC), Neural Network Training Algorithm, Random Forest Classification (RFC), Incremented Random Forest Classification (IRFC), Artificial Neural Network (ANN), Support Vector Machine (SVM) and Weighted Random Forest (WRF), Balanced Random Forest (BRF), etc. are used to resolve data imbalance and improvise performance metrics of classification.

Table 1. Literature review of imbalanced data applications from 2000 to 2020

Real Life Imbalanced Application Scenario with Applied Approach	Imbalanced Category	Application Domain		Author	Year of Study
Artificial Intelligent based Imbalanced application domain study, significance and dealing strategies	Binary and Multiclass Imbalance	Artificial Intelligent Social, Finance, telecommunication, Smart Environment, Medical, security, etc.		Japkowicz et. al.	2000
Expert framework based approaches to deal with Internet of Things, Social, etc. skewed applications	Binary and Multiclass Imbalance	Internet of Things, Social, Finance, Telecommunication, Computer Network, etc.		Estabrooks et al.	2001
Real-time applications dealing with Synthetic minority oversampling technique to balance imbalanced datasets	Binary and Multiclass Imbalance	Social, Finance, telecommunication, Smart Environment, Medical, security, etc.		Ankilash V. Chawla et al.	2002
Skewed applications relating to genomic data sampling approach and the corresponding effect on classification performance assessment in the field of bioinformatics	Binary and Multiclass Imbalance	Bioinformatics		Francisco Azuaje et al.	2003
Current age imbalanced scenarios dealing with multiple sampling approach for classification	Binary and Multiclass Imbalance	Computational Intelligence		Andrew Estabrooks et al.	2004
Incorporation of numerous real-life imbalanced scenarios handled by Machine Learning Techniques (MLT)	Binary and Multiclass Imbalance	Intrusion detection, Security Social, Finance, telecommunication, Smart Environment, Medical, etc.		Sotiris Kotsiantis et al.	2005
Imbalanced applications dealing with the use of Support Vector Machine	Binary and Multiclass Imbalance	Social, Finance, telecommunication, Smart Environment, Medical, security, etc.		Sun et al.	2006
Imbalanced Data Classification through active learning, borderline algorithm, and Oversampling Approaches	Binary Imbalance	Finance, healthcare, social, etc.		Eyda Ertekin et al.	2007
Imbalanced medical decision-making applications dealing with the implementation of Neural Network Training (NNT) algorithm	Binary Imbalance	Medical Decision Making		Maciej A. Mazurowskia et al.	2008
Anomaly Detection using Machine Learning Approach	Binary Imbalance	Security, Intrusion Detection		Mahbod Tavallaee et al.	2009
Diverted data semi-automated classification using random forests for resolving data imbalance	Binary and Multiclass Imbalance	Agriculture		Dimitrios Gounaridis et al.	2010
Highly skewed data applications relating to real-life based on Support Vector Machine (SVM) etc	Binary Imbalance	Social, Finance, telecommunication, Smart Environment, Medical, etc.		Yingchun Liu et al.	2011
Targeted classification related to Medical imbalanced dataset application using Machine Learning Algorithm	Binary Imbalance	Medical		Chunkai Zhang et al.	2012
Imbalanced applications relating to synthetic oversampling and decision tree-based applications and related classification	Binary and Multiclass Imbalance	Social, Finance, telecommunication, Smart Environment, Medical, security, etc.		Ganganwar et al.	2012
Numerous application domains which deal with within data imbalanced characteristics as data intrinsic and data disjoint using hybrid approach	Binary Imbalance	Medicine, Telecommunications, Finance, Ecology, Biology,	Victoria López et al.		2013
Marketing model to diagnose the breast cancer infected patients, credit card applications	Binary Imbalance	Security, Medical	Jia Pengfei et al.		2014

continued on following page

Table 1. Continued

Real Life Imbalanced Application Scenario with Applied Approach	Imbalanced Category	Application Domain	Author	Year of Study
Implementation of N-Hyper Graph Algorithm for classification for classifying imbalanced dataset	Multiclass Imbalance	Medical, Social Application	Feng Hu et al.	2014
Implementation of machine learning techniques for passive remote sensing applications	Multiclass Imbalance	Hyperspectral Applications	Tomohiro Matsuki et al.	2015
Diverted data applications as, uncommon diseases diagnosis, fake telephone calls detection, cataloging of text, information retrieval, and data extraction tasks	Binary and Multiclass Imbalance	Social Media, healthcare, security, finance, etc.	García et al.	2016
Data imbalanced applications dealing with one versus one and one versus all oversampling approaches	Binary and Multiclass Imbalance	Finance, healthcare, social, etc.	Yijing et al.	2017
Handling data imbalance within binary and multiclass healthcare and social application domain using data under-sampling and improved clustering approaches	Binary and Multiclass Imbalance	Social Media, HealthCare	Lu Cao et al.	2019
Malware detection and botnet traffic from a Network flow diverted dataset	Binary Imbalance	Network Security	Antoine et al.	2019
Imbalanced data applications related to Face book and Twitter data analysis	Binary Imbalance	Social Media Applications	Hubert Jegierski et. al	2020
Imbalanced data handling in health science and security applications which deals with class decomposition and synthetics sample generation.	Binary Imbalance	Health life science, security	Eyad Elyan et al.	2020
Anomaly Detection imbalanced applications using machine learning algorithms	Binary Imbalance	Security	Jiawen Kong et al.	2020
Data imbalance relating to smart monitoring of energy consumption, analysis of the resident situation and smart environments and health care applications	Binary Imbalance	Smart Environment, Medical, security,	Rebeen Ali et. al	2020
Imbalanced applications in astrophysics	Binary Imbalance	Science	Jakub Holewik et al.	2020
Major-to-minor Translation of Imbalanced data and Classification related to Twitter data analysis	Binary Imbalance	Social Media	Jaehyung Kim et al.	2020
Imbalanced KDD CUP 1999, NSL-KDD and Power System related applications using IOT techniques	Binary and Multiclass Imbalance	Internet of Things, Computer Network	Mohamed et al.	2020

PERFORMANCE METRICS OF CLASSIFICATION

The performance metrics are listed and elaborated in this section with real life scenario. For analyzing the performance below mentioned metrics of classification are analyzed as per stated formulae 1 to 7.

True Negative Rate $= TN/ (TN +FP)$ ....

$$(1)$$

Figure 8.Machine learning algorithms used for imbalanced data classification

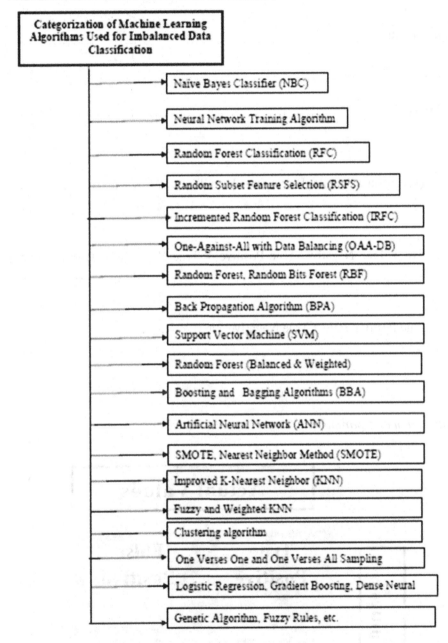

PREFERABLE MACHINE LEARNING ALGORITHMS

True Positive Rate $=$ TP/(TP+FN)..

(2)

Precision $=$ TP/ (TP+FP)..

(3)

Recall $=$ TP/ (TP +FN)..

(4)

F-measure $=2 \times$ (Precision $\times$ Recall)/(Precision + Recall)...

(5)

AUC$=$True Positive + True Negative/(True Positive + True Negative + True Positive + True Positive)... (6)

G-Mean = sqrt (True Positive Rate * True Negative Rate)..

(7)

Figure 9. Confusion matrix parameters

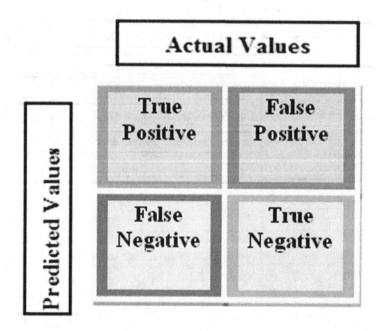

Confusion Matrix Parameters represents the confusion matrix of classification against the actual and predicted values as depicted in Figure 9.

True Positive (TP)

Actual class of data instance is true and the predicted value of the data instance is also true.

Real Life Imbalance Scenario

In case of fraudulent transaction detection, if the transaction is predicted as fraudulent and actually it is fraudulent transaction then it is considered as TP.

True Negative (TN)

Actual class of data instance is False and the predicted value of the data instance is also false.

Real Life Imbalance Scenario

In case of fraudulent transaction detection, if the transaction is predicted as non-fraudulent and actually it is non-fraudulent transaction then it is considered as TN.

False Positives (FP)

Actual class of data instance is False and the predicted value of the data instance is True.

Real Life Imbalance Scenario

In case of fraudulent transaction detection, if the transaction is predicted as non-fraudulent and actually it is fraudulent transaction then it is considered as TN.

False Negatives (FN)

Actual class of data instance is True and the predicted value of the data instance is False.

Real Life Imbalance Scenario

In case of fraudulent transaction detection, if the transaction is predicted as fraudulent and actually it is non-fraudulent transaction then it is considered as FN.

Area under the Curve

Area under the Curve in classification is used for determination of analysis model which predicts the best class.

Geometric Mean

The classification performance metric which measures the balance between majority and minority data sample class is referred to be Geometric Mean.

This variety of performance measures are available to measure the efficiency of the approaches to deal with data imbalance as per the requirement of real time application.

FUTURE RESEARCH DIRECTIONS

The chapter explored the imbalanced data in real time applications, their impact with the variety of solution approaches to resolve and discovered many future research directions which are briefly mentioned here to resolve the data imbalance.

Nowadays, the advancement in technology has transformed the concept of data to the big data. And this advancement of big data era has opened up many research areas with the view of high volume data, variety of data values, from the variety of sources and with the varying speed of arrival. The most challenging research area to manage the imbalanced big data is that volume of data demands the scalable and fast approach with simultaneous management of structured, semi structured and non structured information collected from the different sources at varying speed. Another novel research direction is visualization of multi class and multi-dimensional imbalance data as more than two dimensional visualization is itself challenging one. The time also plays an important role on the presence of distribution of data, so sliding window based data level approach or hybridization approach are in demand to deal data with the timestamp information. The huge data volume opens the area to work in parallel and distributed environment with hybridization of existing approaches.

In big data era, the information is also of many varieties so the effective usage of features can increase the efficiency of approaches. Thus, the class imbalance distribution study is required to analyze the distribution dependency upon the individual feature or correlated features, and feature engineering can be elaborated to resolve the imbalance scenario of the data.

The causal inference is the answer why the particular pattern of data occurs. Therefore, it is also one of the significant open research are to understand the reasoning behind when and why the imbalance in class distribution occurs to utilize in the approach to resolve the data imbalance.

CONCLUSION

Research study carried out in this chapter deals with a detailed literature review of imbalanced data applications relating to real life application domain relating to social, finance, telecommunication, smart environment, medical, security, agriculture, internet of things, intrusion detection, etc. To resolve data imbalance, the detailed literature study showed that numerous approaches such as Down Sampling (DS), Upgrade instance Sampling (Upscale Sampling), Cost Sensitive methods (CSM), Voting Methods Weight based (WVM), Decision Tree Method (DTM), K Nearest Neighbor (KNN), Support Vector Machine (SVM), Bagging and Boosting Methods (BBM), Random Forest Weighted and Balanced (WRF & BRF) and Neural network (NN) etc. are used by the researchers and stated that RFC is one of the best suitable classification for the BImD and MImD Classification. And concluded that in the big data era, still these techniques require the refinements to resolve the data imbalance and also highlighted the open research directions for the researchers.

REFERENCES

Alcalá-Fdez, J., Fernandez, A., Luengo, J., Derrac, J., García, S., Sánchez, L., & Herrera, F. (2011). KEEL Data-Mining Software Tool: Data Set Repository, Integration of Algorithms and Experimental Analysis Framework. *Journal of Multiple-Valued Logic and Soft Computing, 17*(2-3), 255–287.

Angelo, P., Resende, A., & Drummond, A. C. (2018). A Survey of Random Forest Based Methods for Intrusion Detection Systems. *ACM Comput. Surv., 51*(3), 48-48.

Azuaje, F. (2003). Genomic data sampling and its effect on classification performance assessment. *BMC Bioinformatics, 4*(1), 1–14. doi:10.1186/1471-2105-4-5 PMID:12553886

Cao, L., & Shen, H. (2019). Imbalanced Data Classification Using Improved Clustering Algorithm and Under-sampling Method, In *Proceedings of 20th International Conference on Parallel and Distributed Computing, Applications and Technologies*, (pp.361-366). 10.1109/PDCAT46702.2019.00071

Chawla, N. V., Bowyer, K. W., Hall, L. O., & Kegelmeyer, W. P. (2002). SMOTE: Synthetic Minority Oversampling Technique. *Journal of Artificial Intelligence Research, 16*, 321–357. doi:10.1613/jair.953

Delplace, A., Hermoso, S., & Anandita, K. (2019). Cyber Attack Detection thanks to Machine Learning Algorithms, *COMS7507: Advanced Security,* 1-46.

Do, T. N., Lenca, P., & Lallich, S. (2015). Classifying many-class high-dimensional fingerprint datasets using random forest of oblique decision trees. *Vietnam J Comput Sci, 2*(1), 3–12. doi:10.100740595-014-0024-7

Elyan, E., Francisco, C., Garcia, M., & Jayne, C. (2020). CDSMOTE: Class Decomposition and Synthetic Minority Class Oversampling Technique for Imbalanced Data Classification. *Neural Computing & Applications, 33*(7), 2839–2851. doi:10.100700521-020-05130-z

Emanet, N., Öz, H. R., Bayram, N., & Delen, D. (2014). A comparative analysis of machine learning methods for classification type decision problems in healthcare. *Decision Analysis, 1*, 1–20.

Ertekin, S., Huang, J., Bottou, L., & Giles, L. (2007). Learning on the Border: Active Learning in Imbalanced Data Classification. *Proceedings of the sixteenth ACM Conference on information and knowledge management CIKM'07*, 1-77. 10.1145/1321440.1321461

Estabrooks, A., & Japkowicz, N. (2001). A Mixture-of-Experts Framework for Learning from Imbalanced Data Sets. *Proceedings of the 2001 Advances in Intelligent Data Analysis (IDA)*, 34-43. 10.1007/3-540-44816-0_4

Estabrooks, A., Jo, T., & Japkowicz, N. (2004). A Multiple Resampling Method for Learning from Imbalanced Data Sets. *Computational Intelligence, 20*(1), 18–36. doi:10.1111/j.0824-7935.2004.t01-1-00228.x

Fernández, A., Jesus, M. J., & Francisco, H. (2009). Hierarchical Fuzzy Rule Based Classification Systems with Genetic Rule Selection for Imbalanced Datasets. *International Journal of Approximate Reasoning, 50*(3), 561–577. doi:10.1016/j.ijar.2008.11.004

Ferrag, M. A., Maglaras, L., Ahmim, A., Derdour, M., & Janicke, H. (2020). RDTIDS: Rules and Decision Tree-Based Intrusion Detection System for Internet-of-Things Networks. *Future Internet Article,* 1-14.

Ganganwar, V. (2012). An Overview of Classification Algorithms for Imbalanced Dataset. *International Journal of Emerging Technology and Advanced Engineering,* 42–47.

García, V., Sánchez, J. S., Mollineda, R. A., Alejo, R. & Sotoca, J. M. (n.d.). The class imbalance problem in pattern classification and learning. *Pattern Analysis and Learning Group,* 283-291.

Gounaridis, D., Apostolou, A., & Sotirios, K. (2010). Land Cover of Greece, 2010: A Semi Automated Classification using Random Forests. *Journal of Maps, 12*(5), 1055–1062. doi:10.1080/17445647.201 5.1123656

Guo, H., Li, Y., Shang, J., Mingyun, G., Yuanyue, H., & Bing, G. (2017). Learning from class-imbalanced data: Review of methods and applications. *Expert Systems with Applications, 73,* 220–239. doi:10.1016/j. eswa.2016.12.035

Hamad, R. A., Kimura, M., & Lundström, J. (2020). Efficacy of Imbalanced Data Handling Methods on Deep Learning for Smart Homes Environments. *SN. Computer Science, 1,* 204.

He, H., & Garcia, E. A. (2009). Learning from imbalanced data. *IEEE Transactions on Knowledge and Data Engineering, 21*(9), 1263–1283. doi:10.1109/TKDE.2008.239

Holewik, J., Schaefer, G., & Korovin, I. (2020). Imbalanced Ensemble Learning for Enhanced Pulsar Identification. In *Proceedings of International Conference ICSI 2020,* (pp.515-524). Academic Press.

Hu, F., Liu, X., Dai, J., & Yu, H. (2014). A Novel Algorithm for Imbalance Data Classification Based on Neighborhood Hypergraph. *The Scientific World Journal,* 1–13.

Japkowicz, N. (2000). Concept-learning in the presence of between-class and within-class imbalances. In *Proceedings of the Fourteenth Conference of the Canadian Society for Computational Studies of Intelligence,* (pp. 67-77). Academic Press.

Japkowicz, N. (2001). Concept-learning in the Presence of between-class and within-class imbalances, In *Proceedings of the 14th Biennial Conference of the Canadian Society on Computational Studies of Intelligence: Advances in Artificial Intelligence,* (pp. 67-77). 10.1007/3-540-45153-6_7

Japkowicz, N., & Stephen, S. (2002). The class imbalance problem: A systematic study. *Intelligent Data Analysis, 6*(5), 429–449. doi:10.3233/IDA-2002-6504

Jegierski H., & Saganowski, S. (2020). *An ''Outside the Box'' Solution for Imbalanced Data Classification.* Academic Press.

Kim, J., Jeong, J., & Shin, J. (2020). M2m: Imbalanced Classification via Major-to-minor Translation, In *Proceedings of IEEE/CVF Conference on Computer Vision and Pattern Recognition (CVPR),* (pp.13893-13902). IEEE.

Kong, J., Kowalczyk, W., Menzel, S., & Bäck, T. (2020) Improving Imbalanced Classification by Anomaly Detection. Proceedings of Parallel Problem Solving from Nature – PPSN XVI. doi:10.1007/978-3-030-58112-1_35

Kotsiantis, S., Kanellopoulos, D., & Pintelas, P. (2005). Handling imbalanced datasets: A review. *GESTS International Transactions on Computer Science and Engineering*, *30*, 1–13.

Krawczyk, B. (2016). Learning from Imbalanced Data: Open Challenges and Future Directions. *Artificial Intelligence*, 221–232.

Lakshmipadmaja, D., & Vishnuvardhan, B. (2018). Classification Performance Improvement using Random Subset Feature Selection Algorithm for Data Mining. *Big Data Research,* 1-12.

Lars, W., Jochumsen, J., Ostergaard, S., Jensen, H., Clemente, C., & Morten, O. (2016). Pedersen A Recursive Kinematic Random Forest and Alpha Beta Filter Classifier for 2d Radar Tracks. *EURASIP Journal on Advances in Signal Processing*, *82*, 1–12.

Lessmann, S. (2014). Solving Imbalanced Classification Problems with Support Vector Machines. *Inst. of Business Information Systems*, 1-8.

Liu, Y. (2011). Random Forest Algorithm in Big Data Environment. *Computer Modeling and New Technologies*, *18*, 147–151.

López, V., Río, S., Benítez, J. M., & Herrera, F. (2015). Cost-sensitive linguistic fuzzy rule based classification systems under the MapReduce framework for imbalanced big data. *Fuzzy Sets and Systems*, *258*, 5–38. doi:10.1016/j.fss.2014.01.015

Matsuki, T., Yokoya, N., & Iwasaki, A. (2015). Hyperspectral Tree Species Classification of Japanese Complex Mixed Forest With the Aid of Lidar Data. *IEEE Journal of Selected Topics in Applied Earth Observations and Remote Sensing*, *8*(5), 2177–2187. doi:10.1109/JSTARS.2015.2417859

Mazurowskia, M. A., Habasa, P. A., Zuradaa, J. M., Lob, J. Y., Bakerb, J. A., & Tourassib, G. D. (2008). Training Neural Network Classifiers for Medical Decision Making: The Effects of Imbalanced Datasets on Classification Performance. *Neural Network PMC*, 427–436.

More, A. S., & Rana, D. P. (2017). Review of Random Forest Classification Techniques to Resolve Data Imbalance. In *Proceedings of IEEE 1st International Conference on Intelligent Systems and Information Management (ICISIM)*, (pp.72-78). 10.1109/ICISIM.2017.8122151

More, A. S., & Rana, D. P. (2020). An Experimental Assessment of Random Forest Classification Performance Improvisation with Sampling and Stage Wise Success Rate Calculation. Elsevier *procedia. Computer Science*, *167*, 1711–1721.

More, A. S., Rana, D. P., & Agarwal, I. (2018). Random Forest Classifier Approach for Imbalanced Big Data Classification for Smart City Application Domains. *International Journal of Computational Intelligence & IoT*, *1*(2), 261–266.

Peng-fei, J., Chunkai, Z., & Zhen-yu, H. (2014). A new sampling approach for classification of imbalanced data sets with high density. *Proceedings of 2014 International Conference on Big Data and Smart Computing (BIGCOMP)*, 217-222. 10.1109/BIGCOMP.2014.6741439

Somasundaram, A., & Reddy, U. S. (2016). Data Imbalance: Effects and Solutions for Classification of Large and Highly Imbalanced Data, In *Proceedings of International Conference on Research in Engineering, Computers and Technology*, (pp. 28–34). Academic Press.

Sun, Y., Kamel, M. S., & Wang, Y. (2006). Boosting for learning multiple classes with imbalanced class distribution. In *Proceedings of Sixth IEEE Int. Conf. Data Mining*, (pp. 592–602). 10.1109/ICDM.2006.29

Sun, Y., Wong, A., & Kamel, M. S. (2009). Classification of imbalanced data: A review. *International Journal of Pattern Recognition and Artificial Intelligence*, 23(4), 687–719. doi:10.1142/S0218001409007326

Tavallaee, M., Bagheri, E., Lu, W., & Ali, A. G. (2009). A Detailed Analysis of the KDD CUP 99 Data Set. In *Proceedings of the IEEE Symposium on Computational Intelligence on Security and Defense Applications*, (pp. 1-6). 10.1109/CISDA.2009.5356528

Wang, J., Zhang, J., Luo, C., & Chen, F. (2012). Joint Head Pose and Facial Landmark Regression from Depth Images. *Computational Visual Media*, 3(3), 229–241. doi:10.100741095-017-0082-8

Chapter 2
A Survey of Class Imbalance Problem on Evolving Data Stream

D. Himaja

Vignan's Foundation for Science, Technology, and Research (Deemed), Guntur, India

T. Maruthi Padmaja

Vardhaman College of Engineering, Hyderabad, India

P. Radha Krishna
ⓘD https://orcid.org/0000-0002-2764-2818
National Institute of Technology, Warangal, India

ABSTRACT

Learning from data streams with both online class imbalance and concept drift (OCI-CD) is receiving much attention in today's world. Due to this problem, the performance is affected for the current models that learn from both stationary as well as non-stationary environments. In the case of non-stationary environments, due to the imbalance, it is hard to spot the concept drift using conventional drift detection methods that aim at tracking the change detection based on the learner's performance. There is limited work on the combined problem from imbalanced evolving streams both from stationary and non-stationary environments. Here the data may be evolved with complete labels or with only limited labels. This chapter's main emphasis is to provide different methods for the purpose of resolving the issue of class imbalance in emerging streams, which involves changing and unchanging environments with supervised and availability of limited labels.

DOI: 10.4018/978-1-7998-7371-6.ch002

INTRODUCTION

The real-world classification problems, such as fraud and fault detection are characterized by continuously imbalanced evolving streams from non-stationary environments. The combined problem of class imbalance and concept drift, on the other hand, hinders the success of online learners. Learning from unbalanced emerging streams poses a different set of problems than learning from balanced groups. The problem of learning from emerging streams, on the other hand, faces significant challenges such as infinite stream size, varying speed, and concept drift. The method of extracting information from continuous, rapid data records is known as stream learning. It's a huge challenge to learn from these streams. The evolving data may be completely or partially labeled.

Class Imbalance Learning

On standalone training sets, the class imbalance learning (CIL) problem arises when one class of data vastly outnumbers the others, causing the underrepresented class output to suffer. Therefore the classes from over represented class are correctly classified where as from under represented are misclassified. This scenario is common in applications such as fraud and fault detection. Smart building is an example for imbalanced data. It has sensors to detect risky conditions. Any fault in sensors causes a great destruction. The size of smart building is 5000 with two classes namely faulty and good, where only 1% is faulty and remaining 99% is good conditions. A model can be built on this kind of datasets, to predict faults in sensors. But predicting faults is expensive as faulty conditions are underrepresented than good. Figure 1 shows the scenario for class imbalance. Here there are two classes (i.e. blue and yellow). From the figure 1, it is clear that the dataset is highly imbalanced where blue is 70% and remaining 30% is yellow class.

Figure 1. Class imbalance

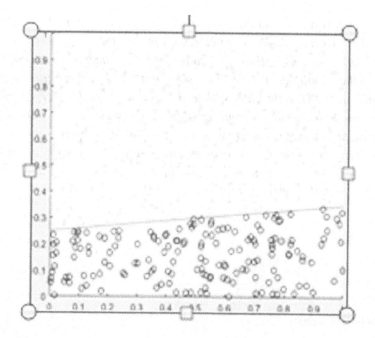

Several researchers examined the behavior of different classifiers on various data attributes like class imbalance (CI), overlapping, minority class disjuncts and data set size, concluded that most of the classifiers favored majority class. Solutions are proposed at both the data and algorithm level to resolve this problem (Haibo & Garcia, 2009; Sun et al., 2009). The data level solutions balance the class distributions either by oversampling or by undersampling approaches. The algorithm level solutions shift the decision boundary towards the under-represented class by applying additional costs or weights to the parameters that represent the minority class. The vast majority of these strategies are usually driven by the degree of imbalance, i.e., the majority to minority class ratio, which can be calculated directly from the data. In addition to these approaches, the literature proposes many combinations of data and algorithm levels, as well as their ensembles (Galar et al., 2012).

Concept Drift (CD)

Concepts drift (CD), which occurs when the underlined concept generation functions shift over time. It is considered to be the most important challenge in stream learning. Let < x, y > be the training set with predicting variable x and output variable y. Real and virtual concept drifts are the two forms of the drifts (Gama et al., 2013).

- In former drift, also known as posterior, changes in distributions cause changes in decision boundaries.
- Where as in latter drift, however a change in distribution does not result in a change in decision boundary, such as change in prior. The dynamic changes in priors are a sort of virtual drift (Khammasi et al., 2018).

Figure 2 illustrates the real-world and virtual concept drifts. There are two classes in this diagram, which are colored blue and yellow. Figure 2(a) shows the $p(y/x)$ drift. On the left side of the figure, the data distribution before the drift is shown, while on the right side, the data distribution after the drift is shown. Due to the drift, the original decision boundary has been impacted, and the previously learned model is no longer adequate. Therefore, the model must be revised. Figure 2(b) depicts the p(y) drift, also known as virtual drift. Prior probabilities for the yellow and blue classes were switched, resulting in a CI. However, as shown in Figure 2, the decision boundary is unchanged. Electricity is an example of a data set with CD. This dataset is 45,312 in size, with a 40% imbalance ratio. It's a binary classification data set with two class labels, and each instance has four features (i.e. up and down). The task at hand is to decide if the price of electricity will rise or fall, which is determined by demand and supply. But the problem here as there is CD in the dataset, the classes can be misclassified which incurs in huge loss.

The imbalance drift is a sort of virtual drift caused due to the dynamic changes of class distributions that change over time (Wang et al., 2018). The learner has no way of knowing what the current state of these distributions ahead of time. Unlike the standalone training sets, the status of CI is not persistent in the stream, from time to time it changes in a dynamic way. Usually, the drifts arrive at different speeds, such as abrupt, gradual, and recurrent. In abrupt drifts, the change in concept occurs suddenly. The gradual change in concept takes place in gradual drifts. In recurrent drifts, the last seen drifts recur over time. Figure 3 depicts the drifts with three different speeds.

In general, active or passive approaches are used to combat concept drift. The latter methods monitor and detect drifts first, then adjust to changes using mechanisms like forgetting and weighing. The former

Figure 2. Real and virtual drifts

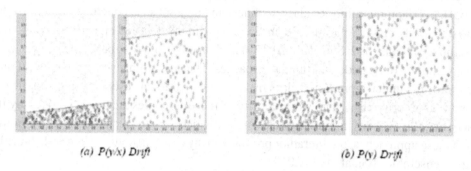

(a) P(y/x) Drift   (b) P(y) Drift

methods do not perform explicit drift detection and allow a learner to adapt to the situations or adding / removing/updating a new classifier from an ensemble.

Class Imbalance and Concept Drift (CI-CD) Problem

Both issues (CI-CD) coexist in real-world situations such as credit card, fraud, intrusion and spam detection. Figure 4 shows the CI-CD drift where both p(y) and p(y/x) exists. Here both drifts occur i.e. (Imbalance drift and concept drift). The decision boundary got changed from the original decision boundary. This change is due to the concept drift but not imbalance drift. The CI-CD drift occurs in both supervised as well as limited labeling settings of evolving streams. As a result, classifiers must constantly adjust to these dynamic (non-stationary) shifts (Wang et al., 2018).

With respect to CI-CD problem, addressing either CI or CD at first is an important issue. Several supervised learning-based drift detection methods were discussed in (Gama et al., 2013). These methods detect drift directly or indirectly in both online and batch modes based on classifier output estimates such as error and precision, but they are unable to sense the drifts that are unbalanced because of low or no prediction from under represented classes (Wang et al., 2018).

There are ensembles approaches (Ditzler & Polikar, 2013; Ditzler & Polikar, 2010) that address the combined CI-CD problem. But these works assume that the stream evolves with the static imbalance and learns batch by batch. However, the authors addressed both batch by batch and online learning and used (Wang & Abraham, 2015; Brezezinski & Stefanowski, 2015) an explicit drift detector to track the drifts. In (Wang & Abraham, 2015), linear four rates (LFR) system was proposed, which tracks four rates with a threshold for detecting drift. A drift will be verified if any rates surpass the threshold. Prequential AUC (PAUC) (Brezezinski & Stefanowski, 2015) suggested a measure of overall measures for online scenarios instead of tracking multiple performance rates for individual class. It does however include historical data. If CD occurs, the online model will be reset and retrained. Despite being built for unbalanced data,

Figure 3. Drifts with different speeds

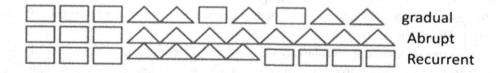

Figure 4. CI-CD drift

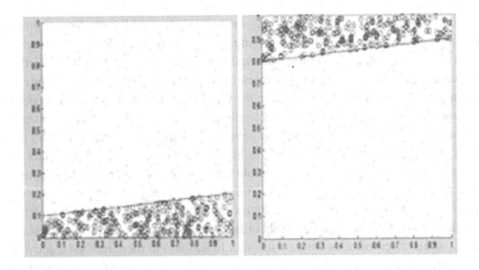

they have no way of dealing with it. It's also unclear how they perform when it comes to using class imbalance strategies.On the other side, (Wang et al., 2015; Ghazikhani et al., 2013) suggested solutions to the issue of dynamic CI. To solve dynamic CI (Wang et al, 2015) used ensemble approaches such as weighted online bagging, undersampling, and oversampling based Online bagging (OOB and UOB). Here oversampling and undersampling rates are guided by time decay class size and recall of each class where as in (Ghazikhani et al., 2013) the online neural network is adjusted to counter the dynamic CI.

Moreover, this chapter focused on supervised and limited labeling algorithms. In the supervised algorithm, outputs are already available. For each and every input data there will be an output. Therefore, for creating a model, the algorithm is supplied with available data and with corresponding outputs which is called as training. After training, the testing phase occurs where the new data is supplied to the already built model to predict the labels. But in real world scenarios, a little amount of data can be labeled because oracle intervention is time consuming and expensive. For example, Zliobaite et al (Zliobaite et al., 2014) introduced an active learning system to control the learning process and coordinate the use of the labelling budget for incremental streaming data. They created the Random Strategy (Ran), Fixed Uncertainty Strategy (FixedUN), Variable Uncertainty Strategy (VarUN), Uncertainty Strategy with Randomization (RanVarUN), and Split Strategy (Split) based on this system. Hence, this chapter aims to review the methods that address the CI-CD problem in both supervised and limited labeling settings.

CLASS IMBALANCE (CI)

On standalone training sets, researchers analyzed the behavior of various classifiers and concluded that not only the degree of imbalance, however other data characteristics such as degree of overlapping of one class with other classes, the length of the minority concept, and the classification algorithm being used are the key issues to aggravate the minority class prediction (Japkowicz & Stephen, 2002; Japkowicz,

2001; Chawla et al, 2003; Wu & Chang, 2003;Prati et al., 2004; Jo & Japkowicz, 2004). Solutions are suggested at both the data and algorithm level to resolve this issue (Haibo & Garcia, 2009; Sun et al., 2009).

The solutions at data level include resampling methods such as undersampling, oversampling and combination of two. The training set is balanced using these resampling techniques, and the performance of the minority class increases. Resampling can be done in two ways: random and selective. Random resampling techniques either replicate random minority samples with or without substitution (oversampling) or exclude random majority samples from the training collection to match the class distribution (under sampling). Both oversampling and under sampling is possible at selective resampling methods. In selective oversampling, the synthetic samples are generated across minority class samples or in between the borders of majority and minority samples. Further, based on the degree of imbalance around each minority and majority regions, the synthetic sample generation can be carried out adaptively. For the selective undersampling, unlike under-sample the training space, the majority class samples focusively under sample from individual regions (clusters) for better performance. The fast KNN searching methods such as Tomak Links, condensed nearest neighbor rule (One sided selection), Neighborhood cleaning rule near-miss, and distinct methods are also adapted. In addition to these methods, active learning on standalone training sets is used for selective under-sampling. The hybrids of random undersampling and oversampling, selective oversampling and selective under sampling are also proposed to increase under represented class prediction rates.

The algorithm level solutions includes adjusting the threshold (Morik et al, 1999), cost sensitive learning (Elkan, 2001; Liu & Zhou, 2006), and novelty detection methods (Lee & Cho, 2006). The viability of the resampling methods and one class learning methods is well studied on real world applications (Dubey et al., 2014; Padmaja et al., 2007) than the other algorithm level solutions.

The ensemble learning methods such as bagging and boosting are also widely investigated to oppose the class imbalance problem. The hybrid ensembles such as under sampling based-boosting (Seiffert et al., 2010), oversample based boosting (Chawla et al.,2003; Guo & Viktor,2004), under sampling based bagging (Hido et al.,2009; Blaszczynski& Stefanowski,2015), oversampling based bagging (Wang & Yao,2009), cost sensitive learning based-boosting (Fan et al.,1999; Sun et al., 2007; Joshi et al., 2001) and hybrids of bagging and boosting, under-over-bagging (Hido et al., 2009; Liu et al.,2009) are proposed to boost the prediction of minority class. The under-sampling based boosting algorithms and meta learners are shown to be successful in predicting the underrepresented target class from fraud/fault detection domains (Gao et al., 2015; Phua et al., 2004).

Stream Mining

A data stream releases the data continuously. The learning of this data can be taken place either by batch or online. Under batch learning, each and every batch carries fixed number of samples. The length of the stream in the real world tends to infinity and moreover the instances at a time t may not be appropriate and time $t+n$ and due to memory constraints all the instances cannot be maintained. The window based mechanisms are employed to maintain the training samples of current time t. The old samples are forgotten or representative samples are only pertained in the window (Gama et al., 2013; Ditzler et al., 2015). Usually window size is either static or dynamic.

Data is delivered in streams or chunks of samples in streaming applications. The data up to a given time step t is used to create/update models, which then forecast the new samples arriving at time step $t + 1$.Based on the number of samples available at the training, batch-based (chunk-based) or online learning algorithms are needed. Chunk-based learning algorithms process a chunk of samples at every time stage, according to (Ditzler et al., 2015). Inorder to learn from the new data in batch learning, a new model has to construct from the start on the new data and this type of learning is called as offline and causes memory constraints. Windowing methods in (Gama et al., 2013; Ditzler et al., 2015), forgets the old data and a new model can be built or already built model can updated on the recent data in batch learning. On the other hand, online learning as soon as new sample is seen the model gets adapted and discards it as soon as adaption hence this supports high-speed processing of data.

Another significant challenge is that underlined data distribution (the concept) can change over time (CD). When it comes to continuously learning and updating their learned model by always using the most recent data, on-line learning algorithms are especially well suited. It's a popular technique in machine learning where training over the entire dataset is computationally impossible. It's also used in situations where the algorithm needs to adapt to new trends in the data on the fly, or when the data is created as a function of time. A key problem in data stream mining is detecting CD.

Based on the implementation of the window and nature of the learning, few learners such as K Nearest Neighbour (KNN), Support Vector Machine (SVM) and Perceptron are adaptable to the changes in the data. For KNN classifier, a window of training of current time t is mandatory due to memory constraint of lazy learning. However the SVM and Perceptron learn only the boundary, which is updated for each new sample. In particular SVM active learning is well studied on learning from non-stationary environments (Tegjyoth & Kantardzic, 2017; Zliobaite et al., 2014). The Perceptron learns a new sample of the stream through online learning (Haykin, 1998). Here, these are referred as adaptive learners. The learners based on statistical theory such as Naive Bayes, and Very Fast Decision Tree (VFDT) (Domingos & Hulten, 2000) simply updates the statistics for each new sample. These algorithms usually do not require a window for incremental learning of streams. Here these are referred as non-adaptive learners. Usually, the non-adaptive learning methods are intended for stationary environments (Haibo & Garcia, 2009; Gama et al., 2013; Wang et al., 2018).

CONCEPT DRIFT (CD)

The real or virtual drifts or either the combination of both are inherent in an evolving stream. Good amount of research is carried out for drift detection, which includes recent surveys (Haibo & Garcia, 2009; Gama et al., 2013; Khammasi et al., 2018). The methods that detect drifts are divided in to two groups (i) active and (ii) passive. The former approaches are focused on drift detection and adaptation, which means that the drift is first detected, and then the learners are revised / reconstructed to adapt to the data change. The drifts can be detected using

- Hypothesis tests: two samples are validated on whether they are from same distribution or not based on the confidence level (Patist, 2007; Nishida & Yamuchi,2007)
- Change-point method: identifying the change point where the underlined distribution starts to change its statistical behavior using statistical techniques. (Hawkins et al.,2003)
- Sequential hypothesis test: Analyze the stream in a sequential manner before there is sufficient faith to accept or deny the null hypothesis (Ditzler & Polikar, 2011).
- Change detection test: This test uses a defined threshold based on either a classification error or a feature value (Hawkins et al., 2003). (Ditzler & Polikar, 2011; Baseville &Nikiforov,1993) have

also looked into the use of Hellinger distance and the adaptive CUmulative SUM (CUSUM) test for detecting changes between data batches.

Drift detection methods are employed either on raw data (Shujian et al., 2018) or the outcomes of the classification such as performance, error, mean, variance, uncertainty (Tegjyoth & Kantardzic, 2017; Costa et al., 2018). Once the drift is detected, it can be addressed by adapting to new knowledge by forgetting the irrelevant samples from the old. This adaptation mechanism either selects random samples to filter or weights samples based on their age, ensuring that the oldest sample is forgotten. When a change is detected in the windowing process, only the samples that are applicable to the current learner are held in the window. However, the window's size is important here. In (Bifet & Gavalda, 2007), ADWIN is proposed as a method for preserving a variable-size window. While there is no change, the algorithm automatically expands the window, and when there is a change, the algorithm shrinks it. In (Alippi et al., 2011), adaptive window sizes are proposed. Further Gama et al proposed DDM in (Costa et al., 2018), which focuses on the identification of changes in overall error rates. It performs well in detecting abrupt drifts where as it can only detect gradual drifts whose change is not very slow but not whose change is slowly gradual.

Concerned with the passive learning approaches, in contrast to explicit detection and adaptation methods, the underlined model continuously adapts the transition by resetting parameters or adding/ removing/ updating a classifier in an ensemble (Ditzler et al., 2015) to maintain the new information and forget the old. Though, the ensemble methods are computationally expensive, they are much more accurate than single learners. Usually, the passive approaches are shown effective in predicting gradual drifts, whereas active approaches are best for batch learning and effective in predicting abrupt drifts (Ditzler et al., 2015).

CLASS IMBALANCE-CONCEPT DRIFT (CI-CD)

This is the combined problem of CI streams evolving with CD. Imbalance may evolve as dynamic. Here the dynamic refers to the change in p(y) (Wang et al., 2018) i.e., degree of imbalance of the classes changes dynamically. The methods that deal with the CI have the inability to change in concept as they are proposed for standalone training sets. The methods that address the real drift are not designed to handle the degree of class imbalance either statically or dynamically. The major challenge here is the change of degree of imbalance dynamically with real concept drift. In (Wang et al., 2018), the CI problem can affect treatment of the CD. The literature for CI-CD problem is covered in the following way:

1. **Without Concept Drift (CD) Detector:**

    a.   Supervised Learning.
    ▪   Batch Learning

Under batch learning, Gao et. al (Gao et al., 2008; Gao et al., 2007) suggested an instance propagation ensemble mechanism, where the previously seen minority class samples are combined with randomly selected majority samples for the current batch and a new classifier ensemble learned on this combined batch. Instead of propagating all earlier seen minority samples, Chen and He (Chen & He, 2009) proposed selection of best *n* minority class samples on the basis of mahalanobis. The combined best under- represented and all over represented samples in the presently available batch are given as input to the bagging based ensemble classifier for training. Lichten and Chawla (Litchenwalter & Chawla, 2010; Hoens & Chawla, 2012; Hoens et al, 2011) also proposed an add-on to Gao et. al's (Gao et al., 2007; Gao et al., 2008) work. Rather than reproducing underrepresented samples alone, they suggested to synthesize misclassified over represented instances of the previous model. Further, they suggested weighing the each ensemble member with the probability of combined change detection test of Hellinger distance and information gain (Litchenwalter & Chawla, 2010). Class information with and without labels are computed based on the Hellinger distance (Hoens & Chawla, 2012).

An instance selection method based on Naive Bayes classifier named HUWRS.IP is proposed in (Hoens et al., 2011). The old minority class samples that are appropriate to the new underrepresented class instances are selected using the Naive Bayes. Recently Pozzolo et al (Pozzolo et al., 2014) stated that Hellinger Distance Decision Trees (HDDT) with HDDT ensemble strategies alone can efficiently deal the imbalance streams in dynamic environments. Ditzler and Polikar (Ditzler & Polikar, 2013) suggested Learn++CDS and Learn++. NIE as an extension to their past proposal Learn++.NSE (Pozzolo et al., 2014) to handle CI-CD problem from evolving stream. Lu et al (Lu et al., 2017) proposed Dynamic Weighted Majority for Imbalance Learning (DWMIL) to deal with both CI and CD. DWMIL takes into account the output of each and every classifier in the current chunk. Further, Lu et al (Lu et al., 2019) suggested an extension to DWMIL, adaptive chunk-based dynamic weighted majority (ACDWM). Here, chunk size is chosen based on the present classifier stability.

- Online Learning

Under online learning, Minku et al (Minku et al.,2010; Wang et al., 2013a) proposed Online Class Imbalance Learning method called Diversity for Dealing with Drifts (DDD) (Minku & Yao, 2012) and a Resampling-Based ensemble to deal with data streams that aren't balanced. They investigated diversity of ensembles on Online Bagging and described a hybrid of over and undersampling to handle the degree of imbalance in evolving streams. However, parameters for tuning over and under sampling rates are not adaptable dynamically. Wang et. al (Wang et al., 2015) proposed OOB and UOB, based on under- represented class Recall and a decay time guides the oversampling and undersampling rates for online bagging. There are single classifier variations of active approaches such as Recursive Least Square Adaptive Cost Perceptron (RLSACP) (Ghazikhani et al., 2013) and Online Neural Network (ONN) (Ghazikhani et al., 2014). CD is dealt with using a forgetting function, and CI is dealt with using adaptive weighing of Perceptron error, either with the classification rate or with the degree of imbalance, and the learners' weights are updated using dynamic voting of the majority. To be able to cope with recurring concept, the learners with lowest weights, with respect to current ensemble are stored in ELM store. Any classifier in the store that outperforms the current ensemble means the underlying pattern has recurred, and the best classifier is applied to the current ensemble. Both Threshold and Hypothesis tests based, drift detection methods are used subsequently to cope with abrupt and gradual drifts. However, it handles static degree of imbalance with concept drift problem only.

Inline, Baruva et al., (Baruva et al., 2015) suggested a Generalized Over-Sampling based online Imbalanced Learning Framework (GOS-IL) to deal with p(y) drift only. The Cost-sensitive Adaptive Random Forest (CSARF) proposed in (Loezer et al., 2020) is a variant of ARF. In CSARF (i) Matthews Correlation Coefficient (MCC) was used to assign weights to each tree in the ensemble instead of using accuracy and a window that slides was introduced to keep an eye on class distributions. Learning process is modified in such a way that each and every tree is trained with minority class samples, and Cost sensitivity can be assigned locally (CSARF-local) or globally (CSARF-global). Before the combination of votes, CSARF-local uses costs that are related to misclassified instances to affect the base classifiers performance. Korycki et al (Korycki et al., 2019) proposed an extension to popular online ensembles by supplementing them with an abstaining option. The confidence level of each incoming instance is monitored and the learners that are greater than a certain threshold are selected. Uncertain classifiers are holdback from predictions which is useful in noise data.

b.   Partially Labeled Data

Under batch learning, according to (Arabmakki, 2016) the performance of the current chunk and the previous chunk is compared. If the difference in their performance is greater than a certain threshold, then a new model is built using top closest samples from the current chunk to borrow (i.e., the union of both SV's and minority samples) which are labeled using an oracle. Here the neighborhood of the top closest samples is increased until there is at least one minority sample. The number of false alarms is more (Arabmakki, 2016). Thwart and Schenck suggested a two-phase active learning algorithm (Thwart & Schenck et al., 2020). New regions are searched for better exposure to minority class space during the exploration process. New points are synthesized in unknown regions during the exploitation process.

Under online learning, Zhang et al (Zhang et al., 2018) proposed OAL-DI. The ensemble is paired with classifiers (i.e. long-term and dynamic) to deal with both sudden and abrupt drifts. A labelling technique that uses both uncertainity and an imbalance strategy has been suggested to select the most useful instances for learning. The margin-based uncertainity and a dynamically modified threshold are used in the uncertainity technique. The imbalance strategy discovers minority category instances using the underlying principle of the last seen data. Asymmetric weighing strategies are proposed in (Zhao & Hoi, 2013; Zhang et al., 2016). In (Zhao & Hoi, 2013), only one weight is assigned to positive class where as in (Zhang et al., 2016), two different weights are assigned to positive and negative class. Figure 5 shows the taxonomy of CI-CD problem in evolving streams without CD detector.

2.   **With Concept Drift (CD) Detector**

a.   Supervised Learning

Under batch learning, In (Shujian et al., 2019) proposed a detection system of two layers, with first layer adapting LFR whereas second layer is dependent on permutation test in which both of the layers are completely labeled. Both approaches rely on monitoring changes in estimators related to completely labeled data, which may lead to false positives due to True Positive rate's susceptibility to dynamic imbalance rather than the drift in case of high degree of imbalance. In (Wang & Abraham, 2015) suggested a LFR, instead of only tracking changes in TPR. The drift signal is activated when a substantial difference in any of the performance rates is observed. In (Brezzinski and Stefanowski, 2015) proposed a Prequential AUC-based drift detection mechanism that uses the Page-Hinkley test to identify the drift in Prequential AUC.

Under online learning, DDM-OCI (Wang et al., 2013b) is a change made to DDM (Costa et al., 2018). Unlike DDM, which looks for changes in the overall error rate, DDM-OCI looks for changes in True Positive Rate, assuming that when the stream is imbalanced, the drift in distribution causes major changes.

b.   Partially Labeled Data

Under batch learning, Margin Density Drift Detection (MD3) algorithm (Tegjyoth & Kantardzic, 2017) was proposed. Here an ensemble of classifiers is used rather than a single classifier. The input space is divided in to subspaces and each subspace is trained with a classifier. A drift is detected if the ensembles disagreement increases while assigning labels to test data. On drift detection, a complete chunk is requested for labeling by an oracle which is costlier and compares the ensembles accuracy. If the ensembles accuracy is less than the certain threshold then a drift is confirmed. As a result, MD3 relies entirely on supervised methods to confirm the drift, while DDAL (Costa et al., 2018) is an Uncertainity-based approach that relies on an unsupervised drift detection method to confirm the drift. To confirm the drift, this algorithm uses an active learning approach called Fixed Uncertainty strategy (FixedUN). (Zliobaite et al., 2014) calculates the density of the most important instances.

A new framework for CD detection is proposed in (Shujian et al., 2018). This framework is made up of two layers. It just uses labels to detect CD when required. It captures the most essential characteristics of the underlying data in Layer-I and adjusts itself in Layer-II, that needs labeled data when required. Two methods are proposed: HHT-CU and HHT-AG in this framework. In limited labelling environments, Lukasz & Krawczyk (Lukasz & Krawczyk, 2020) suggested a solution for multi-class data that tackles both CI and CD. The algorithm employs an active learning technique to identify useful instances, and then requests labels from Oracle, followed by multi-class oversampling. Both the ratios of the current class and the error of the classifier on each class are taken into account when selecting and generating instances. Figure 6 shows the taxonomy of CI-CD problem in evolving streams with CD detector.

PERFORMANCE METRICS

This section provided various performance evaluation metrics. For stream learning, all the performance measures such as recall, accuracy, F-measure etc… (Gama et al., 2013; Fawcett, 2006) are used along with holdout and Prequential evaluation (Gama et al., 2013).

1.   Hold Out
      Hold out is commonly used when testing data (holdout set) is available ahead of time. The rigid criterion in this holdout is that the output of the holdout set must resemble the definition of the training data at each and every time step, or for every few time steps.
2.   Prequential Evaluation
      In Prequential evaluation, each sample is tested on the learned model and after that it is used for training. This is also called as interleaved-test-and-train. In this evaluation, the model built is tested on new samples and does not need any training set. The holdout works well with recent data, but real-world datasets are more difficult to evaluate. A forgetting mechanism may be used in this situation.(Gama et al., 2013).

Figure 5. Taxonomy of CI-CD problem in evolving stream without CD detector

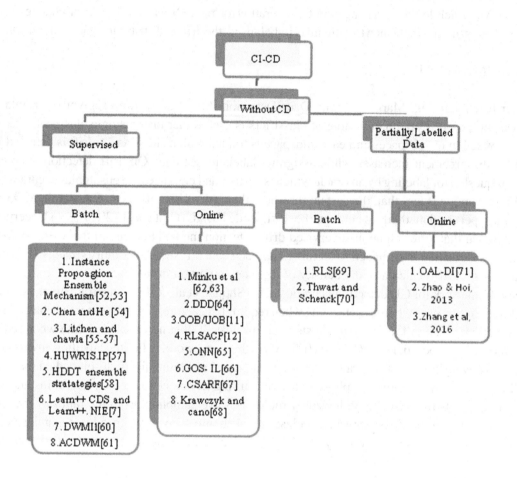

FUTURE RESEARCH DIRECTIONS

New drift detection methods must be developed for detecting CI, CD, and CI-CD drifts at imbalance with high degrees, or established drift detection methods must be fine-tuned for adaptability. Change detection methods based on classification error or efficiency, on the other hand, are vulnerable to imbalance in both static and dynamic states.

The combined CI-CD problem is solved by using both drift detection and solutions that simultaneously solve the problem of CI. At first, CI strategies are used based on the existing degree of imbalance at time t. Drift detection techniques may be used to track the drift (Ditzler et al., 2015 & Gama et al., 2013). If no drift is observed, the current model is updated. Otherwise a new model with the new sample is learned. However, in the case of imbalance with high degrees, the p(y) change could be dynamically captured by an indicator function, and then adaptively countered by methods that fix the problem of CI (Wang et al., 2018).

Figure 6. Taxonomy of CI-CD problem in evolving stream with CD detector

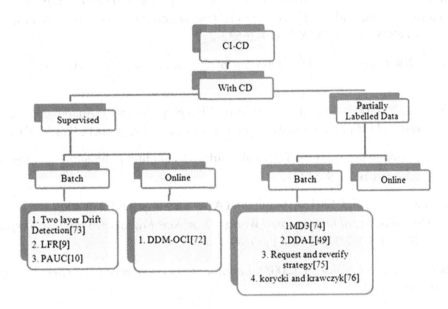

CONCLUSION

This chapter summarizes various approaches for dealing with CI in evolving streams, including both changing and unchanging environments with supervised and limited label availabilty. This survey provides problem descriptions and definitions for both CI and CD. Individual learning challenges and solutions in CI and CD were examined in this chapter, as well as the combined obstacles and current solutions in online CI and CD. The data can be evolved with complete labels (supervised) or with just a few labels (unsupervised).

ACKNOWLEDGMENT

This study was sponsored by India's Defense Research and Development Organization (DRDO) [grant number ERIPR/GIA/17-18/038].

REFERENCES

Alippi, C., Boracchi, G., & Roveri, M. (2011). A just-in-time adaptive classification system based on the intersection of confidence intervals rule. *Neural Networks*, *24*(8), 791–800. doi:10.1016/j.neu-net.2011.05.012 PMID:21723706

Arabmakki, E. (2016). *A reduced labeled samples (RLS) framework for classification of imbalanced concept-drifting streaming data*. University of Louisville. doi:10.18297/etd/2602

Barua, S., Islam, M. M., & Murase, K. (2015). GOS-IL: A Generalized Over-Sampling Based Online Imbalanced Learning Framework. In *Proceedings of International Conference on Neural Information Processing* (pp. 680-687). 10.1007/978-3-319-26532-2_75

Basseville, M., & Nikiforov, V. (1993). *Detection of abrupt changes: Theory and application.* PTR Prentice-Hall.

Bifet, A., & Gavalda, R. (2007). Learning from Time-Changing Data with Adaptive Windowing. *Proceedings of the Seventh SIAM International Conference on Data Mining.* 10.1137/1.9781611972771.42

Blaszczynski, J., & Stefanowski, J. (2015). Neighbourhood sampling in bagging for imbalanced data. *Neurocomputing, 150*(part B), 529-542.

Brzezinski, D., & Stefanowski, J. (2015). Prequential AUC for Classifier Evaluation and Drift Detection in Evolving Data Streams. In *3rd International Workshop on New Frontiers in Mining Complex Patterns* (vol. 8983, pp.87-101) 10.1007/978-3-319-17876-9_6

Chawla, N., Japkowicz, N., & Kolcz, A. (2003). *Learning from Imbalanced Data Sets II. In ICML'2003 Workshop*, Washington, DC.

Chawla, N. V., Lazarevic, A., Hall, L. O., & Bowyer, K. W. (2003). SMOTEBoost: Improving Prediction of the Minority Class in Boosting. *European Conference on Principles of Data Mining and Knowledge Discovery, PKDD 2003: Knowledge Discovery in Databases*, 107-119.

Chen, S., & He, H. (2009). Sera: Selectively recursive approach towards nonstationary imbalanced stream data mining. In *2009 International Joint Conference on Neural Networks* (pp. 522-529). 10.1109/IJCNN.2009.5178874

Costa, A. F. J., Albuquerque, R. A. S., & Santos, E. (2018). A Drift Detection Method Based on Active Learning. *International Joint Conference on Neural Networks.* 10.1109/IJCNN.2018.8489364

Ditzler, G., & Polikar, R. (2010). An incremental learning algorithm for non-stationary environments and class imbalance. In *20th International Conference on Pattern Recognition* (pp. 2997-3000). 10.1109/ICPR.2010.734

Ditzler, G., & Polikar, R. (2011). Hellinger distance based drift detection for nonstationary environments. In *Proceedings of IEEE Symposium on Computational Intelligence in Dynamic and Uncertain Environments* (pp. 41-48). 10.1109/CIDUE.2011.5948491

Ditzler, G., & Polikar, R. (2013). Incremental Learning of Concept Drift from Streaming Imbalanced Data. *IEEE Transactions on Knowledge and Data Engineering, 25*(10), 2283–2301. doi:10.1109/TKDE.2012.136

Ditzler, G., Roveri, M., Alippi, C., & Polikar, R. (2015). Learning in nonstationary environments: A survey. *IEEE Computational Intelligence Magazine, 10*(4), 12–25. doi:10.1109/MCI.2015.2471196

Domingos, P., & Hulten, G. (2000). Mining high-speed data streams. In *Proceedings of 6th ACM SIGKDD international conference on knowledge discovery data mining* (pp. 71-80). ACM.

Dubey, R., Zhou, J., Wang, Y., Thompson, P. M., & Ye, J. (2014). Analysis of sampling techniques for imbalanced data: An n = 648 ADNI study. *NeuroImage*, *87*(15), 220–241. doi:10.1016/j.neuroimage.2013.10.005 PMID:24176869

Elkan, C. (2001). The Foundations of Cost-Sensitive Learning. In *Proceedings of intelligence joint conference on artificial intelligence* (pp.973-978). Academic Press.

Elwell, R., & Polikar, R. (2011). Incremental learning of concept drift in nonstationary environments. *IEEE Transactions on Neural Networks*, *22*(10), 1517–1531. doi:10.1109/TNN.2011.2160459 PMID:21824845

Fan, W., Stolfo, S. J., Zhang, J., & Chan, P. K. (1999). AdaCost: *Misclassification Cost-sensitive Boosting*. *Sixth International Conference of Machine Learning*, 97-105.

Fawcett, T. (2006). An introduction to ROC analysis. *Pattern Recognition Letters*, *27*(8), 861–874. doi:10.1016/j.patrec.2005.10.010

Galar, M., Fernandez, A., Barrenechea, E., Bustince, H., & Herrera, F. (2012). A Review on Ensembles for the Class Imbalance Problem: Bagging-, Boosting-, and Hybrid-Based Approaches. *IEEE Transactions on Systems, Man and Cybernetics. Part C, Applications and Reviews*, *42*(4), 463–484. doi:10.1109/TSMCC.2011.2161285

Gama, J., Sebastiao, R., & Rodrigues, P. P. (2013). On evaluating stream learning algorithms. *Machine Learning*, *90*(3), 317–346. doi:10.100710994-012-5320-9

Gama, J., Zliobaite, I., Bifet, A., Pechenizkiy, M., & Bouchachia, A. (2013). A Survey on Concept Drift Adaptation. *ACM Computing Surveys*, *46*(4), 1–37. doi:10.1145/2523813

Gao, J., Ding, B., Fan, W., Han, J., & Yu, P. (2008). Classifying data streams with skewed class distributions and concept drifts. *IEEE Internet Computing*, *12*(6), 37–49. doi:10.1109/MIC.2008.119

Gao, J., Fan, W., Han, J., & Yu, P. S. (2007). A general framework for mining concept-drifting data streams with skewed distributions. *Proceedings of the Seventh SIAM International Conference on Data Mining*, 3-14. 10.1137/1.9781611972771.1

Gao, K., Khoshgoftaar, T. M., & Napolitano, A. (2015). Investigating Two Approaches for Adding Feature Ranking to Sampled Ensemble Learning for Software Quality Estimation. *International Journal of Software Engineering and Knowledge Engineering*, *25*(1), 115–146. doi:10.1142/S0218194015400069

Ghazikhani, A., Monsefi, R., & Yazdi, H. S. (2013). Recursive least square perceptron model for nonstationary and imbalanced data stream classification. *Evolving Systems*, *4*(2), 119–113. doi:10.100712530-013-9076-7

Ghazikhani, A., Monsefi, R., & Yazdi, H. S. (2014). Online neural network model for non-stationary and imbalanced data stream classification. *International Journal of Machine Learning and Cybernetics*, *5*(1), 51–62. doi:10.100713042-013-0180-6

Guo, H., & Viktor, H. L. (2004). Learning from imbalanced data sets with boosting and data generation: The DataBoost-IM approach. *SIGKDD Explorations*, *6*(1), 30–39. doi:10.1145/1007730.1007736

Haibo, H., & Garcia, E. A. (2009). Learning from Imbalanced Data. *IEEE Transactions on Knowledge and Data Engineering, 21*(9), 1263–1283. doi:10.1109/TKDE.2008.239

Hawkins, D. M., Qiu, P., & Kang, C. W. (2003). The change point model for statistical process control. *Journal of Quality Technology, 35*(4), 355–366. doi:10.1080/00224065.2003.11980233

Haykin, S. (1998). Neural networks: A comprehensive foundation (2nd ed.). Prentice Hall.

Hido, S., Kashima, H., & Takahashi, Y. (2009). Roughly balanced bagging for imbalanced data. *Statistical Analysis and Data Mining, 2*(5-6), 412–426. doi:10.1002am.10061

Hoens, R. T., & Chawla, N. V. (2012). Learning in Nonstationary Environments with Class Imbalance. In *Proceedings of the 18th ACM SIGKDD International Conference on Knowledge Discovery and Data Mining* (pp. 168-176). ACM. 10.1145/2339530.2339558

Hoens, T. R., Chawla, N. V., & Polikar, R. (2011). Heuristic updatable weighted random subspaces for non-stationary environments. In *Proceedings of 11th International Conference on Data Mining* (pp. 241-250). 10.1109/ICDM.2011.75

Japkowicz, N. (2001). Concept-Learning in the Presence of Between-Class and Within-Class Imbalances. In *Advances in Artificial Intelligence, 14th Biennial Conference of the Canadian Society for Computational Studies of Intelligence, AI 2001* (pp. 67-77). 10.1007/3-540-45153-6_7

Japkowicz, N. (n.d.). *Learning from Imbalanced Data Sets*. Technical Report WS-00-05. The AAAI Press.

Japkowicz, N., & Stephen, S. (2002). The Class Imbalance Problem: A Systematic Study. *Intelligent Data Analysis, 6*(5), 429–449. doi:10.3233/IDA-2002-6504

Jo, D. T., & Japkowicz, N. (2004). Class imbalances versus small disjuncts. *SIGKDD Explorations, 6*(1), 40–49. doi:10.1145/1007730.1007737

Joshi, M. V., Kumar, V., & Agarwal, R. (2001). Evaluating Boosting Algorithms to Classify Rare Classes: Comparison And Improvements. *Proceedings of IEEE international conference on data mining*, 257-264. 10.1109/ICDM.2001.989527

Khammasi, I., Mouchaweh, M. S., Hammami, M., & Ghedira, K. (2018). Discussion and Review on Evolving Data Streams and Concept Drift Adapting. *Evolving Systems, 9*(1), 1–23. doi:10.100712530-016-9168-2

Korycki, L., Cano, A., & Krawczyk, B. (2019). Active learning with abstaining classifiers for imbalanced drifting data streams. In *Proceedings of 2019 IEEE International Conference on Big Data* (pp. 2334-2343). Los Angeles, CA: IEEE. 10.1109/BigData47090.2019.9006453

Lee, H., & Cho, S. (2006).). The Novelty Detection Approach for Different Degrees of Class Imbalance. *Lecture Notes in Computer Science, 4233.*

Lichtenwalter, R. N., & Chawla, N. V. (2010). Adaptive methods for classification in arbitrarily imbalanced and drifting data streams. In New Frontiers in Applied Data Mining, Lecture Notes in Computer Science (vol. 5669, pp. 53-75). doi:10.1007/978-3-642-14640-4_5

Liu, X., Wu, J., & Zhou, Z. (2009). Exploratory undersampling for class imbalance learning. *IEEE Transactions on Systems, Man, and Cybernetics. Part B, Cybernetics*, *39*(2), 539–550. doi:10.1109/TSMCB.2008.2007853 PMID:19095540

Liu, X., & Zhou, Z. (2006). The Influence of Class Imbalance on Cost-Sensitive Learning: An Empirical Study. In *Sixth International Conference on Data Mining (ICDM'06)* (pp. 970-974). 10.1109/ICDM.2006.158

Loezer, L., Enembreck, F., Barddal, J. P., & Britto, A. D. S. (2020). Cost sensitive learning for imbalanced data streams. In *Proceedings of SAC '20: Proceedings of the 35th Annual ACM Symposium on Applied Computing* (pp. 498-504). 10.1145/3341105.3373949

Lu, Y., Cheung, Y., & Tan, Y. Y. (2017). Dynamic Weighted Majority for Incremental Learning of Imbalanced Data Streams with Concept Drift. In *Proceedings of the Twenty-Sixth International Joint Conference on Artificial Intelligence* (pp. 2393-2399). 10.24963/ijcai.2017/333

Lu, Y., Cheung, Y., & Tang, Y. Y. (2019). Adaptive Chunk-Based Dynamic Weighted Majority for Imbalanced Data Streams with Concept Drift. *IEEE Transactions on Neural Networks and Learning Systems*, *31*(8), 2764–2788. doi:10.1109/TNNLS.2019.2951814 PMID:31825880

Lukasz, K., & Krawczyk, B. (2020). Online Oversampling for Sparsely Labeled Imbalanced and Non-Stationary Data Streams. In *International Joint Conference on Neural Networks* (pp. 1-8). Academic Press.

Minku, L. L., White, A., & Yao, X. (2010). The impact of diversity on online ensemble learning in the presence of concept drift. *IEEE Transactions on Knowledge and Data Engineering*, *22*(5), 731–742. doi:10.1109/TKDE.2009.156

Minku, L. L., & Yao, X. (2012). DDD: A New Ensemble Approach For Dealing With Concept Drift. *IEEE Transactions on Knowledge and Data Engineering*, *24*(4), 619–633. doi:10.1109/TKDE.2011.58

Morik, K., Brockhausen, P., & Joachims, T. (1999). Combining Statistical Learning with a Knowledge-Based Approach - A Case Study in Intensive Care Monitoring. In *Proceedings of the 16th International Conference on Machine Learning ICML* (pp. 268-277). Academic Press.

Nishida, K., & Yamauchi, K. (2007). Detecting concept drift using statistical testing. In *Proceedings of tenth international conference on discovery science* (pp. 264-269). 10.1007/978-3-540-75488-6_27

Padmaja, TM., Dhulipalla, N., Radha Krishna, P., Bapi, R.S., & Arjith, L. (2007). An Unbalanced Data Classification Model Using Hybrid Sampling Technique for Fraud Detection. *Pattern Recognition and Machine Intelligence*, 341-348.

Patist, J. P. (2007). Optimal window change detection. In *Proceedings of Seventh IEEE international conference on data mining workshops* (pp. 557-562). 10.1109/ICDMW.2007.9

Phua, C., Alahakoon, D., & Lee, V. C. S. (2004). Minority Report in Fraud Detection: Classification of Skewed Data. *SIGKDD Explorations*, *6*(1), 50–59. doi:10.1145/1007730.1007738

Pozzolo, A. D., Johnson, R. A., Caelen, O., Waterschoot, S., Chawla, N. V., & Bontempi, G. (2014). HDDT to avoid instances propagation in unbalanced and evolving data streams. In *IEEE International Joint Conference on Neural Networks IJCNN*. 10.1109/IJCNN.2014.6889638

Prati, R. C., Batista, G. E. A. P. A., & Monard, M. C. (2004). Class Imbalances *versus* Class Overlapping: An Analysis of a Learning System Behavior. In *Mexican International Conference on Artificial Intelligence* (vol 2972, pp. 312-321). 10.1007/978-3-540-24694-7_32

Seiffert, C., Khoshgoftaar, T. M., Hulse, J. V., & Napolitano, A. (2010). RUSBoost: A Hybrid Approach to Alleviating Class Imbalance. *IEEE Transactions on Systems, Man, and Cybernetics. Part A, Systems and Humans*, *40*(1), 185–197. doi:10.1109/TSMCA.2009.2029559

Shujian, Yu., Abraham, Z., Wang, H., Shah, M., Wei, Y., & Principe, J. C. (2019). Concept Drift Detection and adaptation with Hierarchical Hypothesis Testing. *Journal of the Franklin Institute*, *356*(5), 3187–3215. doi:10.1016/j.jfranklin.2019.01.043

Shujian, Yu., Wang, X., & Principe, J. C. (2018). Request-and Reverify: hierarchical hypothesis testing for concept drift detection with expensive labels. In *Proceedings of the Twenty-Seventh International Joint Conference on Artificial Intelligence* (pp. 3033-3039). Academic Press.

Sun, Y., Kamel, M. S., Wong, A. K. C., & Wang, Y. (2007). Cost-sensitive boosting for classification of imbalanced data. *Pattern Recognition*, *40*(12), 3358–3378. doi:10.1016/j.patcog.2007.04.009

Sun, Y., Wong, A. K. C., & Kamel, M. S. (2009). Classification of Imbalanced Data: A Review. *Journal of Pattern Recognition and Artificial Intelligence*, *23*(4), 687–719. doi:10.1142/S0218001409007326

Tegjyoth, S. S., & Kantardzic, M. (2017). On the reliable detection of concept drift from streaming unlabeled data. *Expert Systems with Applications: An International Journal*, *82*(C), 77–99.

Tharwat, A., & Schenck, W. (2020). Balancing Exploration and Exploitation: A novel active learner for imbalanced data. *Knowledge-Based Systems*, *210*, 106500. doi:10.1016/j.knosys.2020.106500

Wang, H., & Abraham, Z. (2015). Concept Drift Detection for Streaming Data. *International Joint Conference of Neural Networks*.

Wang, S., Minku, L. L., Ghezzi, D., Caltabiano, D., Tino, P., & Yao, X. (2013). Concept drift detection for online class imbalance learning. In *International Joint Conference on Neural Networks (IJCNN)* (1-10). 10.1109/IJCNN.2013.6706768

Wang, S., Minku, L. L., & Yao, M. (2015). Resampling-Based Ensemble Methods for Online Class Imbalance Learning. *IEEE Transactions on Knowledge and Data Engineering*, *27*(5), 1356–1368. doi:10.1109/TKDE.2014.2345380

Wang, S., Minku, L. L., & Yao, X. (2013). Online Class Imbalance Learning and Its Applications in Fault Detection. *Special Issue of International Journal of Computational Intelligence and Applications*, *12*(4), 1–19. doi:10.1142/S1469026813400014

Wang, S., Minku, L. L., & Yao, X. (2018). A Systematic Study of Online Class Imbalance Learning with Concept Drift. *IEEE Transactions on Neural Networks and Learning Systems*, *29*(10), 4802–4821. doi:10.1109/TNNLS.2017.2771290 PMID:29993955

Wang, S., & Yao, X. (2009). Diversity analysis on imbalanced data sets by using ensemble models. In *IEEE Symposium on Computational Intelligence and Data Mining* (pp. 324-331). 10.1109/CIDM.2009.4938667

Wu, G., & Chang, E. Y. (2003). Class-boundary alignment for imbalanced dataset learning. *ICML 2003 Workshop on Learning from Imbalanced Data Sets*.

Zhang, H., Liu, W., Shan, J., & Liu, Q. (2018). Online Active Learning Paired Ensemble for Concept Drift and Class imbalance. *IEEE Access: Practical Innovations, Open Solutions*, *99*, 1–1. doi:10.1109/ACCESS.2018.2882872

Zhang, X., Yang, T., & Srinivasan, P. (2016).4 Online Asymmetric Active Learning with Imbalanced Data. In *Proceedings of the 22nd ACM SIGKDD International Conference on Knowledge Discovery and Data Mining* (pp. 2055-2064). 10.1145/2939672.2939854

Zhao, P., & Hoi, S. C. H. (2013). Cost-Sensitive Online Active Learning with application to malicious URL detection. In *Proceedings of the 19th ACM SIGKDD International Conference on Knowledge Discovery and Data Mining* (pp. 919-927). 10.1145/2487575.2487647

Zliobaite, I., Bifet, A., Pfahringer, A., & Holmes, G. (2014). Active learning with drifting streaming data. *IEEE Transactions on Neural Networks and Learning Systems*, *25*(1), 27–39. doi:10.1109/TNNLS.2012.2236570 PMID:24806642

Chapter 3
A Survey on Aspect Extraction Approaches for Sentiment Analysis

Vrps Sastry Yadavilli

National Institute of Technology, Tadepalligudem, India

Karthick Seshadri

National Institute of Technology, Tadepalligudem, India

ABSTRACT

Aspect-level sentiment analysis gives a detailed view of user opinions expressed towards each feature of a product. Aspect extraction is a challenging task in aspect-level sentiment analysis. Hence, several researchers worked on the problem of aspect extraction during the past decade. The authors begin this chapter with a brief introduction to aspect-level sentimental analysis, which covers the definition of key terms used in this chapter, and the authors also illustrate various subtasks of aspect-level sentiment analysis. The introductory section is followed by an explanation of the various feature learning methods like supervised, unsupervised, semi-supervised, etc. with a discussion regarding their merits and demerits. The authors compare the aspect extraction methods performance with respect to metrics and a detailed discussion on the merits and demerits of the approaches. They conclude the chapter with pointers to the unexplored problems in aspect-level sentiment analysis that may be beneficial to the researchers who wish to pursue work in this challenging and mature domain.

INTRODUCTION

With tremendous growth of world wide web and internet, many users are interested to post reviews about a product in social blogs, merchant web sites and social networking sites. Analyzing and identifying emotions and opinions in this review text can give better insights about a product or service to manufacturers or buyers. Sentiment analysis identifies hidden emotion or opinions in the review text. Sentiment analysis could be applied to each review document (document level sentiment analysis), or to

DOI: 10.4018/978-1-7998-7371-6.ch003

each review sentence (sentence level sentiment analysis) or to each feature phrase (aspect level sentiment analysis). Sentiment analysis at document level deals with mining hidden sentiment in a document about a product. Sentence Level Classification identifies polarity labels such as positive, negative, neutral in each sentence. Aspect level sentiment analysis (ALSA) performs inference of opinions at a fine-grained level i.e., it extracts opinions about a feature of a product. Aspect level sentiment analysis mainly deals

Figure 1. A generic model for ALSA

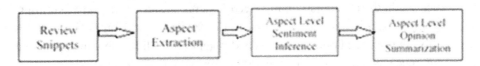

with three phases as shown in figure 1. (i) Aspect Extraction, (ii) Aspect Level Sentiment Inference and (iii) Opinion Summarization of extracted aspects.

The aspect level sentiment inference refers to identification of opinion words e.g., adjectives, adverbs expressed towards each aspect. Aspect Level Opinion summarization is the process of summarizing opinions expressed towards each aspect as a statistical or textual summary. The following example outlines the phases of aspect level sentiment analysis. From the review snippet "This camera is cheap", extracting "price" is an aspect extraction task; inferring the opinion orientation of the aspect "price" as positive is referred to as the aspect level sentimental inference task; summarizing number of such opinions expressed towards the aspect "price" across all the review snippets is considered as the aspect level opinion summarization task. Out of the three tasks, aspect extraction is important and challenging since aspects can either be explicitly mentioned (explicit aspects) in the text or hidden in the text (implicit aspects). Aspect extraction can be thought of as an imbalanced classification problem because the distribution of product aspects over all sentences is not uniform, the users tend to specify few aspects very frequently, leaving some infrequent but popular aspects in review sentences. It is difficult to prepare enough training data to train a classifier to extract implicit aspects which requires extensive domain knowledge as they are implicitly stated in the text. So, extraction of such aspects can try to address the imbalanced data classification issue. Various approaches for aspect extraction are predominantly classified as follows.

- Unsupervised methods
- Supervised methods
- Semi-supervised methods
- Reinforcement Learning methods
- Soft Computing methods
- Hybrid methods

The unsupervised methods extract aspects based on manually curated rules or heuristics or using some statistical techniques. Hu et al. (2004) adopted association rule mining (Agarwal et al.,1994) to find frequent features in product reviews. Quan et.al. (2014) used a combination of PMI (Bouma et al. (2009)) and TF-IDF (Salton et al. (1988)) to identify domain specific features. The features with a score above a preset threshold are declared as aspects. These methods are widely applied in sentiment analysis across various domains and languages.

The supervised methods use some predefined dictionary or machine learning or deep learning methods to perform aspect-oriented sentiment analysis. Kobayashi et al. (2007) used a seed opinion lexicon to get opinion words, Syntactic rules are used to find aspects from opinion words. Brychcín et al. (2014) proposed to extract aspects using a supervised machine learning framework called CRF (Lafferty et al. 2001) for extracting aspects.

The semi supervised methods use partially labelled data as a seed input to perform aspect level sentiment analysis. Such methods use bootstrapping, seed lexicon, graph based and word alignment-based techniques to perform aspect extraction. Wang et al. (2008) used bootstrapping to extract aspects by finding associations between seed opinion words and potential candidate features. Ansari et al. (2020) proposed Label Inference technique (Zhou et al. 2004) for extracting the aspects.

Recently researchers applied reinforcement learning for aspect level sentiment analysis. Such research attempts formulate the task of extraction of aspects as a explore-exploitation phenomenon and applied various reinforcement learning techniques like Hierarchal Reinforcement Learning, Deep Reinforcement learning to perform aspect level sentiment analysis. Wang et al. (2019) proposed to integrate LSTM (Hochreiter et al. 1997) and a Policy Network to perform aspect level sentiment classification.

Soft Computing methods consider the task of aspect extraction as an optimization problem and applied techniques like Ant Colony Optimization (J. Handl et al. 2006) and Particle Swarm Optimization (PSO) (Kennedy et al. 2001) to find an optimal subset of aspects. Gupta et al. (2015) adopted a PSO technique to extract noun phrases as an optimal set of aspects which maximizes the F-score of the sentiment classification task. Chifu et al. (2015) proposed to use ant colony optimization to cluster similar sentences and to extract potential aspects associated with the opinion words.

Hybrid approaches integrate two or more of the approaches cited above in hopes of obtaining a better performance. Wu et al. (2018) proposed to train a bi directional GRU (Cho et al. 2004) with dependency rules (Wu et al. 2009) to find dependencies between aspects and other opinion words through parsing. Ray et al. (2020) proposed to train a Convolution Neural Network (Kim Y. et al. 2014) with the dependency rules (Wu et al. 2009) to extract potential aspects from review snippets. In the subsequent sections the chapter outlines the technical details and merits and demerits of each of the approaches mentioned above.

CERTAIN TOOLS

WordNet (Fellbaum et al. 1998)
This dictionary maps the word pairs into their lexical relations such as synonym, hypernym and hyponym.
Senticnet (Cambria et al. 2016)
It is a sentiment polarity identification framework that can be used to assign polarity scores to various sentiment words.
Probase (Wu et al. 2012)
This framework infers various semantic relations between concepts such as cause-effect, hypernym-hyponym relationships.
Stanford Parser (Stanford, 2008)
This parser is used to find syntactic relationships between words such as amod (adjective modifier) and det (determiner).

Tweepy (Tweepy, 2009)

It is a python client library used to fetch tweets into an application.

Nltk (Nltk, 2002.)

This python library is used for performing various language processing tasks such as stemming and lemmatization.

Genism (Genism, 2009)

This python library is used for topic modelling and assorted language preprocessing tasks.

Spacy (Spacy, 2015)

This python library is used for finding syntactic dependencies through dependency parsing and parts of speech tagging.

ASPECT EXTRACTION APPROACHES

This section outlines the seminal aspect extraction approaches found in the literature.

Unsupervised Methods

The Unsupervised Approaches are classified into the following:

- Frequency Based Methods
- Bootstrapping Based Methods
- Statistical Methods.
- Rule Based Methods

Frequency Based Methods

Hu et al. (2004) proposed to extract aspects based on frequent feature identification as shown in Figure 2. Nouns were treated as potential features. Frequent features having frequency greater than a threshold were considered as aspects using association rule mining (Agarwal et al.1994) and discarded those reviews containing infrequent features. Adjectives were considered as opinion words and sentimental inference of each aspect was done by locating nearby adjectives. The sentiment classification of each opinion word (i.e., positive, negative, neutral) was done using Wordnet (Fellbaum et al. 1998), an opinion lexicon dictionary. After identifying opinion identification of sentences containing each aspect, opin-

Figure 2. Aspect extraction using association rule mining

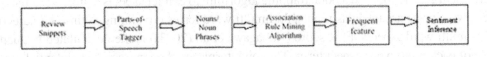

ion summary corresponding to each aspect was generated. This work operates based on the explicitly mentioned aspects in the reviews.

Moghaddam et al. (2010) proposed an unsupervised opinion miner framework to extract aspects from product reviews. Each word is labelled with its corresponding parts of speech tag and noun phrase stems are extracted using Porter's stemming algorithm (Willett et al. 2006). After pruning stop words, Apriori algorithm (Agarwal et al. 1994) is applied on noun phrases to extract frequent multipart noun phrases. Then for each noun phrase adjectives are extracted as opinion words using K-nearest neighbor (K-NN) algorithm and subsequently the sentiment expressed towards each aspect is inferred. Sentimental inference of each aspect across all the sentences in the review snippet is done and subsequently converted into a rating in the range of 1 to 5.

Eirinaki et al. (2012) proposed a High Adjective Count (HAC) algorithm to extract potential features. The algorithm takes review snippets as input, converts the snippets into sentences. Nouns are extracted as features and the nearest adjectives to each feature in a sentence is counted; the features with a high nearest adjective score are regarded as important features. Subsequently, the important features are input to the Max Opinion Score Algorithm, which computes a feature's polarity score as an average opinion score of all nearby adjectives over all the sentences.

Marrese-Taylor et al. (2014) have proposed to use parts of speech tagging and frequent item set mining to extract aspects from sentences. Given review snippets, nouns/noun phrases are extracted from reviews and frequent set mining is adopted (Agrawal et al. 1994) to collect noun phrases with above support threshold as aspects. The opinion orientation of each aspect is inferred as the sum of the opinion scores of nearby adjectives. across all the sentences.

Li et al. (2015) proposed to perform aspect extraction in three phrases namely Frequent Itemset Mining, Order based pruning and Similarity based pruning. Frequent Itemset Mining (Agarwal et al. 1994) is applied on the noun phrases in the review snippet to extract frequent noun phrases with a support greater than a preset threshold as aspects. The term order in each aspect is verified and aspects with irrelevant term order are pruned. Finally, the authors computed the similarity between each aspect and product name, the aspects having high similarity score are retained as final aspects.

Chauhan et al. (2018) prepared a domain specific contextual opinion lexicon, which is a dictionary of opinion words. The noun phrases which are nearer to these opinion words and having frequency greater than threshold are considered as aspects. Subsequently a dependency parser (Stanford, 2008.) and CRF (Lafferty et al. 2001) are used to perform aspect level sentiment classification.

Bootstrapping Based Methods

Bootstrapping based methods consider a seed aspect keyword list to recognize frequently associated opinion words with them. New aspects are also recognized in a similar way with available opinion words as shown in Figure 3.

Bagheri et al. (2013) proposed a bootstrapping algorithm to extract aspects using a seed list of aspect terms. Review snippets are taken as inputs, and multi word terms containing nouns and adjectives are extracted as multi word aspects. FLR score (Nakagawa et al. (2003)) is then calculated to quantify the importance of each multi word aspect term. The top k terms are then extracted as potential aspects. A-Score metric was designed and used to find the correlation between the extracted aspects and product. Irrelevant aspects with correlation less than a threshold are pruned. Aspects which are invalid (i.e., terms those are not related to the product) are pruned.

Figure 3. Aspect extraction using bootstrapping

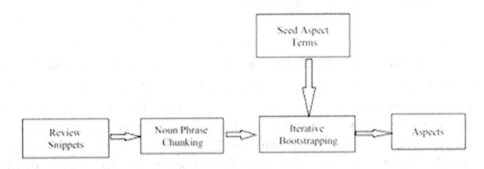

Statistical Methods

These methods use statistical techniques Like PMI, TF-IDF to extract aspects as shown in Figure 4.

Figure 4. Aspect extraction using statistical methods

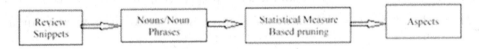

Raju et al. (2009) considered noun phrases from review snippets as aspects and filtered noun phrases that begin with determiner words like "other", "yours", "those" etc. KL divergence (Tomokiyo et al. 2003) between a noun phrase and review corpus to estimate the importance score of each noun phrase is measured. The KL Divergence between two probability distributions P, Q can be computed as given in equation (1) (Tomokiyo et al. 2003).

$$D_{KL}(P \| Q) = \sum_{x \in X} P(x) \log \frac{P(x)}{Q(x)} \dots \dots \dots \tag{1}$$

In equation (1), P, Q are two probability distributions defined on the probability space X.

They clustered the Noun phrases using the Group Average Agglomerative Clustering (GAAC) (Kaufman et al.1999) with the degree of overlap in the number of N-grams as a similarity measure. Finally, those noun phrases with high N-gram overlap scores are extracted as aspects from each cluster.

Zhu et al. (2011) proposed to extract multi word aspect terms using c-value score (Frantzi et al. 2000). The proposed Multi Aspect Bootstrapping algorithm takes review snippets as input, and extracts multi word terms and then it calculates the c-value score (Frantzi et al. 2000) of each multi word term. The c-value score is calculated as given in equation (2) (Frantzi et al. 2000).

$$c - value(t) = \log|t| \cdot frq(t) - \left(\frac{1}{n(S)}\right) \sum_{S} freq(S) \ldots\ldots \tag{2}$$

where $|t|$ .indicates number of words in the multiword term t, $frq(t)$ .gives a count of occurrences of the term t over all the sentences, S gives all the multi words in t .t, n(S) computes the number of terms in S. The multi word terms having a high c-value score are extracted as multi word aspects. Another algorithm entitled multi word aspect segmentation was proposed to cluster the multi aspect words into multi aspect segments based on their lexical similarity. Then the opinion orientation of each extracted aspect is inferred by locating the nearby adjectives and inferring the sentiment of each adjective using a seed lexicon opinion dictionary

Quan et.al. (2014) proposed to use PMI-TFIDF measure to measure the correlation between noun phrase and product term as given in equation (3) (Quan et.al. (2014)).

$$\text{PMI-TFIDF (p, q)} = \ .\log \frac{pr(p,q) \cdot \sum_{k} TFIDF(p,d_k) \sum_{k} TFIDF(q,d_k)}{pr(p) \cdot pr(q)} \ldots\ldots \tag{3}$$

$pr(p,q)$ .denotes the probability of both the terms p, q cooccurring with each other in the review corpus. $\sum_{k} TFIDF(p,d_k)$ .gives the value of significance score of a term p in a corpus. $\sum_{k} TFIDF(q,d_k)$ .computes the value of importance score of a term q in a corpus, $pr(p)$ .gives frequency estimate of the term p over all terms in a corpus. . $pr(q)$ .denotes frequency estimate of term q over all terms in a corpus The noun phrases with correlation scores greater than a threshold are extracted as domain specific aspects. Each sentence is represented in the form of a dependency tree using a dependency parser. aspect, opinion pairs using Dependency rules are used to extract aspects-opinion pairs. The opinion words with a less PMI-TFIDF score are filtered out from the list of Opinion words.

Rule Based Methods

These methods adopt parser-based dependency rules (Wu et al. 2009) to extract aspects as shown in Figure 5.

Figure 5. Aspect extraction using dependency rules

Poria et.al. (2014) proposed to use dependency rules to extract aspects from reviews. Each sentence is represented in the form of a dependency parse tree using the Stanford parser (Stanford,2008.) and lemmatization is then applied on each sentence. Nouns are then extracted from reviews and considered as explicit aspects. They have clustered aspects which are synonyms of one another provided by wordnet (Fellbaum et al. 1998). Opinion words are identified with the help of a seed opinion lexicon dictionary and the relation between each aspect and opinion word is determined using manually curated rules.

Rana et al. (2017) proposed to take Annotated reviews with parts of speech tags are taken as input and then adjectives, frequent nouns / noun phrases are extracted using manually preset rules. Similarity between two noun phrases is measured using the Normalized Google Distance (NGD) as specified in equation (4) (Cilibrasi et al.2007).

$$NGD(x,y) = \frac{max\{\log f(x), \log f(y)\} - \log f(x,y)}{\log N - \min\{\log f(x), \log f(y)\}} \cdots \cdots \cdots \quad (4)$$

The NGD between two noun phrases x and y is calculated as a function of number of web pages on which both noun phrases occur ($f(x,y)$) and number of web pages on which each noun phrases occur (f(x), f(y)) and the total number of web pages searched(N). The noun phrases are grouped using NGD. Each noun cluster is treated as a potential aspect.

Table 1. Summary of unsupervised methods

Author Name	Year	Method Used	Dataset	Language	Precision (%)	Recall (%)
Hu, M., & Liu, B.	2004	Frequency based	Product Reviews (Amazon, 1996a.)	English	53	49
Raju, S.	2009	Frequency based	Product Reviews (Amazon, 1996b.)	English	67	61
Moghaddam, S.	2010	Frequency based	Product Reviews (Epinions,1999.)	English	80	87
Zhu, J.	2011	Boot Strapping	Product Reviews (DianPing, 2010.)	English	69	56
Eirinaki, M.	2012	HAC	Product Reviews (Bing et al. 2004)	English	82	85
Bagheri, A.	2013	Bootstrapping	Product Reviews (Amazon, 1996a.)	English	81	68
Marrese-Taylor, E.	2014	Frequency based	Tourism Reviews (Tripadvisor,2000.)	English	90	93
Poria, S.	2014	Rule based	Product Reviews (Bing et al. 2004)	English	89	91
Quan, C.	2014	PMI	Product Reviews (Bing et al. 2004)	English	84	91
Li, Y.	2015	Bootstrapping	Product Reviews (Bing et al. 2004)	English	95	88
Rana, T.	2017	Two-fold rule based	Product Reviews (Bing et al. 2004)	English	87	92
Chauhan, G.S.	2018	Contextual opinion Lexicon + Dependency Parser	Product Reviews (Amazon,1996b.)	English	86	85

Table 1 shows that Bootstrapping approach provides a high precision and moderate recall due to partial supervision in the form of the initial set of seed opinion words. The frequency-based methods achieve a low precision and recall on Product Reviews because less frequent but important terms are ignored by these methods. The rule-based methods achieve moderate precision and a high recall on product reviews since the performance of rule-based methods depends on the quality of the rules chosen.

Supervised Methods

The supervised methods generally adopted for aspect extraction are based on the following methods:

- Sequence labelling
- Machine learning
- Deep learning

Sequence Labelling Based Methods

Kobayashi et al. (2007) used dependency rules for extracting aspects. The opinion words are identified using a predefined seed lexicon dictionary. Subsequently the authors identified strength of association between extracted opinion words and noun phrases to collect aspects using their cooccurrence frequencies.

A lexicalized HMM model (Cutting et al. 1992.) was leveraged by Jin et al. (2009) for extracting aspect-opinion pairs and for performing aspect level sentiment classification. After tagging each word with its part-of-speech, a hybrid tag sequence is used to identify whether it is an opinion word or aspect with the help of HMM (Cutting et al. 1992). Adjectives that are in the vicinity of an aspect are retrieved as opinion words and sentences without any opinion word are pruned. The authors then performed sentimental inference of each opinion word using a seed opinion lexicon dictionary.

In a subsequent research work done by Li et al. (2010), Linear CRF (Lafferty et al. 2001), Skip Chain CRF (Sutton et al. 2006) and Skip tree CRF (Sutton et al. 2006) were employed for the aspect-opinion pair extraction. A CRF (Lafferty et al. 2001) is a probabilistic graphical model based on conditional distribution $p(z|t)$.as given in equation (5) (Lafferty et al. 2001).

$$P(z|t) = \frac{\exp\left(\sum_{k=1}^{l} U(t_k, z_k) \cdot \sum_{k=1}^{l-1} V(z_k, z_{k+1})\right)}{Z(t)} \dots\dots\dots\dots(5).$$

z .gives a vector of random variables over class labels. t .gives observed feature vectors. $Z(t)$ .s a normalization factor. $V(z_k, z_{k+1})$ specifies how likely the label z_{k+1} .can be seen after the label z_k . $U(t_k, z_k)$ denotes the joint likelihood of the variable t_k .and the label z_k .

The authors adopted a Linear CRF to identify the polarity orientation between two continuous words, (i.e., if they are connected by the conjunction" and" the words represent similar sentiment polarity; however, if they are connected by" but" to the words are considered to have opposite polarities). Skip chain CRF was used to model the semantic relationship between two text sequences which are connected by a conjunction having same parts of speech tag. A sentence is depicted in the form of a dependency tree using tree CRF. Finally, SkipTreeCRF is used to give a combined representation of these two structures Skip chain CRF and tree CRF to extract aspect and opinion pairs that are semantically connected by conjunctions and exhibit syntactic dependencies in a sentence.

Li et al. (2012) proposed to construct parse tree from each sentence using a dependency parser and by supplying opinion words as predicate list. The irrelevant opinion targets are pruned using some heuristic rules. Then the extraction of the potential opinion targets was considered as a binary classification problem to infer aspects.

Brychcín et al. (2014) proposed to extract aspects using CRF ((Lafferty et al. 2001) by labelling each sentence using BIO tagging. and opinion orientation of each aspect is determined by finding out opinion words occurring within a contextual window of ten words in each sentence. Given a predefined set of categories an implementation of maximum entropy binary classifier (Konkol et al. 2014) was used for determining each aspect category. Then aspect category of a sentence is taken as an assembled result of individual classifiers.

Machine Learning Based Methods

Agarwal et al. (2016) adopted information gain (Lerman et al. 1984) and minimum redundancy Maximum Relevance mrMR (Ding et al. 2005) measures for aspect extraction as given in equations (6) -(8) (Ding et al. 2005).

$$A = MI\left(f_m, c\right) = \sum_{f_m, c} p\left(f_m, c\right) \log \frac{p\left(f_m, c\right)}{p\left(f_m\right) \cdot p\left(c\right)} \ldots \ldots \ldots (6).$$

$$B = MI\left(f_i, f_j\right) = \sum_{f_i, f_j} p\left(f_i, f_j\right) \log \frac{p\left(f_i, f_j\right)}{p\left(f_i, f_j\right)} \cdot \ldots \ldots \ldots \tag{7}$$

'A' indicates the correlation between a feature f_m and the class label c. 'B' denotes the correlation between two features namely f_i, f_j. Mutual Information Difference (MID) measure can be computed using equation (8) (Ding et al. 2005).

$$MID \text{ (Mutual Information Difference)} = \max\left(A - B\right) \ldots \ldots \tag{8}$$

$$Information\,Gain\left(S, a\right) = H\left(S\right) - H\left(S|a\right) \ldots \ldots (9).$$

$$H\left(S\right) = \sum_{I-1}^{C} - P_i \log P_i \ldots \ldots \ldots \ldots \ldots \tag{10}$$

In equation (9) (Lerman et al. 1984) H(S) is the entropy of dataset S before observing any feature. $H(S \mid a)$. denotes the entropy of S after observing the feature 'a'. In equation (10) (Lerman et al. 1984) P_i.refers to the probability of the class 'i'.The following types of features are extracted: (i) unigrams, (ii) bi-grams, (iii) bi-tagged and (iv) dependency features as shown in Figure 5. Clustering of features is done using the feature's semantic orientation for which Pointwise Mutual Information (Bouma et al. 2009) is adopted as a similarity measure. The feature scores are calculated using information gain and MID measures. Those features with a score greater than the threshold are extracted as prominent aspects.

Manek et.al. (2017) adopted a decision tree- based Gini index (Lerman et al. 1984) measure as the feature selection method for aspect extraction. The movie reviews are pre-processed, and features are extracted from the reviews. Each feature is weighted using Gini index measure as given in equation (11) (Lerman et al. 1984).

$$Gini\ index = 1 - \sum_i 1 - p_i^2 \dots\dots\dots \tag{11}$$

Gini index measures the level of impurity i.e., a randomly chosen element is wrongly classified under a particular class. p_i indicates the probability that a variable is classified under the class 'i'. The top-k features for opinion classification are extracted based on these Gini index weights.

Deep Learning Based Methods

Figure 6. Aspect extraction using deep neural network

Wang et al. (2015) adopted a deep learning framework for extracting aspects as shown in Figure 6. Bag-of-words based sentence representation is given to a neural network which outputs a probability distribution over aspects. Then these word vectors are scaled based on aspects. CNN (Kim Y. et al. 2014) is then used to perform a convolution (Weighted Sum) operation on a window of 'h' sequential words. After iterating over all the words in a sentence, a feature vector is generated, then Max Pooling operation is performed to select the maximum value as a sentiment orientation associated with each aspect.

Ma et.al. (2018) adopted a Hierarchal LSTM (Hochreiter et al. 1997) for extracting the aspects. Each word in a sentence is converted to its word embeddings (Mikolov et al. 2013). These word vectors are fed into a LSTM network (Hochreiter et al. 1997) which converts the embeddings into a sequence of hidden outputs. A target level attention (Bahdanau et al. 2014) is proposed to obtain a target vector to identify corresponding target expressions (opinion expressions). The aspect embeddings and target vectors are concatenated to represent a sentence vector for each aspect-target pair. Subsequently, this representation is given to a SoftMax layer for sentiment classification. The authors incorporated common sense knowledge from SenticNet (Cambria et al. 2016) to enhance the accuracy of sentiment classification.

Table 2. Summary of supervised methods

Author Name	Year	Method Used	Dataset	Language	Precision (%)	Recall (%)	Limitation of Methodology
Kobayashi, N.	2007	Dependency Tree	Product Reviews (Amazon, 1996a .)	Japanese	72	62	Sentence needs to follow predefined dependency grammar
Jin, W.	2009	Lexicalized HMM	Camera Reviews (Amazon, 1996b.)	English	75	70	Does not deal with out of vocabulary words
Li, F.	2010	Skip tree-CRF	Movie Reviews (Amazon, 1996a.)	English	86	69	Expensive to train
Li, S.	2012	Shallow Semantic Parsing	Web Services (Mitre,1958.)	English	89	52	It takes more processing time to build the semantic graph
Brychcín, T.	2014	CRF+MaxEntropy Classifier	Product Reviews (Cornell,2002.)	English	77	82	Expensive to train
Wang, B.	2015	MLP+CNN	Product Reviews (Cornell,2002.)	English	52	50	Performance degrades when reviews are not available while testing
Agarwal, B.	2016	Information Gain+mrMR	Movie Reviews (Cornell,2002.)	English	78	65	It overfits the model when there are several unique values for an attribute
Manek, A. S	2017	Gini Index+NB+SVM	Movie Reviews (Cornell,2002.)	English	80	81	Time Complexity in building ensemble architecture is quite high.
Ma, Y.	2018	Hierarchal LSTM	Product Reviews (Cornell,2002.)	English	82	81	Requires an extensive training set.

Table 2 shows that we can observe that the shallow semantic parsing-based method achieves a high precision but suffers from a low recall. An ensemble of classifiers achieves a high precision and recall. Deep learning models like Hierarchal LSTM achieves a high precision and recall for the sentiment classification task, as Hierarchal LSTMs are good at sequence modeling which can remember long range dependencies between aspects and opinion words

Semi-Supervised Methods

The semi-supervised approaches for aspect extraction are normally classified as follows:

- Bootstrapping based methods
- Word alignment-based methods

- Graph based methods.

Bootstrapping Based Methods

Wang et.al. (2008) proposed a modified mutual information (Church et al. 1990) measure to find strength of correlation between aspects and opinion words. A seed opinion lexicon is used to identify correlated noun phrases(aspects). Subsequently these aspects are used to generate correlated opinion words. Subsequently aspects with low frequency are pruned by applying some linguistic rules. Implicit aspects are mapped to explicit aspects with the help of opinion words.

Wu et al. (2009) proposed to represent each sentence in the form of a dependency tree using a dependency parser (Stanford, 2008). Adjectives are taken to be the opinion words located near frequent nouns(aspects). After constructing a dependency parse tree, a separate kernel function (Culotta et al. 2004) is adopted to find the lowest common ancestor of aspects and opinion words to identify the relation between them. A kernel function was incorporated into SVM (Mullen et al. 2004) for finally performing an aspect level sentiment classification.

Qiu et.al. (2009) adopted double propagation for the task of aspects and opinion words extraction. The authors have considered a seed opinion lexicon to recognize noun phrases, which have close association with this opinion words. These noun phrases are termed as aspects. The new opinion words are extracted which are closely associated with these aspects. The same procedure is repeated until no new aspects, opinion words are found. As this process propagates through both opinion words and aspects, it is referred to as "Double Propagation".

Zhang et al. (2010) introduced additional patterns like whole-part pattern, no pattern to improve the performance of double propagation. The whole-part relationship is identified to exist between a product and an aspect. For instance, consider the review snippet, "the location of the hotel", whole-part relationship exists between the entity "hotel" and the aspect "location". The "no pattern" is adopted to identify aspects. For example, in the review snippet "no color"," color" is the aspect followed by "no" keyword". HITS algorithm is used (Kleinberg et al. 1999) to measure importance score of aspects and the aspects are finally ranked based on their important scores.

Yu et.al. (2011) recognized the nouns/noun phrases using a Sandford Parser (Stanford, 2008) Then a synonym-based clustering is performed on the aspects. The frequency of each aspect is estimated in reviews expressing both positive and negative sentiments and the opinion orientation of each aspect over all reviews.

d is known as damping factor, typically has value equal to 0.85, N indicates the total count of vertices in a graph. $M(p_i$ indicates number of edges connected to the vertex $p_i . L(p_j)$ denotes the number of outgoing edges the vertex p_j an have. The features with an importance score above a predefined threshold are considered as aspects. The authors expanded each aspect term using a seed synonym lexicon dictionary and identified potential implicit aspects from the expanded synonym sets.

Ansari et.al. (2020) adopted a graph-based approach for aspect extraction task. Each word in reviews is represented as a feature vector containing features such as frequent terms, orthogonal features, stop words etc. which are used as clues for potential aspect terms. Similarity between feature vectors is estimated and a K-nearest Neighbor graph is constructed. Subsequently, some of the terms are labelled as aspects and Label Propagation algorithm (Zhou et al. 2004) is adopted to infer whether a word is an aspect or not.

Table 3. Summary of semi-supervised methods

Author Name	Year	Method Used	Dataset	Language	Precision (%)	Recall (%)
Wang, B.	2008	Bootstrapping	Product Reviews (it168,2017.)	Chinese	56	49
Wu, Y.	2009	Dependency Parsing	Product Reviews (Bing et al. 2004)	English	57	44
Qiu, G.	2009	Double Propagation	Product Reviews (Bing et al. 2004)	English	70	60
Zhang, L.	2010	Rules +Double Propagation	Product Reviews (Bing et al. 2004)	English	72	54
Yu, J.	2011	Shallow Dependency Parser	Product Reviews (cnet, 1994.)	English	68	81
Hai, Z.	2012	Bootstrapping	Product Reviews (Crunchbase, 2015.)	English	68	81
Liu, K.	2013	Word Alignment Model	Product Reviews (Tripadvisor,2000.)	English	80	85
Xu, L.	2013	Partially Supervised Word Alignment Model	Product Reviews (Amazon,1996a.)	English	78	84
Ma, B.	2013	LDA + Seed Lexicon	Product Reviews (Bing et al. 2004)	English	75	73
Yan, Z.	2015	PageRank Model	Product Reviews (jd, 1998.)	English	80	70
Ansari, G.	2020	Label Propagation	Product Reviews (Bing et al. 2004)	English	70	68

Table 3 shows a summary of the different semi supervised methods for aspect extraction. The word alignment model gives an optimal precision and recall among all others. Although extended page rank method provides a good precision it suffers from a low recall because it filters out the terms with low page rank scores.

Reinforcement Learning Based Methods

Wang, T. et.al. (2019) proposed an aspect level sentiment classification using reinforcement learning. Each sentence was divided into segments and each segment is fed into Bi-LSTM (Hochreiter et al. 2004) to get hidden state vectors for each segment, then a multi-layer perceptron (MLP) was used to reduce the dimensionality of each segment hidden state vector and finally it was passed to SoftMax layer for sentiment prediction. Then aspect segments were extracted using a Policy Network which defines a policy for aspect segment extraction and LSTM (Hochreiter et al. 2004) was adopted for state representation. Then policy gradient (Sutton et al. 1999) was used to update the parameters of policy network and cross entropy (Li et al. (1993)) was used as a loss function.

Wang, J. et.al. (2019 b) proposed a hierarchal reinforcement learning (Sutton et al. 1999) for document level aspect sentiment classification. A two-level policy framework was used in which a high-level policy was used to select aspect specific clauses, the cosine similarity was used to select aspect specific clauses in a review sentence whereas low-level policy selects opinion words in each clause. Two LSTM (Hochreiter et al. 2004) networks were used for each of these policies.

Table 4 shows that the SR-LSTM + Policy Network performs better than LSTM + Hierarchical Reinforcement Learning because the former extracts each aspect segment at a sentence level and assigns polarity to each aspect segment thus improves overall aspect level sentiment classification.

Table 4. Summary of reinforcement learning based methods

Author Name	Year	Method Used	Dataset	Language	Precision (%)	Recall (%)
Wang, T.	2019	State Representation LSTM + Policy Network	Product Reviews (SemEval, 2014)	English	83	80
Wang, J.	2019	Hierarchal Reinforcement Learning + LSTM	Product Reviews (SemEval, 2014)	English	80	85

Soft Computing Based Methods

Gupta et al. (2015) proposed to apply PSO (Kennedy et al. 2001) for aspect extraction and CRF (Lafferty et al. 2001) for sentiment prediction. Each review sentence is labelled with the parts of speech tagging and a feature vector of each word is constructed with its context (preceding and following two words), prefix and suffix of length (up to three characters), orthographical features (a word is capitalized or not) etc. as features. Binary Particle Swarm Optimization (PSO) (Kennedy et al. 2001) technique is adopted to find an optimal set of aspects maximizing F-measure as an objective function. CRF (Lafferty et al. 2001) is applied for performing aspect level sentiment analysis. Their approach is domain independent in nature.

Chifu et al. (2015) proposed to apply ant colony optimization (J. Handl et al. 2006) technique to group similar sentences and extract potential aspects that are associated with opinion words. Extended neural network named Growing Hierarchical Self-Organizing Maps (Kohonen et al. 2012) is adopted to represent a hierarchal relationship between aspects and opinion words. The root node is a Product Name, Child nodes are aspect names, whereas the Leaf nodes are Opinion words (Positive, Negative Labels).

Rana, T. et al. (2015) proposed to label each review sentence with a parts of speech tagger, some sequential pattern rules (J. Pei et al. 2004) are used to find correlations between different words and opinion words. Google similarity distance (Cilibrasi et al. 2007) based method was adopted to find synonyms of the extracted aspects. The sets of aspects with a similarity value above a predefined threshold

Table 5. Summary of soft computing based methods

Author Name	Year	Method Used	Dataset	Language
Gupta, D.	2015	CRF + PSO	Product Reviews (SemEval, 2014)	English
Chifu, E.	2015	ACO + GHSOM	Product Reviews (SemEval, 2014)	English
Rana, T.	2015	Rule based method + PSO	Product Reviews (Bing et al., 2004)	English
Akhtar,M.	2017	PSO + ensemble classifiers	Product Reviews (SemEval, 2014)	English

are given to Particle Swarm Optimization algorithm as input (Kennedy et al. 2001) to find an optimal set of aspect clusters.

Akhtar et.al. (2017) taken a set of aspects from a training set and an optimal set of aspects are obtained using PSO (Kennedy et al. 2001) solver with F-measure as the objective function. The three ensemble classifiers namely ME (Nigam et al. 1999), CRF (Lafferty et al. 2001) and SVM (Mullen et al. 2004) are used. A PSO based ensemble with a majority voting and PSO based ensemble with majority weighting methods are used to find a good subset of ensemble classifiers for an accurate sentiment prediction.

Table 5 shows that combining genetic algorithm with traditional aspect extraction approaches yields better results. Combining Conditional Random Field with Particle Swarm Optimization yields a high precision and nominal recall since the aspect and opinion word dependencies in a sentence are better captured through sequence labelling, thus improving the accuracy of the aspect level sentiment classification.

Hybrid Methods

Wu et al. (2018) extracted aspects using some dependency rules (Wu et al., 2009). Each review sentence is annotated with its parts of speech and noun phrases are extracted. The domain correlation of the extracted noun phrases is checked using cosine similarity between these phrases and product terms. The noun phrases are extracted as potential aspects which have a frequency greater than a threshold. These aspects are then converted into word embeddings (Mikolov et al., 2013) and are used in training a bidirectional GRU (Cho et al. 2004) for aspect extraction.

Ray et al. (2020) labelled each review sentence with its parts-of-speech. A skip-gram model (Mikolov et al., 2013) is adopted to convert each word into a 300-dimensional word vector. Then these word embeddings are fed into a 7-layer CNN (Kim et al., 2014) to predict the aspect categories in each sentence. CNN is trained with the Stanford dependency rules (Wu et al., 2009) for extracting aspects. Sentiwordnet (Cambria et al., 2014) is used for sentiment prediction. Sentiment scores of aspects are calculated using some predefined rules (Wu et al., 2009).

Chauhan et al. (2020) integrated linguistic rules and deep learning techniques to improve the accuracy of aspect extraction. The noun phrases are fetched from reviews and extended noun phrases are obtained using some linguistic rules. Then a frequency pruning step filtered out the infrequent nouns. Domain correlation pruning is done to prune domain irrelevant terms by measuring cosine similarity between aspects and product terms. Subsequently, these aspects are used to train a bi-directional LSTM network (Hochreiter et al., 1997) with attention (Bahadanu et al., 2014) mechanism for aspect extraction.

Table 6 illustrates the hybrid methods. Combining two or more existing aspect extraction approaches can yield better results on aspect extraction compared to individual aspect extraction approaches. From

Table 6. Summary of hybrid methods

Author Name	Year	Method Used	Dataset	Language	Precision (%)	Recall (%)
Wu, C.	2018	Dependency Parser + Bi GRU	Product Reviews (SemEval, 2014)	English	63	73
Ray, P.	2020	Rule based method + CNN	Product Reviews (SemEval, 2014)	English	90	86
Chauhan, G. S.	2020	Rule based method + Bi LSTM	Product Reviews (SemEval, 2014)	English	68	75

the table we can infer that combining rule-based methods with CNN achieves a high accuracy and recall, since CNN can be suitable for finding minimal optimal set of features for sentiment classification.

FUTURE RESEARCH DIRECTIONS

In this section, we outline some research directions which can be pursued by researchers working in the domain of sentiment analysis.

Implicit Aspect Level Opinion Identification

Extracting implicit aspects from review snippets is a challenging task. This is because the user implicitly mentions the occurrence of aspects through opinion words. For example, the review snippet "The phone requires frequent charging" implicitly mentions the aspect "battery" and an opinion "negative" towards the aspect "battery". Extracting implicit opinions corresponding to implicit aspects is underexplored in the literature.

Dynamicity of Aspect Level Sentiment Inference

The preferences of users on different aspects of a product change over time as users change their opinions through their experience of using the product or by consulting with their friends or relatives. Hence, modeling the way sentiments towards aspects change over time is a challenging task.

Aspect Identification from Objective Sentences

Identification of aspects from objective sentences is a challenging task because we do not have any clue words. For example, consider the following hotel review statement "There are many ants in the room" discuss about the aspect "cleanliness".

Multi Implicit Aspect Identification

A review snippet can have more than one implicit aspect in it. For example, consider the following review snippet "The phone display is good, but it is too tiny to put into my pocket", mentions about two aspects namely "screen" and "size".

CONCLUSION

This chapter provided a brief introduction to and motivation behind Aspect Level Sentiment Analysis and then subsequently explored various aspect extraction techniques. We categorized these techniques according to the nature of the statistical model they adopted and provided a summary of these techniques with a relative comparison with respect to the performance metrics like precision and recall. Finally, the chapter highlights some open research challenges to be addressed by researchers in aspect level sentiment analysis. Since Implicit aspect extraction is a challenging task, incorporating domain knowledge into the aspect extraction task can yield a better performance as typically aspects are domain specific in nature. Due to the generic nature of the existing seed opinion lexicon frameworks like Senticnet and WordNet, these frameworks can't be applied to specific domains. It is safe to remark that sentimental inference with the domain specific opinion words can potentially improve the accuracy of the aspect level sentiment classification tasks.

REFERENCES

Agrawal, R., & Srikant, R. (1994). Fast algorithms for mining association rules. *Proc. 20th int. conf. very large data bases, VLDB, 1215*, 487-499.

Akhtar, M. S., Gupta, D., Ekbal, A., & Bhattacharyya, P. (2017). Feature selection and ensemble construction: A two-step method for aspect-based sentiment analysis. *Knowledge-Based Systems, 125*, 116–135. doi:10.1016/j.knosys.2017.03.020

Amazon. (1996a). http://www.amazon.com

Amazon. (1996b). http://www.amazon.in

Ansari, G., Saxena, C., Ahmad, T., & Doja, M. N. (2020). Aspect term extraction using graph-based semi-supervised learning. *Procedia Computer Science, 167*, 2080–2090. doi:10.1016/j.procs.2020.03.249

Bouma, G. (2009). Normalized (pointwise) mutual information in collocation extraction. *Proceedings of GSCL*, 31-40.

Bagheri, A., Saraee, M., & De Jong, F. (2013). Care more about customers: Unsupervised domain-independent aspect detection for sentiment analysis of customer reviews. *Knowledge-Based Systems, 52*, 201–213. doi:10.1016/j.knosys.2013.08.011

Bahdanau, D., Cho, K., & Bengio, Y. (2014). *Neural machine translation by jointly learning to align and translate.* arXiv preprint arXiv:1409.0473.

Bing, L. (2004). *Opinion Mining, Sentiment Analysis and Opinion Spam Detection.* http://www.cs.uic.edu~liub/FBS/sentiment-analysis.html

Blei, D. M., Ng, A. Y., & Jordan, M. I. (2003). Latent dirichlet allocation. *The Journal of Machine Learning Research, 3*, 993-1022.

Brown, P. F., Della Pietra, S. A., Della Pietra, V. J., & Mercer, R. L. (1993). The mathematics of statistical machine translation: Parameter estimation. *Computational Linguistics, 19*(2), 263–311.

Brychcín, T., Konkol, M., & Steinberger, J. (2014). Uwb: Machine learning approach to aspect-based sentiment analysis. *Proceedings of the 8th International Workshop on Semantic Evaluation (SemEval 2014)*, 817-822. 10.3115/v1/S14-2145

Cambria, E., Poria, S., Bajpai, R., & Schuller, B. (2016). SenticNet 4: A semantic resource for sentiment analysis based on conceptual primitives. *Proceedings of COLING 2016, the 26th international conference on computational linguistics: Technical papers*, 2666-2677.

Cambria, E., Olsher, D., & Rajagopal, D. (2014). SenticNet 3: a common and common-sense knowledge base for cognition-driven sentiment analysis. *Proceedings of the AAAI Conference on Artificial Intelligence*, 28-35.

Church, K., & Hanks, P. (1990). Word association norms, mutual information, and lexicography. *Computational Linguistics, 16*, 22–29.

Culotta, A., & Sorensen, J. (2004). Dependency tree kernels for relation extraction. *Proceedings of the 42nd Annual Meeting of the Association for Computational Linguistics (ACL-04)*, 423-429. 10.3115/1218955.1219009

Chauhan, G. S., & Meena, Y. K. (2018). Prominent aspect term extraction in aspect based sentiment analysis. *2018 3rd International Conference and Workshops on Recent Advances and Innovations in Engineering (ICRAIE)*, 1-6. 10.1109/ICRAIE.2018.8710408

Chauhan, G. S., Meena, Y. K., Gopalani, D., & Nahta, R. (2020). A two-step hybrid unsupervised model with attention mechanism for aspect extraction. *Expert Systems with Applications, 161*, 113673. doi:10.1016/j.eswa.2020.113673

Chifu, E. Ş., Leţia, T. Ş., & Chifu, V. R. (2015). Unsupervised aspect level sentiment analysis using Ant Clustering and Self-organizing Maps. *2015 International Conference on Speech Technology and Human-Computer Dialogue (SpeD)*, 1-9. 10.1109/SPED.2015.7343075

Cho, K., Van Merriënboer, B., Gulcehre, C., Bahdanau, D., Bougares, F., Schwenk, H., & Bengio, Y. (2014). Learning phrase representations using RNN encoder-decoder for statistical machine translation. doi:10.3115/v1/D14-1179

Cilibrasi, R. L., & Vitanyi, P. M. (2007). The google similarity distance. *IEEE Transactions on Knowledge and Data Engineering, 19*(3), 370–383. doi:10.1109/TKDE.2007.48

cnet. (1994). http://www.cnet.com

Cornell. (2002). *Movie Review Data*. http://www.cs.cornell.edu/people/pabo/movie-review-data/

Crunchbase. (2015.). *lvping*. https://www.crunchbase.com/organization/lvping

Cutting, D., Kupiec, J., Pedersen, J., & Sibun, P. (1992). A practical part-of-speech tagger. *Third Conference on Applied Natural Language Processing*, 33-140.

Deerwester, S., Dumais, S. T., Furnas, G. W., Landauer, T. K., & Harshman, R. (1990). Indexing by latent semantic analysis. *Journal of the American Society for Information Science, 41*(6), 391–407. doi:10.1002/(SICI)1097-4571(199009)41:6<391::AID-ASI1>3.0.CO;2-9

DianPing. (2010). http://www.DianPing.com

Ding, C., & Peng, H. (2005). Minimum redundancy feature selection from microarray gene expression data. *Journal of Bioinformatics and Computational Biology, 30*(2), 185–205. doi:10.1142/S0219720005001004 PMID:15852500

Dunning, T. E. (1993). Accurate methods for the statistics of surprise and coincidence. *Computational Linguistics, 19*(1), 61–74.

Eirinaki, M., Pisal, S., & Singh, J. (2012). Feature-based opinion mining and ranking. *Journal of Computer and System Sciences*, *78*(4), 1175–1184. doi:10.1016/j.jcss.2011.10.007

Epinions. (1999). http://www.Epinions.com

Fellbaum, C. (1998). A semantic network of English verbs. *WordNet: An Electronic Lexical Database*, *3*, 153-178.

Frantzi, K., Ananiadou, S., & Mima, H. (2000). Automatic recognition of multi-word terms. the c-value/nc-value method. *International Journal on Digital Libraries*, *3*(2), 115–130. doi:10.1007007999900023

Genism. (2009). *Topic Modelling for Humans*. https://radimrehurek.com/gensim/

Gupta, D. K., Reddy, K. S., & Ekbal, A. (2015). Pso-asent: Feature selection using particle swarm optimization for aspect based sentiment analysis. *International conference on applications of natural language to information systems*, 220-233.

Hai, Z., Chang, K., & Cong, G. (2012). One seed to find them all: mining opinion features via association. *Proceedings of the 21st ACM international conference on Information and knowledge management*, 255-264. 10.1145/2396761.2396797

Hochreiter, S., & Schmidhuber, J. (1997). Long short-term memory. *Neural Computation*, *9*(8), 1735–1780. doi:10.1162/neco.1997.9.8.1735 PMID:9377276

Hu, M., & Liu, B. (2004). Mining and summarizing customer reviews. *Proceedings of the tenth ACM SIGKDD international conference on Knowledge discovery and data mining*, 168-177.

Handl, J., Knowles, J., & Dorigo, M. (2006). Ant-based clustering and topographic mapping. *Artificial Life*, *12*(1), 35–62. doi:10.1162/106454606775186400 PMID:16393450

it168. (2017). http://it168.com

jd. (1998). http://www.jd.com

Jin, W., Ho, H. H., & Srihari, R. K. (2009). A novel lexicalized HMM-based learning framework for web opinion mining. *Proceedings of the 26th annual international conference on machine learning*, *10*, 1553374-1553435. 10.1145/1553374.1553435

Joachims, T. (1999). Transductive inference for text classification using support vector machines. ICML, 99, 200-209.

Kaufman, L., & Rousseeuw, P. J. (2009). Finding groups in data: an introduction to cluster analysis. John Wiley & Sons.

Kennedy, J., & Eberhart, R. C. (2001). *Swarm Intelligence*. Morgan Kaufmann Publishers Inc.

Kim, Y. (2014). Convolutional Neural Networks for Sentence Classification. *Proceedings of the 2014 Conference on Empirical Methods in Natural Language Processing (EMNLP)*, 1746-1751. 10.3115/v1/D14-1181

Kleinberg, J. M. (1999). Authoritative sources in a hyperlinked environment. *Journal of the Association for Computing Machinery*, *46*(5), 604–632. doi:10.1145/324133.324140

Kobayashi, N., Inui, K., & Matsumoto, Y. (2007). Extracting aspect-evaluation and aspect-of relations in opinion mining. *Proceedings of the 2007 Joint Conference on Empirical Methods in Natural Language Processing and Computational Natural Language Learning (EMNLP-CoNLL)*, 1065-1074.

Kohonen, T. (2012). Self-organizing maps. Science & Business Media, Springer.

Konkol, M. (2014). Brainy: A machine learning library. *International Conference on Artificial Intelligence and Soft Computing*, 490-499. 10.1007/978-3-319-07176-3_43

Lafferty, J., McCallum, A., & Pereira, F. C. (2001). Conditional random fields: Probabilistic models for segmenting and labeling sequence data. *Proceedings of the 18th International Conference on Machine Learning 2001 (ICML 2001)*, 282-289.

Langville, A. N., & Meyer, C. D. (2008). Google's PageRank and beyond: The science of search engine rankings. *The Mathematical Intelligencer, 30*(1), 68–68. doi:10.1007/BF02985759

Lerman, R. I., & Yitzhaki, S. (1984). A note on the calculation and interpretation of the Gini index. *Economics Letters, 15*(3), 363–368. doi:10.1016/0165-1765(84)90126-5

Li, F., Han, C., Huang, M., Zhu, X., Xia, Y., Zhang, S., & Yu, H. (2010). Structure-aware review mining and summarization. *Proceedings of the 23rd International Conference on Computational Linguistics (Coling 2010)*, 653-661.

Li, S., Wang, R., & Zhou, G. (2012). Opinion target extraction using a shallow semantic parsing framework. *Proceedings of the AAAI Conference on Artificial Intelligence, 26*(1).

Li, Y., Qin, Z., Xu, W., & Guo, J. (2015). A holistic model of mining product aspects and associated sentiments from online reviews. *Multimedia Tools and Applications, 74*(23), 10177–10194. doi:10.100711042-014-2158-0

Li, C., & Lee, C. (1993). Minimum cross entropy thresholding. *Pattern Recognition, 26*(4), 617–625. doi:10.1016/0031-3203(93)90115-D

Liu, B. (2011). Opinion mining and sentiment analysis. In *Web Data Mining* (pp. 459–526). Springer. doi:10.1007/978-3-642-19460-3_11

Liu, K., Xu, L., & Zhao, J. (2013). Syntactic patterns versus word alignment: Extracting opinion targets from online reviews. *Proceedings of the 51st Annual Meeting of the Association for Computational Linguistics, 1*, 1754-1763.

Ma, B., Zhang, D., Yan, Z., & Kim, T. (2013). An LDA and synonym lexicon based approach to product feature extraction from online consumer product reviews. *Journal of Electronic Commerce Research, 14*(4), 304.

Ma, Y., Peng, H., & Cambria, E. (2018). Targeted aspect-based sentiment analysis via embedding commonsense knowledge into an attentive LSTM. *Proceedings of the AAAI Conference on Artificial Intelligence, 32*(1).

Manek, A. S., Shenoy, P. D., Mohan, M. C., & Venugopal, K. R. (2017). Aspect term extraction for sentiment analysis in large movie reviews using Gini Index feature selection method and SVM classifier. *World Wide Web (Bussum)*, *20*(2), 135–154. doi:10.100711280-015-0381-x

Marrese-Taylor, E., Velásquez, J. D., & Bravo-Marquez, F. (2014). A novel deterministic approach for aspect-based media (SocialNLP). *Expert Systems with Applications*, *41*(17), 7764–7775. doi:10.1016/j.eswa.2014.05.045

Mikolov, T., Sutskever, I., Chen, K., Corrado, G., & Dean, J. (2013). *Distributed representations of words and phrases and their compositionality.* arXiv preprint arXiv:1310.4546.

Mitre. (1958). https://www.mitre.org/publications/

Moghaddam, S., & Ester, M. (2010). Opinion digger: an unsupervised opinion miner from unstructured product reviews. *Proceedings of the 19th ACM international conference on Information and knowledge management*, 1825-1828. 10.1145/1871437.1871739

Moon, T. K. (1996). The expectation-maximization algorithm. *IEEE Signal Processing Magazine*, *13*(6), 47–60. doi:10.1109/79.543975

Mullen, T., & Collier, N. (2004). Sentiment analysis using support vector machines with diverse information sources. *Proceedings of the 2004 conference on empirical methods in natural language processing*, 412-418.

Nakagawa, H., & Mori, T. (2003). Automatic term recognition based on statistics of compound nouns and their components. *Terminology. International Journal of Theoretical and Applied Issues in Specialized Communication*, *9*(2), 201–219.

Nigam, K., Lafferty, J., & McCallum, A. (1999). Using maximum entropy for text classification. IJCAI-99 workshop on machine learning for information filtering, 1(1), 61-67.

Nltk. (2002). *Natural Language Toolkit.* https://www.nltk.org/

Pei, J., Han, J., Mortazavi-Asl, B., Wang, J., Pinto, H., Chen, Q., ... Hsu, M. C. (2004). Mining sequential patterns by pattern-growth: The prefixspan approach. *IEEE Transactions on Knowledge and Data Engineering*, *16*(11), 1424–1440. doi:10.1109/TKDE.2004.77

Poria, S., Cambria, E., Ku, L. W., Gui, C., & Gelbukh, A. (2014). A rule-based approach to aspect extraction from product reviews. *Proceedings of the second workshop on natural language processing for social media (SocialNLP)*, 28-37. 10.3115/v1/W14-5905

Qiu, G., Liu, B., Bu, J., & Chen, C. (2009). Expanding domain sentiment lexicon through double propagation. *IJCAI (United States)*, *9*, 1199–1204.

Quan, & Ren, F. (2014). Unsupervised product feature extraction for feature-oriented opinion determination. *Information Sciences*, *272*, 16-28.

Raju, S., Pingali, P., & Varma, V. (2009). An unsupervised approach to product attribute extraction. *European Conference on Information Retrieval*, 796-800. 10.1007/978-3-642-00958-7_88

Rana, T. A., & Cheah, Y. N. (2015). Hybrid rule-based approach for aspect extraction and categorization from customer reviews. *2015 9th International Conference on IT in Asia (CITA)*, 1-5. 10.1109/CITA.2015.7349820

Rana, T. A., & Cheah, Y. N. (2017). A two-fold rule-based model for aspect extraction. *Expert Systems with Applications*, *89*, 273–285. doi:10.1016/j.eswa.2017.07.047

Ray, P., & Chakrabarti, A. (2020). A mixed approach of deep learning method and rule-based method to improve aspect level sentiment analysis. *Applied Computing and Informatics*, 1-9.

Salton, G., & Buckley, C. (1988). Term-weighting approaches in automatic text retrieval. *Information Processing & Management*, *24*(5), 513–523. doi:10.1016/0306-4573(88)90021-0

SemEval. (2014). https://alt.qcri.org/semeval2014/task-4/

Spacy. (2015.). Industrial-Strength Natural Language Processing. https://spacy.io/

Sutton, C., & McCallum, A. (2006). An introduction to conditional random fields for relational learning. *Introduction to Statistical Relational Learning*, *2*, 93-128.

Sutton, R. S., McAllester, D. A., Singh, S. P., & Mansour, Y. (1999, November). Policy gradient methods for reinforcement learning with function approximation. NIPs, 99, 1057-1063.

Stanford. (2008). http://nlp.stanford.edu:8080/parser/

Tomokiyo, T., & Hurst, M. (2003). A language model approach to keyphrase extraction. *Proceedings of the ACL 2003 workshop on Multiword expressions: analysis, acquisition and treatment*, 33-40. 10.3115/1119282.1119287

Tripadvisor. (2000). http://www.tripadvisor,in

Tweepy. (2009). https://www.tweepy.org/

Wang, B., & Wang, H. (2008). Bootstrapping both product features and opinion words from chinese customer reviews with cross-inducing. *Proceedings of the Third International Joint Conference on Natural Language Processing*.

Wang, B., & Liu, M. (2015). Deep learning for aspect-based sentiment analysis. Stanford University report

Wang, J., Sun, C., Li, S., Wang, J., Si, L., Zhang, M., . . . Zhou, G. (2019). Human-like decision making: Document-level aspect sentiment classification via hierarchical reinforcement learning. arXiv preprint arXiv:1910.09260. doi:10.18653/v1/D19-1560

Wang, T., Zhou, J., Hu, Q. V., & He, L. (2019). Aspect-level sentiment classification with reinforcement learning. In *2019 International Joint Conference on Neural Networks (IJCNN)*, 1-8.

Webb, G. I. (2010). Naïve Bayes. Encyclopedia of Machine Learning, 15, 713-714.

Wiebe, J., Bruce, R., & O'Hara, T. P. (1999). Development and use of a gold-standard data set for subjectivity classifications. *Proceedings of the 37th annual meeting of the Association for Computational Linguistics*, 246-253. 10.3115/1034678.1034721

Willett, P. (2006). *The Porter stemming algorithm: then and now*. Academic Press.

Wright, R. E. (1995). *Logistic regression*. Springer.

Wold, S., Esbensen, K., & Geladi, P. (1987). Principal component analysis. *Chemometrics and Intelligent Laboratory Systems*, 2(1), 37–52. doi:10.1016/0169-7439(87)80084-9

Wu, C., Wu, F., Wu, S., Yuan, Z., & Huang, Y. (2018). A hybrid unsupervised method for aspect term and opinion target extraction. *Knowledge-Based Systems*, *148*, 66–73. doi:10.1016/j.knosys.2018.01.019

Wu, Y., Zhang, Q., Huang, X. J., & Wu, L. (2009). Phrase dependency parsing for opinion mining. *Proceedings of the 2009 conference on empirical methods in natural language processing*, 1533-1541.

Wu, W., Li, H., Wang, H., & Zhu, K. Q. (2012). Probase: A probabilistic taxonomy for text understanding. *Proceedings of the 2012 ACM SIGMOD International Conference on Management of Data*, 81-492. 10.1145/2213836.2213891

Xu, L., Liu, K., Lai, S., Chen, Y., & Zhao, J. (2013). Walk and learn: a two-stage approach for opinion words and opinion targets co-extraction. *Proceedings of the 22nd International Conference on World Wide Web*, 95-96. 10.1145/2487788.2487831

Yan, Z., Xing, M., Zhang, D., & Ma, B. (2015). EXPRS: An extended pagerank method for product feature extraction from online consumer reviews. *Information & Management*, *52*(7), 850–858. doi:10.1016/j.im.2015.02.002

Yu, J., Zha, Z. J., Wang, M., & Chua, T. S. (2011). Aspect ranking: identifying important product aspects from online consumer reviews. *Proceedings of the 49th annual meeting of the association for computational linguistics: human language technologies*, 496-1505.

Zar, J. H. (2005). Spearman rank correlation. Encyclopedia of Biostatistics, 7.

Zhang, L., Liu, B., Lim, S. H., & O'Brien-Strain, E. (2010). Extracting and ranking product features in opinion documents. In *Coling 2010* (pp. 1462–1470). Posters.

Zhou, D., Bousquet, O., Lal, T. N., Weston, J., & Schölkopf, B. (2004). Learning with local and global consistency. *Advances in Neural Information Processing Systems*, *16*(16), 321–328.

Zhu, J., Wang, H., Zhu, M., Tsou, B. K., & Ma, M. (2011). Aspect-based opinion polling from customer reviews. *IEEE Transactions on Affective Computing*, 2(1), 37–49. doi:10.1109/T-AFFC.2011.2

zol. (2010). https://www.zol.com/

Chapter 4
Mitigating Data Imbalance Issues in Medical Image Analysis

Debapriya Banik
Jadavpur University, India

Debotosh Bhattacharjee
Jadavpur University, India

ABSTRACT

Medical images mostly suffer from data imbalance problems, which make the disease classification task very difficult. The imbalanced distribution of the data in medical datasets happens when a proportion of a specific type of disease in a dataset appears in a small section of the entire dataset. So analyzing medical datasets with imbalanced data is a significant challenge for the machine learning and deep learning community. A standard classification learning algorithm might be biased towards the majority class and ignore the importance of the minority class (class of interest), which generally leads to the wrong diagnosis of the patients. So, the data imbalance problem in the medical image dataset is of utmost importance for the early prediction of disease, specifically cancer. This chapter attempts to explore different problems concerning data imbalance in medical diagnosis. The authors have discussed different rebalancing strategies that offer guidelines for choosing appropriate optimal procedures to train the samples by a classifier for an efficient medical diagnosis.

INTRODUCTION

The data imbalance problem is prevalent in medical image analysis. The training of machine learning (ML) algorithm from an imbalanced medical data set is an inherently challenging task(Mena & Gonzalez, 2006). A classifier in ML's objective is to learn and predict the unseen output class of an unknown instance with good generalization capability. The mining of knowledge in a machine learning paradigm is accomplished by a set of $\mathfrak{D}$ input instances such as $\eta_1, \eta_2, \eta_3, \ldots, \eta_{\mathfrak{D}}$ described by k features

DOI: 10.4018/978-1-7998-7371-6.ch004

$\lambda_1, \lambda_2, ..., \lambda_k \in F$ whose intended output class labels $\mathcal{O}_j \in C$ { $c_1, c_1, .., c_m$. A mapping function $F^k \rightarrow C$, implies the learning algorithm which is known as a classifier(Galar, Fernandez, Barrenechea, Bustince, & Herrera, 2011). This is a general idea for how a supervised learning algorithm performs its task. The imbalanced distribution of the data in medical image datasets happens when a specific disease type in a dataset appears in a small section of the entire dataset(C. Zhang, 2019). Hence, analyzing medical data posed severe challenges in the classification of a disease. A standard ML classifier will be skewed against the majority class and underestimate the importance of the minority class because the minority class has a lesser number of instances compared to the majority class. However, the minority class is generally referred to as the class of interest(Napierala & Stefanowski, 2016) in medical image analysis. So, the minority class is of utmost importance for the early prediction of disease. This problem influences all supervised classification algorithms. A well-balanced medical image dataset is very crucial for designing a reliable and standard prediction model. Typically, real-world medical data, specifically cancer data, usually suffer from data imbalance, leading to the degradation of ML algorithms' generalization. These eventually degrade the efficiency and accuracy of the computer-aided early prediction of cancer. The biaseness of the medical data in healthcare domain due to individual diversity can cause missclassification which may affect early diagnosis of cancer and disease risk prediction(Zhao, Wong, & Tsui, 2018). However, the imbalanced class problem is generally ignored in Conventional Learning(CL) algorithms. Those algorithms give the same priority to both classes: the majority class and the minority class. However, when the majority class and the minority class are highly imbalanced, it is very challenging to build a good classifier using CL algorithms(Krawczyk, 2016). It is a significant concern in most medical datasets where patients at high-risk tend to be in the minority class, and so the cost in miss-classification of the minority classes is higher than that of the majority class. In Figure 1 a graphical representation of the distribution of majority class and the minority class is shown. The noisy data is a small part of the minority class, which significantly impacts the performance of the classifier(López, Fernández, García, Palade, & Herrera, 2013).

Figure 1. Pictorial representation of a class imbalanced dataset

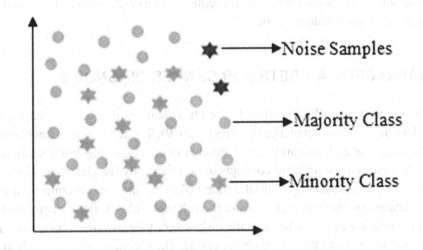

Cancer is a formidable disease. Recently, there is a high incidence and mortality rate due to cancer. Early diagnosis of the disease at a primary stage before metastasis and growth can save more lives. However, the survival rate drastically declines in its advanced stage. Due to the rise in artificial intelligence (AI) techniques for computer-aided early cancer prediction, various researchers worldwide have focused more on various factors affecting the learning algorithms due to imbalanced data. So analyzing medical datasets with imbalanced data is a significant challenge for the machine learning classifiers(Mena & Gonzalez, 2006). It is seen that the learning classifiers are biased towards the class having more samples (majority class), i.e., healthy data, with the perception that the dataset is well-balanced. However, it can be observed that the learning classifiers are inefficient in handling imbalanced data. The classifiers tend to classify the majority class false positively due to imbalanced data, which generally leads to the patients' wrong diagnosis. But an optimal classifier should accurately classify the disease, which typically belongs to the minority class, with a higher degree of accuracy(Ali, Shamsuddin, & Ralescu, 2013). So, the primary goal of a learning classifier in diagnosing a disease is to improve the accuracy of the minority class. Incorrect labeling of class labels(cancer/noncancer) in an imbalanced medical dataset is costly as a cancerous patient will be labeled as noncancerous and vice-versa, which is a significant matter of concern(J. Zhang, Chen, & Abid, 2019).

This chapter is an attempt to explore different problems concerning data imbalance in medical diagnosis, specifically in cancer diagnosis. The chapter will also introduce different rebalancing strategies that offer guidelines for choosing appropriate optimal procedures to train the samples by a computer-aided learning classifier for an efficient medical diagnosis. The rest of the chapter is organized as follows. The next Section, various imbalanced medical datasets available for the diagnosis of cancer are described. In the following Section, an overview of the various steps followed for computer-aided diagnosis systems, precisely diagnosing a cancer disease is diagrammatically represented for the ease of understanding. In next Section, different significant rebalancing techniques available to balance imbalanced medical datasets are elaborately described. In further Section, various recent state-of-the-art(SOTA) AI-based techniques, specifically deep learning-based techniques and hand-crafted feature selection-based approaches for ML employed to handle data imbalance for accurate classification of a disease and thus provides an efficient medical diagnosis are elaborately described with a detailed result analysis in tabulated form. Finally, the chapter's concluding remarks are concisely presented with a description of future work that can be explored to address the data imbalance issues.

MAJOR IMBALANCED DATASETS FOR CANCER DIAGNOSIS

Most medical image analysis tasks, specifically the classification of a cancer disease, suffer from a significant problem due to class imbalance (C. Zhang, 2019). The images of target classes of interest, e.g., cancer data, appear in a significantly lesser number compared to the entire medical dataset. The target class usually represents significant concepts to be learned by the classifier. There are generally two common issues in a medical image classification task. The first issue is concerned with manually labeled training datasets by medical experts from the relevant field. A significantly lesser number of labeled training datasets are available because the task is very tedious, time-consuming, and laborious and mostly suffers from inter and intraobserver variations. The second issue is the high imbalance ratio (IR) between minority and majority class as minority class data acquisition is very costly. Generally, the medical image classification task is a 2 class problem, but it may be multi-class where there are many minority classes, which is very difficult to resolve (Wang & Yao, 2012). This study has considered some of the significant cancer diseases that have shown a high incidence rate, as reported by Global Cancer Observatory (GCO) 2020 (GLOBOCAN project, 2020), which is diagrammatically represented in pie-chart as shown in Figure 2. The GCO is a platform highlighting cancer statistics from across the globe to enhance cancer research. It provides a complete assessment based on incidence rate, mortality rate, and prevalence rate.

Figure 2. The incidence rate of various cancers as per GCO 2020

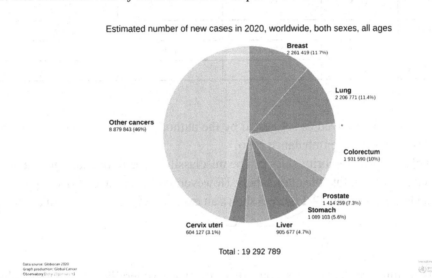

Estimated number of new cases in 2020, worldwide, both sexes, all ages

Total : 19 292 789

The imbalanced datasets of various types of cancers highlighted in this study as per the global statistics of the incidence rate are breast cancer, lung cancer, colorectum cancer, prostate cancer, stomach cancer, liver cancer, and cervix uteri cancer. In Table 1 various significant medical datasets and the type of imaging modality are considered based on the incidence rate of different types of cancers. The imbalance ratio (IR) is also calculated for the considered medical datasets, which may be defined as the ratio between the majority and minority classes present in the dataset (Charte, Rivera, del Jesus, & Herrera, 2015). From Table 1, it can be noticed that the Lung cancer dataset has the highest IR, which signifies that the dataset is the most imbalanced, and the classifier will be skewed towards the majority class, which may result in miss diagnosis of the disease. Furthermore, the cervix cancer dataset, which comprises pap smear images, has the lowest IR. But the dataset is imbalanced, although the minority class instances are more than the majority class. The IR has a significant impact on the performance of the learning classifier. The more the IR, the higher is the imbalance effect (Leevy, Khoshgoftaar, Bauder, & Seliya, 2018).

Some of the significant concerns pertaining to the class imbalance problem in medical image datasets that hinders the classifier learning ability include (Galar et al., 2011):

- Samples with small training data: Medical datasets generally do not have adequate minority samples, as shown in Table 1, which affects the classification model's efficiency. However, the prob-

Table 1. Summary of the imbalanced medical datasets

Cancer Type	Modality	Total Images	Majority Class	Minority Class	IR
Breast (Al-Dhabyani, Gomaa, Khaled, & Fahmy, 2020)	Ultrasound	780	620	210	2.95
Lung (Ausawalaithong, Thirach, Marukatat, & Wilaiprasitporn, 2018)	X-Ray	108899	103907	4992	20.81
Colorectum (Awan et al., 2017)	WSI	139	71	68	1.04
Prostate (Yoo, Gujrathi, Haider, & Khalvati, 2019)	MRI	427	252	175	1.44
Stomach (Iizuka et al., 2020)	WSI	4128	2179	1949	1.11
Liver (Jansen et al., 2019)	MRI	213	125	88	1.42
Cervix (L. Zhang et al., 2017)	WSI	917	242	675	0.35

lem can be minimized or resolved as suggested by the authors (Krawczyk, 2016) to increase the minority samples, balancing the imbalance ratio.

- Overlapping of classes: The minority class can be misclassified due to overlapping classes as discriminative rules cannot separate the class labels. However, in the absence of overlapping classes, the classifier can learn very quickly. Figure 3 shows an example of class overlap in an imbalanced dataset.

- Small disjuncts of minority class: This concern of disjuncts generally arises in an imbalanced dataset when a concept demonstrated by a minority class contains subconcepts (Weiss & Provost, 2003). As the instances in the dataset are not balanced, it increases the complexity of the problem implicitly. Figure 4 shows an example of small disjuncts in an imbalanced dataset.

- Borderline samples: The samples located at the majority's borderlines and minority classes' overlapping regions impact the classification algorithms (López et al., 2013). The algorithms have difficulty classifying the classes during the training process accurately. Thus, it tends to wrong diagnosis of the patients. Figure 5 shows an example of borderline samples in an imbalanced dataset.

PROCEDURE FOR AN EFFICIENT COMPUTER-AIDED MEDICAL DIAGNOSIS

The early detection of a disease is the only way to cure the disease or improve the patients' prognosis rate (Croft et al., 2015). With the advancement in different medical imaging modalities, disease diagnosis becomes more comfortable and less intrusive. There is a steady move on diagnostic approaches with emerging imaging modalities. The digital imaging modalities also allow the computerized diagnosis of a disease, which overcomes a human perception system's limitations. Among various deadliest diseases, cancer incidence and mortality rates are very high (CancerStatistics, 2020). But these diseases are very

Figure 3. Class overlap in an imbalanced dataset

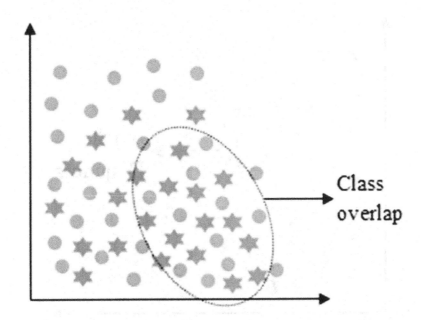

much curable if diagnosed in their early stage of development. A computer-aided decision support system (CADSS) can serve as a supportive tool for accurate and early cancer diagnosis by medical experts/ clinicians, which is the critical demand of the current medical system. Figure 6 shows the block diagram of a CADSS for early prediction of cancer.

Medical imaging and its processing have emerged as a powerful early disease diagnosis approach in the latest medical and bio-medical research field. In the advanced technological era, medical image processing is an umbrella term covering different aspects of digital image processing techniques such as segmentation, classification, registration, etc., to process and analyze medical images for early prediction of disease.

The collection of valid medical images from different imaging modalities with proper annotation by a medical expert, which serves as a ground-truth, is a primary step for any research in the biomedical domain (Willemink et al., 2020).

Medical images are generally more complex to understand due to improper acquisition by not maintaining standard protocol, the presence of unwanted noise, and the presence of different artifacts. Pre-processing of the images by low-level operations like de-noising, manual cropping of unwanted regions, and image enhancement will mitigate such effects with minimal data loss.

Current trends of high-level, complex image processing techniques can effectively solve real-world problems in medical image analysis. Segmentation is a classical problem in medical image analysis, where minor variation between segmented regions (region of interest (ROI)) and the actual region (ground-truth) can lead to misdiagnosis of the patients. The segmentation techniques can be broadly categorized as thresholding-based, clustering-based, Active contour model, edge-based, Neural network, etc. After segmentation of the abnormal regions, suitable handcrafted features are extracted from the ROI. The examination of the ROI is a necessary requisite for determining whether a cancer is benign or malignant

Figure 4. Small disjuncts in an imbalanced dataset

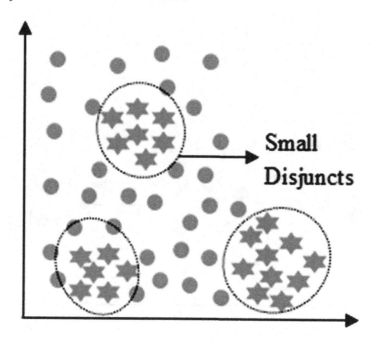

Besides analyzing the medical images using handcrafted features, Deep learning has driven medical image analysis advancements to detect lesions and, hence, predict them as normal or abnormal (Litjens et al., 2017). Besides, deep learning has shown exceptional capabilities in achieving higher diagnostic accuracy in detecting and classification the lesions compared to many handcrafted techniques. The deep neural network (DNN) can extract relevant features with versatile capabilities regardless of the complex color, texture, shape of medical images. Thus deep learning techniques play a crucial role in the computer-assisted diagnosis of lesions for early prediction of the disease.

Computer-aided diagnosis of disease and classification can technically act as a supporting tool for the clinician to take further treatment and improve its quality. The extracted features are fed into the traditional classifiers like support vector machine (SVM) (Noble, 2006), Decision Tree (DT) (Swain & Hauska, 1977), Multilayer perceptron Neural Network (MLPNN) (Orhan, Hekim, & Ozer, 2011), etc., to discriminate between benign and malignant class. So an imbalanced dataset will always be skewed towards the majority class and ignore the minority class (class of interest), which is a severe problem in computer-aided diagnosis of a disease (Fotouhi, Asadi, & Kattan, 2019).

A proper quantification of the classification output is very crucial for an effective diagnosis of a disease. So, to test the performance of the CADSS, a confusion matrix is generally considered. The confusion matrix includes the classifier's actual and predicted output (Moraes, Valiati, & Neto, 2018). Table 2 shows the confusion matrix for the two-class problem.

The classifiers' training process is generally done with leave N-out cross-validation, where the value of N is altered to generate different training and testing sets. A single performance measure alone cannot evaluate the performance of the classifier. So, various performance evaluation measures such as accuracy, specificity, and sensitivity are generally considered to evaluate the classifiers' performance (Moraes et al., 2018). The accuracy is termed as a significant measure, but it alone cannot justify the efficacy of the

Figure 5. Borderline samples in an imbalanced dataset

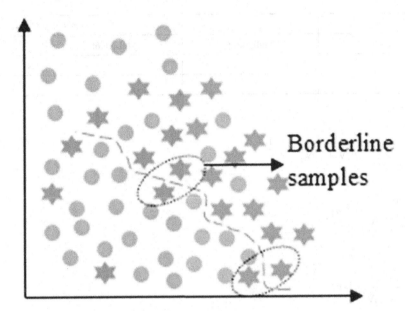

classifier's performance as it may be biased due to imbalanced data (Fotouhi et al., 2019). A classifier may achieve high accuracy in a high IR dataset as it can classify the majority class data, which is not the class of interest. So specificity (True Negative Rate), sensitivity or recall (True Positive Rate), precision, geometric mean, BAlanced accuracy (BAC), F-Score, AUC, and AUPRC are also taken into account to evaluate the classifiers' performance. The geometric mean tends to optimize the accuracy of each of the two classes (Kim, Kang, & Kim, 2015). It may be noted that AUPRC is much more informative than AUC, and it may mislead when there is a small minority class available in the dataset. The accuracy, specificity, sensitivity, precision, geometric mean, balanced accuracy, and F-Score are calculated as:

Figure 6. Block diagram of the computer-aided system for cancer diagnosis

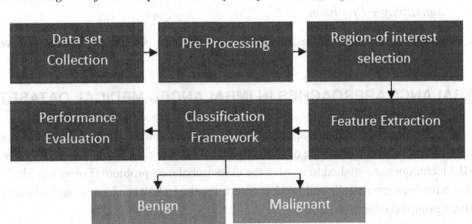

Table 2. The confusion matrix

Actual Class		Predicted Class	
	Malignant	Malignant	Benign
	Benign	TP	FN

$$Accuracy . \frac{TP+TN}{TP+FP+FN+TN} \times 100 .$$ (1)

$$Specificity . \frac{TN}{FP+TN} \times 100 .$$ (2)

$$Sensitivity . \frac{TP}{TP+FN} \times 100 .$$ (3)

$$Precision . \frac{TP}{TP+FP} \times 100 .$$ (4)

$$Geometric\ mean . \sqrt{\frac{TP}{TP+FN} \cdot \frac{TN}{FP+TN}} .$$ (5)

$$Balanced\ Accuracy . \frac{Sensitivity+Specificity}{2} \times 100 .$$ (6)

$$F-Score . \frac{2 \times Sensitivity \times Precision}{Sensitivity+Precision} .$$ (7)

TP, TN, FP, and FN represent true positive, true negative, false positive, and false negative.

DATA REBALANCE APPROACHES IN IMBALANCED MEDICAL DATASETS

The significance of different rebalancing approaches in imbalanced medical image datasets is to maximize the efficacy of diagnosis in the presence of minority class. For the past few decades, different machine learning (ML) techniques are studied to resolve the class imbalance problem (Fotouhi et al., 2019). The strategies that have been empirically followed to determine the imbalance issues can be broadly categorized into three groups (Galar et al., 2011).

1. Algorithm-based approach (or internal): In this strategy, the classifier learning algorithm is either improved to minimize the skewness towards the minority class, or a new learning algorithm is proposed to control the biasness in an imbalanced dataset (Barandela, Sánchez, Garca, & Rangel, 2003). The proposed learning algorithm requires prior knowledge of the application field and the corresponding classifier to justify the classifier's failure case with imbalanced data.

2. Data level-based approach (or external): In this approach, the concern towards dataset imbalance is minimized by resampling the data space. This approach avoids the improvement of the classifier learning algorithm to rectify the biasness. To mitigate the imbalance factor in the dataset, a pre-processing step is applied to the dataset, either by down-sampling the majority class or by up-sampling the minority class (Batista, Prati, & Monard, 2004).

3. Cost-sensitive learning-based approach: This approach falls between the internal and the external level approaches. This approach includes both data-level variations and algorithm-level up-gradation based on the data level modification. In this strategy, the classifier is biased towards the minority class (S. Zhang, Liu, Zhu, & Zhang, 2008). However, this approach's major drawback is the requirement to define the misclassification cost, which is generally unavailable in a dataset.

Apart from the above three stated methods, an ensemble-based method is introduced (Polikar, 2006) to handle the class imbalance problem. It is a hybrid method where the procedure is combined with one of the above-stated approaches. However, the data level-based approach is generally combined with the ensemble-based learning method, which follows a pre-processing step before data is fed into the classifier (Galar et al., 2011). The most popular pre-processing step is the resampling method (Maheshwari, Jain, & Jadon, 2017), where the data distribution is restructured to minimize the biasness. Resampling methods can be classified into three categories.

1. Oversampling: The strength of the minority class is increased through creating new samples or replicates the old instances. The replicating synthetic samples may lead to overfitting since it creates similar samples of the minority class (Galar et al., 2011). A pictorial representation of the oversampling method is shown in Figure 7.

2. Under-sampling: In this technique, the sample size of the majority class is reduced to a level the distribution of the imbalanced training data (majority and minority class) into a ratio of 50:50 (López et al., 2013). However, this method may remove significant majority class examples, which may be a potential instance for the classifier learning algorithm. The under-sampling method of the majority class is shown in Figure 8.

3. Hybrid sampling: This method considers both oversampling and undersampling methods to rectify the biasness between the majority and minority class in an imbalanced training dataset.

The oversampling method stated above to minimize skewness is generally done by generating synthetic samples and including them in the minority class. Different strategies are followed for replicating the samples, either done randomly, or borderline samples present in the border of majority and minority classes are considered (Susan & Kumar, 2020). However, this strategy does not contribute to enhancing the dataset by adding new information. So to overcome such drawback, some improved oversampling methods have been put forward, which are as follows:

Figure 7. Diagrammatic representation of the sampling methods – oversampling

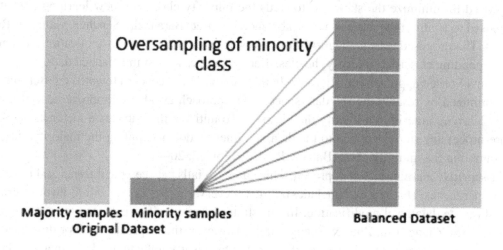

a. Synthetic Minority Oversampling TEchnique (SMOTE) (Chawla, Bowyer, Hall, & Kegelmeyer, 2002): In this technique, the minority samples are generated by interpolating minority class examples with a similar feature space. SMOTE generates minority instances by choosing k-nearest neighbor (KNN) of one of the minority class instances from the interpolation of two instances. This technique thus avoids the overfitting problem as it effectively extends the decision boundary.

b. Safe-Level- Synthetic Minority Oversampling TEchnique (SL-SMOTE) (Bunkhumpornpat, Sinapiromsaran, & Lursinsap, 2009): In this technique, the safe levels of the minority samples are determined prior to the generation of the synthetic examples as per the SMOTE algorithm. This is defined according to the KNN. The most substantial safe level is considered to be nearest to k, and the weakest is nearest to zero.

Figure 8. Diagrammatic representation of the sampling methods-undersampling

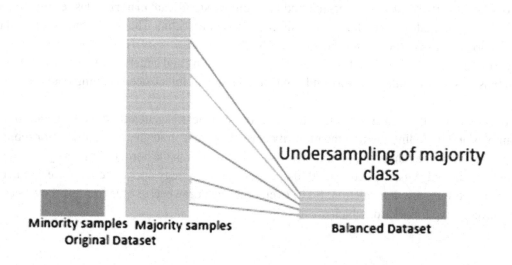

c. Borderline-Synthetic Minority Oversampling TEchnique (B-SMOTE) (Han, Wang, & Mao, 2005): The borderline samples are generally tough to classify from those far away from the borderline. So in this method SMOTE algorithm is applied to the borderline samples, which resample the minority instances.

d. Edited Nearest Neighbor- Synthetic Minority Oversampling TEchnique (ENN-SMOTE) (Fotouhi et al., 2019): The noisy samples are eliminated using this technique. However, it may discard samples from both classes. The misclassified samples are also discarded using KNN, where k is assigned as 3.

e. Tomek Link -Synthetic Minority Over-sampling TEchnique (TL-SMOTE) (Batista et al., 2004): In this technique, the samples composed of Tomek links are being eliminated using SMOTE. Tomek link comprises two samples that are NN but do not belong to the same class. The result of this technique is a balanced dataset.

f. ADAptive SYNthetic Sampling (ADASYN) (He, Bai, Garcia, & Li, 2008): In this technique, a different instance of the minority classes uses a weighted distribution strategy according to their learning difficulty. Therefore, more synthetic samples are generated that are difficult to be learned and lesser for the easier ones.

g. Random Over-Sampling (ROS) (Batista et al., 2004): This technique is the most basic and straight-forward, where random new samples of the minority class are generated. Both classes have an equal distribution of data.

h. Adjusting the Direction Of the synthetic Minority clasS examples (ADOMS) (Fotouhi et al., 2019): In this technique, samples of the minority class are generated as per the first principal component axis of the local distribution of data.

i. Selective Preprocessing of Imbalanced Data (SPIDER) (Stefanowski & Wilk, 2008): This technique includes two steps. At first, the local minority class instances are oversampled, and the noisy samples (hard samples) of the majority class are filtered. The noisy samples (misclassified) are analyzed and labeled by KNN, and then different criteria are stated, such as weak, strong, and relabel. In the weak option, the minority class instances are amplified. In the strong option, the minority classes are amplified strongly, and in relabel option, it strengthens minority class and changes the class labels of the majority class. Finally, the left-out noisy samples are discarded.

The under-sampling method for resampling the imbalanced dataset is generally done by discarding some replicated samples from the majority class randomly or following standard measures. So if a standard measure is followed and the borderline samples are discarded, it gradually reduces the majority class's data space and correctly classifies the minority class. Many under-sampling techniques are being put forward for resampling the dataset, which is as follows:

a. One-Sided Selection (OSS) (Kubat & Matwin, 1997): In this technique, the minority class samples and some hard samples from the majority class, which are misclassified, are chosen by 1NN to detect the Tomek Link. After the detection of the TL, the majority of samples enclosed in the TL are discarded.

b. Condensed Nearest Neighbor (CNN) (Hart, 1968): In this technique, the majority of class samples are eliminated based on some rules, such as samples that are far away from the borderline is the least significant samples. So, by discarding those samples, the dataset size is decreased.

c. Neighborhood Cleaning Rule (NCL) (Agustianto & Destarianto, 2019): In this technique, the majority of class examples are removed by Edited Nearest Neighbor (ENN) algorithm.

d. Random under-sampling (RUS) (Y. Qian, Liang, Li, Feng, & Shi, 2014): In this technique, the majority of class examples are discarded randomly to balance the class.

e. Sampling-Based Clustering (SBC) (Yen & Lee, 2006): In this technique, the class is balanced based on the cluster approach. This rebalancing strategy assumes that one cluster's characteristics differ from the other in a dataset. The cluster may contain both the minority and the majority class examples. But the SBC algorithm picks the majority of samples randomly from the clusters to balance the class.

f. Tomek's Link (TL) (Zeng, Zou, Wei, Liu, & Wang, 2016): In this technique, Tomek's link is being considered, which states that a majority class sample say x and the minority class sample say y is located at a lesser distance from any other sample say z. then a TL is formed between x and y. So the majority of samples are eliminated based on TL to rebalance the dataset.

Table 3 provides a concise overview of different approaches (Maheshwari et al., 2017).

Table 3. Comparative study of different rebalancing approaches

Approach	Method	Learning Algorithm	Remark
Algorithm Level Based	Bagging	Decision Tree and Random Forest	Better classification performance but takes more time and may lead to overfitting
	Boosting	AdaBoost and SMOTEOOST	Boosts the performance of other algorithms but ignore the overall classification performance
Data Level Based	Under Sampling	OSS, CNN, NCL, RUS, SBC, TL	Independent of classifier but may ignore significant useful data
	Over Sampling	SMOTE, SL-SMOTE, B-SMOTE, ADASYN, ROS, ADOMS, SPIDER	Improves the accuracy of the classifier but may lead to overfitting due to overgeneralization
	Hybrid	ENN-SMOTE, TL-SMOTE	Overcomes the problem of overfitting but takes longer training duration
Cost-Sensitive Based	Includes both algorithm level and data level approaches	Cost-Sensitive Boosting Algorithm	Minimizes the classification cost, but it is tentative and not precisely known, so estimation is used

For the last decade, the deep learning (DL) technique, a part of ML, has attained unprecedented popularity in the classification of imbalanced data in many complex domains (Johnson & Khoshgoftaar, 2019). Convolutional Neural Network (CNN) is the current SOTA DL technique for medical image classification tasks (Tajbakhsh et al., 2016). However, CNN's success lies in an extensive training dataset, which is not feasible in the medical domain, where the imbalance is a common problem. It is also challenging for a domain expert to label the unlabelled dataset, specifically disease class (minority class), to correct a patient.

Active learning (Abe, 2003) solves labeling data where a query approach is followed to choose essential samples from the dataset. This technique is an iterative process where, in each iteration, new instances are determined and are labeled by the domain expert. This process improves the classification performance of the deep learning framework (C. Zhang, 2019). The data augmentation technique is generally used to expand the training data. Unified Learning of Feature Representation & Similarity Matrix (Unified LF&SM) (C. Zhang, 2019) is an augmentation scheme that utilizes the similarity between the samples to learn an effective feature representation. Data augmentation schemes generate synthetic samples with different orientations without considering the majority and minority classes (Saini & Susan, 2020).

To overcome such drawback, Generative adversarial networks (GANs) are used, which can generate real samples where data from the minority class can be implicitly generated by considering the majority class distribution structure in the generation of the minority class, which minimizes the chance of data overfitting (Chatziagapi et al., 2019) (Frid-Adar et al., 2018). Another beneficial technique to handle the DL framework's data imbalance is using the weighted loss function, which effectively updates the loss in a classification problem with an imbalanced training dataset (Sudre, Li, Vercauteren, Ourselin, & Cardoso, 2017).

STATE-OF-THE-ART MEDICAL DATASET REBALANCE TECHNIQUES

This section will discuss various recent SOTA approaches proposed by different research groups to effectively handle imbalanced datasets for the correct disease classification to provide an efficient early diagnosis and provide effective treatment. A plethora of research has been done for the last few decades to address this imbalance problem in medical datasets. However, an exact solution is still a subject of research. We elaborately discuss various techniques suggested by different researchers for the prediction of some of the significant cancer diseases which have shown a high incidence rate as reported by GCO 2020 (GLOBOCAN project, 2020), namely breast cancer, lung cancer, colorectum cancer, prostate cancer, stomach cancer, liver cancer, and cervix uteri cancer.

In (Reza & Ma 2018), the authors have proposed a classification model to classify breast histopathology images using a deep convolutional neural network. The imbalanced dataset is rebalanced using different techniques such as SMOTE, ADASYN, Oversampling with replacement and, Under Sampling methods. The resampling techniques improve the performance of CNN during parameter learning. Another study (Wu, Wu, Cox, & Lotter, 2018) proposed a classification model for malignancy prediction in mammograms. Data augmentation scheme (horizontal, rescaling, and flipping) is used to improve the dataset size. The authors have also introduced a multi-scale class-conditional GAN with mask infilling to enhance the class labels and generating synthetic samples. (J. Zhang et al., 2019) overcome data imbalance in predicting breast cancer using a hybrid under-sampling scheme of K-means clustering and Boosted C5.0, named K-Boosted C5.0. The K-means clustering algorithm clusters the majority and the minority class instances and chooses a similar number of instances from the cluster, and Boosted C5.0 uses a classification learning algorithm to predict the malignant breast samples.

A lung cancer classification network with imbalanced computed tomography (CT) data is proposed in the work of (Q. Qian, 2020). The skewness in the dataset, which may lead to patients' wrong diagnosis, is minimized using the minority class's oversampling technique and a weighted loss function. The author has used the D-LSTM network to classify the malignant and benign samples. An improved Random Forest (RF) classifier is proposed by (Paing & Choomchuay, 2018) for the imbalanced classification of lung nodules to predict lung cancer. Authors have used bootstrap sampling and three traditional feature selection algorithms such as ReliefF, Genetic Algorithm (GA), and Particle Swarm Optimization (PSO).

In (Ausawalaithong et al., 2018), authors have proposed a deep learning network to predict lung cancer from x-ray images. They have trained the DenseNet-121 with pre-trained weights of ImageNet and re-trained with the lung cancer image databases. The imbalance datasets are rebalanced with an augmentation scheme (randomly flipping horizontally) and weighted binary classification loss.

(Koziarski, 2020) proposed a two-stage resampling technique to handle the imbalanced histology data of colorectal cancer. In the first stage, oversampling method (SMOTE) is applied to introduce an expansion of synthetic data, and the enhanced data is fed into a deep network, namely MobileNet, and on the head of the fully connected layer, an undersampling technique (RUS) is applied. A data mining technique for colon cancer classification using gene expressions collected from DNA microarray is proposed by (Loey, Jasim, El-Bakry, Taha, & Khalifa, 2020). The reduction of several features (genes) as this dataset has fewer samples. Still, a huge number of genes is done by information gain, which selects significant features and optimization of the features using the grey wolf optimization (GWO) algorithm. Finally, optimized features are fed into the SVM classifier for the classification of colon cancer. In (Shapcott, Hewitt, & Rajpoot, 2019), authors have proposed a deep CNN with pre-trained weights to predict colon cancer from an imbalanced WSI dataset. The authors have proposed two sampling techniques to rebalance the dataset. The 1st technique is random sampling, which provides uniform weighing to the samples, and the 2nd technique is systematic random sampling, which considers spatial dependencies.

A study conducted by (Barlow, Mao, & Khushi, 2019) to predict high-risk prostate cancer patients using the machine learning method has handled the imbalanced digital rectal screening (DRE) dataset of prostate cancer patients. Authors have evaluated a wide variety of over and under sampling methods after evaluating different scaling methods on the dataset to select an optimal scaling method for a sampling method. The experimental results show that SMOTE oversampling method has shown significant results. They have also evaluated various ML classifier learning algorithms of which SVM outperforms other traditional methods. In (Lemaitre, Martí, Rastgoo, & Mériaudeau, 2017), authors have proposed an ML method to detect prostate cancer from an imbalanced MRI dataset. The authors have balanced the feature set using a different variant of an undersampling method, namely NearMiss (NM) and instance-hardness-threshold (IHT). A different variation of the oversampling method, namely SMOTE, is also applied to the dataset. The ML classifier used in the study is an ensemble of learning classifiers, namely AdaBoost (AdB) and Gradient Boosting (GB). Authors (Chandana, Leung, & Trpkov, 2009) proposed a novel technique to analyze the stage of prostate cancer. Different features are extracted based on PCA, GA, and RS, and the imbalanced dataset is rebalanced using an under-sampling method and SMOTE. Finally, SVM and KNN classifier is used to classify the class. However, authors have also combined the classification models based on Dempster-Shafer (DS) theory, where the genetic algorithm ensures the choice of the learning model.

Recently, (Iizuka et al., 2020) conducted a study to classify histopathology gastric epithelial tumor using a Deep learning framework. Authors have used the Inception-v3 network to classify a patch, and then they have aggregated the prediction score from all the patches to obtain final classification using an RNN and max-pooling. The imbalance issue is addressed using different augmentation schemes, sampling of class labels, and a weighted cross binary entropy loss function. The weights were used to minimize the imbalance in the patch labels. In another work, a study was conducted by (Kanavati et al., 2020) for gastric signet ring cell carcinoma (SRCC) classification using a deep model in WSI. The authors have balanced the training dataset using an oversampling method. The samples are fed into the EfficientNet-B1 CNN model with pre-trained weights from ImageNet. (Fan, Qi, & Tie, 2020) proposed a technique to classify gastric cancer using imbalanced DNA methylation data of gastric cancer.

Authors have handled the imbalanced data using balanced feedback sampling, followed by the Tomek Link technique to discard the noise and obtain optimal data. Lasso algorithm is being used for feature extraction, and the extracted features are fed into different learning classifiers such as multi-Grained Cascade Forest (gcForest), CNN, RF, and SVM. The gcForest classifier outperforms other classifiers in the classification of gastric cancer

A study was conducted by (Zhen et al., 2020) for an accurate diagnosis of liver malignancy based on MRI imaging. The study authors have used a deep learning technique (Inception V3 network) to classify the liver tumors in seven classes. However, the imbalanced private MRI dataset was handled using augmentation schemes such as rotation, flipping, scaling, shifting, and shearing. Recently, another study (Lu & Daigle Jr, 2020) proposed a prognostic analysis of WSI images of hepatocellular carcinoma using pre-trained CNN models such as VGGNet, Inception, and ResNet. Before the training, data is downsampled and augmented to increase the variety of samples to minimize the imbalanced data problem. The extracted features are fed in an SVM learning classifier for the classification between benign and malignant cells. A rebalanced technique was reported by (Bilic et al., 2019) from the Liver Tumor segmentation (LiTS) challenge organized by ISBI2017 and MICCAI 2017 on CT images. Most of the teams participated in the challenge focused on the deep learning framework. The data imbalance is minimized using Weighted cross-entropy and augmentation schemes such as shifting, flipping, rotating, scaling, cropping, and elastic deformation.

A study is conducted by (Rehman, Ali, Taj, Sajid, & Karimov, 2020) for automated cervical cancer classification using cervical cells from the Papanicolaou smear test. The study was conducted using a deep learning model with pre-trained weights from ImageNet Dataset. The features extracted from the final layer of CNN are fed into three different ML classifiers: softmax regression, SVM, and GentleBoost ensemble decision trees (GEDT). The authors have handled the imbalanced cervical cell dataset using an augmentation scheme and normalization for better generalization during the model's training. (Jia, Li, & Zhang, 2020) proposed a method for the detection of cervical cancer using the ML and CNN technique. Authors have used a CNN, namely LeNet-5, to extract features and extract some traditional handcrafted features using GLCM, Fourier transform, Gabor Transform, MRF. The features are fused with the CNN features (multi-feature fusion) and fed into SVM for classification. However, the authors have handled the imbalance issue using sample amplification strategy by augmentation scheme (rotation, scaling, random crop, and shear-warp transformation). Another study on the same Herlev imbalanced dataset was done by (Chen, Li, Gao, & Shen, 2020). In this method, the authors have used transfer learning-based CNN using ResNet pre-trained on ImageNet and then combined with a snapshot ensemble named TLSE. The authors have handled the imbalanced dataset using a rotation augmentation scheme with 36 degrees for minority samples and 18 degrees for majority samples.

In Table 4 different rebalance techniques available in the literature for efficient medical image analysis are summarized with a performance analysis on different medical imbalanced datasets.

CONCLUSION AND FUTURE DIRECTIONS

This chapter elaborated various problems concerning data imbalance in medical image datasets to diagnose a disease, specifically cancer. Different medical datasets with imbalanced class distribution and their impact on patients' incorrect diagnoses are discussed in this work. The IR in datasets can significantly hinder the performance of the classifier learning algorithm. A framework for a computer-

Table 4. Summary of different state-of-the-art rebalance techniques for medical datasets

Cancer Type	Image Modality Type	Rebalance Techniques	Classification Model	Dataset & Performance
Breast	Histopathology	SMOTE, ADASYN, Oversampling with replacement, Under Sampling	CNN	**Invasive Ductal Carcinoma Dataset** Sensitivity:0.8085 Specificity:0.9012 F-Score:0.8478 Accuracy:0.8584 BAC:0.8548 **BreakHis Dataset** Sensitivty:0.9090 Specificity:0.8034 F-Score:0.8634 Accuacy:0.8562 BAC:0.8562
	Mammogram	Data Augmentation and infilling GAN	ResNet-50	**DDSM** AUC:0.896
	FNA (Histopathology)	K means clustering	Boosted C5.0	**Wbcd Dataset** Accuracy:98.2% Sensitivity:93.75% Specificity:100% G-mean:96.82% MCC:95.6% **Bcwo dataset.** Accuracy:97.48% Sensitivity:100% Specificity:96.17% G-mean:98.06% MCC:93.6%
Lung	CT	Oversampling, weighted loss function	Distance-LSTM (D-LSTM)	**NLST** ROC curve
	CT	Bootstrap sampling, feature selection using ReliefF, Genetic Algorithm (GA), and Particle Swarm Optimization	Improved Random forest	**LIDC-IDRI** Accuracy:89.9% TNR:89.9% TPR:90.4% Precision:65.3% F1:75.8%
	X-ray	Augmentation (flipping) Weighted binary loss	DenseNet-121	**ChestX-ray14 and JSRT** Accuracy:74.43% Specificity:74.96% Sensitivity:74.68%
Colorectum	Histological	Oversampling(SMOTE) followed by Undersampling (RUS)	Mobile-Net	Accuracy:0.9152 CBA:0.8898 MAvG:0.9050
	DNA microarrays	Feature Selection+ grey wolf optimization (GWO) algorithm	SVM	**Kent Ridge Bio-Medical Data Set** Accuracy:95.35%
	Histology	Random sampling and Systematic Random sampling	Pre-trained CNN (Cifar10)	**TCGA colon cancer data set** Accuracy:0.76
Prostate	DRE	Scaling, SMOTE,	SVM, AdaBoost	**NCIPLCO Dataset** AUC:0.748 Accuracy: 0.855 Sensitivity:0.735 Specificity:0.855 PPV:0.223 NPV:0.983 F1:0.342
	MRI	Undersampling (NM, IHT) and oversampling (SMOTE)	AdB and GB	**Private Dataset** AUC:0.836
	Biopsy	Undersampling and SMOTE	SVM and KNN	**Cerner** Accuracy:90.1% AUC:0.864
Stomach or gastric	Histopathology	Sampling of labels+ weighted cross binary entropy loss	CNN (Inception v3) for patch classification followed by RNN and max-pooling for the final class label.	**Private dataset** AUC Adenocarcinoma:0.97 Adenoma:0.99
	Histopathology	Oversampling+ Augmentation	CNN (EfficientNet-B1model)	**DigestPath2019** AUC:0.9912
	DNA microarray	Balanced feedback sampling and Tomek link	SVM, RF, gcForest, and CNN	**TCGA Database** Best classifier:gcForest Recall:94.3% Precision:96.2% Accuracy:95.1% F-score:95.2%

continued on following page

Table 4. Continued

Cancer Type	Image Modality Type	Rebalance Techniques	Classification Model	Dataset & Performance
Liver	MRI	Augmentation (rotation, flipping, scaling, shifting, and shearing)	CNN (Inception-ResNetV2)	**Private dataset** Accuracy:86.1% Kappa:0.829 Z score:25.1 P-value<0.01
	Histopathology	Downsampling and Augmentation to improve the variety of samples	3 CNNs (VGG 16, Inception V3, and ResNet50) for feature extraction and SVM for classification	**TCGA-LIHC Dataset** ROC
	CT	Weighted cross-entropy and Augmentation (shifting, flipping, rotating, scaling, cropping, and elastic deformation)	CNN approach and Supervised learning	**ISBI 2017HCI dataset** Best Results Dice: 0.8290 Precision: 0.409 Recall:0.408
Cervix	Histopathology	Weighted Data augmentation and normalization	ConvNet+SR,SVM,GEDT	**Herlev Dataset** ConvNet+SVM Accuracy:99.5% Sensitivity:99.38% Specificity:99.20% ConvNet+GEDT Accuracy:99.6% Sensitivity:99.30% Specificity:99.35%
	Histopathology	Augmentation (rotation, scaling, random crop, and shear-warp)	LeNet-5 + GLCM+ fourier transform +Gabor transform +MRF for feature extraction and SVM for classification	**Herlev Dataset** Accuracy:99.3% Sensitivity:98.9% Specificity:99.4% **Private Dataset** Accuracy:94.9% Sensitivity:93.3% Specificity:93.3%
	Histopathology	Augmentation (Rotation of 36 degree for minority samples and rotation of 18 degree for majority samples)	snapshot ensemble + transfer learning (Inception ResNet)	**Herlev Dataset** Accuracy:65.56%

aided diagnosis of a disease is also presented in this study. Different performance evaluation techniques are also discussed to evaluate the classifier performance. Major rebalancing techniques available for balancing an imbalanced dataset are elaborately described for useful classification by ML and DL techniques. A comparative study among the various rebalancing techniques is also provided in this study. Some of the recent SOTA techniques for combating the class imbalance problem in medical datasets to diagnose various types of cancers are highlighted with performance analysis on different datasets. The study shows that most researchers have applied different rebalancing techniques before the classification of the disease using Deep learning-based techniques or Machine learning-based techniques. However, most of the datasets are focused on two-class problems. So in the future, an investigation on the multi-class imbalanced classification problem in imbalanced medical datasets will be executed, which is an essential topic of research. Active deep learning framework can also be explored to combat the class imbalance and small labeled training image set to develop more accurate diagnosis decisions and plan further course of treatment. Furthermore, GANs have also shown a significant improvement in handling class imbalance problems in imbalanced training medical datasets.

ACKNOWLEDGMENT

The first author is thankful to CSIR for the award of SRF (ACK No. 143416/2K17/1, File No. 09/096(0922)2K18 EMR-I). All the authors are thankful for the Indo-Austrian joint project grant No.

INT /AUS-TRIA /BMWF /P-25 /2018 funded by the DST, GOI, and the SPARC project (ID: 231) supported by MHRD, GOI.

REFERENCES

Abe, N. (2003). Sampling Approaches to Learning from Imbalanced Datasets: Active Learning, Cost Sensitive Learning and Beyond. *Proc. of the ICML-KDD'03 Workshop: Learning from Imbalanced Data Sets.*

Agustianto, K., & Destarianto, P. (2019). Imbalance Data Handling using Neighborhood Cleaning Rule (NCL) Sampling Method for Precision Student Modeling. *2019 International Conference on Computer Science, Information Technology, and Electrical Engineering (ICOMITEE)*, 86–89. 10.1109/ICOMITEE.2019.8921159

Al-Dhabyani, W., Gomaa, M., Khaled, H., & Fahmy, A. (2020). Dataset of breast ultrasound images. *Data in Brief*, *28*, 104863. doi:10.1016/j.dib.2019.104863 PMID:31867417

Ali, A., Shamsuddin, S. M., & Ralescu, A. L. (2013). Classification with class imbalance problem. *Int. J. Advance Soft Compu. Appl*, *5*(3).

Ausawalaithong, W., Thirach, A., Marukatat, S., & Wilaiprasitporn, T. (2018). Automatic lung cancer prediction from chest X-ray images using the deep learning approach. *2018 11th Biomedical Engineering International Conference (BMEICON)*, 1–5.

Awan, R., Sirinukunwattana, K., Epstein, D., Jefferyes, S., Qidwai, U., Aftab, Z., Mujeeb, I., Snead, D., & Rajpoot, N. (2017). Glandular morphometrics for objective grading of colorectal adenocarcinoma histology images. *Scientific Reports*, *7*(1), 1–12. doi:10.103841598-017-16516-w PMID:29203775

Barandela, R., Sánchez, J. S., Garca, V., & Rangel, E. (2003). Strategies for learning in class imbalance problems. *Pattern Recognition*, *36*(3), 849–851. doi:10.1016/S0031-3203(02)00257-1

Barlow, H., Mao, S., & Khushi, M. (2019). Predicting high-risk prostate cancer using machine learning methods. *Data*, *4*(3), 129. doi:10.3390/data4030129

Batista, G. E., Prati, R. C., & Monard, M. C. (2004). A study of the behavior of several methods for balancing machine learning training data. *SIGKDD Explorations*, *6*(1), 20–29. doi:10.1145/1007730.1007735

Bilic, P., Christ, P. F., Vorontsov, E., Chlebus, G., Chen, H., Dou, Q., . . . Hesser, J. (2019). *The liver tumor segmentation benchmark (lits).* ArXiv Preprint ArXiv:1901.04056.

Bunkhumpornpat, C., Sinapiromsaran, K., & Lursinsap, C. (2009). Safe-level-smote: Safe-level-synthetic minority over-sampling technique for handling the class imbalanced problem. *Pacific-Asia Conference on Knowledge Discovery and Data Mining*, 475–482.

CancerStatistics. (2020). *National Cancer Institute.* doi:10.32388/VSUMBC

Chandana, S., Leung, H., & Trpkov, K. (2009). Staging of prostate cancer using automatic feature selection, sampling and Dempster-Shafer fusion. *Cancer Informatics, 7*.

Charte, F., Rivera, A. J., del Jesus, M. J., & Herrera, F. (2015). Addressing imbalance in multilabel classification: Measures and random resampling algorithms. *Neurocomputing, 163*, 3–16. doi:10.1016/j.neucom.2014.08.091

Chatziagapi, A., Paraskevopoulos, G., Sgouropoulos, D., Pantazopoulos, G., Nikandrou, M., Giannakopoulos, T., … Narayanan, S. (2019). Data Augmentation Using GANs for Speech Emotion Recognition. *Interspeech*, 171–175.

Chawla, N. V., Bowyer, K. W., Hall, L. O., & Kegelmeyer, W. P. (2002). SMOTE: Synthetic minority over-sampling technique. *Journal of Artificial Intelligence Research, 16*, 321–357. doi:10.1613/jair.953

Chen, W., Li, X., Gao, L., & Shen, W. (2020). Improving Computer-Aided Cervical Cells Classification Using Transfer Learning Based Snapshot Ensemble. *Applied Sciences (Basel, Switzerland), 10*(20), 7292. doi:10.3390/app10207292

Croft, P., Altman, D. G., Deeks, J. J., Dunn, K. M., Hay, A. D., Hemingway, H., ... Petersen, S. E. (2015). The science of clinical practice: Disease diagnosis or patient prognosis? Evidence about "what is likely to happen" should shape clinical practice. *BMC Medicine, 13*(1), 1–8. doi:10.118612916-014-0265-4 PMID:25637245

Fan, Y., Qi, L., & Tie, Y. (2020). *Classification of Cancer Subtypes Based on Imbalanced Data Sets.* EasyChair.

Fotouhi, S., Asadi, S., & Kattan, M. W. (2019). A comprehensive data level analysis for cancer diagnosis on imbalanced data. *Journal of Biomedical Informatics, 90*, 103089. doi:10.1016/j.jbi.2018.12.003 PMID:30611011

Frid-Adar, M., Diamant, I., Klang, E., Amitai, M., Goldberger, J., & Greenspan, H. (2018). GAN-based synthetic medical image augmentation for increased CNN performance in liver lesion classification. *Neurocomputing, 321*, 321–331. doi:10.1016/j.neucom.2018.09.013

Galar, M., Fernandez, A., Barrenechea, E., Bustince, H., & Herrera, F. (2011). A review on ensembles for the class imbalance problem: Bagging-, boosting-, and hybrid-based approaches. *IEEE Transactions on Systems, Man and Cybernetics. Part C, Applications and Reviews, 42*(4), 463–484. doi:10.1109/TSMCC.2011.2161285

GLOBOCAN Project. (2020). *International Agency for Research on Cancer.* Retrieved January 13, 2021, from https://gco.iarc.fr/today/home

Han, H., Wang, W.-Y., & Mao, B.-H. (2005). Borderline-SMOTE: a new over-sampling method in imbalanced data sets learning. *International Conference on Intelligent Computing*, 878–887.

Hart, P. (1968). The condensed nearest neighbor rule (corresp.). *IEEE Transactions on Information Theory, 14*(3), 515–516.

He, H., Bai, Y., Garcia, E. A., & Li, S. (2008). ADASYN: Adaptive synthetic sampling approach for imbalanced learning. *2008 IEEE International Joint Conference on Neural Networks (IEEE World Congress on Computational Intelligence)*, (pp. 1322–1328). IEEE.

Iizuka, O., Kanavati, F., Kato, K., Rambeau, M., Arihiro, K., & Tsuneki, M. (2020). Deep learning models for histopathological classification of gastric and colonic epithelial tumours. *Scientific Reports*, *10*(1), 1–11.

Jansen, M. J. A., Kuijf, H. J., Veldhuis, W. B., Wessels, F. J., Viergever, M. A., & Pluim, J. P. W. (2019). Automatic classification of focal liver lesions based on MRI and risk factors. *PLoS One*, *14*(5), e0217053.

Jia, A. D., Li, B. Z., & Zhang, C. C. (2020). Detection of cervical cancer cells based on strong feature CNN-SVM network. *Neurocomputing*, *411*, 112–127.

Johnson, J. M., & Khoshgoftaar, T. M. (2019). Survey on deep learning with class imbalance. *Journal of Big Data*, *6*(1), 1–54.

Kanavati, F., Ichihara, S., Rambeau, M., Iizuka, O., Arihiro, K., & Tsuneki, M. (2020). *Deep learning models for gastric signet ring cell carcinoma classification in whole slide images*. ArXiv Preprint ArXiv:2011.09247.

Kim, M.-J., Kang, D.-K., & Kim, H. B. (2015). Geometric mean based boosting algorithm with oversampling to resolve data imbalance problem for bankruptcy prediction. *Expert Systems with Applications*, *42*(3), 1074–1082.

Koziarski, M. (2020). *Two-Stage Resampling for Convolutional Neural Network Training in the Imbalanced Colorectal Cancer Image Classification*. ArXiv Preprint ArXiv:2004.03332.

Krawczyk, B. (2016). Learning from imbalanced data: Open challenges and future directions. *Progress in Artificial Intelligence*, *5*(4), 221–232.

Kubat, M., & Matwin, S. (1997). Addressing the curse of imbalanced training sets: One-sided selection. *ICML*, *97*, 179–186.

Leevy, J. L., Khoshgoftaar, T. M., Bauder, R. A., & Seliya, N. (2018). A survey on addressing high-class imbalance in big data. *Journal of Big Data*, *5*(1), 1–30.

Lemaitre, G., Martí, R., Rastgoo, M., & Mériaudeau, F. (2017). Computer-aided detection for prostate cancer detection based on multi-parametric magnetic resonance imaging. *2017 39th Annual International Conference of the IEEE Engineering in Medicine and Biology Society (EMBC)*, 3138–3141.

Litjens, G., Kooi, T., Bejnordi, B. E., Setio, A. A. A., Ciompi, F., Ghafoorian, M., ... Sánchez, C. I. (2017). A survey on deep learning in medical image analysis. *Medical Image Analysis*, *42*, 60–88.

Loey, M., Jasim, M. W., El-Bakry, H. M., Taha, M. H. N., & Khalifa, N. E. M. (2020). Breast and colon cancer classification from gene expression profiles using data mining techniques. *Symmetry*, *12*(3), 408.

López, V., Fernández, A., García, S., Palade, V., & Herrera, F. (2013). An insight into classification with imbalanced data: Empirical results and current trends on using data intrinsic characteristics. *Information Sciences*, *250*, 113–141.

Lu, L., & Daigle, B. J. Jr. (2020). Prognostic analysis of histopathological images using pre-trained convolutional neural networks: Application to hepatocellular carcinoma. *PeerJ, 8*, e8668.

Maheshwari, S., Jain, R. C., & Jadon, R. S. (2017). A review on class imbalance problem: Analysis and potential solutions. *International Journal of Computer Science Issues, 14*(6), 43–51.

Mena, L. J., & Gonzalez, J. A. (2006). Machine Learning for Imbalanced Datasets: Application in Medical Diagnostic. *Flairs Conference*, 574–579.

Moraes, R., Valiati, J. F., & Neto, W. P. G. (2018). *Unbalanced sentiment classification: an assessment of ANN in the context of sampling the majority class*. PeerJ Preprints.

Napierala, K., & Stefanowski, J. (2016). Types of minority class examples and their influence on learning classifiers from imbalanced data. *Journal of Intelligent Information Systems, 46*(3), 563–597.

Noble, W. S. (2006). What is a support vector machine? *Nature Biotechnology, 24*(12), 1565–1567.

Orhan, U., Hekim, M., & Ozer, M. (2011). EEG signals classification using the K-means clustering and a multilayer perceptron neural network model. *Expert Systems with Applications, 38*(10), 13475–13481.

Paing, M. P., & Choomchuay, S. (2018). Improved random forest (RF) classifier for imbalanced classification of lung nodules. *2018 International Conference on Engineering, Applied Sciences, and Technology (ICEAST)*, 1–4.

Polikar, R. (2006). Ensemble based systems in decision making. *IEEE Circuits and Systems Magazine, 6*(3), 21–45.

Qian, Q. (2020). *A Deep Learning Pipeline for Lung Cancer Classification on Imbalanced Data Set*. Academic Press.

Qian, Y., Liang, Y., Li, M., Feng, G., & Shi, X. (2014). A resampling ensemble algorithm for classification of imbalance problems. *Neurocomputing, 143*, 57–67.

Rehman, A., Ali, N., Taj, I., Sajid, M., & Karimov, K. S. (2020). An Automatic Mass Screening System for Cervical Cancer Detection Based on Convolutional Neural Network. *Mathematical Problems in Engineering*.

Reza, M. S., & Ma, J. (2018). Imbalanced histopathological breast cancer image classification with convolutional neural network. *2018 14th IEEE International Conference on Signal Processing (ICSP)*, 619–624.

Saini, M., & Susan, S. (2020). Deep transfer with minority data augmentation for imbalanced breast cancer dataset. *Applied Soft Computing, 97*, 106759.

Shapcott, M., Hewitt, K. J., & Rajpoot, N. (2019). Deep learning with sampling in colon cancer histology. *Frontiers in Bioengineering and Biotechnology, 7*, 52.

Stefanowski, J., & Wilk, S. (2008). Selective pre-processing of imbalanced data for improving classification performance. *International Conference on Data Warehousing and Knowledge Discovery*, 283–292.

Sudre, C. H., Li, W., Vercauteren, T., Ourselin, S., & Cardoso, M. J. (2017). Generalised dice overlap as a deep learning loss function for highly unbalanced segmentations. In *Deep learning in medical image analysis and multimodal learning for clinical decision support* (pp. 240–248). Springer.

Susan, S., & Kumar, A. (2020). The balancing trick: Optimized sampling of imbalanced datasets—A brief survey of the recent State of the Art. *Engineering Reports*, e12298.

Swain, P. H., & Hauska, H. (1977). The decision tree classifier: Design and potential. *IEEE Transactions on Geoscience Electronics*, *15*(3), 142–147.

Tajbakhsh, N., Shin, J. Y., Gurudu, S. R., Hurst, R. T., Kendall, C. B., Gotway, M. B., & Liang, J. (2016). Convolutional neural networks for medical image analysis: Full training or fine tuning? *IEEE Transactions on Medical Imaging*, *35*(5), 1299–1312.

Wang, S., & Yao, X. (2012). Multiclass imbalance problems: Analysis and potential solutions. *IEEE Transactions on Systems, Man, and Cybernetics. Part B, Cybernetics*, *42*(4), 1119–1130.

Weiss, G. M., & Provost, F. (2003). Learning when training data are costly: The effect of class distribution on tree induction. *Journal of Artificial Intelligence Research*, *19*, 315–354.

Willemink, M. J., Koszek, W. A., Hardell, C., Wu, J., Fleischmann, D., Harvey, H., ... Lungren, M. P. (2020). Preparing medical imaging data for machine learning. *Radiology*, *295*(1), 4–15.

Wu, E., Wu, K., Cox, D., & Lotter, W. (2018). Conditional infilling GANs for data augmentation in mammogram classification. In *Image analysis for moving organ, breast, and thoracic images* (pp. 98–106). Springer.

Yen, S.-J., & Lee, Y.-S. (2006). Under-sampling approaches for improving prediction of the minority class in an imbalanced dataset. In *Intelligent Control and Automation* (pp. 731–740). Springer.

Yoo, S., Gujrathi, I., Haider, M. A., & Khalvati, F. (2019). Prostate cancer detection using deep convolutional neural networks. *Scientific Reports*, *9*(1), 1–10.

Zeng, M., Zou, B., Wei, F., Liu, X., & Wang, L. (2016). Effective prediction of three common diseases by combining SMOTE with Tomek links technique for imbalanced medical data. *2016 IEEE International Conference of Online Analysis and Computing Science (ICOACS)*, 225–228.

Zhang, C. (2019). *Medical image classification under class imbalance*. Academic Press.

Zhang, J., Chen, L., & Abid, F. (2019). Prediction of Breast Cancer from Imbalance Respect Using Cluster-Based Undersampling Method. *Journal of Healthcare Engineering*.

Zhang, L., Lu, L., Nogues, I., Summers, R. M., Liu, S., & Yao, J. (2017). DeepPap: Deep convolutional networks for cervical cell classification. *IEEE Journal of Biomedical and Health Informatics*, *21*(6), 1633–1643.

Zhang, S., Liu, L., Zhu, X., & Zhang, C. (2008). A strategy for attributes selection in cost-sensitive decision trees induction. *2008 IEEE 8th International Conference on Computer and Information Technology Workshops*, 8–13.

Zhao, Y., Wong, Z. S.-Y., & Tsui, K. L. (2018). A framework of rebalancing imbalanced healthcare data for rare events' classification: A case of look-alike sound-alike mix-up incident detection. *Journal of Healthcare Engineering*.

Zhen, S., Cheng, M., Tao, Y., Wang, Y., Juengpanich, S., Jiang, Z., ... Lue, J. (2020). Deep learning for accurate diagnosis of liver tumor based on magnetic resonance imaging and clinical data. *Frontiers in Oncology, 10*, 680.

Chapter 5
Effective Multi–Label Classification Using Data Preprocessing

Vaishali S. Tidake

(iD) https://orcid.org/0000-0003-4543-6361

MVPS's KBT College of Engineering, Nashik, India

Shirish S. Sane

K. K. Wagh Institute of Engineering Education and Research, Nashik, India

ABSTRACT

Usage of feature similarity is expected when the nearest neighbors are to be explored. Examples in multi-label datasets are associated with multiple labels. Hence, the use of label dissimilarity accompanied by feature similarity may reveal better neighbors. Information extracted from such neighbors is explored by devised MLFLD and MLFLD-MAXP algorithms. Among three distance metrics used for computation of label dissimilarity, Hamming distance has shown the most improved performance and hence used for further evaluation. The performance of implemented algorithms is compared with the state-of-the-art MLkNN algorithm. They showed an improvement for some datasets only. This chapter introduces parameters MLE and skew. MLE, skew, along with outlier parameter help to analyze multi-label and imbalanced nature of datasets. Investigation of datasets for various parameters and experimentation explored the need for data preprocessing for removing outliers. It revealed an improvement in the performance of implemented algorithms for all measures, and effectiveness is empirically validated.

INTRODUCTION

Many scenarios in the real-life today depict applications of multi-label data. A document may be related to health as well as education, according to its text. A piece of news may focus on new technology that is helpful for safety as well. An image may contain several objects like roads, shops, buildings, etc. Contents of a paper may be relevant to multiple domains. A video may focus on topics of networking

DOI: 10.4018/978-1-7998-7371-6.ch005

along with virtualization. Thus many objects reveal multiple semantic meanings. Many researchers are working for the last few decades on multi-label classification. It is a task that assigns with a thing a set of predefined labels as per its properties.

BACKGROUND

The related work about multi-label classification and label imbalance is presented here. For multi-label classification, there exist methods that use the *transformation* approach. It changes multi-label data such that methods for single-label classification can be used. Sometimes multi-label data is not modified. Thus *adaptation* methods modify the process of dealing with such data. There also exists an approach that ensembles multiple existing methods. CC (Read, 2009), MLkNN (Zhang & Zhou, 2007) and RAkEL (Tsoumakas et al., 2011) are examples of these three approaches respectively.

For few decades, many researchers have worked in the field of multi-label classification (Tsoumakas & Katakis, 2007) (Tsoumakas et al., 2009) (Trohidis et al., 2008) (Tsoumakas et al., 2010) (Madjarov et al., 2012) (Zhang & Zhou, 2014) (Tidake & Sane, 2018). K nearest neighbor has also been the choice of many researchers for multi-label classification. From the study, it is noticed that neighbors are obtained using only features always. In contrast, the scenario is different for data that is multi-label. Each instance belongs to a predefined set of labels. Hence it is possible to consider labels along with features for obtaining neighbors.

Zhang and Zhou discuss an approach in (Zhang & Zhou, 2007). It follows an *algorithm adaptation* approach. It is an improved version of the well-known nearest neighbor algorithm. Several researchers use it to perform multi-label classification. It utilizes feature similarity to determine nearest neighbors (Zhang & Zhou, 2005) (Zhang & Zhou, 2007) (Spyromitros-Xioufis et al., 2008). In the case of multi-label classification, since the instances are associated with multiple labels, label dissimilarity may also help determine a set of nearest neighbors.

Class imbalance also poses problems to multi-label classifiers and may lower their performance. According to Spyromitros-Xioufis (2011), label skew is considered a class imbalance when considering each class individually. Francisco et al. (2013) have proposed how to measure the level of imbalance in a multi-label scenario. They have also presented two dataset preprocessing methods specially designed for multi-label datasets. They used sampling and LP for preprocessing. Those label sets that occur in a majority (minority) were reduced (increased). A method was suggested by Huang et al. (2015) for the improvement of multi-label classifier involving several binary classifiers. It can be used for feature selection also. SOSHF was extended from structured forests (Zachary et al., 2017). At each node, it has used transformation followed by split action to tackle class imbalance. An imbalance ratio was defined using positive and negative samples (Zhang et al., 2018). This ratio and label correlation was considered to improve BR models. Liu and Tsoumakas (2018) have handled the imbalance faced by ECC. They used an ensemble of CC with random under-sampling that helps to balance the distribution of each class. COCOA method explored joint label correlation and imbalance ratio from skewness between positive and negative samples (Zhang et al., 2020). It induced an imbalanced multi-class classifier per label.

MAIN FOCUS OF THE CHAPTER

A novel algorithm adaptation approach called MLFLD (Sane & Tidake, 2020) considered features and labels of instances to determine nearest neighbors while assigning weights to the neighbors. When two instances possess similar features, the chances of its selection as the nearest neighbor is more. Though labels of these instances are different, the possibility of its choice as nearest neighbor is low. The experimentation presented has shown the importance of using both features and labels to improve the classifier's performance. It has also demonstrated how the usage of particular distance measure affected the performance of devised algorithms.

Datasets may have an imbalance in the form of feature values. That can be checked by examining the existence of outliers. At the same time, multi-label datasets may have an imbalance in the form of labels also. This imbalance was measured using MLE (multi-label examples), skew and outliers, among other characteristics. The first two parameters are introduced in this chapter. These parameters computed using experiments helped to analyze the multi-label and imbalanced nature of datasets. Datasets were preprocessed to remove outliers. The performance of algorithms before and after preprocessing was analyzed, keeping an eye on the dataset characteristics. There is a need to explore how to handle imbalance.

In the subsequent sections, the work adopted by authors for the handling of multi-label data is presented. Six variants of experiments for developed algorithms are also focused on. Then multi-label datasets and their properties are described. Next, experimental results are discussed, followed by a conclusion.

DEVISED PARAMETERS AND ALGORITHMS FOR MULTI-LABEL CLASSIFICATION

Before presenting the work adopted by authors to handle multi-label data, different general and introduced parameters for measuring the multi-label and imbalanced nature of datasets are shown in the current section. Then two devised algorithms are presented, followed by two conventional and one introduced distance measures used by algorithms.

Parameters to Measure Multi-Label and Imbalance Nature of Multi-Label Datasets

Along with general parameters, two introduced parameters helped to analyze the multi-label and imbalanced nature of datasets.

Let AL denotes the actual label set present in dataset D. Let E and F be numbers of examples and features in D, respectively, as in Table 1. A proposed parameter MLE denotes the number of Multi-Label Examples: those with a count of labels more than 1 (Eq. (1)). A more considerable value shows more multi-label examples.

$$MLE(D) = \frac{1}{|E|} \sum_{i=1}^{|E|} V(|AL_i| > 1).$$

(1)

Here $V(.) = 1$ if a count of labels associated with instance i is more than 1, otherwise it is 0. Another proposed parameter is *skew* that denotes the proportion of the most frequent label set (Eq. (2)). A smaller value shows an imbalanced label set nature.

$$Skew(D) = \frac{1}{|E|} \max_{AL_i, AL_j \in D} \{AL_i | \mu(AL_i) > \mu(AL_j), \forall AL_j\}. \tag{2}$$

Here $\mu(x)$.denotes occurrence count of label set x in dataset D. One more parameter used is an *outlier* that tells a number of features having std. deviation ± 1.5 (3) from the mean (Eq. (3)). A larger value shows imbalanced nature in the form of feature values.

$$Outlier(D) = \frac{1}{|F|} \sum_{i=1}^{|F|} V(\tilde{A}_i \geq \pm 1.5). \tag{3}$$

Here $V(.) = 1$ if the standard deviation of feature i is more than ± 1.5, else it is 0. Weka (Hall et al., 2009) and Mulan (Tsoumakas et al., 2011) libraries were used for computation of these parameters. Table 1 shows these parameters that give a glance at the multi-label and imbalanced nature of used datasets.

Algorithm MLFLD

An algorithm for Multi-Label classification by exploring Feature Similarity and Label Dissimilarity (MLFLD) was designed for selecting proper neighbors for improving the performance of a multi-label classifier. MLFLD took the following parameters as input: a multi-label dataset (*MLDB*) with q instances, threshold (*Th*), number of neighbors (k), smoothing factor (p), and the distance measure for label dissimilarity (*Ldistance*). It operated in two stages.

In stage one, prior probabilities of each label c were obtained using Eq. (4)-(5). $cnt^{(c)}$.for label c was obtained from known instances.

$$P(H_c = 1) = \left(p + cnt^{(c)}\right) / (2 \times p + q). \tag{4}$$

$$P(H_c = 0) = 1 - P(H_c = 1). \tag{5}$$

Then MLFLD has used available labels of those instances that are already known. While searching for the neighbors, MLFLD utilized their features. Required data were obtained from these neighbors for each label and stored in $F_1^{(c)}[j]$.and $F_1^{(c)}[j]$.arrays. This information was utilized for the estimation of likelihood probabilities (Eq. (6)-(7)).

$$P\left(\mathrm{E} = \mathrm{j}|H_c = 1\right) = \frac{\mathrm{p} + F_1^{(c)}[j]}{p\,x\left(1+\mathrm{k}\right) + \sum_{r=0}^{k} F_1^{(c)}[r]}, 0 \le j \le k. \tag{6}$$

$$P\left(E = j|H_c = 0\right) = \frac{p + F_0^{(c)}[j]}{p\,x\left(1+\mathrm{k}\right) + \sum_{r=0}^{k} F_0^{(c)}[r]}, 0 \le j \le k. \tag{7}$$

In stage two, estimated probabilities of label c were utilized to predict label c for an unlabeled instance using Eq. (8)-(9).

$$j = \sum_{m=1}^{k} N_m^{(c)}. \tag{8}$$

$$t_c = 1, if \left(\frac{P\left(H_c = 1\right) \times P\left(E = j|H_c = 1\right)}{P\left(H_c = 1\right) \times P\left(E = j|H_c = 1\right) + P\left(H_c = 0\right) \times P\left(E = j|H_c = 0\right)} \right) \ge Th. \tag{9}$$

Algorithm MLFLD-MAXP

In most of the applications involving multi-label data, it is expected that an instance belongs to a minimum of one label (Read, 2010) (Godbole & Sarawagi, 2004) (Zhu et al., 2005) (Kiritchenko, 2005) (Ghamrawi & McCallum, 2005). Algorithm MLFLD was expanded to avoid the prediction of no label. Authors expanded algorithm MLFLD with MAXimum Probability (MLFLD-MAXP) that predicted the most probable label from the label set for an instance under consideration, using Eq. (10) (Tidake & Sane, 2021).

$$x = \arg max_c \left(\frac{P\left(H_c = 1\right) \times P\left(E = j \mid H_c = 1\right)}{P\left(H_c = 1\right) \times P\left(E = j \mid H_c = 1\right) + P\left(H_c = 0\right) \times P\left(E = j \mid H_c = 0\right)} \right). \tag{10}$$

Distance Metrics for Label Dissimilarity

From the study, it has been noticed that neighbors were obtained using features always. While the scenario for multi-label data is that each instance is relevant to a predefined set of labels. Hence both devised algorithms have used labels and features of known instances to locate neighbors. They computed feature similarity using Euclidean distance (Han & Kamber, 2012) and label dissimilarity using distance measures, namely Hamming, Jaccard and SimIC as shown in Eq. (11)-(13).

Hamming distance obtains a difference between a total number of distinct and shared labels between the two instances (Read et al., 2008) (Godbole & Sarawagi, 2004). Jaccard distance (Han & Kamber, 2012) uses a ratio of intersection of labels to their union to compute distance (Pesquita et al., 2007) (Veloso et al., 2007). SimIC (Similarity of Information Content) is motivated from SimGIC distance (Aleksovski et al., 2009). It computed information for label c using its probability in the dataset.

$$\text{Hamming}\left(X_i, X_j\right) = \frac{\left|Labels\left(X_i\right) \cup Labels\left(X_j\right)\right| - \left|Labels\left(X_i\right) \cap Labels\left(X_j\right)\right|}{c}. \tag{11}$$

$$\text{Jaccard}\left(X_i, X_j\right) = 1 - \left(\frac{\left|Labels\left(X_i\right) \cap Labels\left(X_j\right)\right|}{\left|Labels\left(X_i\right) \cup Labels\left(X_j\right)\right|}\right). \tag{12}$$

$$\text{SimIC}\left(X_i, X_j\right) = 1 - \left(\frac{IC\left(Labels\left(X_i\right) \cap Labels\left(X_j\right)\right)}{IC\left(Labels\left(X_i\right) \cup Labels\left(X_j\right)\right)}\right). \tag{13}$$

For a set of labels $A = \{L_1, L_2 \ldots L_n\}$. $IC\left(A\right)$ .was obtained from the sum of the information content of $L_1, L_2 \ldots L_n$ .each from Eq. (14).

$$IC\left(c\right) = -\log\left(p\left(c\right)\right). \tag{14}$$

RESULTS AND DISCUSSION

Before discussion of results, an overview of used multi-label data is taken in the current section. Different values obtained through experiments for introduced parameters along with general characteristics of data are presented. The nature of datasets is analyzed based on these values. Then the performance of devised algorithms for six variants of distance measures is compared with MLkNN. Among six variants, the variant performing best is used in further data preprocessing experiments to analyze outliers' effect.

Multi-Label Data

Benchmark datasets are provided by resources such as Mulan (Tsoumakas et al., 2011) and MEKA (Read & Peter, 2012) (Tidake & Sane, 2016). Table 1 describes used multi-label datasets having numeric features only. All the datasets were normalized before use.

General characteristics of the benchmark datasets are shown in Table 1. Only the CAL500 dataset has labels approx. three times more than features. The rest of the datasets have feature count lesser or equal to label count. Also, it is essential to notice that in CAL500, each label set occurs precisely once. Hence the %Unique is 100.

Table 1. Characteristics of datasets

Datasets	Type	F	L	E	Cardinality	Density	% Unique	%Ex/ Label	% MLE	% Skew	% Outlier
Emotions	Media	72	6	593	1.868	0.311	4.6	31.0	70.0	13.7	18.9
Image	Media	294	5	2000	1.236	0.247	1.0	24.7	22.9	18.9	86.2
Scene	Media	294	6	2407	1.074	0.179	0.6	17.9	7.4	16.8	72.2
Yeast	Bio	103	14	2417	4.237	0.303	8.2	30.2	98.7	9.8	29.6
CAL500	Media	68	174	502	26.044	0.15	100.0	14.9	100	0.2	16.3
F: #Features, L: #Labels, E: #Examples											

Table 1 shows Label Cardinality and Label Density of datasets (Zhang & Zhou, 2007) (Carvalho & Freitas, 2009) (Read et al., 2009). They represent an average number of labels/example, and Cardinality/number of labels, respectively. Unique (some researchers denote it as label diversity) (Tsoumakas & Katakis, 2008) shows distinct combinations of labels present in the dataset.

From Figure 1(a), Emotions, Image and Scene, have Cardinality one. Many instances in them have only one label. In Yeast, Cardinality 4 shows many instances have approx. 4 labels. Only CAL500 has Cardinality 26, while the rest datasets have Cardinality less than five. All datasets have minimal Density, except Emotions and Yeast followed by Image. The first two datasets have around 30%, while the third dataset has about 25% labels associated with almost every example. Each label set in CAL500 occurs only once, which means its labelling scheme is very irregular than the remaining datasets.

From Figure 1(b), Scene and Image have only 7% and 22% records associated with more than one label, respectively. The remaining datasets contain more than 70% MLE.

%Skew shows that Scene and Image have higher label skew comparatively than that of Yeast and Emotions. More examples are associated with the most frequent label combination, whereas the remaining examples are associated with rare label combination. Skew in CAL500 is less.

Outliers deviate the performance of a classifier (M. Hall et al., 2009). From Table 1, both Image and Scene contain more %outliers shown by 86 and 72, respectively.

In Figure 2(a), %Skew shows conflicting performance than %Ex/Label. For more skew, %Ex/label is less and vice-versa. Scene and Image datasets have comparatively less unique and more skew label sets, as shown in Table 1. As in Figure 2(b), datasets contain 3-26 labels. But most datasets contain examples

Figure 1a. Label statistics

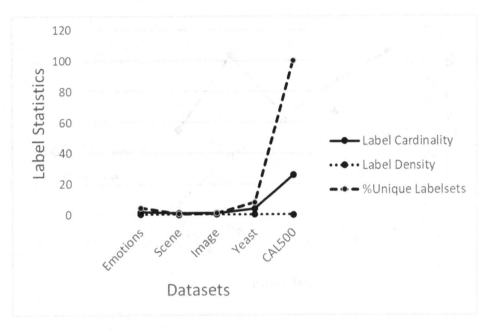

Figure 1b. Multi-label examples of datasets

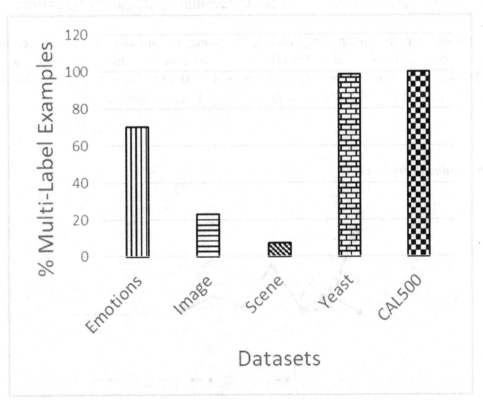

Figure 2a. Label distribution

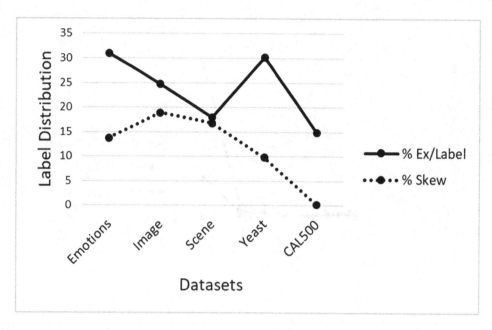

associated with very few labels. Used datasets have 14-31% examples per label, but unique label sets are 1-8% only except CAL500.

Comparison of Performance for Label Dissimilarity Distance Measures

As three measures for label dissimilarity, namely Hamming, Jaccard and SimIC distance, were used, their effect is observed in this section. Ten criteria were used for performance evaluation as shown in Table 2 (Tsoumakas & Katakis, 2007) (Tsoumakas et al., 2009) (Trohidis et al., 2008) (Tsoumakas et al., 2010) (Madjarov et al., 2012) (Zhang & Zhou, 2014) (Tidake & Sane, 2018).

Figure 2b. Cardinality of labels

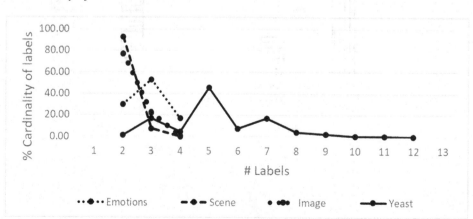

Table 2a. Effect of label dissimilarity on hamming loss (↓)

Dataset	MLkNN	MLFLD			MAXP		
		Hamming	Jaccard	SimIC	Hamming	Jaccard	SimIC
Emotions	0.1959	**0.1938**	0.1989	0.1952	**0.1938**	0.1952	0.1944
Image	0.1690	0.1631	0.1632	**0.1620**	0.1656	0.1661	0.1657
Scene	0.0861	0.0797	0.0795	**0.0792**	0.0812	0.0811	0.0807
Yeast	**0.1940**	0.1981	0.1967	0.2036	0.1977	0.1961	0.2041
CAL500	**0.1388**	0.1394	0.1393	0.1409	0.1394	0.1393	0.1409
Average	0.1568	**0.1548**	0.1555	0.1562	0.1555	0.1556	0.1572
Rank	6	1	2	5	3	4	7

Table 2b. Effect of label dissimilarity on ranking loss (↓)

Dataset	MLkNN	MLFLD			MAXP		
		Hamming	Jaccard	SimIC	Hamming	Jaccard	SimIC
Emotions	0.1959	**0.1938**	0.1989	0.1952	**0.1938**	0.1952	0.1944
Image	0.1690	0.1631	0.1632	**0.1620**	0.1656	0.1661	0.1657
Scene	0.0861	0.0797	0.0795	**0.0792**	0.0812	0.0811	0.0807
Yeast	**0.1940**	0.1981	0.1967	0.2036	0.1977	0.1961	0.2041
CAL500	**0.1388**	0.1394	0.1393	0.1409	0.1394	0.1393	0.1409
Average	0.1568	**0.1548**	0.1555	0.1562	0.1555	0.1556	0.1572
Rank	6	1	2	5	3	4	7

During the experimentations, the primary aim was to explore how measures of label dissimilarity influence MLFLD and MLFLD-MAXP. First, Euclidean and Hamming were used for feature similarity and label dissimilarity. Then Hamming was replaced by Jaccard and SimIC in further experiments. Obtained 6 variants were compared with each other and MLkNN.

Table 2c. Effect of label dissimilarity on one error (↓)

Dataset	MLkNN	MLFLD			MAXP		
		Hamming	Jaccard	SimIC	Hamming	Jaccard	SimIC
Emotions	0.2699	**0.2492**	0.2508	0.2610	**0.2492**	0.2508	0.2610
Image	0.3000	0.2916	0.2916	**0.2901**	0.2916	0.2916	0.2901
Scene	0.2256	0.2050	0.2050	**0.2046**	0.2050	0.2050	0.2046
Yeast	**0.2300**	0.2378	0.2311	0.2506	0.2378	0.2311	0.2506
CAL500	0.1176	0.1160	**0.1140**	0.1240	0.1160	**0.1140**	0.1240
Average	0.2286	0.2199	**0.2185**	0.2261	0.2199	**0.2185**	0.2261
Rank	7	3	1	5	3	1	5

Table 2d.Effect of label dissimilarity on coverage (↓)

Dataset	MLkNN	MLFLD			MAXP		
		Hamming	Jaccard	SimIC	Hamming	Jaccard	SimIC
Emotions	1.7764	**1.7102**	1.7542	1.7576	**1.7102**	1.7542	1.7576
Image	0.9390	**0.8964**	0.8964	0.8999	**0.8964**	0.8964	0.8999
Scene	0.4753	**0.4258**	0.4288	0.4304	**0.4258**	0.4288	0.4304
Yeast	**6.2750**	6.2905	6.3183	6.3697	6.2905	6.3183	6.3697
CAL500	130.564	130.524	**130.512**	130.652	130.524	**130.512**	130.652
Average	28.0059	**27.9694**	27.9819	28.0219	**27.9694**	27.9819	28.0219
Rank	5	1	3	6	1	3	6

Table 2e.Effect of label dissimilarity on average precision (↑)

Dataset	MLkNN	MLFLD			MAXP		
		Hamming	Jaccard	SimIC	Hamming	Jaccard	SimIC
Emotions	0.8034	**0.8183**	0.8094	0.8061	**0.8183**	0.8094	0.8061
Image	0.8030	0.8105	**0.8106**	0.8104	0.8105	**0.8106**	0.8104
Scene	0.8652	0.8785	0.8785	0.8785	0.8785	0.8785	0.8785
Yeast	0.7650	0.7648	**0.7663**	0.7550	0.7648	**0.7663**	0.7550
CAL500	**0.4942**	0.4918	0.4927	0.4871	0.4915	0.4927	0.4871
Average	0.7462	**0.7528**	0.7515	0.7474	0.7527	0.7515	0.7474
Rank	7	1	3	5	2	3	5

In this section, the performance was studied for ten folds using six variants for label dissimilarity. It is detailed in Table 2(a)-2(k) with a summary at the end. For comparison, two criteria, namely minimum average rank and a maximum number of wins, were used.

Table 2f.Effect of label dissimilarity on accuracy (↑)

Dataset	MLkNN	MLFLD			MAXP		
		Hamming	Jaccard	SimIC	Hamming	Jaccard	SimIC
Emotions	0.5340	0.5483	0.5158	0.5401	**0.5627**	0.5463	0.5619
Image	0.4937	0.5588	0.5709	0.5702	0.6169	**0.6187**	0.6179
Scene	0.6635	0.7083	0.7194	0.7110	0.7599	0.7604	**0.7615**
Yeast	0.5162	0.5116	0.5172	0.4862	0.5140	**0.5195**	0.4899
CAL500	0.1972	0.2023	0.1951	**0.2077**	0.2023	0.1951	**0.2077**
Average	0.4809	0.5059	0.5037	0.5030	**0.5312**	0.5280	0.5278
Rank	7	4	5	6	1	2	3

Table 2g. Effect of label dissimilarity on subset accuracy (↑)

Dataset	MLkNN	MLFLD			MAXP		
		Hamming	Jaccard	SimIC	Hamming	Jaccard	SimIC
Emotions	0.2934	0.3051	0.2915	0.3068	0.3136	0.3017	**0.3169**
Image	0.4090	0.4632	0.4657	0.4702	**0.5108**	0.5063	0.5093
Scene	0.6248	0.6629	0.6758	0.6696	0.7117	0.7150	**0.7171**
Yeast	0.1874	0.2046	0.2033	0.1954	**0.2046**	0.2037	0.1959
CAL500	0.0000	0.0000	0.0000	0.0000	0.0000	0.0000	0.0000
Average	0.3029	0.3272	0.3273	0.3284	**0.3481**	0.3453	0.3478
Rank	7	6	5	4	1	3	2

Table 2h. Effect of label dissimilarity on Ex-F1 (↑)

Dataset	MLkNN	MLFLD			MAXP		
		Hamming	Jaccard	SimIC	Hamming	Jaccard	SimIC
Emotions	0.6141	0.6274	0.5901	0.6155	**0.6441**	0.6279	0.6415
Image	0.5223	0.5916	0.6070	0.6044	0.6532	**0.6572**	0.6551
Scene	0.6764	0.7235	0.7340	0.7249	0.7761	0.7756	**0.7763**
Yeast	**0.6204**	0.6109	0.6165	0.5819	0.6145	0.6201	0.5875
CAL500	0.3240	0.3311	0.3212	0.3377	0.3311	0.3212	**0.3377**
Average	0.5514	0.5769	0.5738	0.5729	**0.6038**	0.6004	0.5996
Rank	7	4	5	6	1	2	3

From Figure 3 and Table 2(k), <MLFLD-MAXP, Hamming, Euclidean> triplet topped among seven experiments with average rank 1.5 and 7 wins. To brief,

- All six variants got a better average rank than MLkNN. It showed 6.7 average rank and 0 wins.

Table 2i. Effect of label dissimilarity on macro-F1 (↑)

Dataset	MLkNN	MLFLD			MAXP		
		Hamming	Jaccard	SimIC	Hamming	Jaccard	SimIC
Emotions	0.6226	0.6584	0.6399	0.6596	0.6609	0.6534	**0.6667**
Image	0.5815	0.6287	0.6358	0.6358	0.6482	**0.6507**	0.6496
Scene	0.7364	0.7683	0.7718	0.7696	**0.7795**	0.7789	0.7793
Yeast	**0.3853**	NaN	NaN	NaN	NaN	NaN	NaN
CAL500	**0.1714**	NaN	NaN	NaN	NaN	NaN	NaN
Average	0.4994	0.6851	0.6825	0.6883	0.6962	0.6943	**0.6985**
Rank	7	5	6	4	2	3	1

Table 2j. Effect of label dissimilarity on micro-F1 (↑)

Dataset	MLkNN	MLFLD			MAXP		
		Hamming	Jaccard	SimIC	Hamming	Jaccard	SimIC
Emotions	0.6610	0.6727	0.6476	0.6665	**0.6766**	0.6633	0.6745
Image	0.5842	0.6259	0.6346	0.6328	0.6449	**0.6483**	0.6461
Scene	0.7332	0.7617	0.7641	0.7621	0.7706	0.7702	**0.7709**
Yeast	0.6471	0.6426	0.6477	0.6218	0.6439	**0.6492**	0.6227
CAL500	0.3209	0.3294	0.3182	**0.3377**	0.3294	0.3182	**0.3377**
Average	0.5893	0.6065	0.6024	0.6042	**0.6131**	0.6098	0.6104
Rank	7	4	6	5	1	3	2

- For all metrics, variants of implemented algorithms exceeded MLkNN except hamming and ranking loss along with coverage.
- MLFLD and MLFLD-MAXP showed the same behavior for the first five measures.

From Table 1, Yeast and CAL500 were the most multi-label as implied by larger MLE values. But at the same time, their most frequent label set was associated with fewer examples indicated by smaller skew, inferring an imbalance label set. In contrast, these datasets have a lesser imbalance in terms of feature values. The emotions dataset also has a larger MLE. Simultaneously it has better skew and lesser outlier values. In Table 2(a)-2(k), MLkNN is better for datasets with very large MLE and smaller skew, while devised algorithms could not. They seemed evidenced better for datasets with lesser MLE but with more outliers.

Table 2k. Summarized performance for label dissimilarity

Performance Metric		MLkNN	MLFLD			MAXP		
			Hamming	Jaccard	SimIC	Hamming	Jaccard	SimIC
Hamming Loss	(↓)	0.1568	**0.1548**	0.1555	0.1562	0.1555	0.1556	0.1572
Ranking Loss	(↓)	0.1509	**0.1452**	0.1466	0.1494	**0.1452**	0.1466	0.1494
One Error	(↓)	0.2286	0.2199	**0.2185**	0.2261	0.2199	**0.2185**	0.2261
Coverage	(↓)	28.006	**27.969**	27.982	28.022	**27.969**	27.982	28.022
Avg. Precision	(↑)	0.7462	**0.7528**	0.7515	0.7474	**0.7528**	0.7515	0.7474
Accuracy	(↑)	0.4809	0.5059	0.5037	0.5030	**0.5312**	0.5280	0.5278
Subset Accuracy	(↑)	0.3029	0.3272	0.3273	0.3284	**0.3481**	0.3453	0.3478
Ex-F1	(↑)	0.5514	0.5769	0.5738	0.5729	**0.6038**	0.6004	0.5996
Macro-F1	(↑)	0.4994	0.6851	0.6825	0.6883	0.6962	0.6943	0.6985
Micro-F1	(↑)	0.5893	0.6065	0.6024	0.6042	**0.6131**	0.6098	0.6104
Exec. Time	(↓)	17	60	62	65	58	52	55
Avg. Rank	(↓)	6.7	3	3.9	5.1	**1.5**	2.7	3.9
#Wins	(↑)	0	4	1	0	**7**	1	1

Figure 3. Performance comparison for distance measures used for label dissimilarity

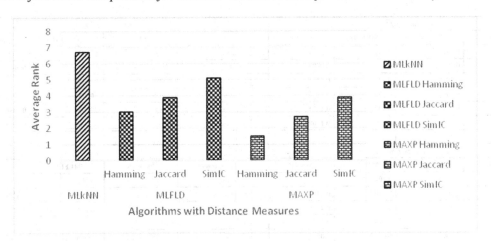

Performance After Outlier Removal

In the previous section, devised algorithms were seemed influenced mainly by the presence of more outliers. To check their influence, outliers were removed during preprocessing. The goal was to examine their performance on datasets of different nature. Here, devised algorithms were noticed for Hamming and Euclidean distance as their performance was seen to exceed compared to others. After removing outliers, datasets were supplied to three algorithms to be evaluated.

Summarized Table 3(b) has shown that both algorithms have defeated MLkNN after outlier removal from datasets. MLFLD-MAXP was seen much better than MLFLD. Figure 4(a)-4(e) has shown that for the first five metrics, devised algorithms behaved the same. For the rest five metrics, MLFLD-MAXP has surpassed MLFLD, as in Figure 4(g)-4(j). To summarize,

- Table 3 has illustrated that MLFLD always was better than MLFLD-MAXP for hamming loss enhancement, while MLFLD-MAXP appeared better after outlier removal.
- Both algorithms behaved the same for average precision, coverage, ranking loss, and one error (shown in Figure 4) with 2, 10, 33, and 37 percent increase than MLkNN, respectively. With MLFLD-MAXP and MLFLD, the highest enhancement was spotted as 46% and 35% for subset accuracy, and the same for accuracy was 32% and 24%, respectively. MLFLD-MAXP beat MLFLD for micro-F1 and ex-F1 with (21, 18) and (28, 21) percent, respectively. They have improved than MLkNN except for two datasets for macro-F1.
- The execution time was comparable for all experiments.

In Table 3(a)-3(b), after removing outliers, the scenario appeared very different. For all the metrics, both devised algorithms surpassed MLkNN. Thus, the imbalance of feature values influenced the designed algorithms for datasets with larger MLE and smaller label set skew.

Table 3a. Effect of outlier removal

(a) Hamming loss (↓)

Dataset	MLkNN	MLFLD	MAXP
Emotions	0.1878	0.1115	**0.1104**
Scene	0.1052	0.0914	**0.0877**
Image	0.1919	**0.1444**	0.1474
Yeast	0.1967	**0.1522**	0.1522
CAL500	0.1394	**0.1324**	0.1324
Average	0.1642	0.1264	**0.1260**
Rank	3	2	1

(b) Ranking loss (↓)

Dataset	MLkNN	MLFLD	MAXP
Emotions	0.1582	**0.0502**	0.0502
Scene	0.0946	**0.0669**	0.0669
Image	0.2089	**0.1537**	0.1537
Yeast	0.1638	**0.0971**	0.0971
CAL500	0.1837	**0.1696**	0.1696
Average	0.1618	**0.1075**	0.1075
Rank	3	1	1

(c) One Error (↓)

Dataset	MLkNN	MLFLD	MAXP
Emotions	0.2599	**0.1042**	0.1042
Scene	0.2910	**0.2302**	0.2302
Image	0.3765	**0.2815**	0.2815
Yeast	0.2222	**0.1147**	0.1147
CAL500	0.1095	**0.0597**	0.0597
Average	0.2518	**0.1581**	0.1581
Rank	3	1	1

(d) Coverage (↓)

Dataset	MLkNN	MLFLD	MAXP
Emotions	1.7959	**1.1792**	1.1792
Scene	0.5612	**0.4154**	0.4154
Image	1.0545	**0.8259**	0.8259
Yeast	6.2599	**5.1735**	5.1735
CAL500	131.057	**130.036**	130.036
Average	28.1457	**27.5260**	27.5260
Rank	3	1	1

(e) Average Precision (↑)

Dataset	MLkNN	MLFLD	MAXP
Emotions	0.8073	**0.9278**	0.9278
Scene	0.8301	**0.8700**	0.8700
Image	0.7568	**0.8201**	0.8201
Yeast	0.7696	**0.8634**	0.8634
CAL500	0.4946	**0.5369**	0.5369
Average	0.7317	**0.8036**	0.8036
Rank	3	1	1

(f) Accuracy (↑)

Dataset	MLkNN	MLFLD	MAXP
Emotions	0.5665	0.7276	**0.7380**
Scene	0.6060	0.6667	**0.7407**
Image	0.3937	0.5722	**0.6630**
Yeast	0.5058	0.6235	**0.6236**
CAL500	0.1936	**0.2385**	0.2385
Average	0.4531	0.5657	**0.6008**
Rank	3	2	1

(g) Subset Accuracy (↑)

Dataset	MLkNN	MLFLD	MAXP
Emotions	0.3223	0.5083	**0.5167**
Scene	0.5701	0.6189	**0.6907**
Image	0.3501	0.5148	**0.5963**
Yeast	0.1805	**0.2806**	0.2806
CAL500	0.0000	0.0000	0.0000
Average	0.2846	0.3845	**0.4169**
Rank	3	2	1

(h) Ex-F1 (↑)

Dataset	MLkNN	MLFLD	MAXP
Emotions	0.6458	0.7948	**0.8059**
Scene	0.6179	0.6826	**0.7574**
Image	0.4084	0.5920	**0.6858**
Yeast	0.6111	0.7206	**0.7209**
CAL500	0.3186	**0.3781**	0.3781
Average	0.5204	0.6336	**0.6696**
Rank	3	2	1

(i) Macro-F1 (↑)

Dataset	MLkNN	MLFLD	MAXP
Emotions	0.6404	0.8166	**0.8196**
Scene	0.6336	0.6998	**0.7397**
Image	0.4455	0.5961	**0.6153**
Yeast	**0.3858**	NaN	NaN
CAL500	**0.1957**	NaN	NaN
Average	0.4602	0.7042	**0.7249**
Rank	3	2	1

(j) Micro-F1 (↑)

Dataset	MLkNN	MLFLD	MAXP
Emotions	0.6814	0.8220	**0.8247**
Scene	0.6715	0.7225	**0.7514**
Image	0.4768	0.6414	**0.6700**
Yeast	0.6396	0.7403	**0.7404**
CAL500	0.3147	**0.3831**	0.3831
Average	0.5568	0.6619	**0.6739**
Rank	3	2	1

FUTURE RESEARCH DIRECTIONS

In this work, multi-label data was observed for MLE, skew and outlier along with other properties. These were obtained through experimentation. It exhibited how performance was affected due to these properties. Multi-label data can be preprocessed further for a feature and instance selection or handling of skew nature. Observations of dataset characteristics showed that more MLE implied more skew. But

Table 3b. Summarized performance after outlier removal

Performance Metric		MLkNN	MLFLD	MAXP
Hamming Loss	(↓)	0.1642	0.1264	**0.1260**
Ranking Loss	(↓)	0.1618	**0.1075**	**0.1075**
One Error	(↓)	0.2518	**0.1581**	**0.1581**
Coverage	(↓)	28.146	**27.526**	27.526
Avg. Precision	(↑)	0.7317	**0.8036**	0.8036
Accuracy	(↑)	0.4531	0.5657	**0.6008**
Subset Accuracy	(↑)	0.2846	0.3845	**0.4169**
Ex-F1	(↑)	0.5204	0.6336	**0.6696**
Macro-F1	(↑)	0.4602	0.7042	**0.7249**
Micro-F1	(↑)	0.5568	0.6619	**0.6739**
Exec. Time	(↓)	6	8	8
Avg. Rank	(↓)	3	1.6	**1**
#Wins	(↑)	0	4	**10**

at the same time, when MLE was less, outliers were more. It needs further investigation and empirical evaluation because experimentation was done on only five datasets.

CONCLUSION

Being associated with multiple labels, the use of label dissimilarity with feature similarity by MLFLD-MAXP has exceeded its performance. While the computation of label dissimilarity was observed for three distance measures, Hamming distance has shown maximum enhancement. When data was seen for outlier existence, its removal seemed more beneficial on MLFLD and MLFLD-MAXP. All the experiments implied that both the algorithms were sensitive to the presence of outliers. They were also affected by skew and the unique characteristics of datasets. It can be concluded that devised algorithms seemed more susceptible to datasets having very high MLE. The imbalance of feature values influenced the designed algorithms for datasets with larger MLE and smaller label set skew. Different forms of preprocessing on multi-label data can be further applied and observed.

Figure 4. Performance after outlier removal

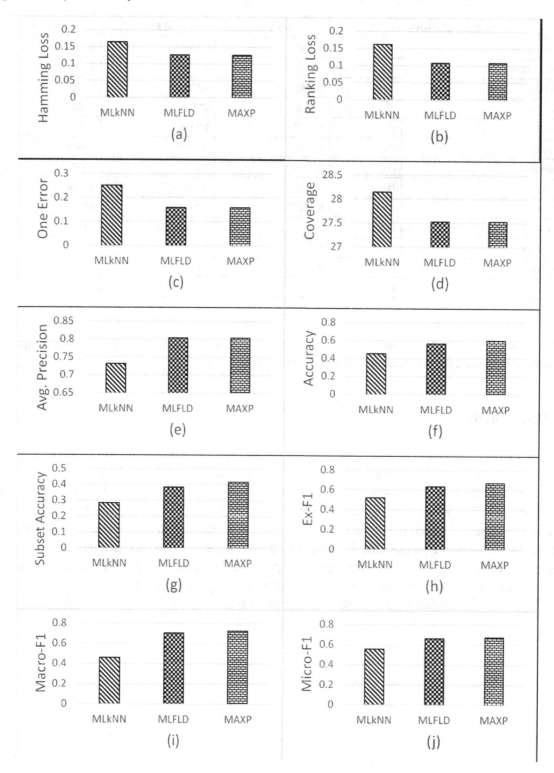

REFERENCES

Aleksovski, D., Kocev, D., & Dzeroski, S. (2009). Evaluation of distance measures for hierarchical multilabel classification in functional genomics. *Proceedings of the 1st workshop on learning from multi-label data (MLD) held in conjunction with ECML/PKDD*, 5–16.

Charte, F., Rivera, A., del Jesus, M. J., & Herrera, F. (2013). A First Approach to Deal with Imbalance in Multi-label Datasets. HAIS 2013, LNAI 8073, 150–160.

Daniels, Z. A., & Metaxas, D. N. (2017). Addressing Imbalance in Multi-Label Classification Using Structured Hellinger Forests. *Proceedings of the Thirty-First AAAI Conference on Artificial Intelligence (AAAI-17)*.

de Carvalho, A., & Freitas, A. A. (2009). A tutorial on multi-label classification techniques. In A. Abraham, A. E. Hassanien, & V. Snasel (Eds.), *Studies in Computational Intelligence 205* (pp. 177–195). Springer.

Ghamrawi, N., & McCallum, A. (2005) Collective multi-label classification. In *CIKM '05: 14th ACM International Conference on Information and Knowledge Management*. ACM Press. 10.1145/1099554.1099591

Godbole, S., & Sarawagi, S. (2004). *Discriminative methods for multi-labeled classification, Advances in Knowledge Discovery and Data Mining*. Springer.

Hall, M., Frank, E., Holmes, G., Pfahringer, B., Reutemann, P., & Witten, I. H. (2009). The WEKA data mining software: An update. *SIGKDD Explorations, 11*(1), 10–18. doi:10.1145/1656274.1656278

Han, J., & Kamber, M. (2012). *Data Mining: Concepts and Techniques*. The Morgan Kaufmann Series in Data Management Systems.

Huang, J., Li, G.-R., Huang, Q.-M., & Wu, X.-D. (2015). Learning label specific features for multi-label classification. *Proc. IEEE Int. Conf. Data Min.*, 181–190. 10.1109/ICDM.2015.67

Kiritchenko, S. (2005). *Hierarchical Text Categorization and its Application to Bioinformatics* (PhD thesis). Queen's University, Kingston, Canada.

Liu, B., & Tsoumakas, G. (2018). *Making Classifier Chains Resilient to Class Imbalance*. ACML.

Madjarov, G., Kocev, D., Gjorgjevikj, D., & Džeroski, S. (2012). An extensive experimental comparison of methods for multi-label learning. *Pattern Recognition, 45*(9), 3084–3104. doi:10.1016/j.patcog.2012.03.004

Pesquita, C., Faria, D., Bastos, H., Falcao, A. O., & Couto, F. M. (2007). Evaluating GO-based Semantic Similarity Measures. *The 10th Annual Bio-Ontologies Meeting, ISMB/ECCB*.

Read, J. (2008). Multi-label classification using ensembles of pruned sets. *Proc. of 8th IEEE Int. Conf. on Data Mining*, 995-1000. 10.1109/ICDM.2008.74

Read, J. (2010). *Scalable Multi-label Classification*. The University of Waikato.

Read, J., & Peter, R. (2012). *MEKA: A multi-label extension to WEKA*. http://meka.sourceforge.net

Read, J., Pfahringer, B., Holmes, G., & Frank, E. (2009). Classifier chains for multi-label classification. In *Proc. of European Conf. on Machine Learning and Knowledge Discovery in Databases: Part II. ECML PKDD '09*. Springer-Verlag. 10.1007/978-3-642-04174-7_17

Sane, S. S., & Tidake, V. S. (2020). Efficient Multi-label Classification using Attribute and Instance Selection. *Biosc. Biotech. Res. Comm. Special Issue*, *13*(14), 221–226. doi:10.21786/bbrc/13.14/52

Spyromitros-Xioufis, E. (2011). *Dealing with Concept Drift and Class Imbalance in Multi-label Stream Classification*. Thesis.

Spyromitros-Xioufis, E., Tsoumakas, G., & Vlahavas, I. (2008). An empirical study of lazy multi-label classification algorithms. *Proc. 5th Hellenic Conf. Artif. Intell.*, 401–406.

Tidake, V. S., & Sane, S. S. (2016). Multi-label learning with MEKA. *CSI Communications*, *2016*(August issue), 33–37.

Tidake, V. S., & Sane, S. S. (2018). Multi-label Classification: A Survey. *International Journal of Engineering and Technology*, *7*(4.19), 1045-1054.

Tidake, V. S., & Sane, S. S. (2021). Effect of Distance Metrics on Multi-label Classification. In *Proceeding of First Doctoral Symposium on Natural Computing Research, Lecture Notes in Networks and Systems 169*. Springer Nature Singapore Pte Ltd.

Trohidis, K. (2008). Multi-Label Classification of Music into Emotions. *ISMIR, 8*.

Tsoumakas, G. (2010). *Mining multi-label data*. In O. Maimon & L. Rokach (Eds.), *Data Mining and Knowledge Discovery Handbook* (pp. 667–686). Springer.

Tsoumakas, G., & Katakis, I. (2007). Multi-label classification: An overview. *International Journal of Data Warehousing and Mining*, *3*(3), 1–13. doi:10.4018/jdwm.2007070101

Tsoumakas, G., & Katakis, I. (2008). Effective and efficient multi-label classification in domains with large number of labels. *Proc. Work. Notes ECML PKDD Workshop MMD*.

Tsoumakas, G., Katakis, I., & Vlahavas, I. (2011). Random k-Labelsets for Multi-Label Classification. *IEEE Transactions on Knowledge and Data Engineering*, *23*(7), 1079–1089. doi:10.1109/TKDE.2010.164

Tsoumakas, G., Spyromitros-Xioufis, E., Vilcek, J., & Vlahavas, I. (2011). MULAN: A Java library for multi-label learning. *Journal of Machine Learning Research*, *12*, 2411–2414.

Tsoumakas, G., Zhang, M. L., & Zhou, Z. H. (2009). *Tutorial on learning from multi-label data, in ECML PKDD*. Available: http://www.ecmlpkdd2009.net/wpcontent/uploads/2009/08/learning-from-multi-label-data.pdf

Veloso, A., Meira, W. Jr, Goncalves, M., & Zaki, M. (2007). Multi-label lazy associative classification. In *PKDD '07: 11th European Conference on Principles and Practice of Knowledge Discovery in Databases*. Springer

Zhang, M. L., Li, Y.-K., Liu, X.-Y., & Geng, X. (2018). Binary relevance for multi-label learning: An overview. *Frontiers of Computer Science*, *12*(2), 191–202. doi:10.100711704-017-7031-7

Zhang, M. L., Li, Y.-K., Yang, H., & Liu, X.-Y. (2020). Towards Class-Imbalance Aware Multi-Label Learning. *IEEE Transactions on Cybernetics*, *2020*, 1–13. doi:10.1109/TCYB.2020.3027509 PMID:33206614

Zhang, M. L., & Zhou, Z. H. (2005). A k-nearest neighbor based algorithm for multi-label classification. *IEEE International Conference on Granular Computing*, 718-721. 10.1109/GRC.2005.1547385

Zhang, M. L., & Zhou, Z. H. (2007). ML-KNN: A lazy learning approach to multi-label learning. *Pattern Recognition*, *40*(7), 2038–2048. doi:10.1016/j.patcog.2006.12.019

Zhang, M. L., & Zhou, Z. H. (2014). A Review on Multi-Label Learning Algorithms. Knowledge and Data Engineering. *IEEE Transactions on.*, *26*(8), 1819–1837. doi:10.1109/TKDE.2013.39

Zhu, S., Ji, X., Xu, W., & Gong, Y. (2005). Multi-labelled classification using maximum entropy method. *SIGIR: '05: 27th Annual ACM Conference on Research and Development in Information Retrieval*, 274-281.

Chapter 6
Leaf Disease Detection Using AI

Praveen Kumar Maduri
Galgotias College of Engineering and Technology, India

Tushar Biswas
Galgotias College of Engineering and Technology, India

Preeti Dhiman
Galgotias College of Engineering and Technology, India

Apurva Soni
Galgotias College of Engineering and Technology, India

Kushagra Singh
Galgotias College of Engineering and Technology, India

ABSTRACT

Plants play a significant role in everyone's life. They provide us essential elements like food, oxygen, and shelter, so plants must be supervised and nurtured properly. During cultivation, crops are prone to different kinds of diseases which can severely damage the whole yield leading to financial losses for farmers. In last 10 years, researchers have used different machine learning techniques to detect the disease on plants, but either the methods were not efficient enough to be implemented or were not able to cover the wide area in which plant diseases can be detected. So, the author has introduced a method which is efficient enough to easily detect plant disease and can be implemented in large fields. The author has used a combination of CNN and k-means clustering algorithms. By using this method, crops disease is detected by analyzing the leaves, which notifies users for action in the initial stage. Thus, the proposed method prevents whole crops from getting damaged and saves time and energy of farmers as disease will be identified way before a human eye can detect it on a large farm.

DOI: 10.4018/978-1-7998-7371-6.ch006

INTRODUCTION

Industries are growing faster day by day and new technologies are also being developed by researchers for the ease of the workers. Nowadays, Machine learning is a very known and vast method for analyzing of data which is used in various sectors among which agricultural sector is one of them. This sector is a very vast sector which includes many important things and in all these important things, the plant's health is very much important. Plant's health could get disturbed by incomplete or wrong treatment during irrigation.

In countries such as India where 70% of the total population's income depends on agriculture, it is very important to keep the crops and plants protected from diseases in present scenario. It is done with the help of pesticides and insecticides. Pesticides and Insecticides are sprayed beforehand to keep the crops protected but regular use of these synthetic chemicals is slowly poisoning the fruit of the plant and when consumed by humans can cause many harmful effects. To overcome this problem, a method is designed in which the disease is detected in early stage and the medicine is sprayed only on the infected area. In this chapter, Author discusses about the method used to detect the disease with the use of the machine learning and its various algorithms.

The detection of the leaves and crops plays an imperative role in the betterment of the plant's health, as plant are essential part of our day to day lives. This chapter contains the methodology that is used for the leaf disease detection and also contains the information about how the models (K-means clustering and convolution neural networks) are being trained. This chapter is very helpful for the specialists present in the agricultural department, where they can observe a leaf and can easily evaluate the disease that the leaf is suffering from. With the early detection of leaf disease, they can take proper steps/ measures to cure the plant or the crop from that particular disease.

The method used in this chapter is an integration of two algorithms: K-means clustering and Convolution neural network (CNN). K-means clustering being the first is used for the color extraction of the leaf. Further, CNN is used for the comparison of the extracted color image with the images present in this dataset that is been used for training of the unsupervised model.

The steps which are used for the detection of disease in the leaves of the particular classes are followed as:

1. Image segmentation
2. Extract dominant colors
3. Applying K-means
4. Make clusters
5. Apply CNN.

This chapter is about explaining the above steps in detail and also proves that how much this model is accurate for the detection of the disease of the leaves.

The dataset that has been used in this research has 5 directories: -

1. Bacteria
2. Fungi
3. Nematodes
4. Normal

5.   Virus

These directories are used to give us a clear vision about the class of plant disease. These directories contain many images of different types of diseases which may affect the growth of the plant. These files or images are being used by the CNN for detection of the disease. The directories developed have many images of a particular disease in different plants/ crops which is used by Convolution Neural Network to compare the input image formed by k- means clustering along with the dataset which is used to obtain the results.

This chapter also explains the hardware portion which consist of the microcontroller, camera, technique which makes this chapter or research more clear. It also contains the future scopes indicating various techniques which could be used in future to enhance the research or to implement this work at some places where it could be useful for the detection of the plant's disease.

ALGORITHMS USED

K-Means

1.   **History**: The standard calculation of k-implies was given by Stuart Lloyd (1957) of Bell Labs however that beat code balance diary was not distributed till 1982. Edward W. Forgy (1965) distributed k-implies strategy, that is the reason it is here and there called Lloyd–Forgy calculation. K-implies was first utilized or implemented by James MacQueen (1967).
2.   Algorithms:
       a.   Standard algorithm (naïve k-means):

The Standard calculation utilizes an iterative refinement procedure, since it is normal. Along these lines, it is known as "the k-implies calculation"; it is otherwise called Lloyd's calculation, in the software engineering local area and at times additionally called as "Innocent k-implies".

The calculation has merged when the tasks presently don't change. Yet, this calculation doesn't affirm to track down the ideal.

The calculation is introduced as the closest group by distance. Utilizing an alternate distance apart from (squared) Euclidean distance can preserve the calculations combined. In this technique, it is ascertained that the mean qualities and expecting one of the bunches are their mean.

Illustration of the Basic Algorithm:

In figure 1, three diverse k methods are beginning to frame which are of various shading's: one is red, second is green, and third is blue. Figure 2 addresses the k bunches which are made by associating each perception with the closest mean. The allotments addresses the Voronoi chart produced by the methods which is imperative to isolate the tones in the picture. Figure 3 addresses the centroid of the K bunch turning into another mean. The means appeared in figure 2 and 3 are rehashed until union has been reached as demonstrated in figure 4.

The calculation does not have the option to figure the specific estimation of the grouping. The yield of the grouping is completely founded on the underlying bunch. As the calculation is quick, it is not difficult to run it on numerous occasions with various starting bunch. However, in couple of cases, it

Figure 1. K starting are normally composed inside the data

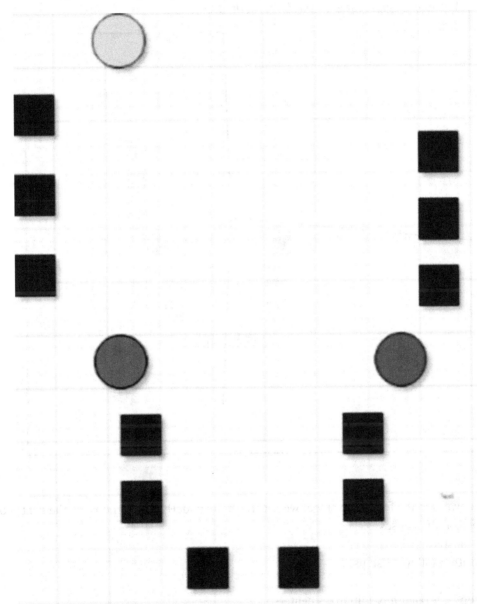

tends to be moderate: specifically in particular point in datasets and for two/ more measurements which are joined with outstanding time, i.e. $2\omega(n)$.

b.   Initialization Method:

Usually utilized strategies are: - Forgy and Random Partition.

In the Forgy strategy, we arbitrarily consider the k worth from the dataset and use it as its underlying methods. This Random Partition strategy depends on a group to every perception. Afterward when

Figure 2. K bunches are made by associating each perception using the closest mean. The allotments addresses the Voronoi graph created through the methods.

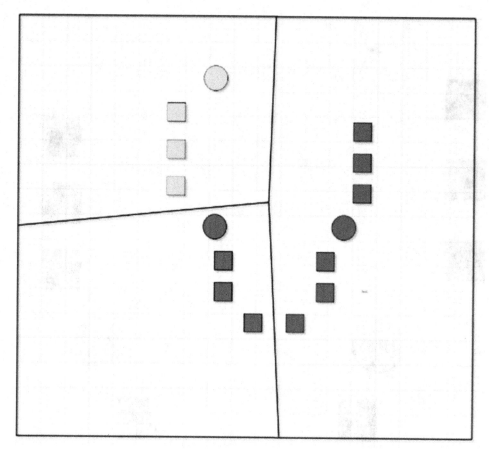

we proceed onward to the following stage, we ascertain the underlying intend to be the centroid of the bunches haphazardly focuses.

K-means clustering:

This algorithm follows 4 steps:

i.   First step is, it randomly initializes centers.
ii. ii. It calculates the distance between each point and each center and associates the point to that center from which its Euclidian distance is minimum. If 'r' being the Euclidean Distance between both the two points (x, y), (a, b), then the formula or the techniques for calculating the distance between the two points is:

$$r = \sqrt{(x-a)^2 + (y-b)^2} \,.$$

Figure 3.Converting each K group centroid to new mean

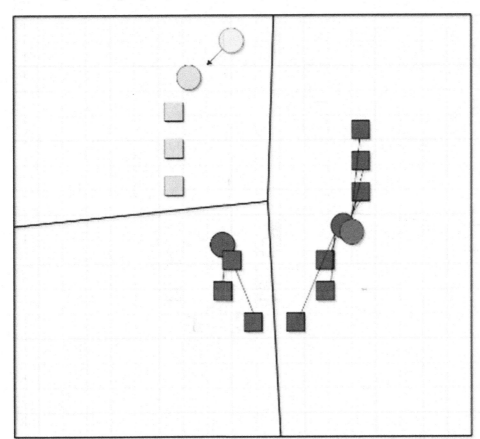

iii.   After associating all points with the centre, the value of centre got changed. New value of centre will be the mean value of all the points associated with it. After changing all the centres, the points associated with it are been removed.

iv.   Step (ii) and (iii) are again performed until the optimum state is reached.

As we clearly see in figure 5 that if p be the center and the q be the point at which the color exists then the distance between them is r.

3.   Hartigan–Wong Method:

Hartigan and Wong's strategy is the technique which shows assortment in k-implies calculation which advances towards a nearby of the base amount of squares issue with various arrangement refreshes. The strategy is a neighbourhood search that iteratively endeavours to move an example into an alternate bunch as long as this interaction improves the goal work. At the point, when no example can be migrated into an alternate group with an improvement of the level headed, the technique stops (in a nearby least).

Figure 4. Stages 2 and 3 are rehashed until combination has been reached.

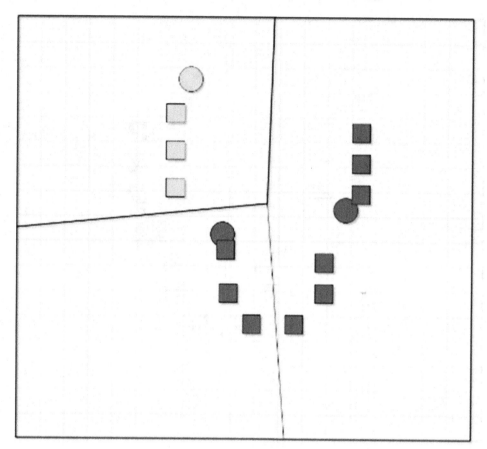

Along these lines as the traditional k-implies, the methodology stays a heuristic since it does not really ensure that the last arrangement is worldwide ideal.

4.   Termination:

Termination represents a point at which the algorithm is less than zero, which simply means there is no more change in pixels. To accomplish this point, various strategies and procedure can be utilized. In a first technique, any best moving positions can be applied, though in a best procedure, all positions will be tried and simply the best one is applied. The previous methodology favors speed, regardless of whether the last methodology by and large kindnesses arrangement quality to the detriment of extra computational time.

CNN (Convolution Neural Network)

This type of Convolution is a neural network type and is of favorable response which is also called as CNN and another name of CNN is ConvNet. It is another type of network or we can say that it is a neural network type which is used for detecting the images. CNN consists of various inputs, outputs and multiple

Figure 5. Euclidian distance between both the two points p and q.

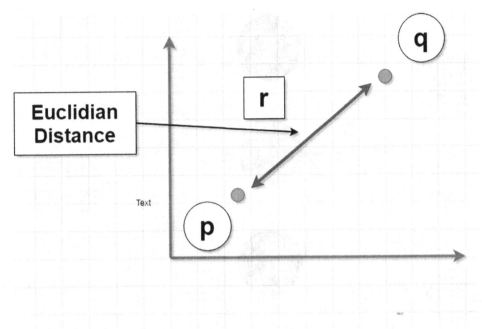

hidden layers. CNN is widely used in audio synthesis and wave net. The convolution networks are used specifically in convolution instead of general matrix multiplication. Image detection is very widely approached part in CNN. The other portions that can also be used are like: analyzing the data and also for classification of the barriers in various problems as well. This property in CNN is stated neural network or artificial neural network that is further classified into different types which are capable of picking up or analyzing forms or the patterns and generates the possible results for them. This analyzing makes the CNN a better method for image detection. As, CNN is an Artificial Neural Network which distinguishes it against the Multi-Layer Perceptron or we can say the MLP. It has its invisible set of layers which are called as convolution layers.

These layers all together comprises of a system that is CNN efficient. CNN may also have many more non-convolutional layers, but the base of the CNN is only convolutional layers.

a.   Layers of Convolution

Convolution layers are the building steps of CNN. As like the different layers a convolutional layer first receives input and then transforms it in other ways possible. The transformed input is further made to fed as an output to the next layer. This transformation is a convolution operation.

As mentioned previously that the convolutional neural networks are capable in detecting the different patterns and images more accurately. They also provide some relevant, low-dimensional space that is used further. More precisely, with every convolutional layer, it is required to provide the number of filters that the layers should have.

As we can see in figure 7 that how the filters are being visualized after 1st layer. By these layers, it can detect multiple corners, shapes, forms, objects etc. for an image. So, one similar type of quote patterns

Figure 6. Layers of Convolution Neural Network (CNN)

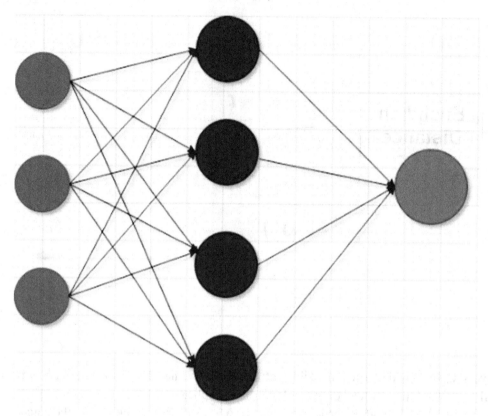

Figure 7. Visualizing filters after 1ˢᵗ layer

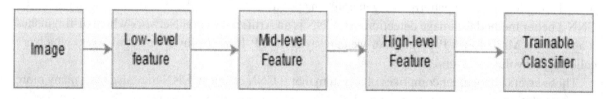

that a filter can detect will be edges of the images and this channel would be called an edge finder. For instance, a few channels can distinguish borders/ some can recognize circles and furthermore different squares and so on too. These typical kind of channels are those which we saw in the start of our organization. The more profound our organization goes, the more straightforward these channels become, so in the more profound layers as opposed to corners in basic shapes these channels might distinguish specific things like eyes and the other body portions of creatures and people, even in more profound layers the channels could identify various sorts of items like full creatures. To comprehend the working of the convolution layers and their specific channels, a model is considered.

Thus, suppose we have CNN that is tolerating the pictures of generally composed digits like from the acquittal ADA set and our organization is sorting them into their separate arrangements of whether the pictures of a 1 2 3 and so on. Let us consider the 1ˢᵗ hidden layer in our model which is a convolutional

Figure 8. Neural network with a hidden layer

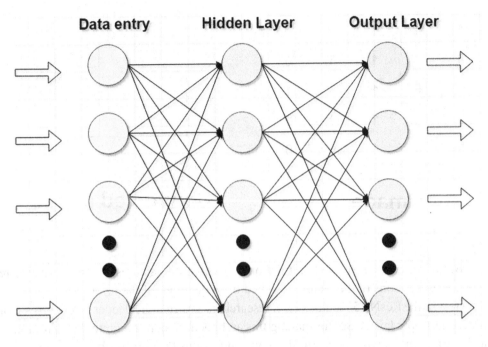

layer. While fixing a convolutional layer to our model, we additionally need to fix the quantity of the channels which are required in the layer.

A channel thinks about a grid which is a small grid, for this we have chosen to give that lattice a specific the number of lines and number of sections that this network ought to have and the qualities in this framework are introduced with the irregular numbers. At the point when a convolution layer gets the information at that point, habitually channel will slide over each 3x3 arrangement of pixels from the actual information until it slides over the 3x3 square of pixels from genuine and full picture. This sliding of channels is really alluded as convolving the picture so truly, it appears like a channel is beginning convolving across each 3 x 3 square of pixels from the accepted contribution as demonstrated in the figure 9.

ResNet50

The ResNet50 stands for "residual network 50". It is a 50-layer residual network. There is other form of this ResNet50 also like ResNet101 and ResNet152. Every year, a competition is organized in which researchers come together and make many architectures to enhance the accuracy of the image classification. ResNet50 is one of the architectures that shows its highest accuracy. Deep neural networks such as ResNet50 have gone through a series of breakthroughs for image classification. From many years, there was a trend which is still going on to go deeper, to solve more complex tasks and to also precise its result or to enhance its accuracy. But it goes more and more deep, the accuracy also gets decreased and the training becomes tougher. So, this residual learning solves both the problems.

The ResNet50 architecture has many layers of convolution between the input image and the output result. Actually in deep learning neural networks, there are many layers that are been stacked and are being trained to conclude the result. The network learns many high/ low/ mid-level features at the end

Figure 9. Convolved matrix

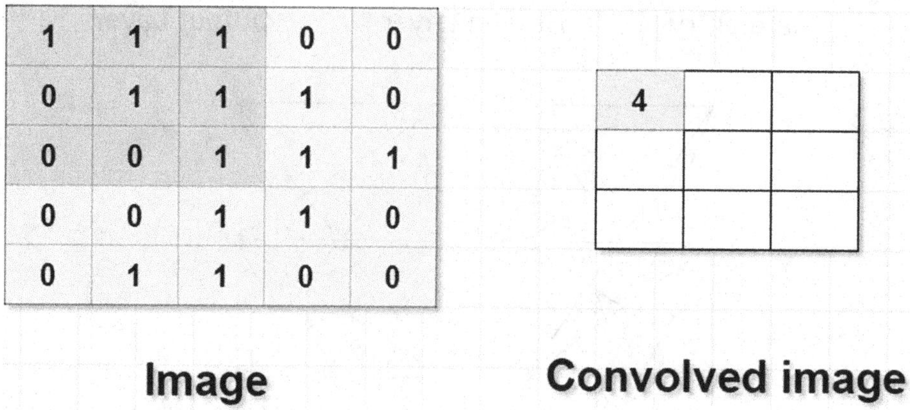

1	1	1	0	0
0	1	1	1	0
0	0	1	1	1
0	0	1	1	0
0	1	1	0	0

4		

Image   ## Convolved image

of the layers. But in the case of ResNet50, it not only learning the features, it also learns the residual. Residuals are the subtractions of the features learned from the input of the layer.

During the test of the ResNet50 architecture, researchers saw that the deeper layers gives more error percentage than the upper layers. So, for making this architecture more accurate they have introduced a deep residual learning framework by using shortcut connections that can perform mappings.

In figure 10, it can be seen that how ResNet50 learns the residuals, it does by using shortcut

Figure 10. ResNet50 residual of the feature

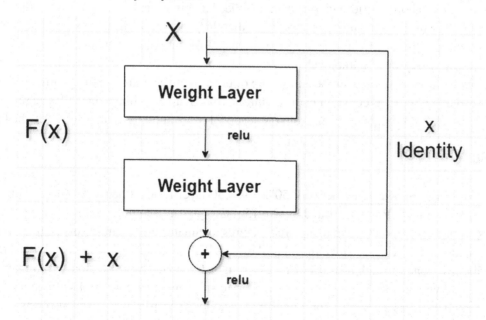

Connections. This proves that training this residual form than training the feature form is much easier and also problem of degrading of the accuracy is also been resolved.

PROPOSED MODEL

In the introduction of this chapter, it has been discussed that our model has been constructed with the help of the integration of two methods Convolution Neural Networks (CNN) and K-means Clustering. The whole procedure is given in figure 11.

Figure 11. Whole model procedure block diagram

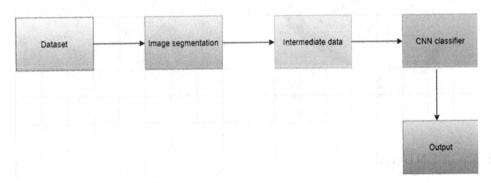

The data set that is used to train the program is taken from internet which is divided into 5 main sections: -

- Bacteria
- Fungi
- Nematodes
- Normal
- Virus

The program is trained not for all diseases but for the ones which are most common and dangerous to plants growth. These diseases first attack the leaves then slowly moves towards the stem and finally decay the roots suffocating the plant to death.

The first method which is used for the image segmentation for extracting the dominant colours is K-means clustering, with the use of these 6 colours that are being separated from leaf's image we can limit the colours of the separation of the colours like we can separate 3 colours, 8 colours, 5 colours etc. In this model, 6 colours are been separated because the accuracy of this model is maximum in this case.

As it can be seen in the results in figure 12 that how colours have been extracted using the image segmentation method from the leaves which is the intermediate state of the whole model. The image thus produced is ready for comparison to the dataset which is pre learned by the programming. The colour extraction method using k-means clustering is very crucial because it can change the efficiency of the whole system. If the image produced is not the replica of the original leaf then the disease detection will not be accurate thus it is very useful to extract image with the help of k-means.

Figure 12. Leaves after the image segmentation and after extracted the dominant colours by K-means

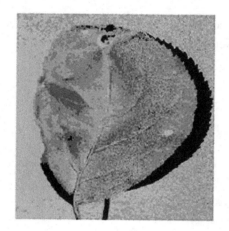 

IMAGE SEGMENTATION

In this model, image segmentation has been done by the K-means. This segmentation process includes many stages by which an image is being processed. This process starts with reading the image and converts it into a 2D array and then the K-means is applied which helps to extract the dominant colours from the image. The dominant colours then get merged together to form a new image and then at last reshaping it into the original size of the image. The block diagram shown in figure 13 states the above process very clearly.

Figure 13. Image segmentation procedure block diagram

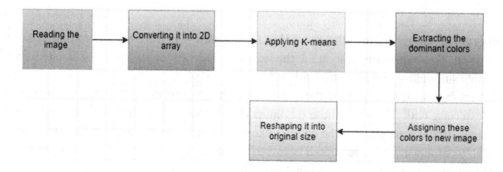

a.   Example:

    i.   Let us assume that there is an image in which blue colour is dominant. Each point in that image is characterized by pixels.

    ii.   Since blue colour is dominant, so all the blue colour points will have same pixel value.

iii. When K-means have been applied to it, all those blue colour points are grouped into a cluster as these points are similar.

iv. Similarly, if another image has more than one dominant colour, then this algorithm groups all the similar pixel points together into clusters.

v. In this way, this algorithm helps to find the dominant colours of an image.

Note: Different number of colours can be chosen to produce the intermediate data by extracting those colors from the image.

In Figure 14, it can be seen that how the dominant colors are grouped as clusters after the image segmentation process and by applying K-means also. Figure 14 shows three different group of clusters which are blue, green and red. When the image will be formed using this data the area around the cluster will be of that color only converting it into an image.

Figure 14. Dominant colour extracted after the image segmentation process and formation of clusters after applying K-means.

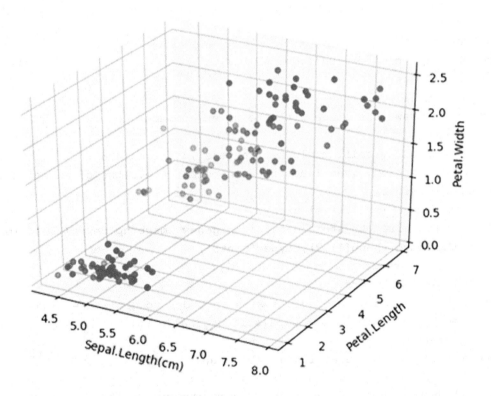

CODE

```
import os
from csv import writer
import pandas as pd
import cv2
import numpy as np
import matplotlib.pyplot as plt
from sklearn.cluster import KMeans
class Segmentation:
def __init__(self,image,dom_colors):
#since cv2 reads image in BGR mode, it is necessary to convert into RGB mode.
self.image=cv2.cvtColor(image,cv2.COLOR_BGR2RGB)
self.orginal_size=image.shape
#flatenning the image in order to make it compatible for KMeans class
self.pixel_array=self.image.reshape((-1,3))
self.dom_colors=dom_colors
#Created an instance of KMeans
self.km=KMeans (n_clusters=self.dom_colors)
#created a model here
self.km.fit(self.pixel_array)
#this function draws the image with the given dominant colors
def draw_image(self):
self.centers=np.array(self.km.cluster_centers_,dtype='uint8')
#here predict function gives label to each point, i.e., the given point is
nearer to which center
pred=self.km.predict(self.pixel_array)
#creaed an empty array to store data of imagenew_image=np.zeros((self.image.
shape[0]*self.image.shape[1],3),dtype='uint8')
        for i in range(new_image.shape[0]):
new_image[i]=self.centers[pred[i]]
#new_image is reshaped into original size in order to get whole image together
        new_image=new_image.reshape(self.orginal_size)
            return new_image
#we have normalized our data with google Imagenet data statistics
```

The above code shows that how the image segmentation has been initiated. The following steps elaborates the whole procedure of this image segmentation: -

1.   Import certain libraries like pandas, numpy, cvs import writer, matplotlib. pyplot etc.
2.   Declare a class as segmentation.
3.   Cv2 reads the image in BGR mode but it has to be convert it into RGB mode.
4.   Flatten the image in order to make the image compatible for K-means class.

5.   Create an instance of K-means.
6.   Create a model which will draw the dominant colors from the image.
7.   This function gives label to each point, i.e., the given point is nearer to which center.
8.   Create an empty array to store the data of the image and create a new image.
9.   The new image is reshaped into original size in order to get whole image together.

```
data = fastai.vision.ImageDataBunch.from_folder (path, size=256, train='train',
valid='val').normalize(imagenet_stats)
#loading resnet50 CNN Architecture
learn = cnn_learner(data, models.resnet50, metrics=accuracy,callback_
fns=ShowGraph)
# finding optimal learning rate
learn.lr_find()
learn.recorder.plot()
```

The above code shows that the Convolutional Neural Network (CNN) architecture has been created and the Learning Rate (LR) find is being initiated.

#we have normalized our data with google imagenet data statistics

```
data = fastai.vision.ImageDataBunch.from_folder(path, size=256,train='train',
valid='val').normalize(imagenet_stats)
```

The above code shows that the data has been fed to the model and the weights have been normalized.

```
learn.recorder.plot(suggestion=True)
best_clf_lr = learn.recorder.min_grad_lr
lr=best_clf_lr
```

The above code selects in which Learning Rate (LR), the train loss will be less.

```
#training
learn.fit_one_cycle(10, max_lr=lr)
# checking top losses
interp = ClassificationInterpretation.from_learner(learn)
losses,idxs = interp.top_losses()
```

The above code shows the training of LR and checking the top losses.

Figure 15 shows the results of Learning Rate (LR) in which the loss is less. If both the graphs are enlarged then we can clearly see the training loss.

The graphs in figure 16 shows the Learning Rate (LR) in which the loss is minimum and how much loss is there in that Learning Rate (LR) in the training period.

Figure 15. Shows the result of training

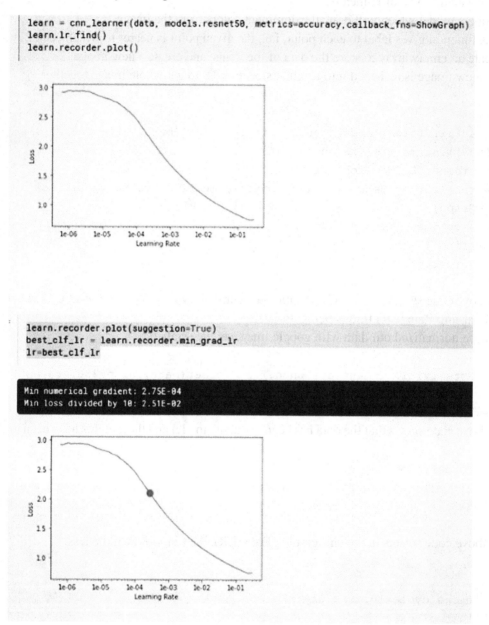

Figure 16. Learning rate (LR) vs loss graph

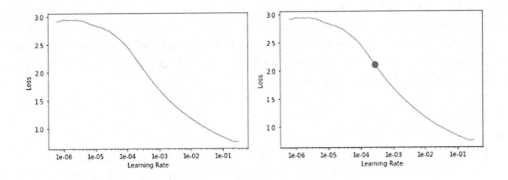

HARDWARE

Computational System

The computational devices are the devices that are used in order to process the output as per the calculated input. There is a very large variety of computational devices that are widely used nowadays. In this model, a Raspberry pi 4 has been used so as to bring more and more advancement in this field of invention.

1. Raspberry pi:

    a. The raspberry pi model was invented back in around 2012.
    b. The invention of latest raspberry pi foundation has invented a latest technology of the raspberry pi edition that is Raspberry pi 4 which comes in many variant like 2 GB, 4 GB, 8 GB.
    c. The latest raspberry pi model which is named as "Raspberry pi 4" was invented in May, 2020. The cost of this model is around $75.
    d. There are many other kind or we can say there are many other modules of raspberry pi which are being used for different kind of Machine Learning (ML) projects as per need of the project.
        i. Specifications of raspberry pi:

    • High in performance – the new raspberry pie consists of 8 GB RAM unlike other models with around 2 GB RAM in it.
    • Compact size and structure - the size of the raspberry pie is small as a deck of card so you get a very compact size which consists of arm-based CPU, many ports, WI-FI, Bluetooth.
    • Operation – the raspberry pie works in 32-bit kernel which can also be further improved to 64 bits kernel so that the 8 GB RAM can be used successfully.

2. Camera:

    Later, cameras were used for capturing beautiful and memorable moments. Nowadays, cameras are being used for detection of object in machine learning algorithm. As technology is growing day by day, the need of cameras are increasing. Nowadays cameras are invented to detect motion, diseases in plants and many other things like detecting images for security purpose and also for detection of other objects which makes a good and innovative use of cameras.

The proposed model contains a camera called wyze cam V2. The wyze cam is smart and of compact size. It is a low-cost camera which is used mainly in home security systems. The wyze cam V2 was invented in around February, 2018. The model of leaf disease detection use this camera module for capturing the images from the top of the plants.

a. Specifications of camera:

i. The wyze camera consists of 2.2 by 1.9 by 1.9 inches, in measurement.
ii. Consisting of a magnetic batch, it can be used for attaching the camera at any surface of the ground.
iii. The price of Wyze cam V2 is around $20.
iv. The cam with V2 consists of a CMOS SENSOR that gives a higher resolution picture of 1080p with a 15 fps. Alos, it has a bidirectional microphone and a speaker. The Wyze cam V2 has a 110 degre camera angle.
v. It also consists of 8x Zoom that helps to objectify a very tiny material.
vi. It also consists of two four infrared LEDs that provides the best night view.
vii. The wyze cam V2 provides dubbed motion tagging which further adds a box aroound that particular object.
viii. It also consists of an inbuilt microSD card slot inside the camera.
ix. There is also a hood that can be used to connect WIFI radio to the home device network.
x. This camera provides you a free cloud storage path for better storing capacity that lasts for around 14 days.
xi. One can also view photos or videos recorded in it with the help of notification button
xii. For installing the wyze cam one needs a mobile phone. Install the mobile app and add a new account in it and follow out the further steps for the process for activation of camera and then pressing the setup button. As you press the setup button the yellow LED light will pop-up. After this a voice is heard which says camera is ready to capture.

3. Drone:

The proposed system contains a drone as a hardware which is used for clicking the picture of plant's leaves for the detection. For this task, a drone which should have high efficiency and support good loading power is required to be built.

As per the requirements, a drone has been built for clicking the pictures of leaves by carrying the previously mentioned camera module which makes this project more innovative and also more effective and attractive. As for the better stability of the drone, we have built a hexacopter. The below figure 17 is the design of the drone which have been used for this project.

The red cylinder shows the propellers of the drone. In the project, we are using 6 propellers because this drone is a hexacopter drone, the purple part is the main controller part which is use to take images in a particular time periods and send it in the system connected with the microcontroller through the communication medium, the brown lines shows the stand of the drone when it will be in rest then the legs will support the drone to stand still, the blue gradient portion shows the wyze camera module which has been used to take still and clear picture of the leaves and is placed.

a. Specifications of drone:

Figure 17. Drone architecture.

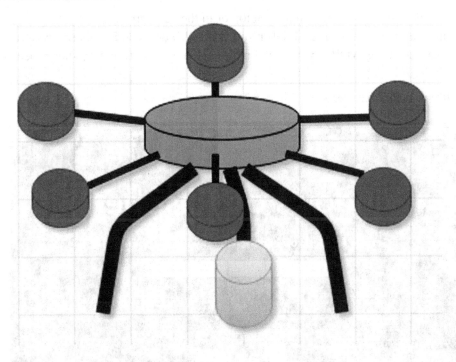

i.   Lithium polymer battery of 6000 mAh.
ii.   6 brushless motors of min. 1900kV, weight will be 57g approx.
iii. Propellers will be of 12*4.5".
iv.   Body of drone made of plastic which makes it light in weight and also it is cheap in cost.
v.   Flight controller.
vi.   Radio frequency transceiver- 9 channel, 12 v.

IMPLEMENTATION OF OPERATING SYSTEM IN RASPBERRY PIE

There are many ways for creating an environment in the raspberry pi, but the method of implementation of windows in raspberry pi 4 that is used for building this project consist of some steps which are being followed for creating the environment in the a microprocessor.

The steps for implementation are as follows:

1. Firstly take a Raspberry pi module whether it is 3B, 3B+ or 4. As we are using the module 4 for the better processing of the input. The microcontroller that has been used in this contains 8 GB RAM which helps it to process the code properly without any kind of obstacle.
2. A micro SD card containing storage of minimum 16 GB is required which helps it to save very big files of windows in it.
3. Fix the SD card with a card reader in the laptop or in the desktop
4. Open the internet and search for the WOR projects.ml (Windows on Raspberry pi projects.ml) and then the interface of the WOR can be seen on the screen like the figure 18 shown below.

Figure 18. WOR project.ml interface.

5. After having the above kind of interface, we have to download the latest version of the windows on raspberry. The windows which is present in this site will be in the form of Google drive link. When we click that link then only, we can move to that downloading interface of the windows.
6. After downloading the particular files for the windows on raspberry, extract these files into the system only which can take some time because the size of the file is very big 13 GB approximately.
7. Once the files got extracted then send those files to the micro-SD card which can be connected on the system earlier and after the files are been sent to the card unplug the SD card.
8. When the extracted files got transferred in the SD card then the SD card must inserted to the raspberry pi 4 module and connect the module with the system and plug it in the system with the help of USB cable.
9. Install the windows on the raspberry pi module by clicking on one of the items in one of the files that has been downloaded from the WOR site.

10. After running that item on the file installation of the windows get started and after completion of some of formalities which we use while installing the windows in the laptops or in desktops the installation is almost done.

11. Finally, after finishing the installing part, now the module is ready to get coded for all kind of machine learning and deep learning programs.

RESULTS

Figure 19. Accuracy graph

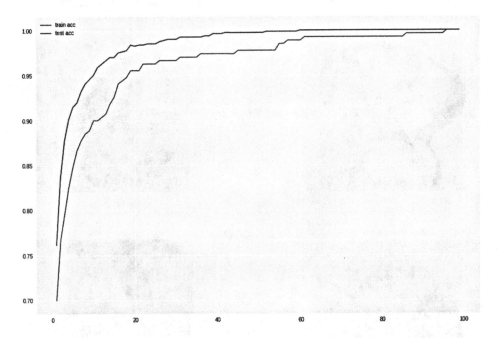

Figure 19 shows the accuracy percentage of the model which is 99.259% which is much more accurate as compared to other models. As this model is the integration of two methods CNN (Convolution Neural Networks) and K-means clustering so these both models together show the maximum accuracy. We can see the accurate percentage in both the cases in training period and also in the testing period. The program was tested and implemented on jupyter. In figure 20, we can clearly see the results that this proposed model is giving after the certain image segmentation process and after the CNN process.

As the dataset contained these classes of the disease, after the detection of the leaves the above results are being displayed. (as shown in figure 20).

Figure 20. Results

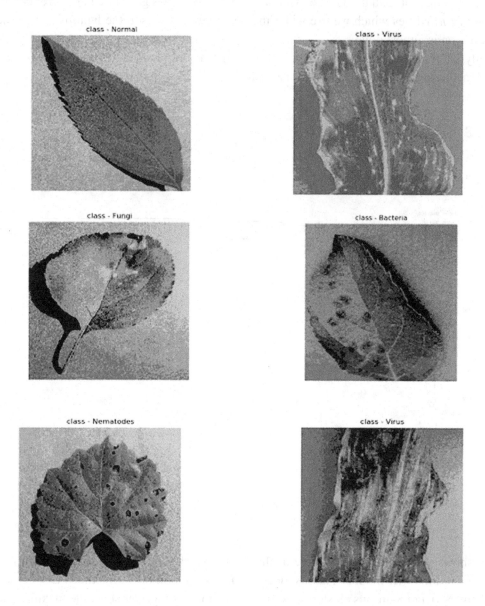

CONCLUSION

In this chapter, it has been concluded that the detection of the disease is very accurate as compared to other models as this model shows an accuracy of 99.259% which is really a very good percentage. So, it can be concluded that the detection of the disease of the leaves could be accurate by integrating two of the methods for the better accuracy. In this chapter, the study of the architecture of CNN (ResNet50) and K-means algorithms is done and the image segmentation process for the detection of the disease of the leaves has been discussed. The coding portion of this model is also explained which elaborates this research or this chapter more. By studying and implementing all these concepts, a researcher can understand that how detection has been done with the use of machine learning which gives better results. As Machine learning is widely used for the image detection and for many other uses nowadays, this chapter discusses about the use of machine learning in image detection and processing for detecting diseases in plants.

FUTURE SCOPE

This project or research work consists of a type of implementation of this project only, there are many other forms that can be used to build this project. This chapter consists of drone type image capturing mechanism which can be enhance to the spider camera image capturing mechanism which can carry a load of 20-30 kg which helps the inventor to carry the heavy cameras for the crystal-clear image and also the rotating cameras which are being fixed at the center of the field with a high resolution. Many other types are listed below for the completion of this project.

Figure 21. Spider camera leaf detection

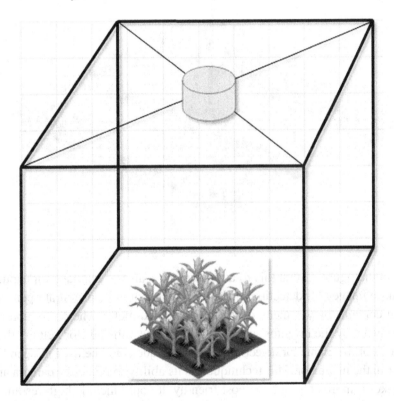

In figure 21, the spider camera technique is shown having the camera with its controller. The light blue portion in the figure is the camera which is facing downwards to take the picture of the leaves of the plants at certain time period and also from certain directions. This could be more costly as it contains high resolution and big cameras whose fps would be good. The rods or we can say the ropes that could be used in this proposed system are for taking picture of leaves from different positions by rotating the camera at every corner on the roof side like the camera that we see in the international cricket and in many sports also. These things make this project more costly and also more innovative also. The disadvantage of this technique is that it needs four corners for giving support to the camera. Due to this reason, it can be better in the green houses and also in incubators which provides four corners for it. This technique could be very effective in future for the diseases detection in the plants as it has high resolution camera which makes the image capturing process for the disease detecting much better and more efficient. The alternative of this is to replace the ropes with rods and rollers, these rollers help the camera to move freely at every corner of the room and stops at given time for capturing the images and then the camera send that image to the microcontroller for further processing.

Figure 22. Rotating camera leaf detection

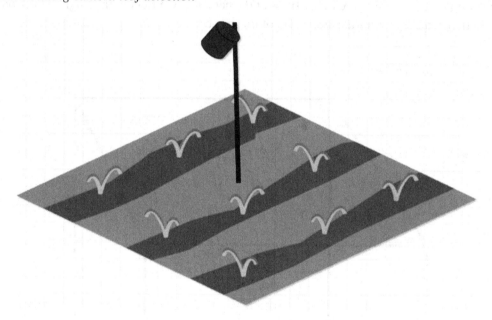

It can be seen in the figure 22 that this rotating camera is also a technique for capturing the images and forwarding those images for detection of the disease. It could be useful at open fields for observing the plants as it contains only camera, controller and servo motor. The servo motor rotates itself as per the instruction given by the inventor and stops as per the commands for helping the camera to take pictures of the leaves or the plants for detection. This technique could be used in open fields and also in the green house or in the incubator. This technique has its ability to rotate the camera at the 360-degree rotation which makes it more efficient and cost friendly. It could include high resolution camera containing gimbal inside it or we can say that gyroscope in it which stabilizes the camera and the camera could easily take good and crystal-clear images of the plants. The camera should be waterproof because of the rain. The pole at which the camera has been situated could be adjustable as per the crop height. So, this technique is also useful for the detection of the disease of the plants.

So, these are some of the techniques which could be used for making this detecting procedure into a new level. There could be many more other types of techniques which could be more efficient but the above-mentioned techniques could be the most common among all the techniques which could be implemented in future and also these techniques are the most efficient one from all.

REFERENCES

Ashok, S., Kishore, G., Rajesh, V., Suchitra, S., Sophia, S. G., & Pavithra, B. (2020, June). Tomato Leaf Disease Detection Using Deep Learning Techniques. In *2020 5th International Conference on Communication and Electronics Systems (ICCES)* (pp. 979-983). IEEE.

Bradley, P. S., & Fayyad, U. M. (1998, July). Refining initial points for k-means clustering. In ICML (Vol. 98, pp. 91-99). Academic Press.

Dasgupta, S. (1999, October). Learning mixtures of Gaussians. In *40th Annual Symposium on Foundations of Computer Science (Cat. No. 99CB37039)* (pp. 634-644). IEEE. 10.1109/SFFCS.1999.814639

Dasgupta, S., & Schulman, L. (2013). *A two-round variant of em for gaussian mixtures.* arXiv preprint arXiv:1301.3850.

Dey, A. (2016). Machine learning algorithms: A review. *International Journal of Computer Science and Information Technologies*, 7(3), 1174–1179.

Dixon, S. R., Wickens, C. D., & Chang, D. (2005). Mission control of multiple unmanned aerial vehicles: A workload analysis. *Human Factors*, 47(3), 479–487. doi:10.1518/0018720057748600005 PMID:16435690

Durmuş, H., Güneş, E. O., & Kırcı, M. (2017, August). Disease detection on the leaves of the tomato plants by using deep learning. In *2017 6th International Conference on Agro-Geoinformatics* (pp. 1-5). IEEE. 10.1109/Agro-Geoinformatics.2017.8047016

Faber, V. (1994). Clustering and the continuous k-means algorithm. *Los Alamos Science*, 22(138144.21), 67.

Fukenaga, K. (1990). Introduction to statistical pattern recognition (2nd ed.). Academic Press.

Han, J., Ngan, K. N., Li, M., & Zhang, H. J. (2005). Unsupervised extraction of visual attention objects in color images. *IEEE Transactions on Circuits and Systems for Video Technology*, 16(1), 141–145. doi:10.1109/TCSVT.2005.859028

Horng, W. B., Peng, J. W., & Chen, C. Y. (2005, March). A new image-based real-time flame detection method using color analysis. In Proceedings. 2005 IEEE Networking, Sensing and Control, 2005 (pp. 100-105). IEEE.

Inaba, M., Imai, H., & Katoh, N. (1996, May). Experimental results of randomized clustering algorithm. In *Proceedings of the twelfth annual symposium on Computational geometry* (pp. 401-402). 10.1145/237218.237406

Kanungo, T., Mount, D. M., Netanyahu, N. S., Piatko, C. D., Silverman, R., & Wu, A. Y. (2002). An efficient k-means clustering algorithm: Analysis and implementation. *IEEE Transactions on Pattern Analysis and Machine Intelligence*, 24(7), 881–892. doi:10.1109/TPAMI.2002.1017616

Khirade, S. D., & Patil, A. B. (2015, February). Plant disease detection using image processing. In *2015 International conference on computing communication control and automation* (pp. 768-771). IEEE. 10.1109/ICCUBEA.2015.153

Na, S., Xumin, L., & Yong, G. (2010, April). Research on k-means clustering algorithm: An improved k-means clustering algorithm. In *2010 Third International Symposium on intelligent information technology and security informatics* (pp. 63-67). IEEE. 10.1109/IITSI.2010.74

Nemati, A., & Kumar, M. (2014, June). Modeling and control of a single axis tilting quadcopter. In *2014 American Control Conference* (pp. 3077-3082). IEEE. doi:10.1109/ICECA.2017.8212855

Padol, P. B., & Yadav, A. A. (2016, June). SVM classifier based grape leaf disease detection. In *2016 Conference on advances in signal processing (CASP)* (pp. 175-179). IEEE. 10.1109/CASP.2016.7746160

Protas, E., Bratti, J. D., Gaya, J. F., Drews, P., & Botelho, S. S. (2018). Visualization methods for image transformation convolutional neural networks. *IEEE Transactions on Neural Networks and Learning Systems*, *30*(7), 2231–2243. doi:10.1109/TNNLS.2018.2881194 PMID:30561353

Pugoy, R. A. D., & Mariano, V. Y. (2011, July). Automated rice leaf disease detection using color image analysis. In *Third international conference on digital image processing (ICDIP 2011)* (Vol. 8009, p. 80090F). International Society for Optics and Photonics.

Qian, Y., Dong, J., Wang, W., & Tan, T. (2016, September). Learning and transferring representations for image steganalysis using convolutional neural network. In 2016 IEEE international conference on image processing (ICIP) (pp. 2752-2756). IEEE. doi:10.1109/ICIP.2016.7532860

Rastogi, A., Arora, R., & Sharma, S. (2015, February). Leaf disease detection and grading using computer vision technology & fuzzy logic. In *2015 2nd international conference on signal processing and integrated networks (SPIN)* (pp. 500-505). IEEE. 10.1109/SPIN.2015.7095350

Sarangdhar, A. A., & Pawar, V. R. (2017, April). Machine learning regression technique for cotton leaf disease detection and controlling using IoT. In *2017 International conference of Electronics, Communication and Aerospace Technology (ICECA)* (Vol. 2, pp. 449-454). IEEE.

Sardogan, M., Tuncer, A., & Ozen, Y. (2018, September). Plant leaf disease detection and classification based on CNN with LVQ algorithm. In *2018 3rd International Conference on Computer Science and Engineering (UBMK)* (pp. 382-385). IEEE. 10.1109/UBMK.2018.8566635

Singh, A., Kumar, P., Pachauri, K., & Singh, K. (2020*).* Drone Ambulance. In *2nd International Conference on Advances in Computing, Communication Control and Networking (ICACCCN)*. IEEE. 10.1109/ICACCCN51052.2020.9362879

Smith, J. R., & Chang, S. F. (1995, October). Single color extraction and image query. *Proceedings - International Conference on Image Processing*, *3*, 528–531.

Tammy & Wimpee. (2017, Dec 9). *Convolutional Neural Networks (CNNs) Explained* [Video post]. Deeplizard. https://deeplizard.com/learn/video/YRhxdVk_sIs

Wen, L., Li, X., & Gao, L. (2019). A transfer convolutional neural network for fault diagnosis based on ResNet-50. *Neural Computing & Applications*, 1–14.

Chapter 7
Limitations and Implications of Doubling Time Approach in COVID–19 Infection Spreading Study:
A Gradient Smoothing Technique

Apurbalal Senapati
Central Institute of Technology, Kokrajhar, India

Soumen Maji
Central Institute of Technology, Kokrajhar, India

Arunendu Mondal
Central Institute of Technology, Kokrajhar, India

ABSTRACT

To control the spread of COVID-19, around the world, many countries imposed lockdowns. Numerous studies were reported on COVID-19 in different disciplines with various aspects. The doubling time is a mathematical technique to estimate the current rate of spread of the disease. Researchers used the doubling technique to address the COVID-19 pandemic situation. The larger doubling period represents a low spreading rate, whereas the smaller doubling period represents a high spreading rate. In other words, high infection implies the low doubling period and low infection implies the high doubling period. So, there is an inverse relationship between doubling time and the infection rate. But the real-life data does not follow such a rule properly in various domains. The data shows that after a certain time when the infection is high, the doubling period is also high, which misleads our general concept of doubling time. This chapter addressed this issue by investigating the real-time COVID-19 data. To overcome this limitation, a gradient smoothing technique has been proposed.

DOI: 10.4018/978-1-7998-7371-6.ch007

INTRODUCTION

Researchers have tried to address the epidemic diseases using mathematical modeling for a long (Britton, 2010; Kermack et al., 1927). In any epidemic disease, a fundamental question is, how fast the infection is spreading? One way to address this question is to look at how long it takes the infection count to get double the current count. This time is termed as doubling time (Patel and Patel, 2020) that is used to estimate the rate of spread of infection. This technique is used in Romania in 2006 for the avian influenza subtype H5N1(Ward et al., 2009) and a similar study carried out for the SARS epidemic in 2003 (Galvani et al., 2003). The concept of doubling time comes from exponential growth or a particular growth model where the doubling time remains constant. For a given day, the doubling time says the number (t_d). of days passed since the number of cases was half ($n/2$) of the current number (n) or the number will be doubled ($2n$) after doubling time (t_d). in days.

The doubling time gives an interpretation of the intensity of infection spreading and it changes over days. But sometimes doubling time gives a misinterpretation especially in the boundary cases i.e. at the beginning and the end of the pandemic period. In this context, we have introduced the concept of infection spreading based on the gradient smoothing technique. Smoothing is a mathematical approach that is used for various purposes like eliminating noise and outliers from datasets, forecasting the patterns more noticeable or expose the patterns, etc. Sometimes the trend of data points is not visible but after smoothing, the patterns are exposed. There are several methods of smoothing, like random method, moving average, random walk, exponential, exponential moving average, etc.

In our cases, we have used the gradient smoothing technique. In time-series data if the gradients are calculated of each pair of points it sometimes shows the direction is ups-and-down and it depends on data. In the COVID-19 data set if gradients are calculated of each pair of points, the gradients or growths are ups-and-down shown in Figure 2. Here we have done the gradient smoothing to expose the growth pattern properly. In this smoothing technique, we have used a window of length seven to calculate the gradient. It is fixed with the window size seven by the heuristic approach i.e. it started with window size one, then two, and so on, and seeing the corresponding growth graph it is fixed with window size seven (Figure 3).

There are various smoothing techniques used in various disciplines based on the applications. According to Hitchcock et al. (2006), smoothing provides accuracy and also shows the effects on data clustering. On the other hand, Hitchcock et al. (2007), and Ghosal et al. (2014) used the smoothing technique in noise images, whereas Scott et al. (1989) used it in the curve fitting. The concepts are also used by Liu et al., (2008) in several other domains like solid mechanics, hydrodynamics by Mao et al. (2019), and so on.

The smoothing does not always offer an interpretation of the themes or patterns but sometimes it helps to recognize. In a continuous growth or continuous decline of the time series data this technique will not help much, it depends on the characteristic of the data points. In a smoothing technique, there is a chance to overlook some usable data points.

This study is an alternate approach to represent or describe the spread of a pandemic disease. It gives a better visualization of the infection spreading for a complete data set and in the case of the partial data set, it gives the trend of infection.

BACKGROUND

There are several works found in the literature on COVID-19 using doubling time. They have used the technique in several perspectives to explain the pandemic (Pellis et al, 2020). It was also used (Walls et al., 2020) for regional short-term prediction and monitoring the regional trend of the COVID-19 pandemic. Pellis et al. (2020) discussed the short doubling time along with the long delay to control Covid-19 and used doubling time to interpret the COVID-19 cases. The doubling times are also used to assess the effectiveness of the intervention in a country like Nepal (Bhandary, 2020). Sarkar (2020) done the relative comparison of doubling times of the COVID-19 pandemic in various countries. Also, the authors explained the trajectories of the COVID-19 infection timeline in India. Lurie et al. (2020) reported the state-wide mitigation strategies with the doubling time. Zhou et al. (2020) used the doubling time as an early epidemic risk assessment tool. Lurie et al. (2020) already used the doubling rate to compare the effect of the lockdown.

MAIN FOCUS OF THE CHAPTER

Calculation of Doubling Time

Though the concept of doubling time is unambiguous, from the implementation point of view, it varies due to the real-life data set and the diverse representation. From a mathematical point of view, it also varies and depends on the continuous or discrete values. But, for this chapter, the authors considered the COVID-19 data as discrete cases. Here doubling time is defined as:

At time t_1. the number of COVID-19 cases is n, and at the time t_2. the number of COVID-19 cases is $2n$, then the doubling time d_t is defined as $d_t = t_2 - t_1$.

Graphically, Figure 1 shows that it can be interpreted as: consider the function $n(t)$.is the infection count at time t. Where, $n(t_2)$ represents the infection count at the time t_2 .and $n(t_1)$ represent the half of earlier infection count ($i.e. = n(t_2)/2$). at time t_1. Hence, the doubling time is $d_t = t_2 - t_1$.

In other words, a relation like $n(t)\left[= \frac{1}{2} nt_0 \right]$.for a unique t where $n(t_0)$.is the initial or count at t_0. can be made.

Issues, Controversies, Problems

Limitation in Doubling Time Representation

As discussed earlier, doubling time is used to interpret the spread of infection. Doubling time is inversely proportional to the infection spread. A *high doubling time* implies the *lower infection spreading* and a *low doubling time* implies the *higher* infection *spreading*. From a theoretical perspective, the above inference is acceptable but in real-life data that can't be always generalized. There are several limitations on that and these are addressed with real-life examples. Here, the authors considered the data of positive COVID-19 cases in India especially highly infected states like Delhi and Maharashtra.

Figure 1. Doubling time representation

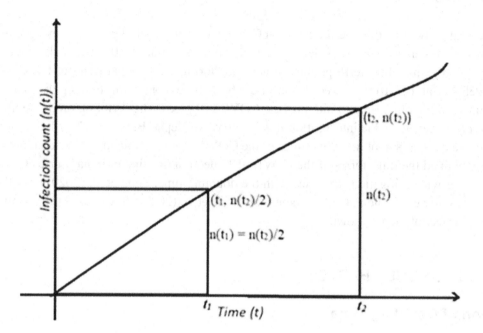

COVID-19 data set of Delhi, India (Table 1) shows that at the very beginning the doubling time is low and spreading rate as well. It contradicts the general phenomenon of doubling time versus infection spreading. The authors defined this problem as the boundary value problem. On the other hand, COVID-19 data set of Maharashtra, India (Table 2) shows that the doubling time is high and daily spreading rate as well. This also contradicts the general phenomenon of the doubling time versus infection spreading. So, it is observed that doubling time interpretation may mislead the conclusion.

The real-valued result (Table1, Table 2, the doubling time is considered in rounded value) shows that it can give the wrong interpretation. To avoid such a problem doubling time is often calculated using the five-day (Tang & Wang, 2020), seven-day, or ten-day moving average (Das, 2020; He et al., 2020) to capture trends over longer periods.

SOLUTIONS AND RECOMMENDATIONS

Proposed Techniques to Represent the Data

Some major drawbacks in doubling time to interpret the infection spreading with the real-time COVID-19 data (Table 1 and Table 2) have already been discussed. This chapter tried to interpret the infection spreading in a new representation that overcomes the earlier limitations.

Data for the experiment: India was one of the most affected countries in the world. The authors have considered data (COVID-19 in India, 2020) from the highly affected states like Maharashtra and Delhi.

Proposed representation of infection spreading: The doubling time can be represented as the exponential growth function and mathematically can be proved that doubling time inversely proportional to

Table 1. COVID-19 data set of Delhi

Date	Positive cases	Doubling time
02-03-2020	1	
03-03-2020	1	
04-03-2020	1	3
05-03-2020	2	
06-03-2020	3	
07-03-2020	3	
08-03-2020	3	4
09-03-2020	4	
10-03-2020	4	
11-03-2020	5	
12-03-2020	6	5
13-03-2020	6	
14-03-2020	7	
15-03-2020	7	
16-03-2020	7	
17-03-2020	8	
18-03-2020	10	6
19-03-2020	12	
20-03-2020	17	
…..	…..	…..

the infection spreading rate. Therefore, for better representation and visualization, a graphical representation of infection spreading over time rather than doubling time over time has been proposed here. The infection spreading is calculated by the new proposed formula *i.e.* maximum doubling time (d_{tmax}). - doubling time (d_t). (the formulation concept is almost similar to the Fuzzy complement (Lowen, 1977)).

For example, consider the doubling times 2, 36, 3, 10, 3, 6, 22, 36, 12, and 14.

The maximum doubling time = 36 (d_{tmax}).

Then the calculated value (d_{tmax}).- d_t . of the infection spreading

(36-2) = 34,

(36-36) = 0,

(36-3) = 33,

(36-10) = 26,

and so on.

Figure 3 shows the graphical representation of the infection spreading of state Delhi.

Table 2. COVID-19 data set of Maharashtra

Date	Positive cases	Doubling time
10-08-2020	515332	
11-08-2020	524513	
12-08-2020	535601	
13-08-2020	548313	
14-08-2020	560126	
15-08-2020	572734	
16-08-2020	584754	
17-08-2020	595865	
18-08-2020	604358	
19-08-2020	615477	> 18
20-08-2020	628642	
21-08-2020	643289	
22-08-2020	657450	
23-08-2020	671942	
24-08-2020	682383	
25-08-2020	693398	
26-08-2020	703823	
27-08-2020	718711	
28-08-2020	733568	
…..	…..	…..

Gradient smoothing technique: The gradient implies the change in y-with respect to the x-direction, which is termed as a slope. It is used to define the growth or growth rate. The gradient of two points (x_1, y_1) .and (x_2, y_2) .is defined as (Eq. 1)

$$m = (y_2 - y_1)/(x_2 - x_1).$$ (1)

Now for the COVID-19 data, it can be interpreted as a set of points (x, y) . Where x represents the date and *y* represents the number of positive cases (or cumulative case) found on that day. In that representation, the gradient represents the growth rate of the infection. Here it is observed that from the Figure 2 that the gradients of each discrete point are not smooth. For the smoothness, considered a window of length seven (Figure 2). Note that, the gradient is calculated by varying the window size and fixed with 'seven' heuristically. This gradient is considered as the growth rate of infections. Here the concern is to fix the window size for gradient smoothing. In this chapter, it is done by increasing the window-size iteratively and fix with size 7 as shown in Figure 3 by the heuristic approach, which is defined as (Eq. 2)

Figure 2. Growth rate of Delhi (window size 1)

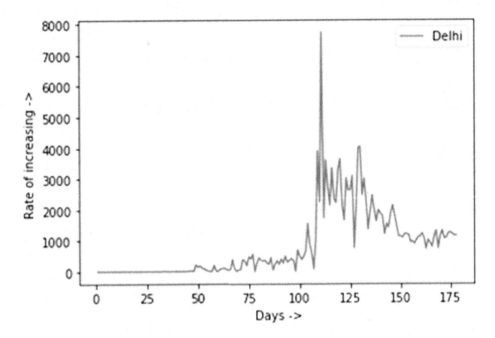

$$m_7 = \left(y_{i+7} - y_i \right) / \left(x_{i+7} - x_i \right). \tag{2}$$

Now, COVID-19 positive cases of the state Delhi till 28th August 2020 has been considered and represented by the three different perspectives *i.e.* Doubling time (as shown in Figure 4), Infection spreading (as shown in Figure 5), and by the Gradient smoothing (as shown in Figure 6).

Figure 4-6 are the representation of the same data *i.e.* COVID-19 positive cases of Delhi up to the date 28th August 2020. Figure 4 and Figure 5 can be treated as complementary to each other (as doubling time is inversely proportional to the spreading). Figure 4 and Figure 5 show that initially there is a highly spreading infection in the early-stage but that was not true. Next, the spreading rate is the almost constant rate for a long time and suddenly decreasing and after a while again increasing. This interpretation is close to the real-life scenario. But if we consider the interpretation of gradient smoothing (as shown in Figure 6), it is a better exposed and more accurate representation compared to the earlier two. It shows that initially, the spreading rate was low, gradually it is increasing. Also, note that Figure 6 shows the correct pick point of the pandemic.

FUTURE RESEARCH DIRECTIONS

This chapter tried to interpret the infection spreading in a new representation using the gradient smoothing technique along with the graphical interpretation. However, the limitation is explained by the COVID-19 data, but mathematically it has not been established yet, which opens the further scope of the investigation.

Figure 3. Growth rate of Delhi (window size 7)

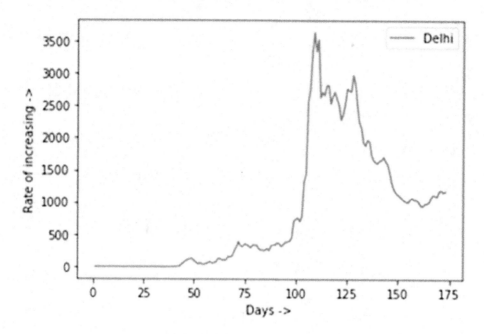

Figure 4. Doubling time of Delhi

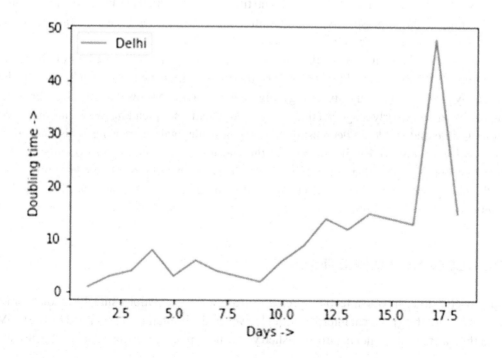

Figure 5. Infection spreading of Delhi

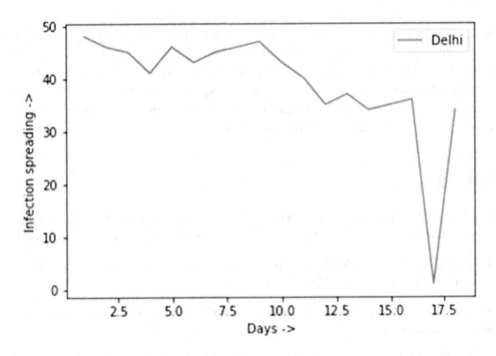

Figure 6. Gradient smoothing of Delhi

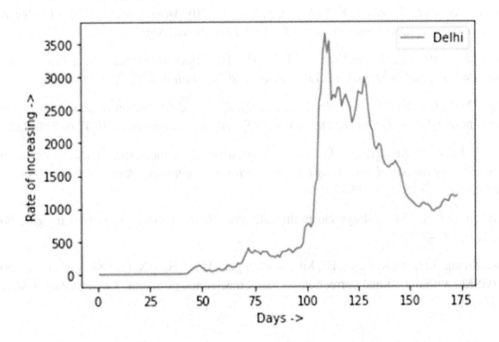

CONCLUSION

The doubling time technique is a popular mathematical tool to analyze the spread of infection which includes identifying the peak of infection and for the short-term prediction. Here authors have identified some drawbacks of this technique, which has been tested with the real-time COVID-19 data. To overcome the said limitations a gradient smoothing technique has been proposed, which gives a better interpretation. This gradient smooth technique may further be extended to apply to a similar type of pandemic, which may give further validation towards our claim.

REFERENCES

Bhandary, S. (2020). Effectiveness of lockdown as COVID-19 intervention: Official and computed cases in Nepal. *Journal of Patan Academy of Health Sciences*, 7(1), 37–41. doi:10.3126/jpahs.v7i1.28861

Britton, T. (2010). Stochastic epidemic models: A survey. *Mathematical Biosciences*, 225(1), 24–35. doi:10.1016/j.mbs.2010.01.006 PMID:20102724

COVID-19 in India. (2020). *Dataset on Novel Corona Virus Disease 2019 in India*. https://www.kaggle.com/sudalairajkumar/covid19-in-india

Das, A. (2020). *COVID-19 Predictions for India An Initial Attempt.* Technical Report. http://cse.iitkgp.ac.in/~abhij/COVID19/report.pdf

Galvani, A. P., Lei, X., & Jewell, N. P. (2003). Severe acute respiratory syndrome: Temporal stability and geographic variation in death rates and doubling times. *Emerging Infectious Diseases*, 9(8), 991.

He, Y. T., He, H., Zhai, J., Wang, X. J., & Wang, B. S. (2020). *Moving-average based index to timely evaluate the current epidemic situation after COVID-19 outbreak.* MedRxiv.

Hitchcock, D. B., Booth, J. G., & Casella, G. (2007). The effect of pre-smoothing functional data on cluster analysis. *Journal of Statistical Computation and Simulation*, 77(12), 1043–1055.

Hitchcock, D. B., Casella, G., & Booth, J. G. (2006). Improved estimation of dissimilarities by presmoothing functional data. *Journal of the American Statistical Association*, 101(473), 211–222.

Kermack, W. O., & McKendrick, A. G. (1927). A contribution to the mathematical theory of epidemics. *Proceedings of the Royal Society of London. Series A, Containing Papers of a Mathematical and Physical Character*, 115(772), 700–721.

Li, M., & Ghosal, S. (2014). Bayesian multiscale smoothing of Gaussian noised images. *Bayesian Analysis*, 9(3), 733–758.

Liu, G. R., Zhang, J., Lam, K. Y., Li, H., Xu, G., Zhong, Z. H., ... Han, X. (2008). A gradient smoothing method (GSM) with directional correction for solid mechanics problems. *Computational Mechanics*, 41(3), 457–472.

Lowen, R. (1977). On fuzzy complements. *1977 IEEE Conference on Decision and Control including the 16th Symposium on Adaptive Processes and A Special Symposium on Fuzzy Set Theory and Applications*, 1338-1342. doi: 10.1109/CDC.1977.271511

Lurie, M. N., Silva, J., Yorlets, R. R., Tao, J., & Chan, P. A. (2020). Coronavirus disease 2019 epidemic doubling time in the United States before and during stay-at-home restrictions. *The Journal of Infectious Diseases*, 222(10), 1601–1606.

Mao, Z., Liu, G. R., & Huang, Y. (2019). A local Lagrangian gradient smoothing method for fluids and fluid-like solids: A novel particle-like method. *Engineering Analysis with Boundary Elements*, 107, 96–114.

Patel, S. & Patel, P. (2020). Doubling Time and its Interpretation for COVID 19 Cases. *National Journal of Community Medicine*, 11(3).

Pellis, L., Scarabel, F., Stage, H. B., Overton, C. E., Chappell, L. H. K., Lythgoe, K. A., Fearon, E., Bennett, E., Curran-Sebastian, J., Das, R., Fyles, M., Lewkowicz, H., Pang, X., Vekaria, B., Webb, L., House, T. A., & Hall, I. (2020). Challenges in control of Covid-19: short doubling time and long delay to effect of interventions. *medRxiv*. doi:10.1101/2020.04.12.20059972

Sarkar, D. (2020). *Doubling times of COVID-19 cases.* https://deepayan.github.io/covid-19/doubling

Scott, L. B., & Scott, L. R. (1989). Efficient methods for data smoothing. *SIAM Journal on Numerical Analysis*, 26(3), 681–692.

Tang, Y., & Wang, S. (2020). Mathematic modeling of COVID-19 in the United States. *Emerging Microbes & Infections*, 9(1), 827–829.

Walls, A. C., Park, Y. J., Tortorici, M. A., Wall, A., McGuire, A. T., & Veesler, D. (2020). Structure, function, and antigenicity of the SARS-CoV-2 spike glycoprotein. *Cell*, 181(2), 281–292.

Ward, M. P., Maftei, D., Apostu, C., & Suru, A. (2009). Estimation of the basic reproductive number (R0) for epidemic, highly pathogenic avian influenza subtype H5N1 spread. *Epidemiology and Infection*, 137(2), 219–226.

Zhou, L., Liu, J. M., Dong, X. P., McGoogan, J. M., & Wu, Z. Y. (2020). COVID-19 seeding time and doubling time model: An early epidemic risk assessment tool. *Infectious Diseases of Poverty*, 9(1), 1–9.

ADDITIONAL READING

Senapati, A., Maji, S., & Mondal, A. (2021). Piece-wise linear regression: A new approach to predict COVID-19 spreading. *6th International Conference on Computers Management & Mathematical Sciences (ICCM 2020)*. 10.1088/1757-899X/1020/1/012017

Senapati, A., Nag, A., Mondal, A., & Maji, S. (2020). A novel framework for COVID-19 case prediction through piecewise regression in India. *International Journal of Information Technology*, 1-8.

KEY TERMS AND DEFINITIONS

COVID-19: It is a new virus which causes pandemic worldwide in the year 2020.

Doubling Time: It is defined as the number of days required to get the number of infections double.

Gradient: Gradient represents direction or slope. For a given two points i.e. (x_1 . y_1). and (x_2 . y_2)., the gradient is calculated as = $\left(y_2 - y_1 \right) / \left(x_2 - x_1 \right)$.

Linear Regression: It is a mathematical model, represent by a straight line $y = mx + c$ (in 2D), where, x and y are the independent and dependent variables respectively. That parameters m and c are estimated from the past data (x_i, y_i) where $i = 1,2,3,\ldots$

Machine Learning: It is a technique of auto-learning and improves from data without being explicitly programmed.

Spreading Rate: It is defined as how much new infection is taking place over time.

Chapter 8
A Novel Feature Correlation Approach for Brand Spam Detection

Bharat Tidke

Sardar Vallabhbhai National Institute of Technology, Surat, India

Swati Tidke

College of Engineering, Pune, India

ABSTRACT

In this age of the internet, no person wants to make his decision on his own. Be it for purchasing a product, watching a movie, reading a book, a person looks out for reviews. People are unaware of the fact that these reviews may not always be true. It is the age of paid reviews, where the reviews are not just written to promote one's product but also to demote a competitor's product. But the ones which are turning out to be the most critical are given on brand of a certain product. This chapter proposed a novel approach for brand spam detection using feature correlation to improve state-of-the-art approaches. Correlation-based feature engineering is considered as one of the finest methods for determining the relations among the features. Several features attached with reviews are important, keeping in focus customer and company needs in making strong decisions, user for purchasing, and company for improving sales and services. Due to severe spamming these days, it has become nearly impossible to judge whether the given review is a trusted or a fake review.

INTRODUCTION

Today, the traditional style of marketing, which is considered as expensive way of promoting, marketing has been taken over by online reviews (Jindal and Liu 2008; Lau et al. 2015). Online reviews are playing a great role in attracting customers and helps in extending communication (Asghar et al. 2020). These reviews are very important part of customer's life, as it helps them to make decisions in purchasing a quality product, Companies harness these reviews to make decisions for improving their businesses. It

DOI: 10.4018/978-1-7998-7371-6.ch008

always looks a great picture when these reviews are true and gets worst if the reviews start getting fake (Fairbanks et al. 2018).

Brand spamming becomes one of the key challenges which increase fake or false reviews. To increase the sales of newly manufactured and launched product, companies generally take support of the existing and famous brands. Though it may not seem wrong, but this biased reviewing describes less about the product and more about supporting product. In case of movie spammer write review about production house. Reviews are not on single attribute of product here. These types of opinions change the direction of reader which may divert to another movie. The proposed work extends effort in detecting these brand spam.

Figure 1. An overview of methodology

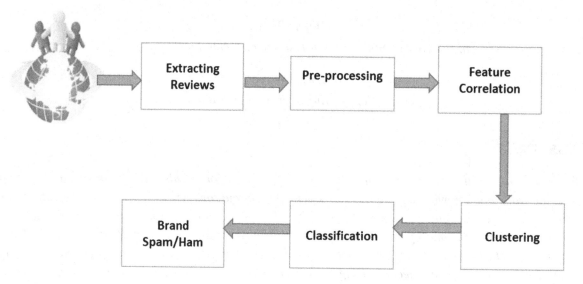

Use of clustering has attracted great attention in recent past from researchers and practitioners due to its usefulness in numerous applications (Xu and Wunsch 2008) as shown in Figure 1. Clustering appears as a capable approach to discover group of objects or individual from diverse data. K-means algorithm is an effective technique for clustering and well known in data mining community. However, if cluster is too large then mining the information from users' contents is very expensive and a large share of the content is basically not worthy.

The paper has been divided into five sections. Section one gives a brief introduction. Section two describes motivation. In the third section, detailed literature survey is presented. The fourth section comprises of proposed work for detecting brand spam using feature correlation. In the end, section five gives a conclusion.

BACKGROUND AND LITERATURE REVIEW

Spam is oozing the web site with several copies of a similar message or same context that force the message on people who would not otherwise need to receive it (Lau et al. 2015). Spam contains industrial advertising, largely for product. Most of the time, these data are paid reviews by competitor, or company itself. There exist various types of spam, that all have completely target product or organization and aim at different goals (Istanto et al. 2020; Wu et al. 2018).

· E-mail Spam

An e-mail spam is in the form of commercial advertising for products, or even broadcasting social comments. Spam filters are widely used, which built into user's e-mail programs and/or mail servers. Techniques consist for detection of keywords, templates, sentence structure, suspicious attachments, etc., that are typical for spam e-mails.

· Web Spam

The objective of web spam is to achieve higher ranking of certain web pages by search engines. Mainly two ways are used to achieve this objective i.e. link spam and content spam.

· Opinion Spam

Fake opinion is given on a certain product or services. Mostly it is found among reviews on e-commerce websites, news websites, review websites, etc. These opinions try to target businesses, products, or services to promote or damage the reputation by posting fake opinions.

Categories of Reviews or Opinions

The Reviews based on users are classified as (Wu et al. 2018).

· **Truthful Review**: These types of reviews contain honest opinions on products.
  ◦ Positive spam review: For promotion of any product some praiseworthy positive opinion on a product are written.
  ◦ Negative review: For helping users to avoid purchase of worst product or watching bad movie such reviews are written.
· **Untruthful Review**: These types of reviews contain fake opinions on products like movie and can change the thinking about product or services (Rout et al. 2017).
  ◦ Positive spam review: For promotion of any product some undeserving positive opinion on a product are written.
  ◦ Negative spam review: To damage the reputation of product by some malicious intension.
· **Non-reviews:** The companies or people often post something irrelevant in review communities to promote any product or business. This can certainly not be considered as a review but is rather some sort of advertisements. These reviews contain no opinions, so these reviews are not useful for the reader and do not serve the purpose of reviews. These reviews may include links which are many

times related to advertisement of other product, services. Also, they may not affect users who read them as they include nothing about product. Most of the time they do not includes any ratings too.

Review Centric Features

· Number of feedbacks, number of helpful feedbacks and percent of helpful feedbacks that the review gets. Feedbacks are useful in judging the quality of review (Jihong et al. 2017).
· Length of review title and length of review body. These features were chosen since longer reviews tend to get more user attention. So, a spammer might use this to his/her advantage.
· Position of the review in the reviews sorted by date, in ascending and descending order. These features were selected for spam detection as earlier reviews posted tend to have more impact on the publicity of movie and which may be exploited by spammers. Other features are also considered as review is the first review or the only review.
· Text related features consider as: Percent of positive and negative synonym words in the review, e.g., \like", \love". Cosine similarity of the review text.

In various online platforms, few feedbacks are posted for a big number of reviews and very less number of reviews are given for huge number of feedbacks. The word 'Fake' is so closely getting associated with reviews. It has clearly got a label of 'Not True'. The reason quite obviously is the misguiding of it to the readers. Just to promote their own product or demote the product of competitor, the companies have started this at a very huge level to give their negative opinions. This new trend of improving own and damaging other's impression in the market has given birth to this review spamming. And this can be seen everywhere. Examples are false reviews, bogus comments, irrelevant page links etc (Sharma and kin 2013; Zubiaga et al. 2018).

Jindal and Liu (2008) demonstrated relation between Reviews, Reviewers and Products which highlight the insights of Product marketing.

· Number of Products Vs Number of Reviews

Smaller numbers of reviews are written for the large number of products whereas large numbers of reviews are written for less number of products. Talking in percentage, it is around 50% of company products blessed with just one review, whereas around 20% products getting 5 reviews.

· Number of Members posting reviews Vs Number of Reviews

Very few reviews are written by big number of reviewers, while there are also few reviewers who posted huge number of reviews. Almost 70% of reviewers posted just one review, while it is 8% of reviewers posting at least 5 reviews.

· Number of Feedbacks Vs Number of Reviews

If user finds the reviews helpful, they do give a feedback to it, considering it as helpful or vice versa. The relativeness of the two follows the power of law distribution.

Jansen et al. (2008) utilizes various classification techniques based on users' brand sentiments data of Twitter to understand the relations between sentiments and commercial businesses. Trattner and Kappe (2013) showed that opinions and sentiments can be useful for purchasing online products. They performed several experiments on Facebook data. Ma et al. (2008) proposed sentiment analysis based on heat diffusion process models.

Proposed Methodolgy

In existing system to sight spam review no of methods are available which supplies the concept regarding however completely different classification rule used with different attribute associated with review. These strategies give the answer that machine learning methodology accustomed sight which kind of spam. Performance (accuracy) of each projected methodology is totally different because the style of spam detection. Some observations enlisted from totally different papers are as below:

· Standard benchmark dataset not available for training dataset.
· No specific feature or standard rules for feature selection.
· Problem in handling of semantic dependencies.

To overcome these challenges architecture for Brand Spam Detection is proposed in this chapter as shown in Figure 2. In first phase data is extracted from online websites. The main challenge lies in preprocessing the data as it contains variety of data in different formats. Similarly, these data are imbalance in nature which negatively affects accuracy for detection of brand spam from the reviews.

Imbalanced Dataset

Imbalanced data has been studied widely in classification problems, when non-uniform distribution of classes occurred. Similarly, if class or data is imbalanced, prediction accuracy of machine learning algorithms that determines the performance may suffer (More et al. 2018). It is observed that while dealing with imbalance data most researchers generally learn at data level, algorithmic level or both. Many approaches such as correct evaluation measures, sampling, ensemble techniques and building new model based on application in hand, can be practical to overcome challenges of imbalanced data. Most of data mining techniques on imbalanced data only work on either static data or small data, and incapable to consider large number of features with data variants. To avoid these, feature correlation techniques is used to reduce similar or duplicate reviews from the dataset.

Feature Correlation

To detect review as spam (fake), or truthful many attached features attached with review are considered. Some of these features are directly present in review, and some of them are not. The features which are not available are extracted for further analysis as follows.

· Question in review
· Product, Companies comparison
· All letters in review are capital

Figure 2. Proposed architecture for brand spam detection

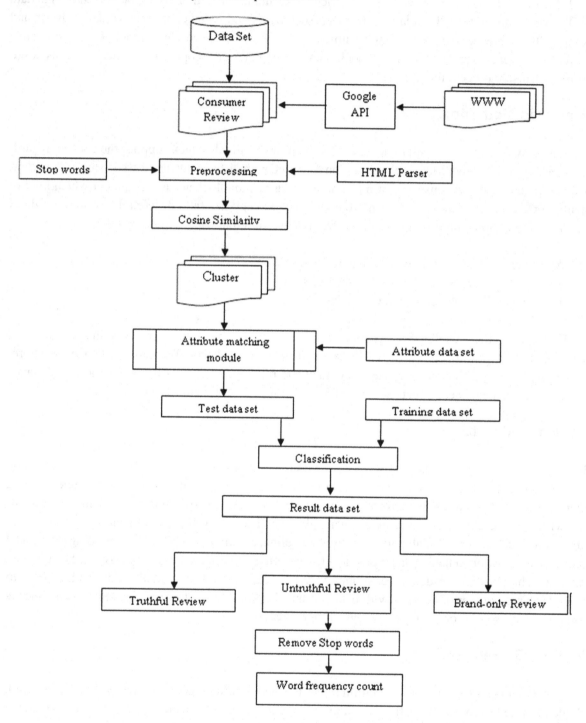

· Link in review for advertisement
· Rating does not match with review, inconsistency
· Determine polarity of opinion, rank opinion on polarity

· All review is positive and only 1 or 2 review is negative
· First review by reviewer in early time.
· Maximum number of reviews by author for day
· Extreme rating
· Rating deviation from average reviewer score
· Total helpful feedback rate.
· Minimum time interval for review by reviewer.

These features are converted into vectors using one -hop encoding technique. Now, the proposed Distance Based Feature Correlation (DBFC) algorithm is applied to remove unwanted features based on the user threshold value.

Algorithm 1. Distance Based Feature Correlation

```
Input: ∈
Output: Correlation Matrix C of order m×n
for i=1: fm,    do
 for j=i+1: fm do

    Compute user node list for feature i and j as Li and Lj respectively

     distanceList = [ ];
       for i=1:n in Li do
        flag=0
        for j=1:n in list Lj do
         if i = j then
          distanceList.append j-i
           flag=1
         end if
         if  flag =0 then
            distanceList.append k+1
          end if
         end for
        end for
return sum(distanceList)
  D = Manhattan Distance (Li,Lj)
    Assign Cji = D in correlation matrix C
    end for
 end for
  Correlation value between feature i and j is same as computing correlation
value
          between feature j and i
for same value of i and j, correlation matrix C do
  Cij = -1
    if i=j then
```

```
        select the feature either i or j
    end if
    end for
  Compute : Min = minimum correlation value from matrix C
  Compute : Max = maximum correlation value from matrix C
    New Min =0,  New Max=1
  for i=1:m do
      for j=1:m do
       if i != j then
          v= [(Cij - Min)/(Max-Min)] * (New Max- New Min) +New Min (7.2)
       Cij=v
     end if
    end for
end for
  return Normalized Correlation Matrix C
  C = Min_Max_Normaliztion (C)
End.
```

Experiments

Dataset

The data is retrieved from IMDB website. The retrieve dataset is related to movie reviews. Reviews available on website for single movie is extracted using Google API. All the extracted reviews will be the dataset considered as an input to the system. For extracting reviews from IMDb website one time authentication application is required. Crowd is application software used for authenticating website access for accessing online reviews from IMDb website. JSoup, a Java library used for extracting and parsing on-line hypertext markup language documents. Various keyword is used to retrieve all the reviews from IMDb website. Two movies i.e., The Imitation Game, Three Idiots and one Web series i.e. Scam 1992: The Harshad Mehta Story reviews are downloaded.

Parsing and Preprocessing

Now HTML file need to be converted to plain text file to process further efficiently. Java HTML, which is a JAVA package used to convert HTML to plain text.

In preprocessing, reviews are clustered using K means clustering to identify similar and duplicate review based on similarity measures. In this work, existing textblob library of python is used to cluster various users based on their sentiment values. Three clusters are generated as positive sentiments, Negative sentiments and Neutral sentiments.

Different cluster provides information for identifying spammers based on their intentions. For example, if spammer wants to advertise his product then he will write positive things about the product and name of that brand will appear a greater number of times. Therefore, cluster with positive sentiment users has the possibility of having such spammer. Clustering will reduce the complexity of searching such user in whole dataset.

Correlation

The feature correlation of various users is carried out to find out similarity among users based on their reviews. Figure 3 shows that user 1 and user 2 have high correlation for all features. Further these users can be merged to avoid the problem of imbalance dataset.

Figure 3. Correlation for features

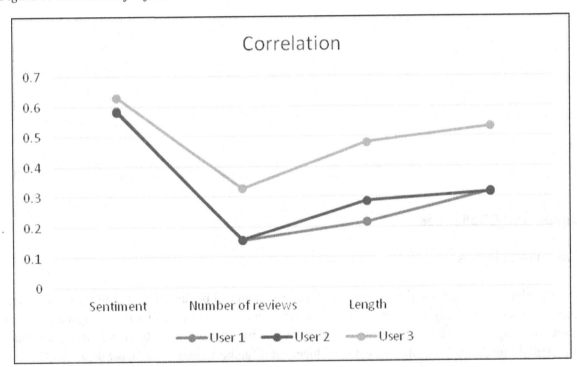

Brand Spam Classification

This study used accuracy metrics to evaluate the performance of the proposed system. The comparison of existing classification techniques with proposed work is shown in Figure 4. The accuracy of proposed model outperformed existing techniques with accuracy of 91%. ID3 performed better when compared with its peer algorithms such as Naïve Bayes' and J 48 classifier.

Figure 4. Proposed architecture performance for brand spam detection

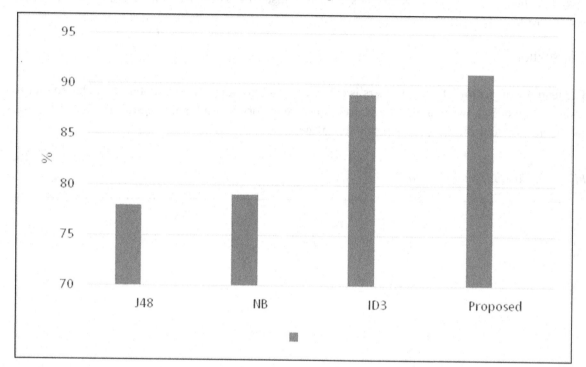

Issues and Challenges

Evaluation Metrics

In computing world, performance of any approach or system can be determined in terms of accuracy, space and time complexity. Real time precise and relevant results are crucial for any organization that desires to compete in digital computing scenarios. Evaluation Metrics can help in overall improvement of system design, processes, enhance trustworthiness and can be leveraging to make decisions.

Contextual Awareness

Advancement of Ubiquitous computing and various social networking sites in recent past, generates vast amounts of contextual data. Contextual aware systems can be categorized into two. First is user-based context where background (job, taste), behavior (activity) and various states (Physiological or Emotional) of different users have been captured. Second is environment-based context where Physical (Time location), Social (neighboring people) and computational resources (devices) taken into consideration.

Load Shedding

Load shedding can be defined as a method used by evolving processing systems, to manage unpredictable spike in size of data that arrives from heterogeneous sources. Many researchers and practitioners investigated on numerous load shedding techniques and algorithms to manage existing computational resources needed by evolutionary data. In addition, advances in storage and processing technology to tackle variant characteristics of Big data makes platforms like Apache Storm, Spark Streaming and Flink to provide distribution of stream data over large number of clusters in real time exist which can be useful to somewhat solve the problem of load shedding.

Data Exploration

The data exploration tools and techniques used to visualize or summarize data by proficiently extracting specific information. The real time data need to intrinsically maintain exploration while loading and searching intriguing patterns. For example, in social networking sites like Twitter, tweets sourced from various locations as a Geo-spatial data, contains co-ordinates or linkage data in terms of graph, for finding relationships among various users. The exploration of continues data over successive time slots supports to understand unknown patterns of application data.

High Dimensional Data

Continuous stream data sourced from heterogeneous sources are mostly high dimensional in nature. Systems, algorithms and techniques have been built and proposed in recent past to overcome the curse of dimensionality. Techniques such as feature selection, subspace clustering and graph embedding) have been effectively used for dimensionality reduction to improve overall system accuracy.

Data Provenance

Recently, data provenance in information systems gain lot of attention. (Glavic 2014; describes various challenges and issues faced by research community. Data provenance can be classified as metadata which refers to lineage data source. The concept of data provenance has great importance for scientists, researchers and engineers to follow origins of errors, for allocating automatic renovation of source to update a data, and to maintain data quality as it may rely on lineage data. However, there are still open issues related to real time data provenance. Modern information management system comprises and integrates data from heterogeneous sources. These systems are distributed and real time in nature which generate complex data workflows. Halevy et al. (2006) argues that analytic provenance is also crucial for data integration and aggregation. Thus, rapid growth of EHSN data sources creates various motivating challenges for data provenance in real time environment.

CONCLUSION

Reviews are meant for both customers and for the Companies. Customers use reviews for purchasing the product while the company uses it to improve its sale. But there are several reasons that add up to the disadvantages to the reviews and thus sums to the motivation to review spam detection. A company has to consistently monitor the reviews on several websites in order to prevent harming of their reputation due to review spamming. With such a big number of businesses of similar products it has got nearly impossible in meeting right people to have a good feedback. Continuous analysis of the feedback is turning out to be troublesome and not proving to be a right way of serving the customers.

This work conducts analysis for on-line review spam detection. Reviews and opinion reemployed by corporations for decision making. However repeatedly review comes/written under malignity like unhealthy promotion, so it's tough to succeed in right people/review for analysis. These entire necessities want to inspire towards detection of opinion spam and opinion sender. This work principally concentrates on review, reviewer centric spam detection that compares the content similarity. The proposed works for classifying lying review, and more truthful review by exploitating similarity measure and features correlation and matching. Analysis of correlation between various features, evaluation metrics, approaches and results are performed to validate selection of features as well as results

REFERENCES

Asghar, M. Z., Ullah, A., Ahmad, S., & Khan, A. (2020). Opinion spam detection framework using hybrid classification scheme. *Soft Computing*, *24*(5), 3475–3498. doi:10.100700500-019-04107-y

Fairbanks, J., Fitch, N., Knauf, N., & Briscoe, E. (2018). Credibility assessment in the news: do we need to read? MIS2'18.

Glavic, B. (2014). Big data provenance: Challenges and implications for benchmarking. In *Specifying big data benchmarks* (pp. 72–80). Springer. doi:10.1007/978-3-642-53974-9_7

Halevy, A., Rajaraman, A., & Ordille, J. (2006, September). Data integration: the teenage years. In *Proceedings of the 32nd international conference on Very large data bases* (pp. 9-16). VLDB Endowment.

Istanto, R. S., Mahmudy, W. F., & Bachtiar, F. A. (2020, November). Detection of online review spam: a literature review. In *Proceedings of the 5th International Conference on Sustainable Information Engineering and Technology* (pp. 57-63). 10.1145/3427423.3427434

Jansen, B. J., Zhang, M., Sobel, K., & Chowdury, A. (2009). Twitter power: Tweets as electronic word of mouth. *Journal of the American Society for Information Science and Technology*, *60*(11), 2169–2188. doi:10.1002/asi.21149

Jindal, N., & Liu, B. (2008, February). Opinion spam and analysis. In *Proceedings of the 2008 international conference on web search and data mining* (pp. 219-230). Academic Press.

Kanwar, P., Mehta, R., & Tidke, B. (2019, November). Correlation Based Multi-Criteria Feature Weighting for Identification of Top-k Investors and Companies. In *2019 9th International Conference on Advances in Computing and Communication (ICACC)* (pp. 271-277). IEEE. 10.1109/ICACC48162.2019.8986183

Lau, R. Y., Liao, S. Y., Kwok, R. C. W., Xu, K., Xia, Y., & Li, Y. (2015). Text mining and probabilistic modeling for online review spam detection. *ACM Transactions on Management Information Systems*, *2*(4), 1–30. doi:10.1145/2070710.2070716

Ma, H., Yang, H., Lyu, M. R., & King, I. (2008, October). Mining social networks using heat diffusion processes for marketing candidates selection. In *Proceedings of the 17th ACM conference on Information and knowledge management* (pp. 233-242). 10.1145/1458082.1458115

More, S, A., P Rana, D., & Agarwal, I. (2018). Random forest classifier approach for imbalanced big data classification for smart city application domains. *International Journal of Computational Intelligence & IoT, 1*(2).

Rout, J. K., Singh, S., Jena, S. K., & Bakshi, S. (2017). Deceptive review detection using labeled and unlabeled data. *Multimedia Tools and Applications, 76*(3), 3187–3211. doi:10.100711042-016-3819-y

Sharma, K., & Lin, K. I. (2013) Review spam detector with rating consistency check. In *Proceedings of the 51st ACM Southeast conference.* ACM. 10.1145/2498328.2500083

Trattner, C., & Kappe, F. (2013). Social stream marketing on Facebook: A case study. *International Journal of Social and Humanistic Computing, 2*(1-2), 86–103. doi:10.1504/IJSHC.2013.053268

Wu, T., Wen, S., Xiang, Y., & Zhou, W. (2018). Twitter spam detection: Survey of new approaches and comparative study. *Computers & Security, 76*, 265–284. doi:10.1016/j.cose.2017.11.013

Xie, J., Wang, G., Lin, S., & Philip, S. (2012). Review spam detection via time series pattern discovery. *ACM Proceedings of the 21st international conference companion on World Wide Web*, 635-636.

Xu, R., & Wunsch, D. (2008). *Clustering* (Vol. 10). John Wiley & Sons. doi:10.1002/9780470382776

You, Z., Qian, T., Zhang, B., & Ying, S. (2016). Identifying Implicit Enterprise Users from the Imbalanced Social Data. In *International Conference on Web Information Systems Engineering* (pp. 94-101). Springer International Publishing. 10.1007/978-3-319-48743-4_8

Zubiaga, A., Aker, A., Bontcheva, K., Liakata, M., & Procter, R. (2018). Detection and resolution of rumours in social media: A survey. *ACM Computing Surveys, 51*(2), 32. doi:10.1145/3161603

Chapter 9
Detection of Bot Accounts on Social Media Considering Its Imbalanced Nature

Isha Y. Agarwal
Sardar Vallabhbhai National Institute of Technology, Surat, India

Dipti P. Rana
https://orcid.org/0000-0002-5058-1355
Sardar Vallabhbhai National Institute of Technology, Surat, India

Devanshi Bhatia
Sardar Vallabhbhai National Institute of Technology, Surat, India

Jay Rathod
Sardar Vallabhbhai National Institute of Technology, Surat, India

Kaneesha J. Gandhi
Sardar Vallabhbhai National Institute of Technology, Surat, India

Harshit Sodagar
Sardar Vallabhbhai National Institute of Technology, Surat, India

ABSTRACT

Social media has completely transformed the way people communicate. However, every revolution brings with it some negative impacts. Due to its popularity amongst tons of global users, these platforms have a huge volume of data. The ease of access with minimal verification of new users on social media has led to the creation of the bot accounts used to collect private data, spread false and harmful content, and also poses many security threats. A lot of concerns have been raised with the increment in the quantity of bot accounts on different social media platforms. Also there is a high imbalance between bot and non-bot accounts where the imbalance is a result of 'normal behavior' of bot users. The research aims at identifying the artificial bots accounts on Twitter using various machine learning algorithms and content-based classification based on features provided on the platform and recent tweets of users respectively.

DOI: 10.4018/978-1-7998-7371-6.ch009

INTRODUCTION

In this modern era of data dominance, the authenticity of data is a major issue for everyone. With the growing presence of Online Social Networks (OSNs), people have started using it as their preferred medium of communication. Everyone and anyone can use these platforms for sharing their personal information, news, opinions and even their current mood. Some of the most popular OSNs are Facebook, Twitter, Instagram, Google Plus, Reddit and LinkedIn. It is not only limited to individuals using it for personal purposes, but governments, organizations, commercial enterprises and even politicians are using these platforms to increase their reach to the masses. It also makes getting response from the audience much easier while making it convenient to convey their messages directly to a wider population. But the popularity of OSNs make them easy targets for malicious objects that are trying to exploit the vulnerabilities of these platforms. The bot accounts are generally made to take advantage of the weaknesses of the network and thus the genuine users become victims of these malicious activities. A social bot is a software made with the purpose of automating user activities. These activities involve generating fake automated posts which look legitimate, re-posting photos, articles etc., adding likes and comments on other posts and increasing their social network by connecting with various different accounts. The level of sophistication of these bots ranges from dummy like bots that aggregate information from posts and re-post them to bots that are capable of infiltrating into actual human conversations. Social bots have their advantages and disadvantages for the users of the OSNs. Thus, it has become necessary to identify these bot accounts on the OSN platforms to preserve the security and privacy of the users.

The next section includes the Background and the Literature Survey followed by the Main Focus of the chapter along with the Issues, Controversies and Problems faced. The chapter also includes the proposed framework of model highlighting the solutions implemented and finally ends with a solid Conclusion along with the Future Work.

LITERATURE SURVEY

Mitigating bot accounts has grabbed the attention and curiosity of a lot of researchers. Therefore, extensive research has been carried out in this direction.

The feasibility of launching automated attacks in correspondence with identity theft: profile cloning and cross-site profile cloning. They then provided solutions and suggestions to protect the privacy of users such as providing more information on the authenticity of the issued requests to the receiver and making the CAPTCHAs more difficult to decode. However, sending detailed information about each user request, i.e., country information based on IP address, profile creation date, leads to high computational overhead. Moreover, in terms of CAPTCHA and reCAPTCHA, not solely do the human interaction abate the communication and probably cause false positives, but also each contribute to a foul client experience, that is that the last thing a website owner needs was discussed (Bilge, Strufe, Balzarotti and Kirda, 2009).

Profile similarity was computed by (Jin, Takabi and Joshi, 2011) after searching and collecting all identity profiles having names similar to the given Input Identity (IID) and a Profile Set. In case, the similarities found for a particular IID was larger than the prescribed thresholds, then it was added to the Suspicious Identity List (SIL) and after suitable verification, it was declared either genuine or non-legitimate. It is believed that the more the connection of a shared network between two users, the greater is their similarity.

A modular approach for detection of bot accounts on social networks was proposed (Kontaxis, Polakis, Ioannidis and Markatos, 2011). The main idea was, it made use of user-specific details, which was obtained from the actual social network profile of the user and this information was used to identify similar profiles across all social networking sites. After obtaining results, depending on the rarity of the profile, suitable methods of inspection for suspects was carried out. At the end, the user was shown a compilation of potential cloned profile along with a similarity score which measures extent to which the profiles were similar.

Bot account detection on social networks was made more efficient by calculating the similarities between user accounts using graph adjacency matrix and then applying the Principal Component Analysis (PCA) algorithm for feature extraction as proposed (Mohammadrezaei, Shiri and Rahmani, 2018). After that, Synthetic Minority Over-Sampling Technique (SMOTE) was used for balancing data. Subsequently, linear Support Vector Machine (SVM), logistic algorithms and Medium Gaussian SVM and regression, were used for classification of the nodes. Weakness of this proposed model however was that it required the bot accounts to work in the network in order to organizet he accounts as legitimate or non-legitimate, by surveying the networks of their friends. Detecting bot accounts before any user activity was hence not possible by this scheme.

A novel unsupervised method of recognizing and segregating bot accounts from legitimate user accounts was presented (Chavoshi, Hamooni and Mueen, 2016). This approach identified bots using correlated user activities. The two-fold procedure included: (1) developing the warped correlation finder and (2) using this finder to detect bots. This system called DeBot guaranteed high precision and was able to detect bots that other methods failed to spot. The presence of highly synchronous cross-user activities revealed abnormalities and was a key to detecting automated accounts according to this scheme. This modular approach however, required iteration over three independent parameters (base window, number of buckets, maximum lag) each time, while keeping the other parameters fixed. This in turn increased computational costs and made the whole system complex.

A technique which utilized sampling of non-uniform features in a machine learning algorithm by adapting a random forest algorithm for the recognition of spammer insiders was put forward(Meda, Ragusa, Gianoglio, Zunino, Ottaviano, Scillia, and Surlinelli, 2016). Integration of bootstrap aggregating techniques with unplanned selection of features is incorporated into this scheme. The dataset collected was based on indefinite user behaviors to check the performance. The features were divided into 2 sub categories, namely, domain expert selection and random selection. The aim was to reproduce two contradictory situations during feature selection. The first group included experts of the domain for choosing features and the second group involved random feature choice. The outputs received revealed the power of enriched feature sampling technique.

A categorization method was proposed (Erşahin, Aktaş, Kılınçand Akyol, 2017) to detect spam Twitter accounts collected manually using the Twitter APIs. Username, number of friends and 4 followers, profile and background image, content of tweets, number of tweets, description of account, etc., were analyzed. The experiment consisted of 499 real accounts and 501 non-legitimate, wherein 16 features were identified from all the data. Two experiments were used to classify the bot accounts. The first experiment was done using the Naive Bayes learning algorithm on the Twitter data which includes all aspects with no discretization and the second experiment performed Naive Bayes learning algorithm on Twitter data after discretization.

A method was initiated by (Gharge and Chavan, 2017), which was classified based on2 new features. First was the identification of spam tweets without any kind of users' data. Second was the study of language on Twitter trending topics, for detection of spam at that particular time. The entire model preprocessing consisted of the following steps: (1) Tweet collection in correspondence to the prevailing trending topics on Twitter. After their storage, analysis of the tweets was done. (2) Labelling of spam was performed across all datasets for detecting malignant URL. (3) Feature extraction using language as a tool for segregating false tweets from real ones. (4) Classification of the dataset was done in order to train and instruct the model for acquiring knowledge for spam detection. (5) Finally, tweets are taken as input and determined whether they are spam or non-spam. The setup for experimentation was analyzed with the system accuracy.

A machine learning framework was presented by (Ferrara, Emilio, Wang, Varol, Flammini and Galstyan, 2016) that leveraged a combination of network, temporal features and metadata to identify the extremist users, and predicted content adopters and interaction reciprocity in social media. They used a distinct dataset which contained several tweets which were generated by thousands of users who were manually reported, identified and/or suspended by Twitter because of their involvement with extremist campaigns. They used learning models like Logistics regression and Random forest for the same.

The author in (Dehade and Bagade, 2015) first shed light into the fact that twitter has become a very attractive target for bots to abuse in the past few years. The author collected data by crawling twitter and based on the recognized features collected through this data, humans, bots and cyborgs can be differentiated on twitter. This is done by observing that humans have complex performance or high entropy while bots and cyborgs have periodic timing or low entropy.

The author (Wang and Alex, 2010) extracted graph-based features like the number of friends and followers for twitter users and also identified relationships between them. They also used the content of users' tweets and applied various algorithms on the content-based and graph-based features for classification.

The author (Varol, Ferrara, Davis, Menczer, and Flammini, 2017) demonstrated a framework for detecting bots on twitter using a system based on machine learning that extracted thousands of features based on six classes: tweet content and sentiment, network patterns, users and friends meta-data, and activity time series (Bessi and Ferrara, 2016).

Moving to bot detection at the tweet-level, and therefore having training large data orders, made the issue of bot detection way more susceptible to the use of deep learning models (Kudugunta, Sneha and Ferrara, 2018). Such techniques benefited from the huge quantities of labeled data, displaying very good performance in several contexts where such resources were obtainable from mastering games to image classification.

In correspondence to the issues presented by the above-mentioned schemes, this research establishes the requirement of an efficient model for the detection of bot accounts on social networks using big data mining tools.

MAIN FOCUS OF THE CHAPTER

The primary goal is to detect bot accounts on social media platforms using a variety of big data mining tools. The aim is to take a random set of user accounts from a social media platform and to filter out the bot accounts using machine learning algorithms. Word Embedding techniques using Python are also carried out to find the similarities between tweets of bot accounts to classify them as non-legitimate. The experimentation is performed on a labelled data set collected from Kaggle (Jain, 2019) to check the accuracy of the proposed model.

Issues, Controversies, Problems

In today's world, social media has gained a lot of popularity. It is not just a platform for interacting anymore, it has evolved a lot. As a result, with more users online, there is more data, and this is collected and manipulated for false information through the help of non-legitimate accounts. These accounts are created for a variety of purposes, for example, collecting personal user data, selling data to third parties, spreading false information about any trending topic/news, etc. Researchers all over the world are trying to identify these fake accounts so that privacy and security of users is preserved. The main motive of this project is to detect bot accounts on social media platform twitter.

PROPOSED FRAMEWORK

As mentioned, there is a need to identify the bot accounts on social media. Here, proposed a model that distinguishes between bot accounts and legitimate user accounts. This section describes the methodology for the implementation of bot detection system model using Twitter dataset. The pictorial representation of the same is given in Figure 1 below. The following sections show the different stages of the proposed framework:

1.   Input Username

    The user of the proposed framework needs to verify the particular username is bot user or legitimate user then he/she has to enter the username in the available user interface. The user interface will check whether the username is available on twitter or not. If yes, then follows the next step, otherwise provide the similar username for the selection.

2.   User Data Extraction

    The proposed framework is requiring the features and the tweets available for the given user, so all the features available on the twitter will be extracted along with the tweets of that user for the further steps. Also, this user will be tested with the available tweeter users, so if the system is used first time, then the same information will be fetched for the maximum users possible. And this information will be kept for the further usage and later only some few latest users information will be collected for the efficient result. The data avail from the twitter is not directly usable by the machine learning algorithm, so further the proposed framework follows the step of data preprocessing to prepare the data for the remaining steps.

3.   Data Preprocessing

    The user's features and tweets are required to process before they apply to the machine learning algorithm to make it usable, by performing the following steps.

a.   Identifying the missing data

Missing data are defined as any values that are not available or entered by the user. A heat map is plotted to showcase which all attributes contain what frequency of null/missing values for further action on them. As shown here in Figure 2, "location", "description", and "url" have the maximum missing values (depicted in yellow) whereas "status" and "has_extended_profile" has only a few of them.

b.   Identifying imbalance in the data

The data analysis shows that whenever the listed count is between the 10,000 to 20,000 from that 5% of them are bots and 95% are non bot/legitimate user accounts as shown in Figure 3. This sets the imbalance in ecosystem. Similarly for the verified case as well, an observation of data imbalance for bots' and non bots' friends and followers was made. The Figure 3 depicts the imbalance of accounts classified as bot and non-bot. This imbalance of accounts, forced the important heuristics to apply which is discussed in step 5.

c.   Feature Extraction and Feature Engineering

The features play very important role in the performance of the model, so to retain the beneficial features and engineered the features in form of the bag of words are required.

Figure 1. Proposed model of bot detection

FLOWCHART

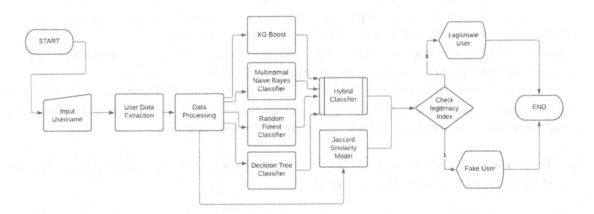

Figure 2. Frequency of null/missing values

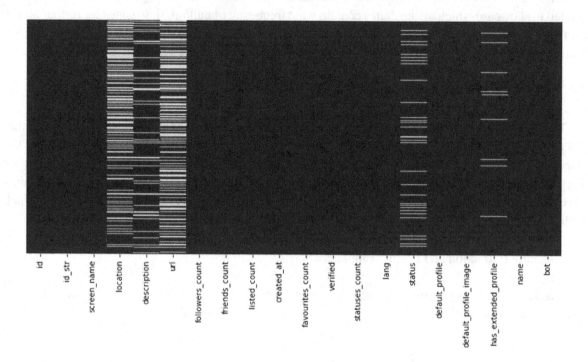

Feature independence method is used to decide the advantageous attributes and here used the Spearman's rank-order correlation technique. It is the nonparametric form of the Pearson product-moment correlation. Spearman's correlation coefficient measures the strength and direction of relationship between two ranked variables. Spearman's correlation, unlike Pearson's correlation, works on determining the direction and strength of the monotonic relationship between two variables. Pearson's correlation, on the other hand, works on determining the direction and strength of the linear relationship between two variables. A monotonic relationship is one where the values of the two variables are such that if one increases, the other also increases, or if one increases the other decreases.

Finally as a part of feature extraction, the unnecessary features after the spearman correlation test are discarded and kept only those with high correlation rank value.

Further, to use the features efficiently, as a part of feature engineering, for most commonly used words created a "bag of words" model for each individual attribute. So, for the selected features, after preprocessing are converted into binary format using the bag of words.

4. Implementing different algorithms - Decision Tree Classifier, Multinomial Naive Bayes Classifier, Random Forest Classifier, XGB Classifier

On the obtained features from the feature extraction and engineering, the variety of classifiers is considered due to their typical characteristics and mix set of attributes. The categorical classifiers considered are Decision Tree Classifier, Multinomial NB classifier, which alone generate poor testing accuracy. The Random Forest Classifier is also considered here though it is complex. Together with the XGB classifier considered which can show the highest training accuracy, precision and recall among all.

Figure 3. Histogram of bot vs. non bot accounts

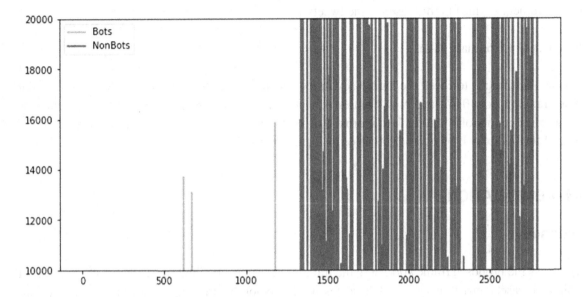

Thus, emphasized to have the hybrid ensemble learning model and used the above mentioned algorithms as weak learning models.

5. Implementing Jaccard Similarity Model

Here, for the proposed framework to identify the user as legitimate or bot, the heuristic considered is that the tweets posted by a bot account should be similar to each other as they are created with a certain agenda. So, together with the classification, the similarity between tweets of a user given account with others is also performed to find out accurate classification of the account into bot or not-bot account.

Generally to find similarity between the texts, cosine similarity or Jaccard similarity can be used. Jaccard similarity takes solely a novel set of words from each document or sentence. In contrast, cosine similarity considers the overall vector lengths. Jaccard similarity is preferred for the cases where repetition of words does not make a difference. In case of significant duplication of words, cosine similarity should be used. In this case, context makes a lot more difference than duplication. Hence the ideal technique to be used is Jaccard similarity.

Jaccard similarity is a statistical method used to find the diversity and similarity between documents using a set of unique words used in the documents.

It measures the proportion of the number of common words in two documents. It is defined as the intersection of the two documents over the union of the two documents as shown in equation 1.

$$J\left(Doc_1, Doc_2\right) = \frac{Doc_1 \cap Doc_2}{Doc_1 \cup Doc_2} \quad \ldots\ldots\ldots\ldots \tag{1}$$

The final output is the Jaccard similarity index ranging from 0 to 1 representing the closeness of the two documents, which in this case are the tweets.

6.   Check Legitimacy Index

The final step is to check the legitimacy index which is the combination of both Jaccard similarity index ranging from 0 to 1 and classification true positive rate ranging from 0 to 1. So, here considered the average ceiling of both which is approx. 0 or 1 and based on this value, the user is classified as bot user, if this index is 1, otherwise classified as legitimate user.

IMPLEMENTATION

Dataset

To assess the proposed framework, here the training dataset is obtained from Kaggle (Jain, 2019). The training dataset consists of 1,321 bot instances and 1,476 non-bot instances.The training dataset sample, with a few columns and rows is shown in the Figure 4 below.

Figure 4. Snapshot of the dataset

Data Preprocessing

Preprocessing of the data was done to clean the tweets and the text attributes available in the data like screen_name, name, description and status. For preprocessing links, images, hashtags, @mentions, emojis, stop words and punctuations were removed. Contractions were expanded, for example, "what's" was converted to "what is". Stemming and tokenizing was done later on as a part of preprocessing.

Exhaustive data analysis discovered the missing data as depicted in the Figure 2 and discarded them. and data imbalance using exploratory data analysis and obtained the graphs and Figure 3.

To decide the advantageous attributes here used the Spearman's rank-order correlation technique. From Figure 5 it can be noted that there is a strong correlation between "verified", "listed_count", "friends_count", "followers_count" and target variable. It also depicts that there is no correlation between "id", "statuses_count", "default_profile", "default_profile_image" and target variable. So these 4 attributes have not been considered into the feature selection process. As correlation for categorical attributes cannot be performed, here considered "screen_name", "name", "description", "status" into feature engineering and use "verified", "listed_count" for feature extraction.

Figure 5. Spearman co-relation plot between features

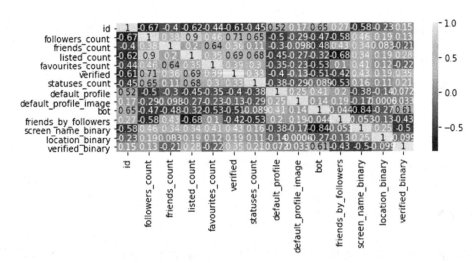

Further, as a part of feature engineering, the authors checked few attributes namely "screen_name", "name", "description" and "status" for most commonly used words and created a "bag of words" model for each individual attribute. To accomplish this, tokenized the screen name, name, description and status and applied lemmatization on the same. Then the attributes are converted into binary format using the bag of words. Finally as a part of feature extraction, the unnecessary features after the spearman correlation test are discarded and kept only those with high correlation rank value.

· Implementation of different machine learning algorithms - Decision Tree Classifier, Multinomial Naive Bayes Classifier, Random Forest Classifier, XGB Classifier

All the machine learning models were implemented in the same order as described in the preceding section and below are the results and ROC curves for each.

· Decision Tree Classifier

The training accuracy was found to be 86.8% and testing accuracy was found to be 86.6%. It also gives training and testing precision of 87.3% and 87.6% respectively. Moreover, the recall obtained for training and testing data is 83.6% and 85.1% respectively. Figure 6 shows the ROC Curve for the Decision Tree Classifier.

Figure 6. Decision tree ROC curve

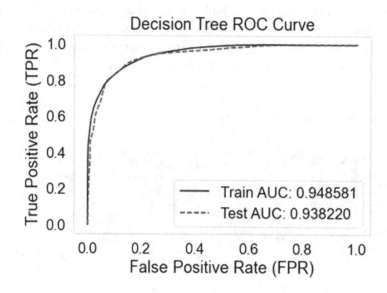

· **Multinomial NB Classifier**

The training accuracy was found to be 67.8% and testing accuracy was found to be 69.7%. It also gives training and testing precision of 59.3% and 62.5% respectively. Moreover, the recall obtained for training and testing data is 96.2% and 97.1% respectively. Figure 7 shows the ROC Curve for the Multinomial NB Classifier.

· **Random Forest Classifier**

The training accuracy was found to be 84.8% and testing accuracy was found to be 84.4%. It also gives training and testing precision of 86.5% and 87.6% respectively. Moreover, the recall obtained for training and testing data is 79.6% and 79.8% respectively. Figure 8 shows the ROC Curve for the Random Forest Classifier.

· **XGB Classifier**

The training accuracy was found to be 98.8% and testing accuracy was found to be 83.5%. It also gives training and testing precision of 99.2% and 84.5% respectively. Moreover, the recall obtained for training and testing data is 98.2% and 82.1% respectively. Figure 9 shows the ROC Curve for the XG Boost Classifier.

· **Hybrid Ensemble Model**

The above mentioned algorithms were used as weak learners to build a hybrid ensemble learning model. The training accuracy was found to be 92.3% and testing accuracy was found to be 90.0%. It

Figure 7. Multinomial NB ROC curve

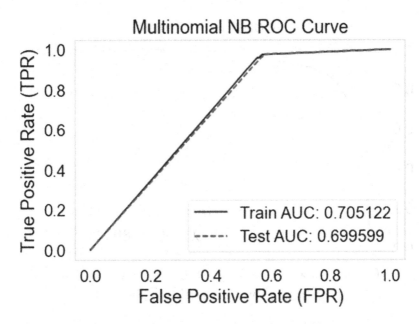

also gives training and testing precision of 91.1% and 88.8% respectively. Moreover, the recall obtained for training and testing data is 92.7% and 91.4% respectively. Figure 10 shows the ROC Curve for the Hybrid Ensemble Model.

Figure 8. Random forest ROC curve

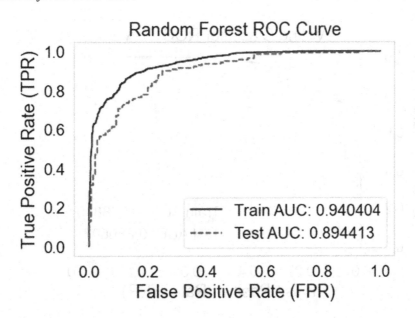

Figure 9. XG boost ROC curve

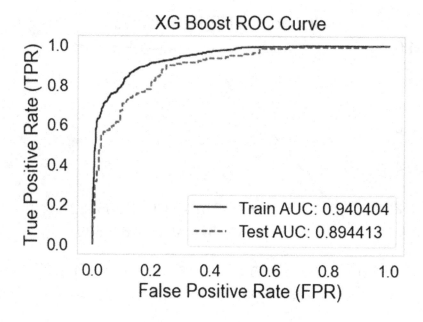

· **Implementation of Jaccard Similarity Model**

Here, to find similarity between the tweets, Jaccard similarity is used. In this similarity test, the experiment depicted the Jaccard similarity score between the 100 most recent tweets of a given Twitter

Figure 10. Voting Classifier ROC curve

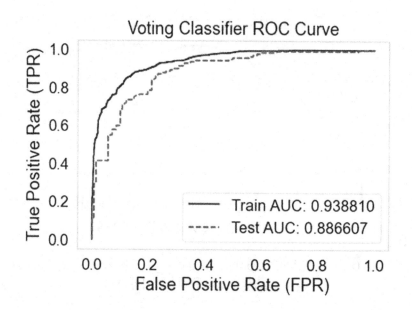

account. Before the similarity score was computed, the tweets made available from the dataset were in their raw form and had to be preprocessed first for effective use.

Further, the tokenizing of the tweets performed using RegExp Tokenizer and lemmatized the tweets using WordNet Lemmatizer from NLTK library. After this, the Jaccard Similarity score was computed. The accuracy up to 93.2% is achieved after combining the results from both the Hybrid model and the Similarity model.

CONCLUSION

This research addresses the issue of presence of artificial bot accounts on the social media platform particularly Twitter and the threat they poses to the privacy of the legitimate users. Social media has become a major source of information and many bot accounts are created with the purpose of spreading misinformation. The primary focus of the research is to build a model that identifies the bot accounts on Twitter which are imbalanced compared to normal user accounts. In the proposed model various machine learning algorithms were used as weak learners to make a hybrid model that could successfully classify 90% of the accounts using the preprocessed Twitter data. The project also consists of classification based on Jaccard Similarity model which uses recent tweets posted by the users. This content based classification along with the hybrid model was able to classify 93.2% accounts correctly. With the help of the model these bot accounts can be identified and removed from the platform to reduce the harm to the society.

FUTURE WORK

Some methods, such as guided learning approaches, were extensively discussed in this work. To comprehend, reinforce or discover new results, several approaches require more exploration. It stimulates the research community to discover new approaches and improve existing approaches. The above model can be utilized for real time applications. With the awareness of bot accounts among users, it would become convenient and highly lucrative for people and organizations to detect them on OSNs. In future, this model will be compared with other available techniques and by including the usage of network information of users.

REFERENCES

Bessi, A., & Ferrara, E. (2016). *Social bots distort the 2016 us presidential election*. Academic Press.

Bilge, L., Strufe, T., Balzarotti, D., & Kirda, E. (2009, April). All your contacts are belong to us: automated identity theft attacks on social networks. *Proceedings of the 18th international conference on World Wide Web*, 551-560. 10.1145/1526709.1526784

Chavoshi, N., Hamooni, H., & Mueen, A. (2016, December). Debot: Twitter bot detection via warped correlation. ICDM, 817-822.

Dehade, S. K., & Bagade, A. M. (2015). A review on detecting automation on Twitter accounts. *European Journal of Advances in Engineering and Technology, 2*, 69–72.

Erşahin, B., Aktaş, Ö., Kılınç, D., & Akyol, C. (2017, October). Twitter fake account detection. *Proceedings of International Conference on Computer Science and Engineering (UBMK)*, 388-392.

Ferrara, E., Wang, W., Varol, O., Flammini, A., & Galstyan, A. (2016). Predicting online extremism, content adopters, and interaction reciprocity. *International conference on social informatics*, 22-39. 10.1007/978-3-319-47874-6_3

Gharge, S., & Chavan, M. (2017, March). An integrated approach for malicious tweets detection using NLP. *Proceedings of International Conference on Inventive Communication and Computational Technologies (ICICCT)*, 435-438. 10.1109/ICICCT.2017.7975235

Jain, C. (2019). *Detecting twitter bot data, Version 1.* Retrieved from https://www.kaggle.com/charvijain27/detecting-twitter-bot-data

Jin, L., Takabi, H., & Joshi, J. B. (2011, February). Towards active detection of identity clone attacks on online social networks. *Proceedings of the first ACM conference on Data and application security and privacy*, 27-38. 10.1145/1943513.1943520

Kontaxis, G., Polakis, I., Ioannidis, S., & Markatos, E. P. (2011, March). *Detecting social network profile cloning. In 2011 IEEE international conference on pervasive computing and communications workshops (PERCOM Workshops), (pp. 295-300).* IEEE.

Kudugunta, S., & Ferrara, E. (2018). Deep neural networks for bot detection. *Information Sciences, 467*, 312–322. doi:10.1016/j.ins.2018.08.019

Meda, C., Ragusa, E., Gianoglio, C., Zunino, R., Ottaviano, A., Scillia, E., & Surlinelli, R. (2016, August). Spam detection of Twitter traffic: A framework based on random forests and non-uniform feature sampling. In *2016 IEEE/ACM International Conference on Advances in Social Networks Analysis and Mining (ASONAM), (pp. 811-817).* IEEE. 10.1109/ASONAM.2016.7752331

Mohammadrezaei, M., Shiri, M. E., & Rahmani, A. M. (2018). Identifying fake accounts on social networks based on graph analysis and classification algorithms. *Security and Communication Networks, 2018*, 1–8. doi:10.1155/2018/5923156

Varol, O., Ferrara, E., Davis, C. A., Menczer, F., & Flammini, A. (2017). *Online human-bot interactions: Detection, estimation, and characterization.* arXiv preprint arXiv:1703.03107.

Wang, A. H. (2010). Detecting spam bots in online social networking sites: a machine learning approach. In *Proceedings of IFIP Annual Conference on Data and Applications Security and Privacy, (pp. 335-342).* Springer. 10.1007/978-3-642-13739-6_25

Chapter 10
Behaviour Anomaly Detection With Similarity–Based Sampling for Imbalanced Data

Isha Y. Agarwal
Sardar Vallabhbhai National Institute of Technology, Surat, India

Dipti P. Rana
iD https://orcid.org/0000-0002-5058-1355
Sardar Vallabhbhai National Institute of Technology, Surat, India

Kshitij R. Suri
Sardar Vallabhbhai National Institute of Technology, Surat, India

Punitkumar Jain
Sardar Vallabhbhai National Institute of Technology, Surat, India

Saumya Awasthi
Sardar Vallabhbhai National Institute of Technology, Surat, India

Krittika Roy
Sardar Vallabhbhai National Institute of Technology, Surat, India

ABSTRACT

Mental health is a major issue in our society, and people treat this issue as a subject that should not be spoken about. So, many such individuals utilize social media as a platform to share their thoughts and fears. This emphasizes the researchers to identify sufferers who require treatment. Many approaches have been devised to detect early markers of mental health illness, some of which include learning algorithms based on the heuristic of equally distributed balanced data. However, they yield biased results towards the majority data (i.e., normal behaviour). Thus, new perception is needed to explore the available data. This research deals with the first identification of such users from weblog data, and the similarity-based sampled data is then given to the classifier. The experiment analysis shows the effectiveness of this work and will provide the user's mental state information early to take timely necessary steps.

DOI: 10.4018/978-1-7998-7371-6.ch010

INTRODUCTION

According to The World Health Organization, around 800,000 people die due to suicide every year ("Suicide data", 2020). That means every 40 seconds one person commits suicide. A first-year Master's student in IIT Madras committed suicide due to academic reasons (Lobo, 2020). A renowned singer committed suicide after suffering from depression for a long time. Unfortunately, several such cases have been reported in the past few years. It is a serious and troubling issue, for the person who commits it, their family, and a loss for the entire Nation. The World Health Organization also states that a person who has committed suicide is likely to have attempted up to 20 times before the actual incident. According to the American Foundation for Suicide Prevention, 5075 percent of the individuals who attempt suicide talk about or express their intentions (Pappas, 2017). Early detection of such behaviour is crucial. Social Media has become one of the most widely used platforms for people to share and express their thoughts and feelings. In the proposed model, with the help of appropriate data mining techniques, the user's data can be analyzed to determine the complex behavioural patterns exhibited by them. The company or institute access logs are used to monitor the frequency of accessing social media websites and the content present in them is analyzed so that users can be classified based on these parameters. With the help of such a model if abnormal behaviour can be tracked down, then these suicides can be prevented and people's lives can be saved.

BACKGROUND

Unstructured text from social media is a common aspect of both clustering and information retrieval-based algorithms. It is imperative to first structure the given data into meaningful categories and then performs algorithm-based analysis. In this section, the different approaches have been discussed that are implemented by prior works to analyze textual data by categorizing its contents.

Content Classification

In order to structure user data by classifying it into meaningful categories, prior works have followed three major approaches, as described below.

Topic-Based Classification

Sergei Koltcov et al. (Koltcov, Koltsova & Nikolenko, 2014) showed that one should be cautious while using the Latent Dirichlet Allocation (LDA) model (Armstrong, 2015), especially for Topic Modelling because the algorithm contains an inherent uncertainty. The authors introduced a new metric of the document and word ratios for evaluating the different aspects of the topic modelling. The use of this new metric decreased the size of vocabulary used in the topic similarity metric based on Kullback–Leibler divergence.

Bo Dao et al. (Dao, Nguyen, Venkatesh & Phung, 2017) presented an approach for analyzing general and mental health-based online communities on social media platforms. These online communities were analyzed based on different categorization methods such as mood tags, text analysis, writing style analysis, and generic words. The data obtained through these categorizations was given to Hierarchical

Dirichlet Process (HDP) algorithm to detect hidden topics. A nonparametric clustering algorithm was utilized to cluster the communities into metacommunities based on the latent topics obtained. It was proposed that such a model could be used to provide guidance and help in mental healthcare to such online communities.

To determine the topics and key points from a very large set of articles and documents related to adolescent substance abuse and depression, ShiHeng Wang et al. (Wang et al., 2016) proposed utilizing the LDA model. The method helped in recognizing the different themes, detecting the terms used in them, and forming a visual word cloud of the terms that belong to the theme. Trend analysis was carried out to detect the cold and hot topics, and hierarchical clustering analysis was used to cluster related topics.

For early risk prediction of depression in users who use social media, Diego et al. (Maupomé & Meurs, 2018) proposed the system based on the topic extraction algorithm, LDA, and neural networks. The author in their system extracted 30 latent topics using unigram, bigram, and trigram frequency. After performing LDA, MLP used to predict the label for each user. The last step of the system involved the decision algorithms that classify users based on setting an absolute threshold of probability. The author shrank this threshold with the fixed ratio at every chunk. The author showed that the limited number of users greatly hinders the predictive power of the MLP.

Text-Based Classification

It is often the case that sentiment extracted from social media predicts the outcomes for a real-world phenomenon. However, most labeling of Twitter sentiment analysis is done on extreme scales of positive, negative and neutral. From the perspective of social sciences, capturing more dimensions of emotions is vital. In this regard, it was proposed by Shubhanshu Mishra et al. (Mishra et al., 2014) to use a novel sentiment classifier, tailored specifically to social causes, that captured sentiment with the level of support (supportive versus no supportive) and degree of enthusiasm (enthusiastic versus passive). Thus with this classifier, various stakeholders associated with social causes can be identified and this information is further used for collective action and advocacy.

In a similar way, (Hasan, Rundensteiner & Agu, 2014) proposed a model that automatically classified the individual's text messages into different emotional classes. Such a model has a large variety of applications, which can be used by healthcare professionals to monitor a patient's emotional states, and to study the public mood of people in a certain region of the country. The model was based on the Circumplex Model and emotions are classified into four categories: HappyActive, HappyInactive, UnhappyActive, and UnhappyInactive. SVM, Naive Bayes, Decision Trees, and KNearest Neighbours used for the classification of data.

To identify depression among users using social media, the authors in (Tadesse, Lin, Xu & Yang, 2019) experimented to understand the relationship between depression and the language used by users using NLP and text classification techniques. They examined both single and combined features to measure any sign of depressions using various text classifying methods. Performance can be improved with proper feature selection and their combinations. For feature extractions, the author used the LIWC dictionary (Pennebaker, Booth, Boyd & Francis, 2015), LDA topics (Blei, Ng & Jordan, 2003), and N-Gram features. After feature selection, the author used different classifying techniques like Logistic Regression (Gortmaker, 1994), (Agresti, 2014), Support Vector Machine (Noble, 2006), Random Forest (Xu et al., 2012), Adaptive Boosting (Freund and Schapire, 1999), and Multilayer Perceptron classifier (Ramchoun, Amine, Idrissi, Ghanou & Ettaouil, 2016) to detect. The author showed that a single feature bigram with the Support Vector Machine (SVM) classifier is best for depression detection, having 80% accuracy and 0.80 F1 scores. For combined features, using a combination of LIWC+LDA+bigram showed the best results, with the Multilayer Perceptron (MLP) classifier having 91% accuracy and 0.93 F1 scores.

Visual and Additional Parameter Classification

Social media is not simply composed of textual information. Generally, to quantify mood at a higher level, studies mainly focused on lexical entries corresponding to human emotion in sentiment analysis. However, users also include emoticons to better convey one's emotions, thus contributing as an important factor for collective mood. The author (Sasahara, 2014) focused on the interactions between emoticons with their associated linguistic representations in Japanese tweets and thereby constructed emoticon networks to quantify the collective mood in social media factoring in emotional information from emoticons. The nodes in the networks represented Japanese emoticons and adjectives, and directed links represented information flow between them. They demonstrated the structural properties of the collective mood before and after the 2011 Japan earthquake.

Additionally, social media content is based more on multiple modalities rather than a single comment or a single activity. To detect cyber bullying episodes on social media, the authors of (Cheng, Silva, Hall & Liu, 2020) introduced new features like considering the MultiModal nature of each session, the Temporal Dynamics, the Levelled Structure of Content, and the Modelling of User Interactions. Processes like point processes, multi-task learning, and burst analysis were used for the analysis of Temporal Dynamics. Language Modelling and construction of networks were recommended to understand user interactions. These features would aid in detecting the defining features of cyber bullying that are a power imbalance between the victim and the bully and repetition of aggressive or unwanted behaviour.

Variety of research are available, emphasize that still research area is open to early identify the social media user's abnormal behaviour to provide the timely help.

MAIN FOCUS OF THE CHAPTER

Across the globe, the number of people who are suffering from mental health disorders is increasing. The most common examples of mental illness are depression and anxiety disorders which are also the main reason for suicides. These disorders also cause a change in people's behaviour so if one can study these changes then able to predict if someone is suffering from mental illness or not. Social media has become a part of day-today life, people use it to share their location, how they feel, what they eat, and all such kinds of information about themselves. So, by studying these activities of an individual one can know about his/her mental health condition.

This research is aiming to create an expert system for the educational institute or employment organization to identify the access based abnormal behaviour of the user using weblog and then social media content which will identify if user activities can be considered as normal or abnormal. It is intended to create a model that analyzes the amount of time spent on social media, what is user posting, how often the user visits the platform and based on these parameters, provides feedback for the user. The major contribution is two-fold. One is identifying the access based behaviour derived from the time spent online and another is a contextual analysis of the content posted in order to determine the state of mind. Thus this is a novel framework that proposes a holistic approach to filter user-based on the time spent online and on contextual analysis so timely help and counseling can be provided to the needful.

PROPOSED FRAMEWORK OF BEHAVIOUR DETECTION

The proposed framework for the analysis of user behaviour for abnormal activities detection is as shown in Figure 1 below. This section describes the methodology for the implementation of an expert system framework for identifying user behaviour.

Figure 1. Proposed framework of behaviour detection

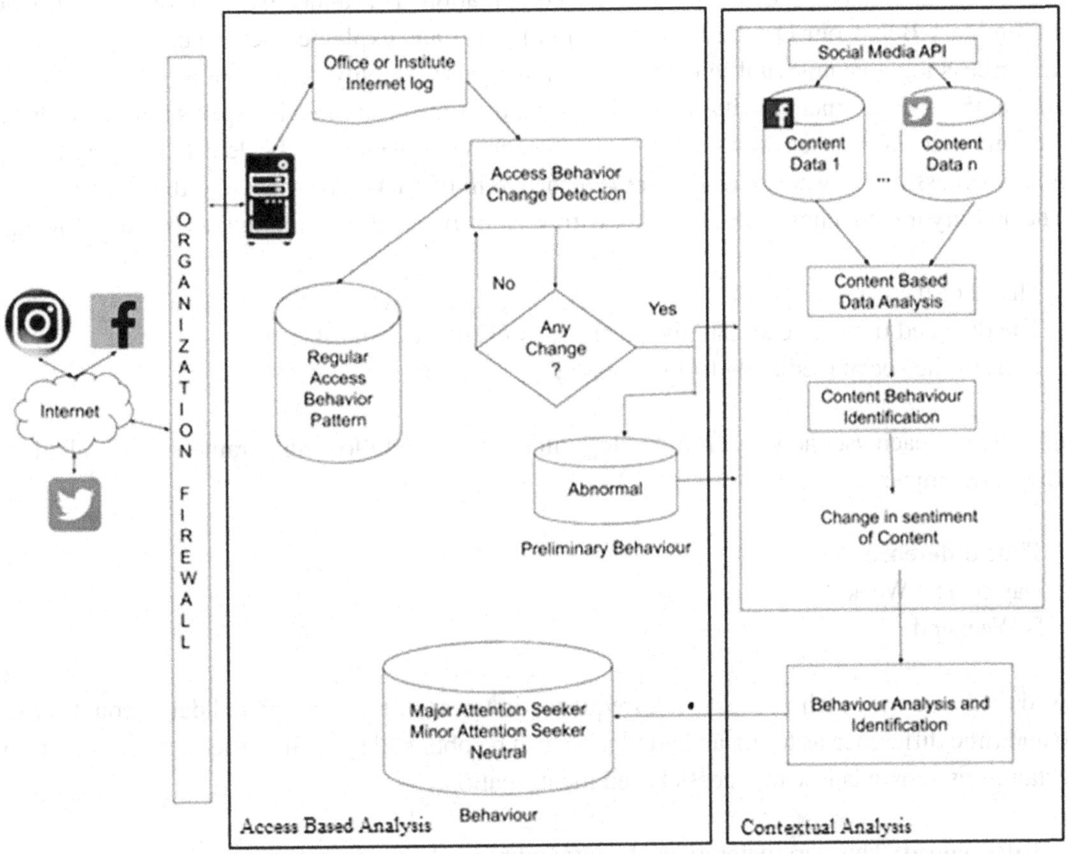

The proposed model is divided into 2 phases:

- Access Based analysis
- Contextual Analysis

Access-Based Analysis

Many offices and higher education institutes provide internet facilities to the people that work or study in their premises with a proper infrastructure of cyber security. The internet surfing activity of such individuals for regular academic or office activity as well as for social media platforms related activity are collected at the central server as internet log. The central server contains complete information regarding the identity of a particular user and the devices owned by him/her. The data present on the social media platforms that users post are managed by the social media application provider.

Several users access social media websites for several days. The information of all users is logged and compared using the Access Based Identification model. The system is made aware of the identification of abnormality in access behaviour of those users whose analysis results in an anomaly. This abnormality is referred to as Access Based behaviour, and convenient as it is utilizing only institute internet log data which can be mined quickly with little memory computation. This abnormality information is stored in the Preliminary Behaviour Database as shown in Figure 1 and explained here in detail.

The access log contains vital information regarding user activity. If one analyzed this activity, it is found that the user internet activity pattern based on the time. The model suspects that the user may be facing some issue if the user shows some change in behaviour which can be detected if there is a change in time of accessing the website or if there is a change in frequency of accessing the website.

The activity log contains multiple fields with various types of information, as listed following:

1. The id of the user
2. The date and time of accessing the particular website i.e. Timestamp
3. URL of the social media platform accessed

Initially, for each user activity from the log information the following parameters are calculated using the timestamps:

- Time difference
- Day of The Week
- Is Weekend

And then again for each user activity, frequency in terms of total_count and daily_counts, weekend ratio and time difference as td_mean and td_max can be obtained by using different calculations on the timestamps as shown below for access based identification.

- **Total_count:** This parameter gives the total number of times a user accesses any website through the institute network till the day the weblog is available.
- **Daily_counts:** This parameter is calculated by taking the median of per day count value for every user.
- **Is_weekend_ratio:** It is the ratio between the total number of times a user accesses a social media website on all weekdays and the total number of times a user visits a social media website on all weekends.
- **Td_mean:** This parameter is calculated by taking the mean of time difference value for each user.

- **Td_max:** This parameter is calculated by taking the maximum value among time difference values for each user.

This information is stored in the Regular Access Behaviour Pattern Database for each user. In the next step, for more fine-grained analysis, intensive resource computed in-depth analysis for the concerned user is done by inspecting the content put by the user on his/her social media platform.

Contextual Analysis

If the user shows some change in internet activity behaviour, then the change can be observed in the content that the user posts on social media. This change in the content is identified by analyzing the sentiment and semantics of content that is shared by the user on these social media applications over the observed time period of abnormality. The content of the user who is suspected to have abnormal behaviour is analyzed. This content includes text posted or reposted, the sender and receiver information. These contents are collected using the social media's API for each social media application for a particular time and provides the required data to the content-based data analysis process to retrieve the content shared by the user. From the content obtained the emotions that it depicts need to be acquired. and After data preprocessing, this process retrieves the sentiment of all the content posted by the user like joy, neutral, sadness, etc. The content behaviour identification process is identifying the change in sentiment of the content. This abnormality in sentiment is referred to as Contextual Based behaviour, and classified using LSTM and CNN. This abnormality information is stored in the Behaviour Database as major attention seeker, minor attention seeker or neutral as shown in Figure 1.

EXPERIMENT SETUP AND RESULT ANALYSIS

Here, this section discusses the experiment setup and result analysis for these two sections: access based analysis and contextual analysis separately.

Access-Based Analysis

This component aims to identify the abnormal use of social media based on user weblogs to give a preliminary analysis of user behaviour. The weblog dataset was made available recently from the authors' institute anonymously and contained three parameters: Time, Username, and URL visited. Data entries from the logs were utilized to construct a Regular Access Behaviour Pattern, which serves as a knowledge base for determining any unusual activity of the user. The derived features like Total_count, Daily_counts, Is_weekend_ration, Td_mean and Td_max are as shown in Figure 2.

After creating the feature set, applied the K-means algorithm to cluster the users into groups. The t-Distributed Stochastic Neighbor Embedding is utilized to convert the multidimensional feature set to a two-dimensional feature set to facilitate further analysis. The sum of squared distances from the centroids is utilized to determine variations of every user relative to all the other clusters. Here, Figure 3 shows the TSNE Plot of sample records.

The points which were at a greater distance from all the clusters were stated as anomalous as shown in Figure 4.

Figure 2. Feature set with sample records

	User Name	total_count	daily_counts	is_weekend_ratio	td_mean	td_max
0	id1	10	1.0	9.000000	469.444444	1127.0
1	id10	48	4.0	1.086957	156.404255	1427.0
2	id11	17	8.5	0.000000	90.187500	1432.0
3	id12	51	13.5	0.000000	90.320000	1334.0
4	id13	18	1.0	17.000000	140.470588	1263.0
5	id14	59	6.5	4.900000	99.655172	1354.0
6	id15	16	8.0	0.000000	86.666667	1296.0
7	id16	78	13.0	6.090909	112.909091	1342.0
8	id17	8	4.0	0.000000	59.428571	163.0
9	id18	12	4.0	0.000000	256.090909	1426.0
10	id19	15	5.0	0.666667	111.571429	1230.0
11	id2	21	9.0	0.750000	93.500000	874.0

Figure 3. TSNE plot for sample records

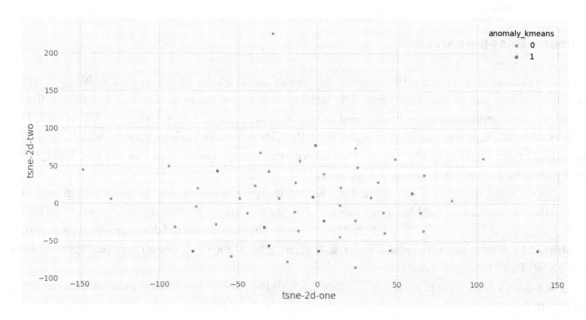

Figure 4. Snapshot of access based behaviour data

	User Name	total_count	daily_counts	is_weekend_ratio	td_mean	td_max	cluster	tsne-2d-one	tsne-2d-two	ssd	anomaly_kmeans
0	id1	10	1.0	9.000000	469.444444	1127.0	0	-30.258148	-56.614037	6.157985	1
13	id21	73	19.5	3.294118	50.597222	1252.0	2	-33.203369	-32.237328	7.101811	1
21	id29	207	18.5	3.404255	20.558252	1271.0	2	-78.805450	-64.059502	6.572077	1
24	id31	17	6.0	0.000000	57.562500	627.0	1	59.428082	13.125393	5.892701	1
31	id38	350	5.0	2.070175	14.959885	1206.0	2	4.353502	-23.526005	5.847614	1
36	id42	79	15.0	5.583333	37.025641	1397.0	2	-2.649386	8.144272	5.624383	1
37	id43	11	11.0	0.000000	7.000000	21.0	1	-62.770298	42.856995	5.725676	1
40	id46	43	5.0	0.000000	38.214286	1110.0	2	-1.092767	76.971939	5.838911	1
43	id49	6	3.0	0.200000	263.600000	1156.0	0	137.717911	-63.114285	8.923941	1
48	id8	6	2.0	1.000000	285.600000	1041.0	0	1.016230	-63.502880	5.877240	1

Results

To achieve the best results, the dataset was tested on three algorithms, SVM, KMeans and Isolation forest. The results obtained were as expected according to the available dataset. As seen in Table 1, KMeans provided maximum accuracy among the three algorithms. Hence, it was used for the Preliminary Behaviour Analysis.

Table 1. Algorithm comparison for weblog analysis

Algorithm	Accuracy	Sensitivity	F1 Score	ROC Score	Specificity
K Means	0.78	0.85	0.48	0.66	0.50
SVM	0.75	0.80	0.33	0.58	0.43
Isolated Forest	0.77	0.78	0.15	0.53	0.50

Context-Based Identification

Evaluation of content brings significant insight into the psyche of the individual. Social media content in the 21st century is widely used to express emotions, thus proving to be a major contributor to determining behaviour change. If the user shows some change in behaviour, then the change can be observed in the content that the user posts on social media. This change in the content is identified by analyzing the sentiment and semantics of content shared by the user on these social media applications over the observed time period of abnormality. Content currently includes tweets posted or reposted, along with the tweet metadata. Twitter's API was used to retrieve the content shared by the user and then passed to the content-based identification system for analysis.

Dataset

A dataset with tweets pertaining to various sentiments was required for the construction of the model. Initially, the top 200 tweets were extracted from the accounts that had committed suicide in the past decade to establish a behaviour pattern for training the model. This was then combined with tweets scraped from Twitter using keywords (for e.g. 'lonely') that indirectly showcase behaviour anomalies in the user. Positive tweets were added into the dataset using Sentiment 140K dataset publicly available from Kaggle with a positive polarity target with the specification: 0 = negative, 2 = neutral, 4 = positive, and for the selection of positive tweets, random sampling is used.

To discretize the tweets collected, the VADER score was used for the detection of sentiments from tweets and segregated into two categories: Negative and Non Negative. The model was then tested against two types of datasets: balanced and imbalanced. The imbalanced dataset contained 100,000 random tweets and 25,000 negative tweets while the balanced dataset contained 25,000 random tweets and 25,000 negative tweets. Dataset was divided such that training: 60%, testing: 20%, and validation: 20%.

Pre-Processing

The tweets made available from the dataset were in their raw form and had to be preprocessed first for effective use. For preprocessing, first all links and images attached with tweets were removed. Using regular expression, hashtags and @mentions were removed. After that, emojis were removed from extracted tweets to keep the data in strict text form. English stop words such as "the", "an", etc, occur frequently in texts but have no semantic importance and were hence removed using Python's stopwords module imported from the Natural Language Toolkit (NLTK) library. Punctuation used in tweets were removed too. It is often the case when tweets may include contractions of words. So the next step involved the expansion of such shortened versions of words. For example "what's" is expanded as "what is". Stemming was then performed which reduces the words to their word stem, base or root form. For example, ran is reduced to run. Finally, tokenizing was carried out to extract individual words through the use of Regular Expressions from Python's RE library.

Tokenizer

Indices were assigned using a tokenizer and infrequent words were filtered out. This was used to produce a map of all distinct words and allocate an index to it. The parameter called num_words indicated that here only considered the top 20000 most frequent words.

Data Analysis

Doing an in-depth analysis of textual data is a complicated task since it is difficult to discern which points are the most important. Data visualization allows communicating this valuable information at a glance and word cloud and frequency charts are preferred visualization techniques to gain insights into the dataset. Figure 5 and Figure 6 shows the frequency chart of the most commonly occurring words in the balanced and imbalanced dataset.

Figure 7 shows the word cloud for the negative tweets present in the dataset. Following that, Figure 8 and Figure 9 shows word clouds of random tweets in the balanced and imbalanced dataset respectively.

Figure 5. Frequency chart for the balanced dataset

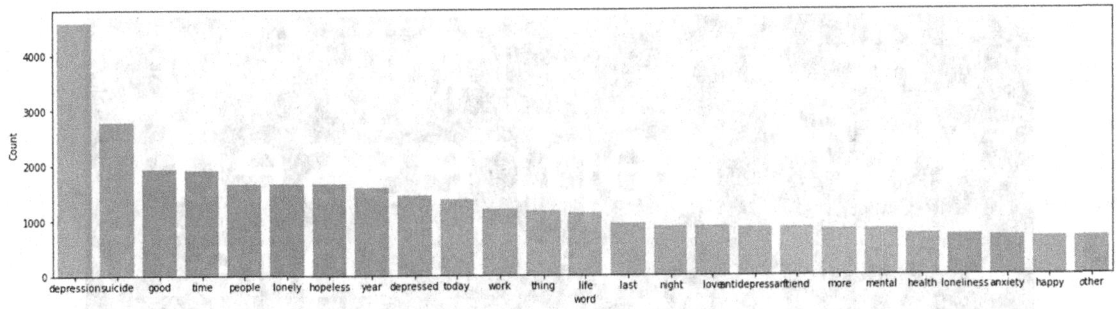

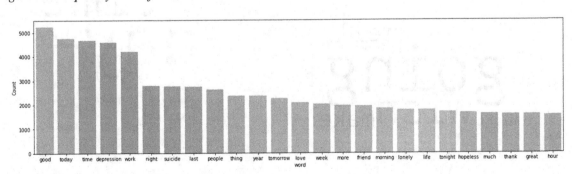

These word clouds can help in gaining insights to accurately analyze one's behaviour or mood. From the positive word cloud, one can know which words are more frequently used to depict positive behaviour. On the other hand, from the negative word cloud, one can know about the words that generally depict a negative behaviour.

VADER Evaluation

VADER score was used for the detection of sentiments from tweets and divided amongst two categories: negative and non-negative. Figure 10 shows the distribution of tweets for the balanced dataset and Figure 11 shows the distribution of tweets for the imbalanced dataset. Sentiment Intensity Analyzer from Vader library in python was used for this discretization.

Embedding Matrix

The embedding matrix was a n x m matrix where n is the number of words and m is the dimension of the embedding. In this case, m=300 and n=20000, for n min between the number of unique words generated by tokenizer and max words in case there are fewer unique words than the max is considered.

Figure 6. Frequency chart for imbalanced dataset

Figure 7. Negative word cloud

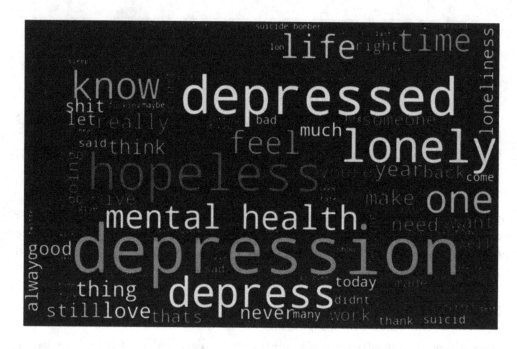

Figure 8. Positive word cloud in the balanced dataset

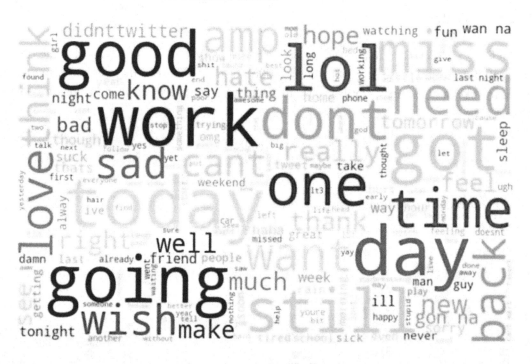

Figure 9. Positive word cloud in the imbalanced dataset

Figure 10. Tweet sentiment distribution for the balanced dataset

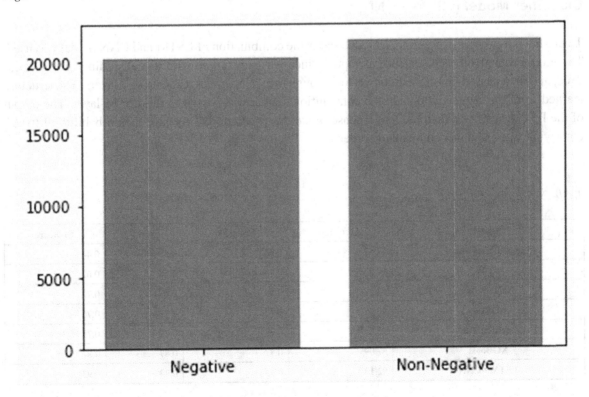

Figure 11. Tweet sentiment distribution for the imbalanced dataset

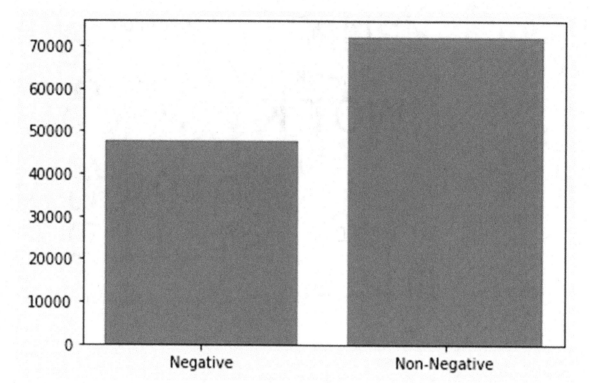

Classifier Model (LSTM + CNN)

To predict if a tweet is depressing, a model that is the combination of LSTM and CNN model was used. The model was given each sentence as input, which was substituted with its embeddings using word-2vec, and then passed this embedding vector through the CNN model made up of 7 layers. The structure learned from the sequential data in the convolutional layer was passed to the LSTM layer. The output of the LSTM layer was then fed into a dense model for prediction. This gave the probability of tweets conveying signs of a mental health disorder.

Table 2. Balanced dataset comparison

Model	Accuracy	Precision	Recall	F1-Score
Logistic Regression	57.52	0.63	0.58	0.44
SVM	67.9	0.78	0.68	0.62
Naive Bayes	67.9	0.84	0.68	0.72
AdaBoost	76.7	0.78	0.77	0.76
Decision Tree	78.8	0.79	0.79	0.79
XGBoost	87.09	0.87	0.87	0.87
LSTM+CNN	92.13	0.93	0.93	0.93

RESULTS

In order to identify the most effective model, the dataset was used on various classifiers and results of which are shown in Table 2 for a balanced dataset and Table 3 for an imbalanced dataset. While accuracy is a good initial measure to use when evaluating a model, a dataset involving mental or physical health will almost certainly be imbalanced, as this one is. In a model that uses imbalanced data, it is likely that the accuracy score will be high but the accuracy score may only reflect the underlying class distribution. So f1_score, precision, and recall were used along with accuracy as the evaluation criteria.

Table 3. Imbalanced dataset comparison

Model	Accuracy	Precision	Recall	F1-Score
Logistic Regression	84.03	0.71	0.84	0.77
SVM	87.44	0.88	0.87	0.84
Naive Bayes	84.53	0.88	0.85	0.86
AdaBoost	88.1	0.88	0.88	0.85
Decision Tree	86.6	0.86	0.87	0.87
XGBoost	93.9	0.94	0.94	0.94
LSTM+CNN	96.54	0.97	0.97	0.96

Figure 12. Model accuracy graph for the balanced dataset

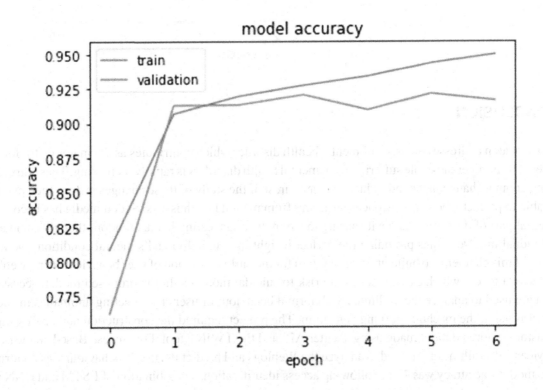

By evaluating the classifiers on combined features it was discovered that the LSTM+CNN model outperforms all the other classifiers with an accuracy of 92.13 and 0.93 f1-score in the balanced dataset as shown in Figure 12 and an accuracy of 96.54 and 0.96 f1-score in the imbalanced dataset as shown in Figure 13.

Figure 13. Model accuracy for the imbalanced dataset

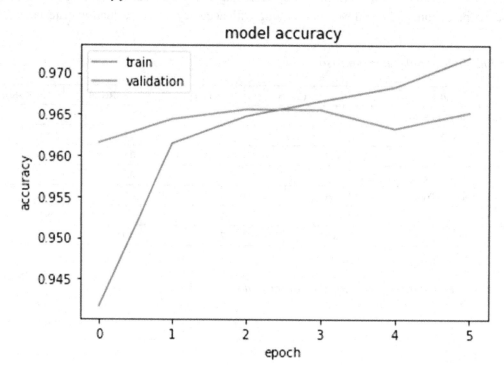

CONCLUSION

This research addresses the issue of mental health disorder which contributes as the major factor for suicides. The number of people suffering from mental health disorders is rapidly increasing. These disorders bring about a change in the individual's behaviour, so if the study of these changes is done then one will be able to predict whether someone is suffering from mental health issues. Social media has become an integral part of daytoday life, be it sharing location, feelings, eating habits, random thoughts, and even individual mindsets, thus providing the perfect insight into an individual's mental condition.The main focus of this chapter is to build an expert system for the early prediction of user behaviour using weblogs and social media which can predict future risk to suicidal thoughts. In the proposed model, access log data are used to analyze the preliminary abnormal behaviour of users by detecting anomalies in access patterns using the machine learning algorithm. The project required the construction and processing of a custom tailored dataset made using Twitter API and the TWINT tool. For Access Based analysis, the K-Means algorithm was utilized to analyze the Weblogs and predict if a user's behaviour was abnormal. The model's accuracy was 78%. Following access identification, a combination of LSTM and CNN was used to analyze the content of user's social media accounts for behaviour analysis, the model had an accuracy of 92.13% for the balanced dataset and 96.54% for the imbalanced dataset.

FUTURE RESEARCH DIRECTIONS

The core focus would be on improving the accuracy of the model and it is aimed to incorporate a network analysis based model in combination with the behavioural analysis model to gain more knowledge regarding the users and make data-oriented decisions. As for real-world based applications, incorporation of the model in universities and schools can help gain behaviour analysis to better provide an efficient and streamlined health service.

REFERENCES

Agresti, A. (2014). *An Introduction to Categorical Data Analysis*. Wiley.

Armstrong, W. (2015). *Using Topic Models to Investigate Depression on Social Media*. University of Maryland.

Blei, D. M., Ng, A. Y., & Jordan, M. I. (2003, March). Latent Dirichlet allocation. *Journal of Machine Learning Research*, *3*, 993–1022.

Cheng, L., Silva, Y. N., & Liu, D. H. (2020). *Session based Cyberbullying Detection: Problems and Challenges*. Arizona State University. *IEEE Internet Computing*.

Dao, B., Nguyen, T., Venkatesh, S., & Phung, D. (2017). Latent sentiment topic modelling and nonparametric discovery of online mental health related communities. *International Journal of Data Science and Analytics*, *4*(3), 209–231. doi:10.100741060-017-0073-y

Freund, Y., Schapire, R., & Abe, N. (1999). A short introduction to boosting. *Jinkō Chinō Gakkaishi*, *14*, 771–780.

Gortmaker, S. L. (1994). Theory and methods–applied logistic regression. *Contemporary Sociology*, *23*(1), 159.

Hasan, M., Rundensteiner, E., & Agu, E. (2014). EMOTEX: Detecting Emotions in Twitter Messages *ASE Bigdata/Socialcom/Cybersecurity Conference*. Stanford University.

India Today. (n.d.). *19-year-old IIT Madras student, depressed over low marks, commits suicide.* https://www.indiatoday.in/india/story/19yearoldiitmadrasstudentdepressedoverlowmarkscommitssuicide161751420191110

Koltcov, S., Koltsova, O., & Nikolenko, S. (2014). Latent Dirichlet Allocation: Stability and Applications to Studies of UserGenerated Content. In *Proceedings of the 2014 ACM Conference on Web Science*, (pp. 161–165). doi:10.1145/2615569.2615680

Maupomés, D., & Meurs, M. (2018, September). Using topic extraction on social media content for the early detection of depression. In *Proceedings of CLEF (Working Notes),* (vol. 2125). Available: https://CEURWS.org

Mental Health and Substance Use: Suicide data. (n.d.). Available: https://www.who.int/teams/mental-healthandsubstanceuse/suicidedata

Mishra, S., Agarwal, S., Guo, J., Phelps, K., Picco, J., & Diesner, J. (2014). Enthusiasm and Support: Alternative Sentiment Classification for Social Movements on Social Media. In *Proceedings of the 2014 ACM conference on Web science* (pp. 261–262). ACM.

Noble, W. S. (2006). What is a support vector machine? *Nature Biotechnology*, *24*(12), 1565.

Pennebaker, J. W., Booth, R. J., Boyd, R. L., & Francis, M. E. (2015). *Linguistic Inquiry and Word Count: LIWC2015*. Pennebaker Conglomerates. Available www.LIWC.net

Ramchoun, H., Idrissi, M. A. J., Ghanou, Y., & Ettaouil, M. (2016). Multilayer perceptron: Architecture optimization and training. *International Journal of Interactive Multimedia and Artificial Intelligence*, *4*(1), 26–30. doi:10.9781/ijimai.2016.415

Sasahara, K. (2014). Quantifying Collective Mood by Emoticon Networks. In *WebSci '14: Proceedings of the 2014 ACM conference on Web science*, (pp. 253–254). 10.1145/2615569.2615658

Suicide: Statistics, Warning Signs and Prevention. (n.d.). Available: https://www.livescience.com/44615suicidehelp.html

Tadesse, M. M., Lin, H., Xu, B., & Yang, L. (2019). Detection of Depression Related Posts in Reddit Social Media Forum. In *IEEE Access* (vol. 7, pp. 44883-44893). doi: 10.1109/ACCESS.2019.2909180

Wang, S., Ding, Y., Zhao, W., Huang, Y., Perkins, R., Zou, W., & Chen, J. J. (2016). Text mining for identifying topics in the literature about adolescent substance use and depression. *BMC Public Health*, *16*, 279.

Xu, B., Ye, Y., & Nie, L. (2012, June). An improved random forest classifier for image classification. In *Proceedings of IEEE International Conference Information Automation* (pp. 795–800). 10.1109/ICInfA.2012.6246927

Chapter 11
Fake News and Imbalanced Data Perspective

Isha Y. Agarwal
Sardar Vallabhbhai National Institute of Technology, Surat, India

Dipti P. Rana
iD https://orcid.org/0000-0002-5058-1355
Sardar Vallabhbhai National Institute of Technology, Surat, India

ABSTRACT

Fake news has grabbed attention lately. In this chapter, the issue is tackled from the point of view of collection of quality data (i.e., instances of fake and real news articles on a balanced distribution of subjects). It is predicted that in the near future, fake news will supersede true news. In the media ecosystem this will create a natural imbalance of data. Due to the unbounded scale and imbalance existence of data, detection of fake news is challenging. The class imbalance problem in fake news is yet to be explored. The problem of imbalance exists as fake news instances increase in some cases more than real news. The goal of this chapter is to demonstrate the effect of class imbalance of real and fake news instances on detection using classification models. This work aims to assist researchers to better resolve the problem by illustrating the precise existence of the relationship between the imbalance and the resulting impact on the output of the classifier. In particular, the authors determine that data imbalance and accuracy are inversely proportional to each other.

INTRODUCTION

"Fake news" has gained a significant research attention worldwide since 2017 (Allcott & Gentzkow, 2017). Although fake news is in the public realization, it is important to note that digitally generated text and content can reach far then expected more than the true news. News or media articles online are less authenticated than that of original news media sources such as magazines or newspapers (Xiao, 2018; Zhang et al., 2019). Massive data is getting produced, either manually or by AI, to have a political or financial gains (Vosoughi et al., 2018; Berinsky, 2015). Fake news is those news stories that claim to

DOI: 10.4018/978-1-7998-7371-6.ch011

be accurate, but contain factual misrepresentations with the intention of arousing emotions, attracting viewership, or deceiving (Mihaylov et al., 2018).

By 2022, more fake information than real information would be processed by most people in developed nations also (Gartner, 2018). This will create imbalance in data in online media ecosystem making people exposed to more of Fake News then Real News.

In recent years, there has been significant contribution in the fake news detection area. Major contributions in this field focus on the detection methodology i.e. feature engineering, model construction and so on. However, one area is yet to be explored in the perspective of fake news i.e. nature of the data at disposal for classification. A severe class disparity among these groups causes one of the major problems faced by current machine learning models used for fake news detection. Therefore, most models struggle to distinguish instances that fall into minority groups correctly. The detection of fake news is difficult because of the infinite magnitude and imbalance nature of news data information. The class imbalance problem in data mining is the biggest problem. The problem of imbalance exists where one of the two groups has more samples than other classes. The algorithm mostly focuses more on classifying major samples while ignoring minority samples or misclassifying them. Minority samples are those that occur occasionally, but are very important. There are various ways to deal with imbalance. In this paper we present evaluation of data oriented methods for imbalance handling i.e. over sampling and under sampling. The goal is to recognize the shortcomings of current approaches to class imbalance; more precisely, the techniques of machine learning.

Many contributions have been dedicated to the issue of classification of imbalance data. In an extensive bulk of literature (Zhi-Hua Zhou & Xu-Ying Liu, 2006; Kaur & Gosain, 2018; Wasikowski & Chen, 2010), many solutions have been proposed that are based on machine learning and data mining algorithms. Class imbalance, however, has remained an unresolved problem (Richhariya & K Singh, 2014; Shuo Wang & Xin Yao, 2012).

In this research, comparative analysis of performance of classifier for imbalance data using is made. Focus is more specifically on data oriented methods with various machine learning algorithms. A research on state-of-the-art technologies currently used in applications was conducted to resolve the issue of imbalance classification. The area for imbalance data chosen here for experimentation is Fake News. Contribution of the work in this book chapter are highlighted in the next section.

Contribution

In this research, comparative analysis of approaches to deal with data imbalance is presented. Precisely the data oriented approaches. The list of unique contributions made by this research work is given below:

- Study the impact of data imbalance on Fake News
- Analysis of existing datasets for imbalance
- Comparative analysis of various techniques of dealing with imbalance
- Analysis and validation of oversampling approach for fake news

In the following background section, summary of research literature related to publicly available datasets for fake news research and methodologies existing for imbalanced classification is reviewed. The proceeding section has detailed description of proposed framework. The next section explains in depth the experimental study including experimental design, the findings and the discussion of solutions' limitations. Lastly, conclusion and future work are listed.

BACKGROUND

This section is divided into three parts: i) Data imbalance issue ii) Data imbalance in existing datasets for fake news detection task and iii) Methodologies existing for imbalanced data classification.

1.   Data Imbalance Issue

Large amounts of data are created with distorted distribution in many real-time applications. A series of results was particularly biased whether the sample of a class was larger than other samples (Wang et al., 2012). In several applications with a decreased rate of positive instances in a class, including chronic disease diagnosis data (Rao, 2006), fraud identification (Wei, 2013), data privacy (Cieslak, 2006) and image recognition, skewed data inevitably exist. The class with more instances is considered a primary class of imbalances whereas the class with comparatively fewer samples or observations or instances is defined a minor class (Chawla, 2004). Applications such as surgical diagnostics are very important than routine therapy for rare yet important diseases. Other fields, such as intrusion detection, banking fraud detection (Galar, 2011), risk management and technological equivalent failure prediction, have been found in similar circumstances. Many of the classifiers are thus prejudicial to the main classes and thus indicate very low ratings in smaller classes. Classifier can also forecast the whole thing as main class and disregard the minor class. Diverse methods were proposed to resolve the class imbalance problems (Seiffert, 2008). These are divided into three fundamental categories: pre-processing of data, the algorithms strategy, and the method of subset selection. In data-preprocessing technique sampling is applied on data in which either new samples are added or existing samples are removed. Second method for solving class imbalance problem is crafting or altering existing classification algorithms. Algorithms cover cost-sensitive methods and techniques focused on recognition, kernel-based learning, such as SVM and a radial base function. It is counterproductive to apply algorithms alone since the data size and the class imbalance ratio are high and a new approach is then used, i.e. combining the sampling procedure with the algorithm. The feature selection techniques selects a subset of 'm' features that are best fit to classifier for attaining best performance, where 'm' is user-defined input. For high-dimensional data sets, it uses filters that score each feature independently based on a rule. Feature selection is a key step for many machine learning algorithms, especially when the data is high-dimensional. Sampling of data is implemented in the data-preprocessing, in which new or current samples are either inserted or taken away. When learning from imbalanced data, it is necessary to investigate the demonstration of minority and majority groups. Krawczyk (2016) suggested that, because of the disproportion of class, good outcomes will be accomplished where all classes are well presented and are not overlapping. The effects from class imbalance were investigated by developing artificial data sets with a wide range of scope, scale and imbalance combinations (Japkowicz, 2000). Here, study of imbalance on one such area of Fake News is explored.

2.   Existing datasets for fake news detection task

Often data quality has restricted the production of new fake news detection solutions. An extensive list of data sets relevant to classification of fake news to testify the imbalance nature of the data on this subject is presented here. This further encourages research for imbalance in this domain. The collection of data could vary significantly due to various research goals and objectives. Some datasets, for instance, only focus on political statements, others consist of news/articles on open domains. Data sets could also differ depending on the labels, how the labels are obtained, and the types of texts. The survey shown below in Table 1 bears a testimony that in case of a political issue like US presidential elections or a medical pandemic COVID-19, Fake News eruption creates imbalance in news ecosystem and fake news then surpasses the existence of the true news.

Table 1.Existing datasets for fake news detection

Dataset	Records	Nature of data
LIAR (Wang, 2017)	12,800	Almost imbalanced
Fake Vs. Satire (Golbeck, 2018)	486	58% Fake
NewsTrustData (Mukherjee, 2015)	82,000	Almost imbalanced
Weibo (Ma, 2016)	4,664	Almost imbalanced
GossipCop (Kochkina, 2018)	3,570	81% Fake
FacebookHoax (Tacchini, 2017)	15,500	60% Fake
BuzzfeedNews (Horne, 2019)	2,282	62% Fake
Emergent (Ferreira, 2016)	2,145	26% Real, 34% Fake, 40% Unverified
KaggleFN (Golbeck, 2018)	13,000	100% Fake

Thus, there is an implicit data imbalance where there is a situation of spread of Fake News. Thus, techniques to detect fake news for this imbalanced data is required. The following subsection enlists the techniques used for the data imbalance issue and classification.

3.   Imbalance Data Classification

In imbalance classification issues, the handling of data imbalance is described as having abundance or majority of one-class observations that make it difficult for the classifier to detect the category of the marginal class or minority samples. Figure 1 below is the taxonomy of the strategies discussed in the literature. Below are also discussed the benefits and weaknesses of each of the techniques.

The strength and limitations of each of the techniques is presented in the Table 2 below.

Researchers have used methods listed in this taxonomy presented for various cases. The following is the summary of work carried out in this area using the aforementioned approaches.

The class imbalance problem has been a well-liked topic amongst the researchers. As a result some solutions were presented. Krawczyk (2016) proposed different ways to go about with the skewed class distribution. The easiest way is to deal with the problem on the data-level itself. Before applying any of the classification algorithms, under-sampling or over-sampling of data is done to balance the classes.

Figure 1. Taxonomy of ways to handle data imbalance

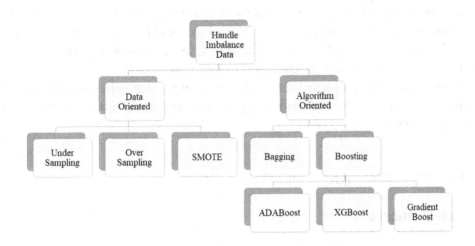

Alternatively, algorithm-level techniques, such as cost-sensitive models, may be used to give the class of minorities or classifying methods higher costs when only the class of minorities is used for training.

Kamaruddin and Ravi suggested a hybrid framework for particle swarm and automotive neural networks (PSOAANN) (2016). Experimental analysis of the proposed work was carried out on Spark computational framework. An approach was presented in Wei (2013) which included three algorithms and demonstrated its efficiency in huge imbalanced data. The approach included contrast pattern mining, decision forest and artificial neural networks. The results of these algorithms were thencombined. Health-insurance deceit dataset was used by Padmaja (2004) to prove the efficiency of their approach. These algorithms were applied on the data that was obtained after over-sampling with replacement.

Table 2. Analysis of techniques to handle data imbalance

	Technique	Strength	Limitations
Data Oriented Techniques	Under Sampling	Reduce the time and space complexity in large humongous training dataset	Dismiss useful information for building rule classifiers which might be relevant. Sample selected by random under-sampling might well be biased. Not precise exemplification of the population
	Over Sampling	No loss of data samples or information Performs better than under sampling	Increases probability of overfitting since it replicates the minority class events
	S.M.O.T.E.	Synthetic data sample observations are added between the chosen point and its nearest neighbors	Applicable for data with numeric features
Algorithm Oriented Techniques	Bagging	Produces numerous different bootstrap training samples with replacement	Time complexity increases
	76Boosting	Combines poor classifiers to create an accurate learner that can make accurate predictions	Does not allow replacement in the samples

Padmaja (2007) concentrated on the problem of fraud detection as a class imbalance. By using K Reverse nearest neighbor, they eliminated the extreme outlines from the minority class. Following that, the minority sample class (SMOTE) and the majority class were merged. They also carried out several experiments focused on various classifiers, such as Naive Bayes and K-Nearest Neighbor (KNN). Chan (1999) suggested a way of dealing with different problems in the identification of fraud. They proposed that separate learned detectors of fraud be combined under a cost model.

In this work, experimentation is carried out on LIAR dataset and data oriented techniques have been focused. The reason for selection of data oriented approach is that for fake news classification, different algorithms are applicable for various cases.

FAKE NEWS WITH IMBALANCE PERSPECTIVE

Data Oriented Methods

A bigger selection of information may provide more balanced view of the groups. Additional examples of minor class samples can be useful for re-sampling data collection. The following performance metrics presents the exactness of your model rather than the conventional classification exactness (Sotto, 2016).

One solution is to test the training set for a balanced class distribution to manage large-scale imbalances. Cost-sensitive and constructive learning techniques are other approaches. Since the exactness of the classification algorithms on imbalanced data sets can be decreased for some reason. The sampling methods are designed to alter imbalanced data through a certain process in balanced distribution. The adjustment happens by changing the scale and the balance of the initial data collection. For the treatment of imbalance data set classification, over-sampling, synthetic data generation, and cost-sensitive learning processes (Huang, 2001; Dubey, 2014).

- **Under Sampling Approach**

Under sampling is a technique to balance the imbalanced nature of the dataset. It balances the data by deleting the majority class samples. This causes loss of information.

The limitation of the study is that data is being discarded from the dominant class and this condition is compounded by the growing degree of the class disparity. Random forest models can be used without data loss during sampling. Many samples are taken from the training data, and for each data set a separate non pruned tree is built (Uniyal, 2014). This form is another function in which a subgroup of predictors is randomly sampled at each split to promote the diversity of the resulting tree. When a new sample is predicted, every tree in the forest produces a prediction which will aggregate the results to generate one prediction for each instance. Bootstrap sampling is used by random forests. If 'n' training set samples occur, the resulting sample selects n replacement samples (Blagus, 2013).

- **Over Sampling Approach**

Over sampling is simple technique to balance the imbalanced nature of the dataset. It balances the data by duplicating the minority class samples. This does not cause any loss of information. The dataset is prone to overfitting as the same information is replicated.

The technique works with this form of statistical learning. Minority class support vectors can less contribute to the final hypothesis. The ideal hyper-plane is also oriented towards the majority class. Techniques for managing imbalances Classification algorithms, which battle with precision to make existing classifiers more probable to the majority class due to their unequal distribution in dependent variable. The algorithms are exact, such that the overall errors made by the minority class are reduced.

Evaluation Metrics

Accuracy is generally the most used output measurement parameter for classification. In this context, however, accuracy is not appropriate, as the classification of data with imbalance is considered. The precise results of fake news detection will alter the calculation of accuracy alone. Precision and Recall are also necessary for the assessment of results and the correctly categorized findings by the minority class. Precision is the amount of exactness of the classifiers and recall is a measure of classifiers completeness. (Hapfelmeier, 2013).

Dataset

LIAR is a novel public dataset for the analysis of fake news. It is compiled from a fact-check website PolitiFact.com. 12.8 K labeled short statements that include research reports and links to each case's source documents. The attributes of LIAR dataset are listed in table 3 below.

Table 3. Attributes of LIAR dataset

Column	Description
id	JSON id of statement
date	Date of the news
speaker	Name of author/editor
source	URL of the news content
label	truth values of statement
title	title of politifact article
statement	Text content
speaker	Source of statement

Features

Learning from multi-dimensional and big data is one of the difficulties in categorizing text. In papers, there are many concepts, works and approaches that contribute to a high computational load on the learning process. In addition, the accuracy and efficiency of the classifiers can be affected by significance and redundancy. It is also better to reduce the feature size to reduce the text and prevent wide space dimensions of the feature. In this study we have examined two separate selection methods of functions, namely Term Frequency (TF) and Inverted Text Frequency (TF-IDF). Term Frequency (TF) Term Frequency is an approach using terms in documents to demonstrate the similarity between documents. For computation of Term Frequency (TF), the same length vector, which includes the words counts, is expressed in each text. The next step is to normalize each vector in such a way that the total of its items adds to it. If a text is present in a specific document, it will be characterized as one, and if it is not in the document, it will be set at zero. Each word count will be translated into the likelihood of a similar word in the documents. Each document is therefore defined by word groups. TF-IDF is a metric of weights that also functions in natural language processing and information retrieval (TF - IDF) is a word frequency inverted text frequency. It is a quantitative calculation that determines the value of a word for a text. With the amount of time a word occurs in the text, the frequency of the word in the corpus reduces this term value. One of the key features of IDF is that it decreases the occurrences and raises the uncommon frequency. The influence of these terms is minimized by using IDF.

Proposed Approach

In all current research domains, class imbalance is very prevalent. This problem fundamentally refers to the kurtosis of the data distribution underlying the algorithms of machine learning. To tackle the emerging issues rising from class imbalance this study presents imbalance situations, imbalanced data set problems with characteristics and the methodologies to deal with that type of data. This paper focuses on one such real life peril of Fake News. In some situation the news ecosystem is imbalanced and fake news supersedes the real news.

Figure 2. Architecture of workflow

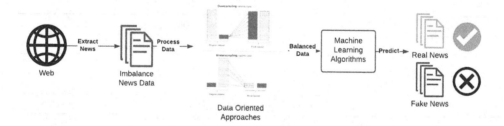

Figure 2 is pictorial representation of the workflow of the experimental analysis carried out in this work. The news from web on a particular situation form a dataset. This is imbalanced as in the news ecosystem instances of Fake News supersede that of true news. Evaluation of machine learning classifiers is done on this dataset to and observation is recorded for the comparative analysis. The data oriented approaches are then experimented on this dataset. The data instance obtained by over-sampling and under-sampling is used for experimental analysis. Performance of classifier for detection of fake news is recorded for the oversampled and under sampled data instance. The classifiers SVM, KNN, Decision trees, Random Forest and Logistic Regression are implemented for performing comparative analysis. The evaluation parameters used are precision, recall and accuracy.

RESULT ANALYSIS

Experimental Specification

The evaluation of the system was done on 64 bit Windows 10 operating system. Processor used 2.40 GHz is Intel Core (i5) with the memory of 4 GB. Coding Language is Python (version 3.5.0).

Results

The evaluation of the proposed model on LIAR dataset was performed using accuracy, precision, recall and specificity measures. For profound analysis of the proposed model, the empirical result has been tested on original dataset as well as over and under-sampled instances. Initial observation comprises of performance of baseline model i.e. performance of classifiers with TF-IDF vectors on imbalance dataset. This was followed by performance evaluation of model given under and over sampled instances of data. There is marginal improvement in performance of classifiers. The impact of sampling was then examined. Figures below show the instances of both the class samples for imbalances data, under and over sampled instances. For imbalanced data, the number of instances of Real news are 2050 and Fake 13002. The percentage of data which comprise of real news is 15.76. This is shown below in figure 3(a). The undersampling and oversampling instances are as shown in figure 3(b) and 3(c) respectively.

*Tota*l samples of Fake and Real after undersampling: i) Fake: 2050 and ii) Real: 2050.

Figure 3.Imbalanced data

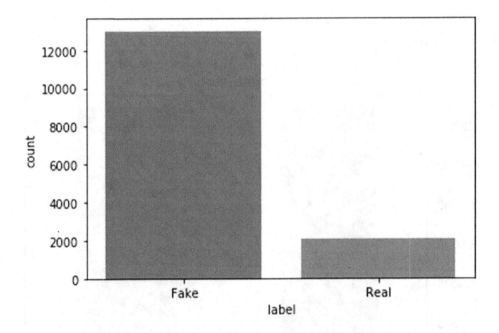

Figure 4. Undersampling

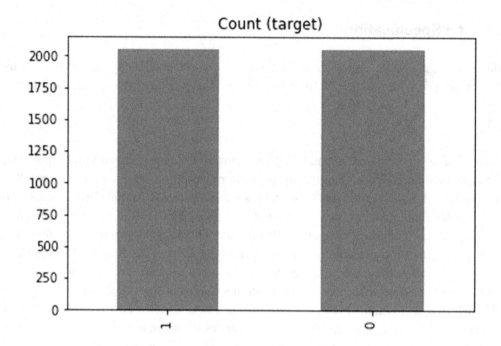

Total samples of Fake and Real after oversampling: i) Fake: 13002 and ii) Real: 13002.

Figure 5. Oversampling

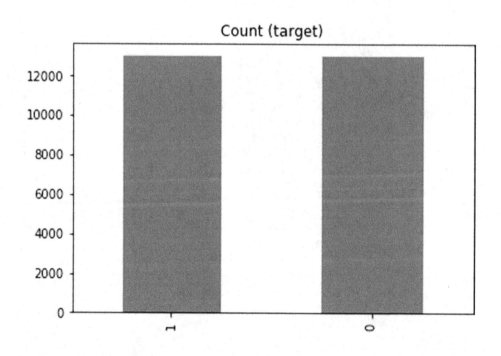

Table 4.Classifiers accuracy measure for all the approaches

Classifiers	Imbalance Dataset	Under Sampling	Over Sampling
Support Vector Machine (SVM)	0.56	0.57	0.70
K-Nearest neighbor	0.52	0.54	0.70
Decision Tree	0.50	0.52	0.87
Random Forest	0.51	0.62	0.82
Logistic Regression	0.53	0.55	0.79

Figure 6. Accuracy Plot

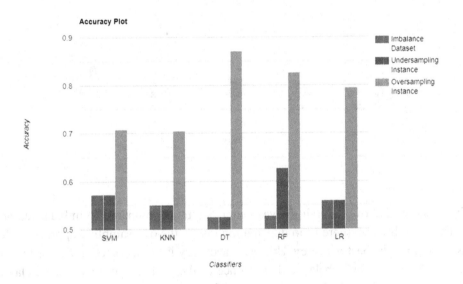

This series of evaluations lead to an inference that there is correlation between sampling and the performance of classifier. Experimentation is carried out on all the above instances of the dataset. Table 4 gives the information about the accuracy evaluation measure of classification of Fake News. This is shown in figure 4.

Table 5.Classifier performance of Precision

Classifiers	Imbalance Dataset	Under Sampling	Over Sampling
Support Vector Machine (SVM)	0.54	0.58	0.68
K-Nearest neighbor	0.52	0.53	0.66
Decision Tree	0.51	0.53	0.80
Random Forest	0.60	0.64	0.86
Logistic Regression	0.53	0.57	0.77

Figure 7. Precision plot

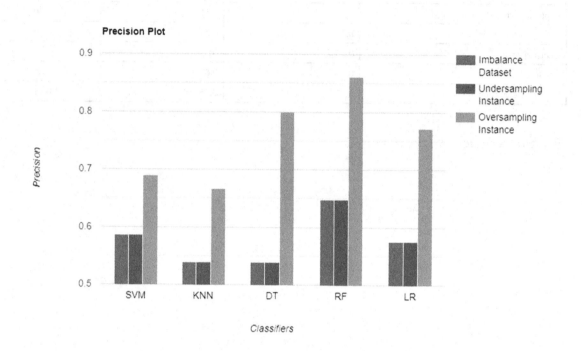

The above shows that oversampling gives better output as compared to imbalanced and the under sampling. This is so because there is no information loss in the oversampling approach. Moreover, tree based classifiers give the best accuracy. However, accuracy is not a correct measure for the evaluation of classifier performance for imbalance data. Hence analysis of the performance of classifier is done with precision as shown in table 5 below. The plot of precision is figure 5.

The performance measure recall of classifier is listed in table 6. Recall plot is shown in figure 6.

Table 6. Classifier performance of recall

Classifers	Imbalance Dataset	Under Sampling	Over Sampling
Support Vector Machine (SVM)	0.57	0.58	0.75
K-Nearest neighbor	0.54	0.56	0.82
Decision Tree	0.54	0.57	0.98
Random Forest	0.67	0.69	0.81
Logistic Regression	0.55	0.59	0.83

From the results obtained, the following inferences can be drawn.

1. Accuracy measure is not efficient to evaluate the performance of classifier for imbalance data.
2. In the particular scenario of Fake News detection, oversampling with random forest classifier gives the best output.

Figure 8. Recall plot

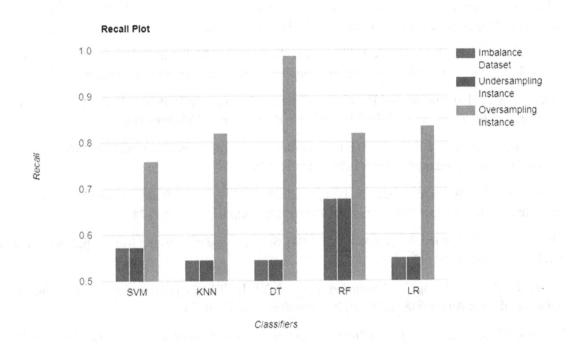

CONCLUSION AND FUTURE RESEARCH DIRECTIONS

This research work explained how in real life scenarios imbalanced datasets can be handled in this expanding digital era by data oriented imbalance dealing and classification techniques. Imbalance is everywhere in real life scenarios. Many important real-world fields of application such as banking, health, network, news and weather have imbalanced data. There are real time issues linked with each of these domain areas such as fraud credit card transaction detection, unusual disease prediction, network intrusion detection, fake news detection and weather forecasting. For combatting these real-time issues, automated approaches are being devised. These approaches are based on the heuristic of balanced data and provide the biased result towards the majority data class, which is not accepted. One such area is explored here of data imbalance in Fake News. Data oriented sampling approaches: Under sampling and oversampling are explored. Oversampling yields better performance than undersampling, as there is loss of data and thus information in undersampling. Experimental analysis justifies that Random Forest classifier gives comparatively best classification accuracy with reduced execution time as compared with the performance of SVM, Naive Bays, Decision Trees, logistic regression and KNN as it is an ensemble based classifier. This work can be further this can be applied for real-world scenarios like bot-detection, fraud credit card transaction detection, anomaly detection, rare disease prediction, etc. As the nature of data is random and not balanced, it has to deal with exponential and big data. Thus this research work can be also implied to address imbalance in Big data applications through incremental parallel approaches.

REFERENCES

Allcott, H., & Gentzkow, M. (2017). Social Media and Fake News in the 2016 Election. *The Journal of Economic Perspectives, 31*(2), 211–236. doi:10.1257/jep.31.2.211

An, A., Cercone, N., & Huang, X. (2001, June). A case study for learning from imbalanced data sets. In *Conference of the Canadian Society for Computational Studies of Intelligence* (pp. 1–15). Springer.

Berinsky, A. (2015). Rumors and Health Care Reform: Experiments in Political Misinformation. *British Journal of Political Science, 47*(2), 241–262. doi:10.10170007123415000186

Blagus, R., & Lusa, L. (2013). SMOTE for high-dimensional class-imbalanced data. *BMC Bioinformatics, 14*, 106. https://doi.org/10.1186/1471-2105-14-106

Chan, P. K., Fan, W., Prodromidis, A. L., & Stolfo, S. J. (1999). Distributed data mining in credit card fraud detection. *IEEE Intelligent Systems & their Applications, 14*(6), 67–74.

Chawla, N. V., Japkowicz, N., & Kotcz, A. (2004). Special issue on learning from imbalanced data sets. *SIGKDD Explorations, 6*(1), 1–6.

Dubey, R., Zhou, J., Wang, Y., Thompson, P. M., & Ye, J. (2014). Analysis of sampling techniques for imbalanced data: An n= 648 ADNI study. *NeuroImage, 87*, 220–241.

Ferreira, W., & Vlachos, A. (2016, June). Emergent: a novel data-set for stance classification. In *Proceedings of the 2016 conference of the North American chapter of the association for computational linguistics: Human language technologies* (pp. 1163-1168). Academic Press.

Galar, M., Fernandez, A., Barrenechea, E., Bustince, H., & Herrera, F. (2011). A review on ensembles for the class imbalance problem: Bagging-, boosting-, and hybrid-based approaches. *IEEE Transactions on Systems, Man and Cybernetics. Part C, Applications and Reviews, 42*(4), 463–484.

Golbeck, J., Mauriello, M., Auxier, B., Bhanushali, K. H., Bonk, C., & Bouzaghrane, M. A. G. (2018, May). Fake news vs satire: A dataset and analysis. In *Proceedings of the 10th ACM Conference on Web Science* (pp. 17-21). Academic Press.

Hapfelmeier, A., & Ulm, K. (2013). A new variable selection approach using random forests. *Computational Statistics & Data Analysis, 60*, 50–69.

Horne, B. D., & Adali, S. (2019, July). Nela-gt-2018: A large multi-labelled news dataset for the study of misinformation in news articles. In *Proceedings of the International AAAI Conference on Web and Social Media* (*Vol. 13*, pp. 630-638). Academic Press.

Japkowicz, N. (2000, June). The class imbalance problem: Significance and strategies. In *Proc. of the Int'l Conf. on Artificial Intelligence* (*Vol. 56*). Academic Press.

Kaur, P., & Gosain, A. (2018). Issues and challenges of class imbalance problem in classification. *International Journal of Information Technology*. doi:10.100741870-018-0251-8

Kochkina, E., Liakata, M., & Zubiaga, A. (2018). *All-in-one: Multi-task learning for rumour verification*. arXiv preprint arXiv:1806.03713.

Krawczyk. (2016). Learning from imbalanced data: Open challenges and future directions. *Prog. Artif. Intell*.

Krawczyk, B. (2016). Learning from imbalanced data: Open challenges and future directions. *Progress in Artificial Intelligence*, *5*(4), 221–232.

Liar, Liar, Pants on Fire? Psychophysiological Deception Detection Unraveled. (2017). *Psychophysiology*, *54*, S12-S13. doi:10.1111/psyp.12928

Ma, J., Gao, W., Mitra, P., Kwon, S., Jansen, B. J., Wong, K. F., & Cha, M. (2016). *Detecting rumors from microblogs with recurrent neural networks*. Academic Press.

Mihaylov, T., Mihaylova, T., Nakov, P., Màrquez, L., Georgiev, G., & Koychev, I. (2018). The dark side of news community forums: Opinion manipulation trolls. *Internet Research*, *28*(5), 1292–1312. doi:10.1108/intr-03-2017-0118

Mukherjee, S., & Weikum, G. (2015, October). Leveraging joint interactions for credibility analysis in news communities. In *Proceedings of the 24th ACM International on Conference on Information and Knowledge Management* (pp. 353-362). ACM.

Padmaja, T. M., Dhulipalla, N., Bapi, R. S., & Krishna, P. R. (2007, December). Unbalanced data classification using extreme outlier elimination and sampling techniques for fraud detection. In *15th International Conference on Advanced Computing and Communications (ADCOM 2007)* (pp. 511-516). IEEE.

Phua, C., Alahakoon, D., & Lee, V. (2004). Minority report in fraud detection: Classification of skewed data. *SIGKDD Explorations*, *6*(1), 50–59.

Rao, R. B., Krishnan, S., & Niculescu, R. S. (2006). Data mining for improved cardiac care. *SIGKDD Explorations*, *8*(1), 3–10.

Richhariya, P., & Singh, K, P. (2014). Evaluating and Emerging Payment Card Fraud Challenges and Resolution. *International Journal of Computers and Applications*, *107*(14), 5–10. doi:10.5120/18817-0215

Seiffert, C., Khoshgoftaar, T. M., Van Hulse, J., & Napolitano, A. (2008, December). A comparative study of data sampling and cost sensitive learning. In *2008 IEEE International Conference on Data Mining Workshops* (pp. 46-52). IEEE.

Silverman, C., & Strapagiel, L. (2016). Hyperpartisan Facebook pages are publishing false and misleading information at an alarming rate. Buzzfeed News 20.

Sotto, L. F., Coelho, R. C., & de Melo, V. V. (2016, July). Classification of cardiac arrhythmia by random forests with features constructed by kaizen programming with linear genetic programming. In *Proceedings of the Genetic and Evolutionary Computation Conference 2016* (pp. 813-820). Academic Press.

Tacchini, E., Ballarin, G., Della Vedova, M. L., Moret, S., & de Alfaro, L. (2017). *Some like it hoax: Automated fake news detection in social networks.* arXiv preprint arXiv:1704.07506.

Uniyal, N., Eskandari, H., Abolmaesumi, P., Sojoudi, S., Gordon, P., & Warren, L. M. (2014). Ultrasound RF time series for classification of breast lesions. *IEEE Transactions on Medical Imaging, 34*(2), 652–661.

Vosoughi, S., Roy, D., & Aral, S. (2018). The spread of true and false news online. *Science, 359*(6380), 1146–1151. doi:10.1126cience.aap9559

Wang, S., & Yao, X. (2012). Multiclass Imbalance Problems: Analysis and Potential Solutions. *IEEE Transactions on Systems, Man, and Cybernetics. Part B, Cybernetics, 42*(4), 1119–1130. doi:10.1109/tsmcb.2012.2187280

Wang, S., & Yao, X. (2012). Multiclass imbalance problems: Analysis and potential solutions. *IEEE Transactions on Systems, Man, and Cybernetics. Part B, Cybernetics, 42*(4), 1119–1130.

Wang, W. Y. (2017). *"Liar, liar pants on fire": A new benchmark dataset for fake news detection.* arXiv preprint arXiv:1705.00648.

Wasikowski, M., & Chen, X. (2010). Combating the Small Sample Class Imbalance Problem Using Feature Selection. *IEEE Transactions on Knowledge and Data Engineering, 22*(10), 1388–1400. doi:10.1109/tkde.2009.187

Wei, W., Li, J., Cao, L., Ou, Y., & Chen, J. (2013). Effective detection of sophisticated online banking fraud on extremely imbalanced data. *World Wide Web (Bussum), 16*(4), 449–475.

Xiao, H. (2018). *Multi-sourced information trustworthiness analysis: Applications and theory.* Retrieved from https://search.proquest.com/openview/f40c14b131693f2a1ce8cb198041ed99/1?pq-origsite=gscholar&cbl=18750&diss=y

Zhang, Q., Lipani, A., Liang, S., & Yilmaz, E. (2019). Reply-Aided Detection of Misinformation via Bayesian Deep Learning. In *The Web Conference 2019.* ACM Press.

Zhou, Z.-H., & Liu, X.-Y. (2006). Training cost-sensitive neural networks with methods addressing the class imbalance problem. *IEEE Transactions on Knowledge and Data Engineering, 18*(1), 63–77. doi:10.1109/tkde.2006.17

Chapter 12
Impact of Balancing Techniques for Imbalanced Class Distribution on Twitter Data for Emotion Analysis:
A Case Study

Shivani Vasantbhai Vora

CGPIT, Uka Tarsadia University, Bardoli, India

Rupa G. Mehta

Sardar Vallabhbhai National Institute of Technology, Surat, India

Shreyas Kishorkumar Patel

Sardar Vallabhbhai National Institute of Technology, Surat, India

ABSTRACT

Continuously growing technology enhances creativity and simplifies humans' lives and offers the possibility to anticipate and satisfy their unmet needs. Understanding emotions is a crucial part of human behavior. Machines must deeply understand emotions to be able to predict human needs. Most tweets have sentiments of the user. It inherits the imbalanced class distribution. Most machine learning (ML) algorithms are likely to get biased towards the majority classes. The imbalanced distribution of classes gained extensive attention as it has produced many research challenges. It demands efficient approaches to handle the imbalanced data set. Strategies used for balancing the distribution of classes in the case study are handling redundant data, resampling training data, and data augmentation. Six methods related to these techniques have been examined in a case study. Upon conducting experiments on the Twitter dataset, it is seen that merging minority classes and shuffle sentence methods outperform other techniques.

DOI: 10.4018/978-1-7998-7371-6.ch012

INTRODUCTION AND MOTIVATION

Information technology is used in every field of human life and make human's life improved and more accessible. This tool became valued elements of life because it opened many doors to individuals. It firmly entrenched in human lives and facilitated their lives. Continuously growing technology strengthens individual creativity, makes our daily life more accessible, and gives us the facility to predict and cater to our needs. A deep understanding of human behavior is needed in machines and computers to understand our needs. The key part of human behavior is about perceiving and communicating emotions. It also motivates to take actions, influence the quality of decision making, and enhance the ability to empathize and communicate. Machines and computers must deeply understand emotions to anticipate human needs (Chatterjee A et al. (2019)). Emotion recognition and detection are closely related to sentiment analysis. Identification of sentiment intends to detect neutral, negative, or positive feelings from the content (Liu, B. (2012)).

In contrast, Emotion Analysis aims to identify and recognize feelings through text phrases, like joy, happiness, anger, disgust, fear, sadness, surprise, and many more (Picard R. W. (2000)). Recently, an identification of emotion has become a popular application of NLP. It has potential applications in Artificial intelligence (Damani S et al. 2018), Psychology (Druckman J. N. et al. 2008), Human-computer interaction (S. Brave et al.2009), Political science (Valentino N. A. et al. 2011) help in preventing suicide, or measuring the communal well-being (Van der Zanden R. et al. 2014), and Marketing (Bagozzi R. P. et al. 1999) etc.

WhatsApp, Facebook, and Twitter are prominent messaging platforms used by many online users to interact with each other. Statics given by (Statista, 2021) – "by the 3rd quarter of 2020, there are around 187 million daily active users of Twitter worldwide." In varied fields like researchers in marketing, analytics for political parties or social scientists look into twitter data in order to study human behavior in physical world. Tweets are rich sources of textual data containing the emotions of users. These data inherit the imbalanced emotion class distribution. In imbalanced dataset, data samples of one class are higher or lower than that of other group of classes. Figure 1 illustrates an imbalanced data. On encountering a imbalance class distribution problem in the training data, the results of classification task is influenced by majority class (Zhao C. et al. 2020).

Most machine learning classification algorithms are unable to manage imbalanced distribution of classes and are likely to get influenced by majority classes (Kothiya, Y. (2020, July 17)).

In the research literature, various approaches are proposed to cater to the imbalance class distribution issues in the data classification. These approaches are broadly categorized as algorithmic centered approaches and pre-processing methods or data level approaches.

Re-sampling techniques (Kotsiantis S. et al. 2006), reducing redundant data (Y.K. (2019, May 15)), and augmentation of text data are data-level approaches that are included as a solution to handle imbalance distribution of classes. The techniques are utilized to obtain an approximately equal count of samples in the classes. Assumptions created to favor the minority class and change the costs to get the balance classes, is the algorithmic-centered approach. (Kotsiantis S. et al. 2006).

In the machine learning (ML) community, the imbalanced class distribution gained extensive attention as it has produced many research challenges. It demands the experimental comparisons of approaches to take care of the imbalanced data set. A case study focuses on various data-level methods to deal with the imbalance distribution of emotion classes in Twitter data.

Figure 1. Imbalance distribution of class (Zhao C. et al. 2020)

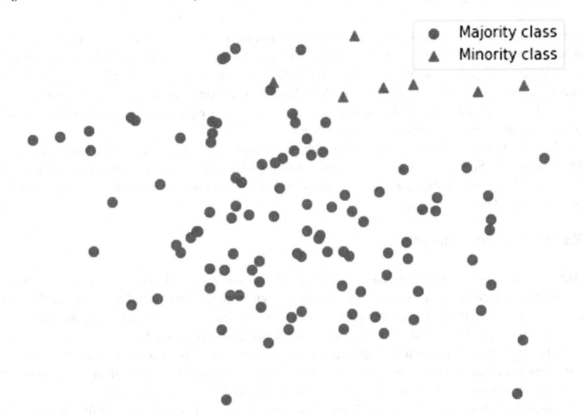

Contribution and Plan of the Report

- A case study focuses on tackling the imbalance multiclass emotion classification of tweets using various techniques such as resampling, reducing redundant data, augmentation of text data. It focuses on effectively processing imbalanced data while including the proposed model that inferred emotions from tweets. The study intends to bridge the gap between imbalanced learning and emotion analysis.
- This study's primary goal is to compare various approaches for balancing classes and enhance the proposed deep learning (DL) based model's efficiency and accuracy.

The rest of this chapter is organized as follows: Section 2 describes a literature review. The Proposed methodology is explained in section 3. Section 4 discusses the experiment setup. The analysis of experimental results is discussed in section5. Section 6 is the conclusion and future work that remarks the findings of this study in the end of the chapter.

LITERATURE REVIEW

In the research literature, Kotsiantis S. et al. 2006 discuss various approaches at the data and the algorithm level for managing class imbalanced data. Many different resampling approaches are proposed at the data level like random over-sampling, Synthetic Minority Over-Sampling (SMOT), and random under-sampling, etc.,. Various classification algorithms and techniques are updated to manage the imbalanced class distribution. Ensemble learning, leveraging the class weights parameter during the training of models, etc., is examples under the latter category.

The study focuses on different data-level methods to deal with imbalanced multiclass emotion analysis for Twitter data. Strategies such as resampling, handling redundant data, data augmentation methods for NLP task are used in the case study for balancing classes and enhance the efficiency and accuracy of the proposed deep learning model.

Twitter Emotion Analysis

Although emotion Recognition based on speech and images has been worked on a lot at this point, text-based emotion detection is in its early stage in natural language processing, including how recently it has drawn ample of attention. The emotion-detection algorithms are at large, put down to two categories, namely, Machine learning (ML) based methods and dictionary based methods.

When the vocabularies such as linguistic rules, ontologies, lexicons, or bags of words are used it is considered as Lexicon based approaches, whereas when the algorithms based on linguistic features, it falls into the category of Machine learning (ML) approaches (Canales L.et al. 2014).

The limitations of lexicon-based methods (Strapparava c. Et al. 2008, ma c. Et al. 2005, Balahur a. Et al. 2011, Sykora m. D. Et al. 2013, Bandhakavi a. Et al. 2017, pp. 102-108, Bandhakavi a. Et al. 2017, pp. 133-142, Chaumartin f. R. 2007, al Masum et al. 2007, Ortony a. Et al. 1988, Neviarouskaya a. Et al. 2010, Deerwester s. Et al. 1990, gill a. J. Et al. 2008, Wang x. Et al. 2013) concerning scalability and domain customization can be overcome by machine learning approaches (Mohri m. Et al. 2012, Hasan m. Et al. 2014, ACM, Sigkdd, Hasan m. Et al. 2014, Wang w. Et al. 2012, Roberts k. Et al. 2012, Suttles j. Et al. 2013, Balabantaray r. C. Et al. 2012, Seol y. S. Et al. 2008, li w. Et al. 2014, lee s. Y. M. Et al. 2010). It can also learn emotional signals that are not explicitly expressed.

The Conventional machine learning techniques required heavy feature engineering as well as a substantial expertise in the domain to create a model to transform raw input into a feature vector which enables a classifier to identify patterns in the input.

Deep learning-based (DL) methods are basically the method of representation learning. It has multiple levels of representation that are obtained by composing non-linear components which transforms a raw input at one level into a abstract higher level (LeCun Y. et al. 2015). The key advantage of deep learning methods is that the layers of features are learned from data using learning procedure. The DL methods perform feature engineering so there is no requirement to design hand-crafted features (LeCun Y. et al. 2015).

Deep learning-based architectures and algorithms have shown considerable success in speech and image domains. They also show favorable results in many NLU tasks such as question answering, topic classification, language translation, and sentiment analysis (LeCun Y. et al. 2015).

Lately, many approaches using deep learning (DL) models for emotion recognition from the text format have been proposed.

In (Zahiri S. M. et al. 2017), the author classifies emotion in a transcript of TV show. Transcripts are well-scripted, but the text data from social media such as tweets and textual dialogue are crowded by internet slang. spell errors etc. Some recent researches are on understanding the various emotions of tweets (Abdul-Mageed M. 2017, Köper M. 2017). In (Felbo B. 2017), authors learn representation based on emojis and uses it for identification of emotions. An author used pretrained LSTM model that is trained with lots of tweets and the emoticons appears in tweets. The work done by Mundra S.2017 is the sole study that addresses the difficulty of emotion identification in textual conversation of English language.

The study says that the deep learning methods give promising results for emotion detection in text. Also, deep learning-based algorithms require very less feature engineering, and so they can conveniently take advantage of available computation and data, as it increases in the amount. It motivated us to move to deep learning approaches for recognized emotion from the text.

Deep Learning Based Emotion Analysis for Imbalanced Class Distribution

Imbalance class distribution is a common problem in classification tasks. Model's performance will degrade due to imbalanced distribution of class. A balanced class distribution is not possible for real-world application domains.

To balance the minority class samples, researchers utilize data over-sampling methods to generate synthetic data from original training data. Method such as synthetic minority oversampling technique (SMOT) performs well for random numerical data (Chawla N. V. et al. 2002) and AdaSyn (He H. et al. 2008). A deep learning model CycleGAN that is the type of generative adversarial networks (GAN) performs well for images (Almahairi, A. et al. 2018). Synthetic text and images generally suffers from semantic or contextual information loss, whereas this is not the case with numeric data. The resulting text frequently turns out to have poor text structure and grammar, thus losing its meaning. Recently, research on tackling imbalanced dataset involves semantic text generation using deep language models. In (Shaikh S. et al. 2021), the authors proposed an LSTM-based model for sentence-level text generation to cater to imbalance distribution of classes in NLP domain applications. Three highly imbalanced datasets from two different domains were used evaluate the performance of LSTM and GPT-2 models for document-level sentence generation. Experimental results show overall improved classification accuracy for the proposed model (Shaikh S. et al. 2021).

In (Cong Q. et al. 2018), authors proposed a model for identification of depression in highly imbalanced social media data. They proposed a deep learning based model (X-A-BiLSTM) that consists of two modules: one is XGBoost module that increases the samples in minority classes and other one is an attention based BiLSTM model that enhances performance of classification task. An author utilizes real-world depression dataset. The dataset used is the Reddit Self-reported Depression Diagnosis (RSDD) dataset. Results illustrate that the approach remarkably performs well with the previous (SOTA) state-of-the-art models on the same dataset.

A research study in (Jamal N. et al. 2019) proposed a hybrid method of a deep learning-based model for emotions recognition on a highly imbalanced tweets data. The proposed model works in four stages:

1. Pre-processing steps are help in getting useful features from raw tweets and filtering out the noisy data.
2. The importance of each feature is computed using entropy weighting method.
3. Further, each class is balanced using a class balancer.

4.   Principal Component Analysis (PCA) is applied to get normalized forms from the high correlated features.

At last the TensorFlow with Keras module is recommended to predict good-quality features for identification of emotions. A data set of 1,600,000 tweets that is collected from the 'Kaggle' was analyzed with the suggested methodology. Upon comparing it with the various states of art techniques on various training ratios, it is seen that the recommended methodology outperforms all of them.

Several researchers in different learning settings have studied imbalanced learning for emotion detection. However, we found very few papers that directly address imbalanced emotion classification for Twitter data (Shaikh S. et al. 2021, Jamal N. et al. 2019).

A study focuses on deep learning-based emotion detection for highly imbalanced Twitter data. The next sections describe the methodology used to balance the imbalanced class distribution of text data.

Handle Redundant Data

Twitter dataset comprises of duplicate tweets and a lots of similar tweets. Discarding identical tweets will help to bring down the size of the majority class. Tweet dataset contains multiple tweets with similar semantic meaning. Removing the redundant tweets will help in balancing the classes. One of the beneficial approaches is that the validation set can remove redundant tweets (Kotsiantis S. et al. 2006). There is a range of techniques to represent tweets like word2vec embedding, TF-IDF embedding, BOW representations, etc. The similarity of tweets is measured using different similarity metrics such as Jaccard similarity, cosine similarity, etc. Siamese LSTM models to find out similar tweets have been proposed in the research domain (Cohen E. (2018, September 16)).

Merge minority classes is the approach to merge multiple minority classes that have numerous overlapping features (Multi-Class Emotion Classification for Short Texts, 2018). This trick may help out to enhance the f1-score of the classification task.

Resample Training Dataset

Oversampling the tweets of minority classes or under sampling tweets of majority classes is the straightforward method for balancing the imbalanced tweet data set. Another resampling method is to make new synthetic tweets from minority classes with SMOTE (Synthetic Minority Over-sampling Technique) (Chawla N. V. et al. 2002) algorithm.

Undersampling is an approach to balance the majority classes by eliminating tweets randomly. It may cause information loss from tweets and lead to inadequate model training (Y.K. (2019d, May 15)).

Oversampling is the process to replicate minority class tweets randomly. Random under-sampling suffers with information loss issue and random over-sampling may cause the problem of over fitting. To be precise, if the instances in the dataset are randomly replicated, then the learned model would fit too closely with the training data, resulting into unseen cases to be less generalized (Hoens T. R. et al. 2013).

To conquer this issue, (Chawla N. V. et al. 2002) came up with a SMOTE approach that creates synthetic data instead of taking same samples that already exist in the dataset. In this algorithm, the synthetic instances are introduced to each sample from the minority class, along the line segments connecting any or all of the nearest neighbours of the k minority class (Chawla N. V. et al. 2002). In the feature space, the Euclidean Distance between its data points help evaluates the nearest neighbours, this is essential for the technique. SMOTE works in the feature space such that it selects close examples and draws a line between them, then at a point along this line it draws a new sample.

Data Augmentation

Recently, research on tackling imbalanced dataset involves data augmentation methods of texts. Data augmentation of text can be done by tokenizing documents into a sentence, shuffling and joining them again to generate new sentences. Semantic text generation is also done by replacing adjectives, verbs, etc., with its synonym. A word's synonym is found using any pre-trained word embeddings or lexical dictionaries such as Wordnet, SentiWordNet, etc. ((I. (2019b, March 1)), (T. (2018a, November 16))).

(Zhang X. et al. 2015), Introduced the use of synonyms in their research work. While experimenting, it is found that text augmentation can be done by replacing words or phrases with their synonyms. In a very time effective way a huge amount of data can be generated if there is leverage existing thesaurus. The geometric distribution helps the authors to replace the selected word with its synonym (Zhang X. et al. 2015). Another interesting way was utilization of K-NN algorithm with cosine similarity to find a analogous word for replacement was suggested by (Wang W. Y. et al. 2015).In place of using static word embedding to replace the target word, (Fadaee M. et al. 2017) used the contextualized word embedding. In their work of data augmentation for machine translation with lower resources, they perform text augmentation to validate the model. The experiment proves that by leveraging text augmentation, the machine translation model gets enhanced.

(Kobayashi S. 2018), proposes to employ a bi-directional language model in the research work of data augmentation using contextual word embedding. Upon having selected the target word, the model predicts all probable substitutions by providing the surrounding words. Author applied the language model (LM) approach with sequential model RNN and convolution model CNN on six datasets, and the results turned out to be positive. (Kafle K. et al. 2017) presented an alternate approach for data augmentation. Here, the whole sentence is generated instead of just replacing a single few words.

Machine language translation is another interesting method of data augmentation for text. The technique helps to increase samples of minority classes. The technique used machine translation model to translate English language text to any language text and again converting back to English text. In this way, the essential details of the input texts are preserved, but word order or sometimes new words with similar meanings are introduced as new records, thus increasing the number of insufficient classes ((T. (2020a, September 7)), (Es, S. (2021b, April 9))). It may help out to enhance the f1-score of the classification task.

A case study focuses on tackling the imbalance multiclass emotion classification of tweets using various techniques such as resampling, reduced redundant data, augmentation of text data. It also focuses on effectively processing imbalanced data while including the proposed model that inferred emotions from tweets. The study intends to bridge the gap between imbalanced learning and emotion analysis.

This study's primary goal is to compare different techniques for balancing classes and enhance the proposed deep learning model's efficiency and accuracy.

PROPOSED APPROACH

Emotion recognition from the tweets is an area in Natural Language Processing (NLP), which is the study of interpreting the emotion expressed in text. A study of emotion detection using a deep learning-based approach is shown in Figure 2.

Proposed approach work in two phases. The first phase balances the dataset's class distribution using different data level strategies such as handling redundant data, resampling techniques, and data augmentation approach.

In second phase, pre-processing of a balanced dataset has been done with different methods and tools. Pre-processing techniques replace contraction words with proper words, remove punctuation, numbers, URLs, replace line space and extra white space, replace emoticons with related appropriate words, and demojized the emojis in tweets using emot library available in python.

The proposed model utilized the pre-trained embedding of GloVe (Global Vectors) as weights of the Embedding layer. The Glove Twitter pre-trained model with 200 dimensions is used to embedding the pre-processed Twitter data.

Glove embedding data fed to recurrent neural network (RNN), a deep learning (DL) based model for the text classification task. For twitter classification, the proposed model utilizes the biLSTM model with different layers.

A sequential model RNN is the type of ANN that specialize in the processing the sequential data. RNNs designed to deal with sequential data by sharing their internal weights. The Long Short-Term Memory networks (LSTMs), an extension of the RNN was introduced In 1997. In LSTM, the vanishing and exploding of the gradient issues are avoided by the unique connection of the recurrent cells (Sepp Hochreiter et al. 1997). Generally the LSTMs maintain information from the past because the sequence is processed in only one direction. The bidirectional LSTM (BiLSTM) combine output from two LSTM layers that processed in opposite directions. One processed forward through time, and another processed backwards through time to retrieve information from both states simultaneously (Schuster M. et al. 1997).

EXPERIMENTAL SETUP

Dataset

Experiments performed on a publically available emotion dataset from Kaggle (Emotion, 2020). The emotion dataset has 40,000 tweets with its 13 emotion labels. The dataset is highly imbalanced with a different number of tweets in each emotion category. Detail of imbalanced dataset provided in Table 1.

For the emotion dataset, 80% used for training, 20% for testing and another 20% used for validation. The training dataset has 25,600 tweets, 6400 tweets are in the validation set, and 8000 tweets are in the test set. The cleaning operations are performed on train, validation and test tweets datasets. Details of the dataset are available in Table 2.

Pre-Processing Techniques

Pre-processing techniques replace contraction words with proper words, remove punctuation, numbers, URLs, replace line space and extra white space, replace emoticons with related appropriate words,

Figure 2. Proposed framework for emotion detection

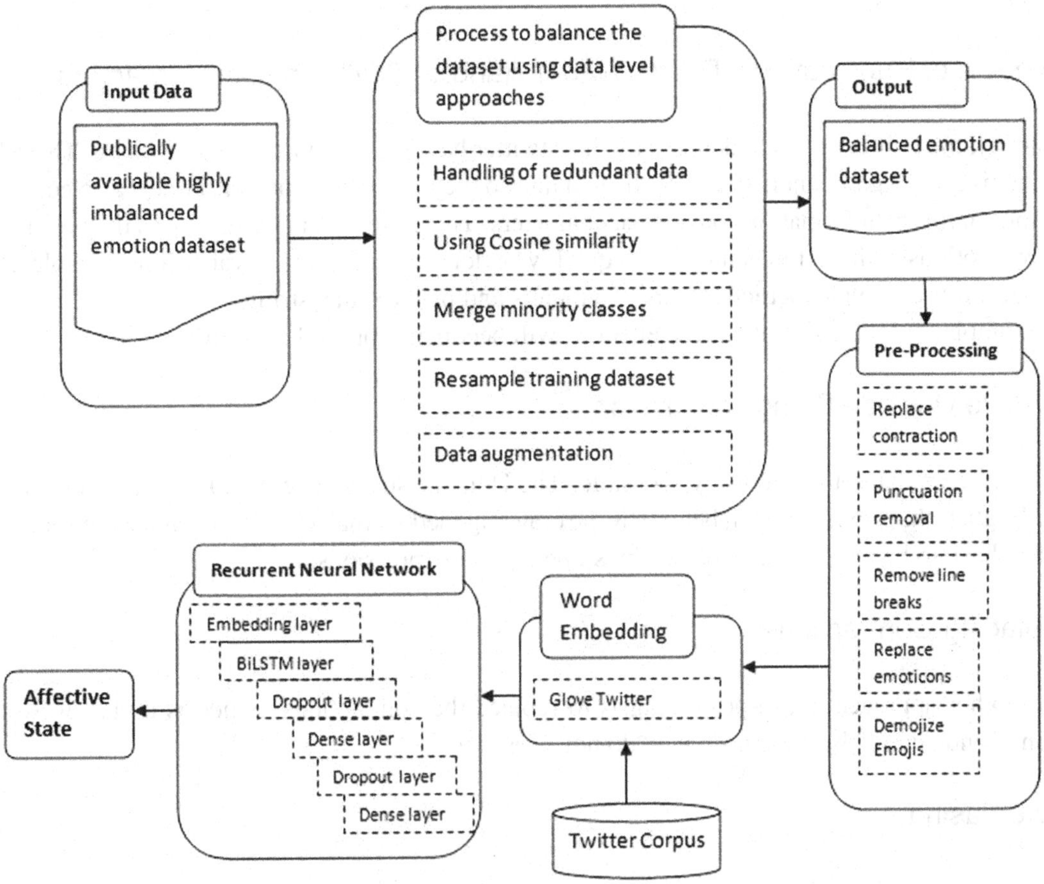

Table 1. Class details of emotion dataset

Emotion Classes	# Tweets	Emotion Classes	# Tweets	Emotion Classes	# Tweets
neutral	8504	love	3837	empty	806
worry	8441	surprise	2178	enthusiasm	758
happiness	5206	fun	1774	boredom	178
sadness	5154	relief	1525		
anger	110	hate	1323		

Table 2. Emotion dataset

Dataset	Classes	Train	Validation	Test
Emotion dataset from Kaggle	13 (neutral, worry, happiness, sadness, anger, love, surprise, fun, relief, hate, empty, enthusiasm, and boredom)	25600	6400	8000

and demojized the emojis in tweets using emot library available in python. Figure 3 describes the pre-processing techniques.

Removal of Punctuations, Digits, Twitter Handles ('@'), Special Characters

Basically, the twitter users are denoted by their twitter handles that start with a '@' sign. These handles do not give any significant meaning to the text and so they are to be removed. Tweets also contain punctuations, numeric information and special characters. These are also unnecessary as they do not convey many emotions with their meaning. It can quickly be done using Regular Expression available in python libraries. It uses simple methods to find characters and patterns in a string.

Example: "@abc 102 Not out Excellent!!" will become "Not out Excellent

Remove Unicode Strings and Noise

To get a clean dataset is not always possible. The Unicode strings like "\u002c" and "\x06" and some non-English characters were left behind by the crawling method that was used to create the dataset. These strings have to be removed or replaced by some regular expressions.

Replacing Contractions

Yet another approach in pre-processing is to replace the contractions, which is replacing words like "won't" and "don't" by "will not" and "do not", respectively.

Lowercasing

A common pre-processing method is to convert all the words into lowercase. This will merge a lot of words thereby reducing the dimensionality of the problem.

Lemmatization

Lemmatization typically refers to doing things correctly using a vocabulary and morphological examination of words, generally aimed solely at eliminating infection endings and restoring the basic term referenced as a lemma. Lemmatization is done by using different modules and available open-source libraries.

Spell Check

Examining the word's spelling is one of the primary necessities for any form of text processing. There are various paths available in Python to check the spelling of terms and correct their respective words.

Removing Stop Words

The function words that have high frequency that it their presence across all the sentences is high are called stop words. This reduces their importance in getting analyzed because they don't hold much nec-

Figure 3. Flow of data pre-processing

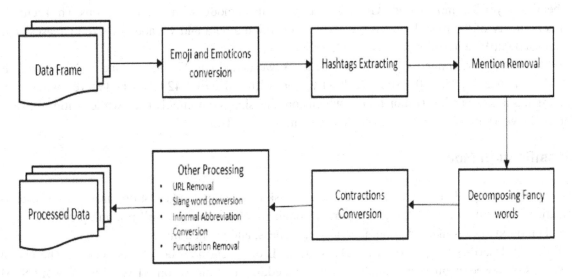

essary information in regards to the sentiment analysis. This collection of words is never pre-defined; it may change by adding or removing some words, based on the application.

Replacing Elongated Words

Sometimes there are words which have characters that have been wrongly (thought purposely) repeated more than once, e.g. "greeeeat", these are called as elongated words. The need is to replace these words with their source words in order to merge them. If this wasn't done then these different words would never be considered in evaluation due to their low frequency of occurrence.

Replacing Emoticons and Demojized Emojis

An emoji is defined as a unique combination of keyboard characters like letters, numbers and punctuation marks to express a human facial expression. They are like small images that can be fitted into text also express an emotion or idea. The name "emoji" is derived from the Japanese characters 'e' for picture + 'mo' for writing + 'ji' for character, making its literal meaning to be 'picture-character' (Subramanian D. (2020b, January 7)).

Emojis and emoticons play a fundamental role in human computer-mediated communications. They use a proxy of emotional communication to process tweets by considering emoticons information. Emot library available in Python libraries used to replace emoticons with appropriate words. With the help of Demojize function of Python, emojis replaced with suitable words.

Pre-Trained Word Embedding – GloVe

Experiments have been done with Glove that is pre-trained with billions of tweets (Pennington J. et al. 2014) word embedding as an embedding layer of the model.

The proposed model used the pre-trained embeddings of GloVe (Global Vectors) as weights of the Embedding layer. The model used a Glove Twitter pre-trained model with 200 dimensions. The accuracy and complexity of the model increase as the size of training data and vocabulary size increases. The model used GloVe embeddings trained with Twitter data.

Glove Twitter pre-trained model trained with 2B tweets and has 27B tokens and 1.2M vocab. It is available in uncased, 25d, 50d, 100d, & 200d vectors with a size of 1.42 GB. The GloVe Twitter Embedding has a dataset of 27 Billion tokens which contains slangs commonly used while writing a tweet. Hence GloVe Twitter is favorable when dealing with Twitter data.

Classification Model

The experimental study is to create a model whose task is to understand emotions as a multiclass classification problem where for the given input through tweets, the model will provide probabilities of varied emotion classes like – neutral, fear, anger, sadness, and joy and more.

Figure 4 describes the proposed EMOTWEET_TL deep learning model architecture. The neural network's proposed architecture comprising the embedding unit and a (biLSTM) bidirectional LSTM unit (64 dim). The LSTM unit learns semantic and sentiment feature representation. Initially, using the pre-trained word embedding, each tweet is given to the bidirectional LSTM. Text-based transfer learning techniques such as Glove embedding used as embedding layer and leverage them to perform effectively on downstream tasks. To predict the final emotion class label, the features proceed through a dense layer with the Relu non-linear function and then through the output layer with the softmax non-linear function. A dropout layer (Srivastava N. et al. 2014) was added between the bidirectional LSTM layer and to the first dense layer with Relu activation function and another dropout layer was added between the dense layer and the prediction layer (p=0.2) to improve the generalization of the network.

The Adam optimizer is used to train the model. For multiclass classification, the categorical cross-entropy loss function is utilized. F1-score, recall and precision were used as performance measures of the model.

Strategies used for Balancing Imbalanced Data

The experimental study focuses on different data-level methods to deal with imbalance multi-class emotion analysis. The strategies used in experiments are discussed below.

Handling of Redundant Data

For handling redundant tweets, the experiments have performed with two techniques. In the first technique, similar tweets are identified from the majority class. Such tweets are either deleted or added to the validation set to reduce the majority class size. The second technique merges similar minority classes.

Using Cosine Similarity

tweets with similar semantic meaning or duplicate tweets are finding out using a cosine similarity measure. The tweets are used in validation sets also. Removing such duplicate and similar semantic meaning

Figure 4. EMOTWEET_TL: Proposed model for inferring emotions from tweets

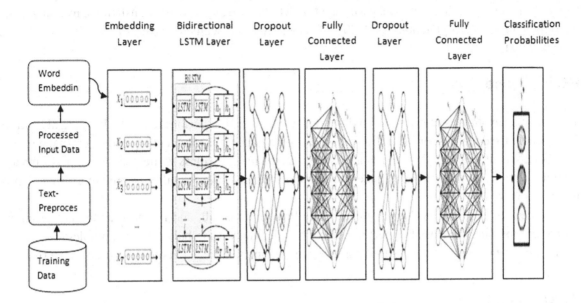

tweets will aid to reduce the size of the majority classes. In an experimental study, the tweets' similarity is identified using a cosine similarity metric with a threshold of 40% similarity.

Merge Minority Classes

It is the approach to merge multiple minority classes that have numerous overlapping features. The 13 emotions have been converted into 5 emotions such as neutral, happy, sad, hate, and anger. (It will add in handling the redundant data-merge similar classes-The native dataset is consists of 40,000 tweets that are divided into 13 emotion classes. These five classes are also the same as in (Bouazizi M. et al. 2017).

Resample Training Dataset

The experimental study used the SMOTE method to generate synthesized new tweets for minority classes. For creation of a new synthetic minority class instance, begin with randomly selecting a minority class instance namely 'p' and figure out its k-nearest class neighbors. Now randomly choose any one of these k-nearest minority neighbors namely 'q' and connect the two together, making a line segment in the feature space. The convex combination of these instances 'p' and 'q' generate the synthetic instance. Experiments have been performed with k=5. All minority classes have been balanced with the same number of tweets of majority class (here neutral class has maximum tweets - 8504 tweets). SMOTE algorithm is used to generate synthesized new data.

Data Augmentation

Simple data augmentation methods are used to increase similar tweets for minority classes. In the first approach, tokenizing tweets into words, shuffling and joining them again to create new tweets. NLTK library is used to tokenize tweets. The second approach replaces words of tweets with synonyms found using Pydictionary. It is a Dictionary Module for Python to get synonyms, translations, meanings, and Antonyms of words (PyDictionary, 2020). The synonym replacement method is helpful to generate semantic texts.

Performance Metrics

The use of an evaluation metrics is a vital to rate the classification performance of a learning algorithm. The broadly used metrics for evaluating classification algorithm is the accuracy and error. In the imbalances datasets, it seen that there exists a bias towards the majority class while, measuring performance. Therefore, these famous metrics' values do not show the classifier's ability to predict examples from minority classes.

Theoretically, various evaluation metrics like Precision, Recall, and F-measure etc. have been put forward to measure the classifier performance while dealing with imbalanced data problems.

To measure the correctly classified positive class samples, a Precision metric is used and defined as:

$$Precision = \frac{TP}{TP + FP}.$$

where TP and FP stands for the count of true-positive and false-positive respectively.

Now the Recall is used to measure the proportion of correctly identified the real positive samples and is calculated using:

$$Recall = \frac{TP}{TP + FN}.$$

where FN stands for the counts of false-negative.

In general, there is a trade-off between precision and recall. This relationship can give an inherent view of the performance of the classifier using the F-measure metrics. F-measure is basically a harmonic mean of precision and recall (Chicco D. et al. 2020). It is calculated using:

$$F - measure = 2 * \frac{Presicion * Recall}{Precision + Recall}.$$

In the experimental study, a highly imbalanced dataset is used so precision, recall and F-measures are used as evaluation metrics for evaluating model performance.

EXPERIMENT RESULTS AND ANALYSIS

Experiments performed on a highly imbalanced emotion dataset. It is balanced using above mentioned techniques and applied to the proposed model EMOTWEET_TL and infer emotion from it. Results are shown in Table 3.

In the study, an emotion dataset with 13 emotion classes is used. Data distributions of classes are highly imbalanced and described in Table1. To balance data distributions of minority classes, different techniques such as resampling, handling redundant data in majority classes, and data augmentation methods are used. After applying the methods mentioned above, the prepared balanced dataset is fed to the proposed EMOTWEET_TL model that infers tweets' emotion.

The experimental study conducted with the baseline method gives an f1-score 0.17. In the Baseline method, the imbalanced dataset is fed to the proposed model and evaluates its performance. The results of the dataset, balanced with the SMOTE method, give poor performance. F1-score is only 0.028. The performance of the model is decreasing with much difference in F1-score.

One observation of SMOTE algorithm's poor performance is that it does not take neighboring samples from other classes while generating synthetic samples. This can lead to an increase in the overlapping of classes and may introduce additional noise. The literature study indicates that the performance of the SMOTE is degrading with text data because the vectors created from the text data has high dimensions, and SMOTE is not very effective for high dimensional data (Chawla N. V. et al. 2002).

The technique's performance that used cosine similarity to filter out similar tweets from majority classes is almost equal to a baseline method. The F1-score of the method is 0.18. The technique finds similar tweets with a cosine similarity threshold of 40%. Due to the small amount of similar tweets identified with a given threshold, the majority class tweets not reduced much in size. So the impact of the method on this dataset is not much as compared to other techniques. A prior experiment was conducted with 65% threshold but identified a very less number of similar tweets.

Data augmentation methods such as shuffle words, shuffle sentences and replacing synonyms in tweets give better results than the baseline method. Their F1-score are 0.36, 0.48 and 0.38 respectively. Almost it is +0.20 points higher than the baseline method. The new tweets generated using these methods are similar to their class tweets, and it is one of the reasons for better performance. The Shuffle sentence method gives better performance than the shuffle words method. In the shuffle words method, a tweet is tokenized and shuffles these tokens and again joining them may change the context of some tweets and may cause the model's effectiveness. Whereas in the shuffle sentences method, tweets are tokenized by sentences and shuffle sentences to create a new tweet, so the context of sentences did not change, and performance may improve. These prominent methods are performed well as a merging minority classes method. The F1-score of this method is 0.48. Similar minority classes are merged, and as a result, it reduces the number of classes in the dataset. The merging method performs well over other methods of experimental study. Better performance of the methods due to below reasons:

CONCLUSION AND FUTURE WORK

Emotion detection from the Twitter dataset is confronted with the class imbalance problem. Most machine learning and deep learning classification algorithms are not equipped to manage imbalanced distribution of classes and are likely to get influenced by majority classes.

Table 3. Performance of the proposed model for different techniques to balancing class distribution of the dataset

Method		Train			Validation			Test		
		Precision	Recall	F1-score	Precision	Recall	F1-score	Precision	Recall	F1-score
Baseline		0.65	0.2	0.30	0.44	0.10	0.18	0.44	0.10	0.17
Handling Redundant Data	Using cosine similarity	0.71	0.22	0.34	0.39	0.12	0.18	0.39	0.12	0.18
	Merging Minority classes	0.78	0.62	0.69	0.53	0.45	**0.49**	0.53	0.44	**0.48**
Resample Training Dataset	SMOTE	0.69	0.014	0.028	0.67	0.012	0.023	0.70	0.014	0.028
Data Augmentation	Shuffle Words	0.80	0.28	0.42	0.73	0.24	**0.37**	0.72	0.24	**0.36**
	Shuffle sentences	0.84	0.30	0.52	0.78	0.35	**0.48**	0.77	0.35	**0.48**
	Synonym	0.86	0.30	0.44	0.78	0.26	**0.39**	0.77	0.25	**0.38**

- It reduces the number of classes of the dataset.
- It balances the distribution of data in all merged classes.

A way to address this challenge is to use different strategies for balancing imbalance class distribution in a case study are handling redundant dataset, resampling training dataset and data augmentation. Five methods related to the techniques mentioned above examined in a case study. In a case study, experiments are conducted on Twitter dataset collecting from Kaggle to infer emotions from the tweets. A Twitter dataset is in the English language. The obtained results show that merging minority classes with similar classes and shuffle sentence methods for data augmentation give better performance than other techniques.

In future work, we intend to extend our study to incorporate more advanced techniques for data augmentation, such as generating new semantic tweets using biLSTM models and using machine language translation techniques.

Reduce the majority classes' size by filtering out semantically similar tweets using the Siamese LSTM model instead of a cosine similarity measure to get the more accurate and efficient performance of the model. An experimental study will perform with more datasets on the same domain and with different domain datasets.

REFERENCES

Abdul-Mageed, M., & Ungar, L. (2017, July). Emonet: Fine-grained emotion detection with gated recurrent neural networks. In *Proceedings of the 55th annual meeting of the association for computational linguistics (volume 1: Long papers)* (pp. 718-728). 10.18653/v1/P17-1067

Al Masum, S. M., Prendinger, H., & Ishizuka, M. (2007, November). Emotion sensitive news agent: An approach towards user centric emotion sensing from the news. In *IEEE/WIC/ACM International Conference on Web Intelligence (WI'07)* (pp. 614-620). IEEE. 10.1109/WI.2007.124

Almahairi, A., Rajeshwar, S., Sordoni, A., Bachman, P., & Courville, A. (2018, July). Augmented cyclegan: Learning many-to-many mappings from unpaired data. In *International Conference on Machine Learning* (pp. 195-204). PMLR.

Bagozzi, R. P., Gopinath, M., & Nyer, P. U. (1999). The role of emotions in marketing. *Journal of the Academy of Marketing Science*, *27*(2), 184–206. doi:10.1177/0092070399272005

Balabantaray, R. C., Mohammad, M., & Sharma, N. (2012). Multi-class twitter emotion classification: A new approach. *International Journal of Applied Information Systems*, *4*(1), 48–53. doi:10.5120/ijais12-450651

Balahur, A., Hermida, J. M., & Montoyo, A. (2011, June). Detecting implicit expressions of sentiment in text based on commonsense knowledge. In *Proceedings of the 2nd Workshop on Computational Approaches to Subjectivity and Sentiment Analysis (WASSA 2011)* (pp. 53-60). Academic Press.

Bandhakavi, A., Wiratunga, N., Massie, S., & Padmanabhan, D. (2017). Lexicon generation for emotion detection from text. *IEEE Intelligent Systems*, *32*(1), 102–108. doi:10.1109/MIS.2017.22

Bandhakavi, A., Wiratunga, N., Padmanabhan, D., & Massie, S. (2017). Lexicon based feature extraction for emotion text classification. *Pattern Recognition Letters*, *93*, 133–142. doi:10.1016/j.patrec.2016.12.009

Bouazizi, M., & Ohtsuki, T. (2017). A pattern-based approach for multi-class sentiment analysis in Twitter. *IEEE Access: Practical Innovations, Open Solutions*, *5*, 20617–20639. doi:10.1109/ACCESS.2017.2740982

Brave, S., & Nass, C. (2009). Emotion in human–computer interaction. In *Human-computer interaction fundamentals* (Vol. 20094635). CRC Press. doi:10.1201/b10368-6

Canales, L., & Martínez-Barco, P. (2014, October). Emotion detection from text: A survey. In *Proceedings of the workshop on natural language processing in the 5th information systems research working days (JISIC)* (pp. 37-43). 10.3115/v1/W14-6905

Chatterjee, A., Gupta, U., Chinnakotla, M. K., Srikanth, R., Galley, M., & Agrawal, P. (2019). Understanding emotions in text using deep learning and big data. *Computers in Human Behavior*, *93*, 309–317. doi:10.1016/j.chb.2018.12.029

Chaumartin, F. R. (2007). UPAR7: A knowledge-based system for headline sentiment tagging. In *SemEval (ACL Workshop)* (pp. pp-422). 10.3115/1621474.1621568

Chawla, N. V., Bowyer, K. W., Hall, L. O., & Kegelmeyer, W. P. (2002). SMOTE: Synthetic minority over-sampling technique. *Journal of Artificial Intelligence Research*, *16*, 321–357. doi:10.1613/jair.953

Chicco, D., & Jurman, G. (2020). The advantages of the Matthews correlation coefficient (MCC) over F1 score and accuracy in binary classification evaluation. *BMC Genomics*, *21*(1), 1–13. doi:10.118612864-019-6413-7 PMID:31898477

Cohen, E. (2018, September 16). *How to predict Quora Question Pairs using Siamese Manhattan LSTM*. Medium. https://blog.mlreview.com/implementing-malstm-on-kaggles-quora-question-pairs-competition-8b31b0b16a07

Cong, Q., Feng, Z., Li, F., Xiang, Y., Rao, G., & Tao, C. (2018, December). XA-BiLSTM: A deep learning approach for depression detection in imbalanced data. In *2018 IEEE International Conference on Bioinformatics and Biomedicine (BIBM)* (pp. 1624-1627). IEEE.

Damani, S., Raviprakash, N., Gupta, U., Chatterjee, A., Joshi, M., Gupta, K., & Mathur, A. (2018). *Ruuh: A deep learning based conversational social agent*. arXiv preprint arXiv:1810.12097.

Deerwester, S., Dumais, S. T., Furnas, G. W., Landauer, T. K., & Harshman, R. (1990). Indexing by latent semantic analysis. *Journal of the American Society for Information Science*, *41*(6), 391–407. doi:10.1002/(SICI)1097-4571(199009)41:6<391::AID-ASI1>3.0.CO;2-9

Druckman, J. N., & McDermott, R. (2008). Emotion and the framing of risky choice. *Political Behavior*, *30*(3), 297–321. doi:10.100711109-008-9056-y

Emotion. (2020, January 7). *Kaggle*. https://www.kaggle.com/icw123/emotion

Es, S. (2021b, April 9). *Data Augmentation in NLP: Best Practices From a Kaggle Master*. Neptune. Ai. https://neptune.ai/blog/data-augmentation-nlp

Fadaee, M., Bisazza, A., & Monz, C. (2017). Data augmentation for low-resource neural machine translation. arXiv preprint arXiv:1705.00440. doi:10.18653/v1/P17-2090

Felbo, B., Mislove, A., Søgaard, A., Rahwan, I., & Lehmann, S. (2017). Using millions of emoji occurrences to learn any-domain representations for detecting sentiment, emotion and sarcasm. arXiv preprint arXiv:1708.00524. doi:10.18653/v1/D17-1169

Gill, A. J., French, R. M., Gergle, D., & Oberlander, J. (2008). Identifying emotional characteristics from short blog texts. In *30th Annual Conference of the Cognitive Science Society* (pp. 2237-2242). Washington, DC: Cognitive Science Society.

Hasan, M., Agu, E., & Rundensteiner, E. (2014). Using hashtags as labels for supervised learning of emotions in twitter messages. ACM SIGKDD workshop on health informatics.

Hasan, M., Rundensteiner, E., & Agu, E. (2014). *Emotex: Detecting emotions in twitter messages*. Academic Press.

He, H., Bai, Y., Garcia, E. A., & Li, S. (2008, June). ADASYN: Adaptive synthetic sampling approach for imbalanced learning. In *2008 IEEE international joint conference on neural networks (IEEE world congress on computational intelligence)* (pp. 1322-1328). IEEE.

Hochreiter, S., & Schmidhuber, J. (1997). Long short-term memory. *Neural Computation, 9*(8), 1735–1780. doi:10.1162/neco.1997.9.8.1735 PMID:9377276

Hoens, T. R., & Chawla, N. V. (2013). Imbalanced datasets: from sampling to classifiers. *Imbalanced learning: Foundations, algorithms, and applications*, 43-59.

I. (2019b, March 1). *NLP (data augmentation)*. Kaggle. https://www.kaggle.com/init927/nlp-data-augmentation#Introduction-to-Data-Augmentation-in-NLP

Jamal, N., Xianqiao, C., & Aldabbas, H. (2019). Deep learning-based sentimental analysis for large-scale imbalanced twitter data. *Future Internet, 11*(9), 190. doi:10.3390/fi11090190

Kafle, K., Yousefhussien, M., & Kanan, C. (2017, September). Data augmentation for visual question answering. In *Proceedings of the 10th International Conference on Natural Language Generation* (pp. 198-202). 10.18653/v1/W17-3529

Kobayashi, S. (2018). Contextual augmentation: Data augmentation by words with paradigmatic relations. arXiv preprint arXiv:1805.06201. doi:10.18653/v1/N18-2072

Köper, M., Kim, E., & Klinger, R. (2017, September). IMS at EmoInt-2017: Emotion intensity prediction with affective norms, automatically extended resources and deep learning. In *Proceedings of the 8th Workshop on Computational Approaches to Subjectivity, Sentiment and Social Media Analysis* (pp. 50-57). 10.18653/v1/W17-5206

Kothiya, Y. (2020, July 17). *How I handled imbalanced text data - Towards Data Science*. Medium. https://towardsdatascience.com/how-i-handled-imbalanced-text-data-ba9b757ab1d8

Kotsiantis, S., Kanellopoulos, D., & Pintelas, P. (2006). Handling imbalanced datasets: A review. *GESTS International Transactions on Computer Science and Engineering, 30*(1), 25–36.

LeCun, Y., Bengio, Y., & Hinton, G. (2015). Deep learning. *Nature, 521*(7553), 436-444.

Lee, S. Y. M., Chen, Y., & Huang, C. R. (2010, June). A text-driven rule-based system for emotion cause detection. In *Proceedings of the NAACL HLT 2010 Workshop on Computational Approaches to Analysis and Generation of Emotion in Text* (pp. 45-53). Academic Press.

Li, W., & Xu, H. (2014). Text-based emotion classification using emotion cause extraction. *Expert Systems with Applications, 41*(4), 1742–1749. doi:10.1016/j.eswa.2013.08.073

Liu, B. (2012). Sentiment analysis and opinion mining. *Synthesis Lectures on Human Language Technologies, 5*(1), 1-167.

Ma, C., Prendinger, H., & Ishizuka, M. (2005, October). Emotion estimation and reasoning based on affective textual interaction. In *International conference on affective computing and intelligent interaction* (pp. 622-628). Springer. 10.1007/11573548_80

Mohri, M., Rostamizadeh, A., & Talwalkar, A. (2012). *Foundations of machine learning*. Academic Press.

Multi-Class Emotion Classification for Short Texts. (2018, March 17). *Github*. https://tlkh.github.io/text-emotion-classification/

Mundra, S., Sen, A., Sinha, M., Mannarswamy, S., Dandapat, S., & Roy, S. (2017, May). Fine-grained emotion detection in contact center chat utterances. In *Pacific-Asia Conference on Knowledge Discovery and Data Mining* (pp. 337-349). Springer. 10.1007/978-3-319-57529-2_27

Neviarouskaya, A., Prendinger, H., & Ishizuka, M. (2010, August). Recognition of affect, judgment, and appreciation in text. In *Proceedings of the 23rd International Conference on Computational Linguistics (Coling 2010)* (pp. 806-814). Academic Press.

Ortony, A., Clore, G. L., & Collins, A. (1988). *The cognitive structure of emotions*. Cambridge University Press.

Pennington, J., Socher, R., & Manning, C. D. (2014, October). Glove: Global vectors for word representation. In *Proceedings of the 2014 conference on empirical methods in natural language processing (EMNLP)* (pp. 1532-1543). 10.3115/v1/D14-1162

Picard, R. W. (2000). *Affective computing*. MIT Press. doi:10.7551/mitpress/1140.001.0001

PyDictionary. (2020, July 9). *PyPI*. https://pypi.org/project/PyDictionary/

Roberts, K., Roach, M. A., Johnson, J., Guthrie, J., & Harabagiu, S. M. (2012, May). EmpaTweet: Annotating and Detecting Emotions on Twitter. In *Lrec* (Vol. 12, pp. 3806-3813). Academic Press.

Schuster, M., & Paliwal, K. K. (1997). Bidirectional recurrent neural networks. *IEEE Transactions on Signal Processing*, *45*(11), 2673–2681. doi:10.1109/78.650093

Seol, Y. S., Kim, D. J., & Kim, H. W. (2008, July). Emotion recognition from text using knowledge-based ANN. In *ITC-CSCC: International Technical Conference on Circuits Systems, Computers and Communications* (pp. 1569-1572). Academic Press.

Shaikh, S., Daudpota, S. M., Imran, A. S., & Kastrati, Z. (2021). Towards Improved Classification Accuracy on Highly Imbalanced Text Dataset Using Deep Neural Language Models. *Applied Sciences (Basel, Switzerland)*, *11*(2), 869. doi:10.3390/app11020869

Srivastava, N., Hinton, G., Krizhevsky, A., Sutskever, I., & Salakhutdinov, R. (2014). Dropout: A simple way to prevent neural networks from overfitting. *Journal of Machine Learning Research*, *15*(1), 1929–1958.

Strapparava, C., & Mihalcea, R. (2008, March). Learning to identify emotions in text. In *Proceedings of the 2008 ACM symposium on Applied computing* (pp. 1556-1560). 10.1145/1363686.1364052

Subramanian, D. (2020b, January 7). *Emotion analysis in text mining | Towards AI*. Medium. https://pub.towardsai.net/emoticon-and-emoji-in-text-mining-7392c49f596a

Suttles, J., & Ide, N. (2013, March). Distant supervision for emotion classification with discrete binary values. In *International Conference on Intelligent Text Processing and Computational Linguistics* (pp. 121-136). Springer. 10.1007/978-3-642-37256-8_11

Sykora, M. D., Jackson, T., O'Brien, A., & Elayan, S. (2013). Emotive ontology: Extracting fine-grained emotions from terse, informal messages. *IADIS Int. J. Comput. Sci. Inf. Syst*, *2013*, 19–26.

T. (2018a, November 16). *Using Word Embeddings for Data Augmentation*. Kaggle. https://www.kaggle.com/theoviel/using-word-embeddings-for-data-augmentation

T. (2020a, September 7). *Using Google Translate for NLP Augmentation.* Kaggle. https://www.kaggle.com/tuckerarrants/using-google-translate-for-nlp-augmentation

Valentino, N. A., Brader, T., Groenendyk, E. W., Gregorowicz, K., & Hutchings, V. L. (2011). Election night's alright for fighting: The role of emotions in political participation. *The Journal of Politics*, *73*(1), 156–170. doi:10.1017/S0022381610000939

Van der Zanden, R., Curie, K., Van Londen, M., Kramer, J., Steen, G., & Cuijpers, P. (2014). Keshia Curie, Monique Van Londen, Jeannet Kramer, Gerard Steen, and Pim Cuijpers. Web-based depression treatment: Associations of clients' word use with adherence and outcome. *Journal of Affective Disorders*, *160*, 10–13. doi:10.1016/j.jad.2014.01.005 PMID:24709016

Wang, W., Chen, L., Thirunarayan, K., & Sheth, A. P. (2012, September). Harnessing twitter" big data" for automatic emotion identification. In *2012 International Conference on Privacy, Security, Risk and Trust and 2012 International Conference on Social Computing* (pp. 587-592). IEEE.

Wang, W. Y., & Yang, D. (2015, September). That's so annoying!!!: A lexical and frame-semantic embedding based data augmentation approach to automatic categorization of annoying behaviors using# petpeeve tweets. In *Proceedings of the 2015 Conference on Empirical Methods in Natural Language Processing* (pp. 2557-2563). 10.18653/v1/D15-1306

Wang, X., & Zheng, Q. (2013, March). Text emotion classification research based on improved latent semantic analysis algorithm. In *Proceedings of the 2nd International Conference on Computer Science and Electronics Engineering* (pp. 210-213). Atlantis Press. 10.2991/iccsee.2013.55

Zahiri, S. M., & Choi, J. D. (2017). *Emotion detection on tv show transcripts with sequence-based convolutional neural networks.* arXiv preprint arXiv:1708.04299.

Zhang, X., Zhao, J., & LeCun, Y. (2015). *Character-level convolutional networks for text classification.* arXiv preprint arXiv:1509.01626.

Zhao, C., Xin, Y., Li, X., Yang, Y., & Chen, Y. (2020). A heterogeneous ensemble learning framework for spam detection in social networks with imbalanced data. *Applied Sciences (Basel, Switzerland)*, *10*(3), 936. doi:10.3390/app10030936

Chapter 13
Indian Judgment Categorization for Practicing Similar Judgment Identification

Jenish Dhanani
Sardar Vallabhbhai National Institute of Technology, Surat, India

Rupa G. Mehta
Sardar Vallabhbhai National Institute of Technology, Surat, India

Dipti P. Rana
https://orcid.org/0000-0002-5058-1355
Sardar Vallabhbhai National Institute of Technology, Surat, India

Rahul Lad
Sardar Vallabhbhai National Institute of Technology, Surat, India

Amogh Agrawal
Sardar Vallabhbhai National Institute of Technology, Surat, India

Karan Chevli
Sardar Vallabhbhai National Institute of Technology, Surat, India

Jashwanth Gummula Reddy
Sardar Vallabhbhai National Institute of Technology, Surat, India

ABSTRACT

Recently, legal information retrieval has emerged as an essential practice for the legal fraternity. In the legal domain, judgment is a specific kind of legal document, which discusses case-related information and the verdict of a court case. In the common law system, the legal professionals exploit relevant judgments to prepare arguments. Hence, an automated system is a vital demand to identify similar judgments effectively. The judgments can be broadly categorized into civil and criminal cases, where judgments

DOI: 10.4018/978-1-7998-7371-6.ch013

with similar case matters can have strong relevance compared to judgments with different case matters. In similar judgment identification, categorized judgments can significantly prune search space by restrictive search within a specific case category. So, this chapter provides a novel methodology that classifies Indian judgments in either of the case matter. Crucial challenges like imbalance and intrinsic characteristics of legal data are also highlighted specific to similarity analysis of Indian judgments, which can be a motivating aspect to the research community.

INTRODUCTION

Due to the advancements in digital and information technologies, a vast amount of data is being produced every day. In the Legal domain, various legal documents are also digitalized and preserved in online and offline repositories for convenient accessibility to Legal communities. There are multiple types of legal documents like Previous Judgments (i.e. court case documents), Laws, Statutes, Constitution, Bills, etc. Here, Legal systems are primarily categorized based on the importance given to the particular legal documents, such as *Common Law System* and *Civil Law System* (Raghav et al., 2016). Civil law system outweighs the codified statute which assists in deriving the judgment in the court as a crucial source of law. In contrast, common low system emphasizes on previous judgments given by the courts. It follows the belief of 'stare decisis' that similar facts and circumstances should be treated in a similar way (Mandal et al., 2018).

The Indian judiciary follows a Common law system where legal judgments are given significant importance, especially when existing laws cannot determine the outcome of a case (Trivedi et al., 2020). Legal professionals typically prepare their strategic arguments for a specific court case by manually finding relevant legal documents or judgments. However, manual identification practice is very tedious and laborious. This challenge demands an automated Legal document retrieval system. Therefore, AI-based Legal information retrieval applications have gained the significant attention from the Legal and information science community, such as identification of Similar Legal documents to a specific legal document (i.e. similar judgment identification in the Common law system) (Kumar et al., 2011; Kumar et al., 2013; Mandal et al., 2018; Raghav et al., 2015; Sugathadasa et al., 2018). This chapter mainly focuses on the application to identify similar Indian judgments given a specific judgment.

By analyzing Indian judgments, it is observed that legal cases be classified among several case matters like *labour*, *rent*, *direct tax*, *service*, etc. However, at a macro level, all the judgments may broadly classify into two categories: *civil* that indicates a case for a non-criminal activity like discrimination, divorces, child custody, property disputes, estate distribution, injury cases; and *criminal* indicates case for criminal offences like theft, assault, robbery, trafficking in controlled substances, murder, etc. In general, judgments with similar case matters can have strong relevance compared to judgments with different case matters. Hence, consideration of a categorized set of judgments (i.e. based on case matter) can potentially restrict the judgment search space to a particular set of judgments. This practice significantly avoids undesirable computational efforts in a similar judgment identification process.

This research proposes a novel judgment categorization approach that aims to classify the set of judgments based on their respective case matter. The judgments from Supreme Court of India (SCI) were collected from the prominent online Legal repository[1], where judgments were not labeled with case matters. Hence, this research first categorizes judgments based on keywords (selected with the help of Legal experts) which are associated with the respective case matter. However, there are still many judgments whose category cannot be derived using keywords. Further, categorized judgments are used to train the linear SVM classifier[2] (Cortes & Vapnik, 1995), which can classify the uncategorized judgments into one category. It is observed that the case matter distribution is highly imbalanced in categorized judgments. Here, the number of civil cases is significantly higher than the number of criminal cases. Moreover, the significant imbalance is also noticed in the contextual and referential information of judgments. This chapter also highlights existing challenges in the field of Legal information retrieval, which demand intensive attention and development from the Legal research community.

The rest of the Chapter is organized as follows: subsequent Section provides the necessary background, and also review the existing work judgment similarity approaches. Section *Judgment Categorization* discusses the proposed approach to categorize Indian judgments and also provides an empirical result. Section *Open Issues in Legal Information Retrieval* highlight the various open challenges associated with Legal information retrieval. Finally, the study is concluded in Section *Conclusion*.

BACKGROUNDAND RELATED WORK

This section concisely introduces to the essential background for analyzing Indian legal documents. The subsection also reviews recent works in the Indian judgment similarity analysis.

Indian Judicial System

India likes several other countries viz. Canada, Singapore, Australia etc. follow the Common law system (Bhattacharya et al., 2020). As discussed earlier, Common Law is the body of law derived from judicial decisions of courts. This means that previously held judgments have equal importance as laws in the current system. The Indian Judiciary is formally structured into a hierarchical format, with the Supreme Court being the apex body. Apart from the Supreme Court there are High Courts, District, session court, Tribunals and Appellate Boards.

Components of a Judgment

Judgments are the court's description of essential information and verdicts of a particular case provided by a judge or a panel of judges with respect to trial or other court proceedings. This results in the judgments being a complex mixture of various legal issues, arguments, facts, and verdicts. It also cites the associated law, acts, sections, articles and previous judgments. Hence, major components of a typical judgment are: Name of judgment, Names of judges, Act, Headnote, case citation, and judgment text (Kumar et al., 2013), as discussed follows:

Name of Judgment: It is assigned in accordance with the names of Plaintiff and Defendant.
Plaintiff: A plaintiff is the organization or person who files a lawsuit in the court.
Defendant: A defendant is the organization or person against whom the case has been filed in the court.
Names of Judges: Every judgment states the names of the judge or bench of judges who delivered the verdict after hearing the difference of opinions between Plaintiff and Defendant.

Act: It determine the legal category that the dispute in the presented case falls into. It defines a law which has been enacted by the legislation, and explains the legal specifications of the matter at hand.

Headnote: It is a brief summary of the judgment.

Citation: It is referred previous judgments, acts, laws, sections, articles, etc. in a particular judgment. Citations are further subdivided into out-citations which mean reference to a previously held judgment and in-citation is a hypothetical term which is an inverse mapping of out-citation.

Judgment Text: It is the textual information like arguments, facts, issues and verdict written in English.

Similar Judgment Analysis

To find similar judgments, recent works attempted *Citation based approaches* that utilize the case citations, and/or *Text based approaches* that utilize the textual information. Citation based approaches formulate a citation network from referred citations, where relevance can be captured with the help of Network based similarity measures like bibliographic coupling (Kumar et al., 2011), co-citation analysis (Kumar et al., 2011), network embedding (Bhattacharya et al., 2020). In bibliographic coupling, two judgments are considered to be bibliographically coupled if they both share one or more common citations. In contrast, co-citation considers the number of judgments which cite the two given judgments together. In the experiments of Kumar et al. (Kumar et al., 2011), the bibliographic coupling has demonstrated better performance compared to co-citations for Indian judgments. Network embedding (Grover & Leskovec, 2016) transforms nodes of a citation network to a vector space such that the network neighborhoods of the nodes are preserved. Bhattacharya et al. (Bhattacharya et al., 2020) exploited citation network and node2vec to capture the relevance among Indian judgments.

Text based approaches measure the syntactic and semantic similarity between the content (i.e. textual information) of the judgments. The judgments are mapped to real-valued vectors using embedding techniques such as TFIDF (Kumar et al., 2011), LDA (Blei et al., 2003), Word2Vec (Mikolov et al., 2013a, 2013b), and Doc2Vec (Le et al., 2014). Majority works have computed the Cosine similarity score to measure the relevance in the text based approaches. Kumar et al. (Kumar et al., 2011; Kumar et al., 2013) utilized the TFIDF to generate the judgment vector space for Indian judgments. In the LDA, each document is characterized by a probability distribution over topics and each topic is characterized by a probability distribution over words. Word2vec learns word vectors space using contextual information to preserve semantic meaning. The semantically similar words' vectors are adjacent in the learned word vector space. Doc2Vec is the advanced variant of Word2Vec, which transform an arbitrary length of text (i.e. paragraph, document, judgment, etc.) into the real-valued vectors. Doc2Vec also learns the semantically rich document vector space by exploiting contextual information, where contextually relevant documents' vectors are in close proximity. Mandal et al. (Mandal et al., 2017) perform the rigorous experimental study using aforesaid embedding techniques for Indian judgments. Doc2Vec has yielded the finest performance in terms of correlation to the Legal expert scores. Many recent studies have attempted to hybridize both textual and citation information to capture the relevance (Kumar et al., 2013, Bhattacharya et al., 2020, Wagh & Anand, 2020).

Judgment Categorization

This section presents a proposed *Judgment Categorization* approach that classifies Indian judgments based on case-matters i.e. *civil* and *criminal*. Judgment categorization aids in pruning the search space;

which can potentially make the similar judgment identification process efficient. For example, if the given query judgment falls in the criminal category then the system will search for similar cases only from judgments categorized as criminal, while the cases labeled as civil will essentially be pruned. As illustrated in Figure 1, The Judgment categorization process is divided into two stages namely, 1) *Keyword based categorization*, and 2) *Machine Learning based categorization*.

Keyword Based Categorization

It is observed that majority of the legal cases contain case matter specific keywords in the first four paragraphs. This can be exploited to differentiate the case into either civil or criminal category. To do so, these case matter specific keywords are identified with the help of legal experts, which are listed in Table 1. This research discriminates the civil judgments which consist of civil case specific keywords in the first four paragraphs. Similarly, criminal judgments are also identified based on criminal case specific keywords. Keyword based categorization is applied to the real-life judgments of SCI, which are collected from an online repository. Out of 48,518 judgments, the 24,294 judgments were labeled as civil and 9,267 judgments were labeled as criminal. However, 14,957 judgments were not categorized to any one of the category, as case specific keywords were not found in the judgment text. So, these set of judgments were labeled as **'unsure'** judgments.

Machine Learning Based Categorization

A significant amount of judgments (30.8% of 48,518) could not be classified, i.e., were labeled as 'unsure'. So, Machine learning based linear SVM classifier is used to categorize those 'unsure' judgments. The SVM model is trained and tested using the judgments which are classified as civil or criminal by the *Keyword based categorization*. Once the proper training is performed, the 'unsure' judgments are then categorized using the trained SVM model. It is noticeable that the proportion of labels (i.e. civil and criminal) in the training data is highly imbalanced. Hence, it demands an appropriate performance measures (i.e. F1-Score and MCC score) to evaluate the trained model.

In the text classification, considering only domain specific features significantly enriches the performance. Hence primarily, this research keeps only *Legal Dictionary*[3] terms in the judgments while the remaining is filtered. Further, Term Frequency Inverse Document Frequency (TFIDF) score is computed, aiming to recognize significant and important words in judgments. This research retains only the top 50% words in each document with the highest TFIDF score. This filtration process potentially reduces the corpus vocabulary (i.e., a unique set of words), which can significantly influence the time and space complexities of the vectorization technique (i.e. Doc2Vec). Judgments have to be transformed into a numerical vector form to train the classifier model. Hence, Judgments were vectored using Doc2Vec embedding technique, as it has an excellent ability to preserve semantic relatedness among the embedded judgment vectors.

A linear SVM classifier was trained using the vectored judgments labeled as civil and criminal in the final step. Here, SVM is a non-parametric supervised method of classifying data points by finding a linearly separating hyper-plane in N-dimensional space. The SVM classifier finds the hyper-plane that acts as a *maximum margin separator*, that is, it maintains the maximum distance between data points of both classes (Cortes & Vapnik, 1995). The margin of the classifier is maximized by using *Support Vectors*, i.e., data points lying closer to the hyper-plane, and thus affects the position of it. The margin of

Figure 1. Architectural flow of judgment categorization

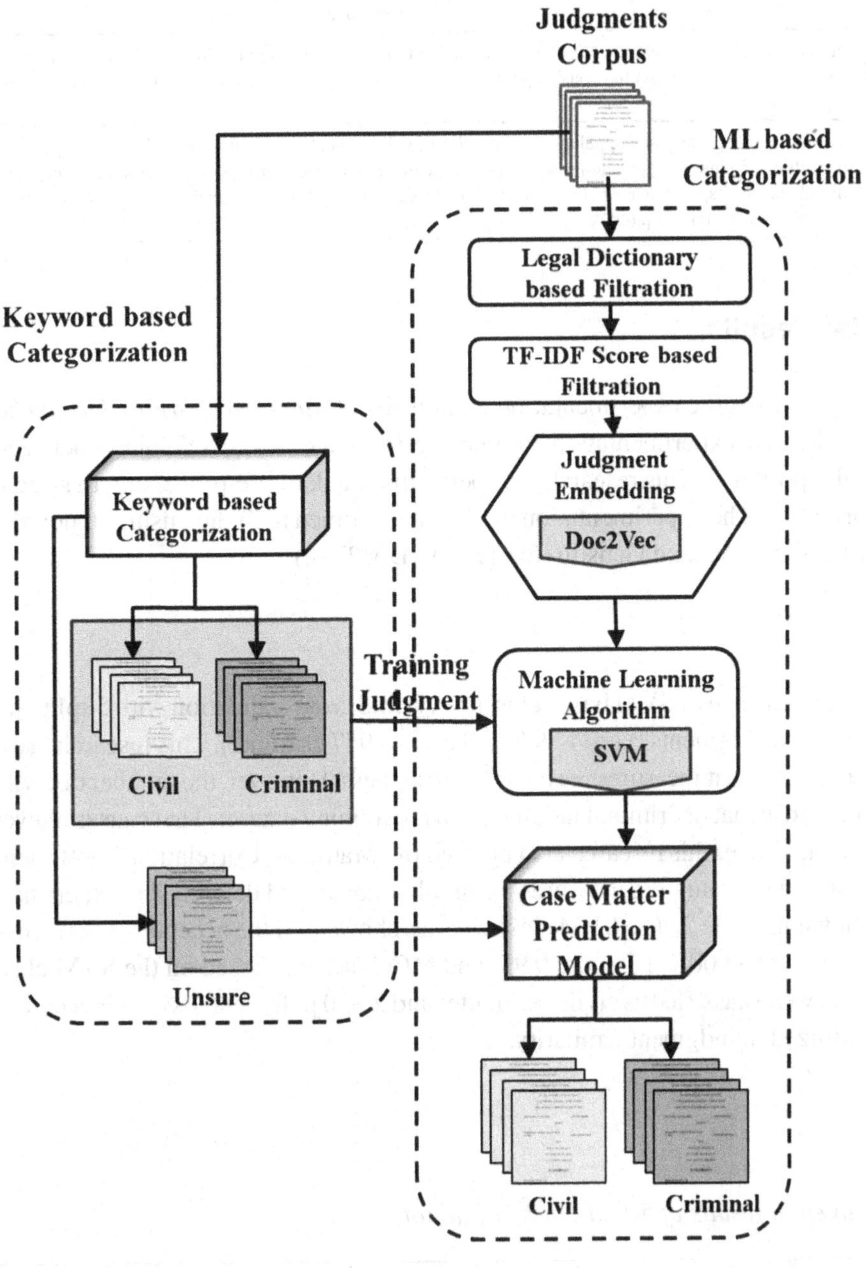

the hyper-plane is therefore the shortest distance between the instances of both classes that are closest to the hyper-plane. Finally, all the unlabeled judgment vectors were categorized as either civil or criminal using the trained SVM classifier model.

Table 1. Case matter specific keywords

Category	Keywords
Civil	'civil appeal', 'civil appellate', 'civil original', 'appeal(civil)', 'appellate jurisdition(civil)', 'appelate civil', 'writ petition(civil)', 'civil miscellaneous', 'special leave petition (civil)', 'slp(civil)', 's.l.p.(civil)', 'special leave petition(c)', 'slp(c)', 's.l.p.(c)'
Criminal	'criminal appeal', 'criminal appellate', 'criminal original', 'appeal (criminal)', 'appeal (crl)', 'appellate jurisdition(criminal)', 'appellate jurisdition(crl)', 'criminal appelate', 'writ petition (criminal)', 'criminal miscellaneous', 'special leave petition(criminal)', 'slp(criminal)', 's.l.p (criminal)', 'special leave petition(crl)', 'slp(crl)', 's.l.p.(crl)', 'w.p.(crl)', 'cr.p.c'

Experimental Results

This subsection discusses the experimentation and results of *Machine Learning based Categorization*. As, discussed earlier, the experimentation has been performed on 48,518 SCI judgments collected from the online Legal repository[1]. This research also performs standard pre-processing to structure and clean the textual information. The experimentation has been performed in Python using standard libraries such as sklearn (for Linear SVM) and Gensim (for TFIDF, Doc2Vec).

Results

To validate the performance of SVM based classifier, k-fold cross-validation with 5 splits was performed on the 33,561 labelled judgments (i.e. 24,294 civil and 14,957 criminal). This research uses Accuracy as a performance measure, as it measures the overall correctness. However, the number of civil judgments is considerably more than that of criminal judgments in the training dataset. That causes a severe imbalance in the training data. Hence, this research also utilized the Matthews Correlation Coefficient (MCC) and F1-Score, as best-suited evaluation measures for highly imbalanced dataset. The experimental results of each fold are shown in Table 2. The SVM classifier has showcased the acceptable performance in terms of average Accuracy of 96.00%, F1-score 0.97, and MCC of 0.90. Based on the SVM classifier model, 12,117 judgments were classified as civil case matter and 2,840 judgments as criminal case matter, which can be further utilized in judgment similarity.

Table 2. Experimental results of 5-fold cross-validation

Fold	True Civil	False Civil	True Criminal	False Criminal	Accuracy	F1-Score	MCC Score
1	5277	106	1311	58	97.57%	0.98	0.93
2	4996	146	1542	68	96.83%	0.98	0.92
3	4794	124	1749	85	96.90%	0.98	0.92
4	4616	271	1783	82	94.77%	0.96	0.88
5	4378	324	1966	86	93.93%	0.95	0.87
Average					**96.00%**	**0.97**	**0.90**

Open Issues in Legal Information Retrieval

This subsection discusses the major issues and challenges specific to the Indian Legal document similarity analysis.

- **Imbalance Judgment Category:** As discussed in the case study, the case matters of the available set of judgments are highly imbalanced, such as civil cases are significantly more in number than the criminal cases. This limits the applicability to ML algorithms (i.e. SVM), as the learned model will be biased towards frequent cases (i.e. civil). Despite the admissible performance of SVM, leaning from properly-balanced data would enhance the functionality of the classification model.
- **Imbalance Content Length and Citations**: By analyzing judgments, it is observed that the length of the judgments is highly skewed. A significant amount of judgments are very small (i.e. consisting of few paragraphs), while many judgments are very large (i.e. consisting of few hundreds of paragraphs). Moreover, an imbalance is also realized in the size of paragraph length, consisting of few words to a substantial number of words. Likewise, in judgment corpus, significant skewness is also noticeable in terms of cited references, ranging differ from zero to several dozens. This imbalance in content and citations may significantly affect the practice of Legal information retrieval.
- **Large number of Legal Documents:** Presently, the large number of legal documents digitally exists from various courts like (Apex court, High courts, Session Courts, District courts, etc.) and legislative organizations. Varieties of legal documents are being produced at high velocity. With aforesaid characteristics, majority of Information retrieval techniques cause challenges for space and process complexity.
- **Intrinsic Characteristics of Legal Documents:** Legal documents are comprehensively quite lengthy compare to other domain's documents. Moreover, available judgments are written in using natural language (i.e. English) and Legal glossary by a different mindset. Thus, Linguistic and structural heterogeneity can be observed in the judgments corpus. Indian judgment text also contains noisy texts i.e. proper nouns, precedent names, abbreviations of various appeals, slips, articles, etc. Recognizing and eliminating such insignificant text from the large volume of judgments is also a challenging task. Also, proper extraction and utilization of inherent referential information in the legal document is also a big challenge.

CONCLUSION

In the Indian Legal system, identifying a set of relevant judgments to a particular judgment is one of the essential requirements for Legal professionals. Hence, Legal information retrieval has gained significant attention from the research community. Indian Legal judgments are classified either in civil case matter or criminal case matter. Judgments hold strong relevancy within a group of judgments having similar case matter. So, this Chapter presented a Judgment Categorization approach to potentially prune the search space by limiting the search within a particular category. The presented approach also showcased the acceptable performance in terms of Accuracy, F1-Score and MCC Score. Despite the encouraging performance, the present Legal information retrieval possesses many challenges such as a severe imbalance in judgment category, content and citations, volume and intrinsic characteristics of available legal documents. Intense attention is strongly desirable from the research community to make fruitful advancements in Legal information retrieval.

REFERENCES

Bhattacharya, P., Ghosh, K., Pal, A., & Ghosh, S. (2020). Hier-SPCNet: A Legal Statute Hierarchy-based Heterogeneous Network for Computing Legal Case Document Similarity. In *Proceedings of the 43rd International ACM SIGIR* (pp. 1657-1660). ACM.

Blei, D. M., Ng, A. Y., & Jordan, M. I. (2003). Latent dirichlet allocation. *Journal of Machine Learning Research*, *3*(Jan), 993–1022.

Cortes, C., & Vapnik, V. (1995). Support-vector networks. *Machine Learning*, *20*(3), 273–297. doi:10.1007/BF00994018

Grover, A., & Leskovec, J. (2016). Node2vec: Scalable feature learning for networks. In *Proceedings of the 22nd ACM SIGKDD international conference on Knowledge discovery and data mining* (pp. 855-864). 10.1145/2939672.2939754

Kumar, S., Reddy, P. K., Reddy, V. B., & Singh, A. (2011). Similarity analysis of legal judgments. In *Proceedings of the Fourth Annual ACM Bangalore Conference* (pp. 1-4). ACM.

Kumar, S., Reddy, P. K., Reddy, V. B., & Suri, M. (2013). Finding similar legal judgements under common law system. In *Proceedings of International workshop on databases in networked information systems* (pp. 103-116). Springer. 10.1007/978-3-642-37134-9_9

Le, Q., & Mikolov, T. (2014). Distributed representations of sentences and documents. In *Proceedings of International conference on machine learning* (pp. 1188-1196). PMLR.

Mandal, A., Chaki, R., Saha, S., Ghosh, K., Pal, A., & Ghosh, S. (2017). Measuring similarity among legal court case documents. In *Proceedings of the 10th annual ACM Indiacompute conference* (pp. 1-9). 10.1145/3140107.3140119

Mikolov, T., Chen, K., Corrado, G., & Dean, J. (2013a). *Efficient estimation of word representations in vector space.* ArXiv Preprint arXiv:1301.3781.

Mikolov, T., Sutskever, I., Chen, K., Corrado, G. S., & Dean, J. (2013b). Distributed representations of words and phrases and their compositionality. *Advances in Neural Information Processing Systems*, 3111–3119.

Raghav, K., Reddy, P. B., Reddy, V. B., & Reddy, P. K. (2015). Text and citations based cluster analysis of legal judgments. In *Proceedings of International conference on mining intelligence and knowledge exploration* (pp. 449-459). Springer. 10.1007/978-3-319-26832-3_42

Raghav, K., Reddy, P. K., & Reddy, V. B. (2016). Analyzing the extraction of relevant legal judgments using paragraph-level and citation information. In Proceedings of AI4JC Artificial Intelligence for Justice (pp. 1-8). Academic Press.

Sugathadasa, K., Ayesha, B., de Silva, N., Perera, A. S., Jayawardana, V., Lakmal, D., & Perera, M. (2018, July). Legal document retrieval using document vector embeddings and deep learning. In *Proceedings of Science and information conference* (pp. 160-175). Springer.

Trivedi, A., Trivedi, A., Varshney, S., Joshipura, V., Mehta, R., & Dhanani, J. (2020). Extracted Summary Based Recommendation System for Indian Legal Documents. In *Proceedings of 2020 11th International Conference on Computing, Communication and Networking Technologies (ICCCNT)* (pp. 1-6). IEEE.

Wagh, R. S., & Anand, D. (2020). Legal document similarity: A multi-criteria decision-making perspective. *PeerJ. Computer Science*, 6, 1–20. doi:10.7717/peerj-cs.262 PMID:33816914

ENDNOTES

[1] https://indiankanoon.org/
[2] https://scikit-learn.org/stable/modules/svm.html
[3] https://dictionary.law.com

Chapter 14
An Experimental Analysis to Learn Data Imbalance in Scholarly Data:
A Case Study on ResearchGate

Mitali Desai

https://orcid.org/0000-0002-3264-6143

Sardar Vallabhbhai National Institute of Technology, Surat, India

Rupa G. Mehta

Sardar Vallabhbhai National Institute of Technology, Surat, India

Dipti P. Rana

https://orcid.org/0000-0002-5058-1355

Sardar Vallabhbhai National Institute of Technology, Surat, India

ABSTRACT

Data imbalance is a key challenge in the majority of real-world classification problems. It refers to the disparity of data instances corresponding to either of the class labels. Data imbalance is studied in detail with respect to many data domains such as transaction data, medical data, e-commerce data, meteorological data, social media data, and web data. But the scholarly data domain is yet to be analyzed pertaining to data imbalance. In this chapter, the scholarly data domain is explored with a focus to study various forms of data imbalance. A well-known and popular scholarly platform, ResearchGate (RG), is targeted to extract real scholarly data. An extensive experimental analysis is performed on the extracted data in order to identify the existence of both data-level and network-level imbalance. The outcome contributes to the learning of various types of data imbalance that exist in scholarly data. Resolving the existing data imbalance will substantially help in achieving efficient and accurate outcomes in many real-world scholarly literature applications.

DOI: 10.4018/978-1-7998-7371-6.ch014

INTRODUCTION

Data imbalance is referred as an unequal distribution of data instances among classes (Kaur et al. 2019). A few data instances fall into the minority class whereas majority class is occupied by a major portion of data instances. Such substantial difference in data distribution leads to a performance bias in the model. It is a crucial issue in many data-intensive applications such as anomaly detection, fraud discovery, spam recognition, natural disaster prediction, image recognition, disease identification and claim prediction (Somasundaram & Reddy, 2016). An intensive work has been carried out to study data imbalance in mentioned data domains.

The proposed solutions to resolve data imbalance majorly fall int two categories: data centric approaches and algorithm centric approaches. Various data centric approaches (Rout et al., 2018; Kotsiantis et al., 2006; Mahmood, 2015) include under sampling, over sampling, cluster-based over sampling, Synthetic Minority Over-sampling Technique (SMOTE). Algorithm centric approaches incorporate bagging based methods, boosting based methods, penalized algorithms and tree-based techniques to address the imbalance issue.

In recent times, applications such as community detection, influence identification, influence ranking, expert finding, recommendation systems and discovering topical authority in the domain of scholarly literature analytic are seeking researchers' interest. The open accessibility, availability and digitization provide researchers a common medium in terms of scholarly platforms to connect, communicate and cooperate. Due to an extensive utilization of various scholarly platforms, there exist massive scholarly data. Such scholarly data that is present across wide range of digitized scholarly platforms provides potential base in scholarly literature analytic.

Numerous studies are present in the realm of the mentioned applications, although identifying the existence and the forms of data imbalance in scholarly data is yet to be focused. Data imbalance leads to many adverse effects that decrease the efficiency of scholarly outcomes. On the other hand, identifying and then resolving various data imbalance will help achieving outperforming results in scholarly literature applications.

In this chapter, the real scholarly data extracted from very popular scholarly platform ResearchGate (RG) is thoroughly analyzed to inspect the data imbalance problem. In data extraction, N number of RG users are targeted and their profile demographics are rendered. Based upon selected demographics, various experimentation scenarios are built to deeply analyze the data imbalance. Further, the RG graph is constructed using the followers/followings relations present among targeted RG users. The RG graph is visualized in order to identify network-level imbalance.

The results disclose that due inherent complex characteristics of scholarly data, various forms of imbalance exist at both data and network level. Identifying such forms of imbalance opens new paradigms of understanding data imbalance in order to develop novel approaches and mechanisms to achieve accurate outcomes for real-world problems in scholarly literature domain.

The remainder of this chapter is systematized as follows: In section Related Research, the recent research that is carried out in different application domains to identify and resolve data imbalance is briefly discussed. The experimental setup and results are described in section Experimentation and Result Analysis. In section Conclusion, this work is concluded.

RELATED RESEARCH

Data imbalance problem has remained at the focus since a long and many researchers have contributed to this domain. In this section, the data domains that are explored in terms of analyzing data imbalance in recent research are briefly discussed.

Gao et al. (2014) worked on semantic extraction from video dataset. The authors have proposed Enhanced and Hierarchical Structure (EHS) method for data imbalance issue. The proposed method outperformed common sampling methods. Nepal & Pathan (2014) worked with anomaly detection application in information security domain. The authors have represented various techniques on resolving data imbalance related to security in cloud systems. Wan et al. (2017) have focused on bioinformatic domain and have discovered an efficient prediction algorithm for proteins' sub-cellular localization. Authors have implemented multi-label classifier using an ensemble called HPSLPred in order to handle imbalanced data. Song et al. (2014) have classified DNA-binding proteins using an ensemble approach nDNA-Prot for imbalanced data. Zakaryazad & Duman (2016), Fu et al. (2016), Kulkarni & Ade (2016) have aimed at credit card fraud detection application. Identifying the inconsistent person responsible for fraud is a crucial task in credit card fraud detection, where imbalance data reduces the accuracy of the task. Abeysinghe et al. (2016) have proposed techniques for detecting insurance fraud while dealing with imbalanced data. Krawczyk et al. (2016) and Yang et al. (2016) worked in the domain of cancer and tumor tissues related research. To deal with unbalanced data, Krawczyk et al. have incorporated the boosting knowledge of under-sample evolution for each of the base classifier. Yang et al. have used balanced sampling and feature selection. Folino et al. (2016) have utilized genetic programming and incremental ensemble to detect cybersecurity drifts.

It is identified from the relevant literature that the domain of scholarly data is yet to be explored with respect to identifying imbalance. Considering the importance of scholarly literature analytic in realistic applications and considering detrimental impact of data imbalance on application performance, this chapter focuses on inspecting various forms of data-level and network-level imbalance in the domain of scholarly data.

Experimentation and Result Analysis

To perform an experimental analysis on data imbalance in scholarly data domain, real RG data is used. Various surveys conducted on numerous scholarly platforms revealed that RG is widely utilized and extremely popular among researchers (Desai et al., 2021). RG is preferable among other available scholarly platforms in terms of usage frequency, activeness of users, number of users, reliability of information, social media like follower/following groups and range of diverse demographics (Gasparyan, 2017; Rapple, 2018; Ortega, 2018 & Jordan, 2019).

RG data is rendered using our developed Data Rendering method (Desai et al., 2021). Total 1544 RG users connected by the means of followers and followings on RG platform are targeted. For each RG user, the demographic information i.e., Name, RGScore, Total Research Interest (TRI), Affiliation, Citations, Reads, Recommendations, Research Items, Projects, Questions, Answers, Followings, Followers, Location, Department and Position is rendered. Rendered data is stored in database with label D.

To analyze the data-level and network-level imbalance in D, cluster analysis was performed. RGScore, TRI, Citations, Reads, Recommendations, Research Items, Projects, Questions, Answers, Followings and Followers are selected to form various clusters. Based on selected demographics, following experimentation scenarios are built. All experiments are conducted on machine having Ubuntu 18.04 LTS (64-bit), 8 GB RAM and Intel Core i7-7700 Processor.

Experiment 1

To identify the data-level imbalance, D is clustered based on the average RGScore value - RG_{Avg}.

The cluster analysis disclosed the following two clusters of RG users as displayed in Figure 1: i) the first cluster contains users having equal or higher RGScore compared to RG_{Avg}. ii) the second cluster contains users having lower RGScore compared to RG_{Avg}.

Figure 1. Cluster formulation based on RGScore

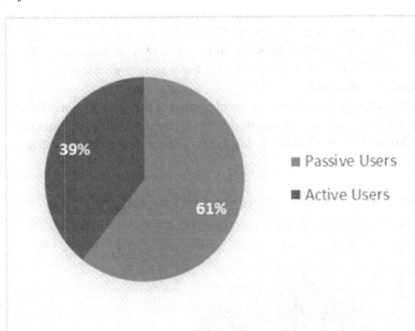

RGScore value represents the overall influence of an active RG user. The first cluster contains RG users who are identified as highly influential based on their RGScore. These users are denoted as "Active Users". The second cluster has users who are identified as lower influential according to their RGScore. These users are represented as "Passive Users".

The results revealed that from the dataset, 39% users are "Active Users" while 61% users are "Passive Users". It signifies that majority of RG users in sample data are just registered users and are not taking active part in the opportunities provided by RG.

This experiment suggests that the high degree of imbalance is found in terms of users' degree of activeness in scholarly activities. In many realistic applications such as community detection, influence identification, recommendation systems, such imbalance might degrade the efficiency of results.

Experiment 2

The clusters of "Active Users" and "Passive Users" formed in Experiment 1 are analyzed further to identify the data-level imbalance in D based on the degree of scientific contributions and technical communications.

To analyze the degree of scientific contributions of RG users, five demographics: citations, reads, recommendations, research items and projects are considered. The other four demographics i.e., questions, answers, followings and followers are taken into account while analyzing RG users' degree of communications.

Based on the mentioned nine demographics, each cluster formed in Experiment 1 is further divided into four clusters: Contributors, Communicators, Both and None.

As displayed in Figure 2, 69% of users are not taking part in any scientific contributions or communication, 11% of users are active as contributor as well as communicator, 10% users are contributor and 10% users are communicator in the cluster of "Passive Users".

In the cluster of "Active Users" as displayed in Figure 3, 69% of users are neither contributors nor communicators, 16% of users are active as both contributor and communicator, 8% users are communicator and 7% users are contributor.

It is noted that in both clusters, there is an equal portion of the users who are "dead users", although for contributors and commutators, the overall degree of participation is substantially higher (70%) in "Active Users" cluster. This experiment reveals that at a great degree, the imbalance is discovered in

Figure 2. Cluster formulation based on RGScore passive users cluster

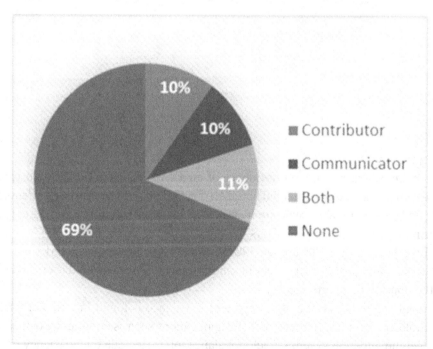

Figure 3. Cluster formulation based on RGScore active users cluster

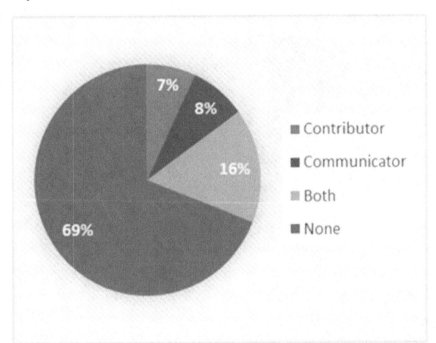

both clusters while analyzing the scientific contributions and technical communications of RG users based on their RGScore.

Experiment 3

Experiment 1 is conducted taking into account TRI instead of RGScore. Same as in Experiment 1, the cluster analysis disclosed two clusters of RG users as displayed in Figure 4: i) the first cluster contains users having equal or higher TRI compared to TRI_{Avg}. ii) the second cluster contains users having lower TRI compared to TRI_{Avg}.

Unlike RGScore, TRI represents specifically the scientific influence of an active RG user. The first cluster contains RG users who have high scientific impact based on their TRI whereas the second cluster has users who have low scientific impact according to their TRI. The first cluster denotes the "Active Users" and the second cluster depicts the "Passive Users".

The results exposed that from the dataset, 14% users are "Active Users" while 86% users are "Passive Users". It signifies that majority of RG users in sample data are just registered users and have lower scientific impact.

This experiment suggests that the high degree of imbalance is found in terms of users' degree of scientific involvement. In many realistic applications such as expert finding, topical authority discovery, subject based recommendation systems, such imbalance might lower the competence of outcomes.

Figure 4. Cluster formulation based on TRI

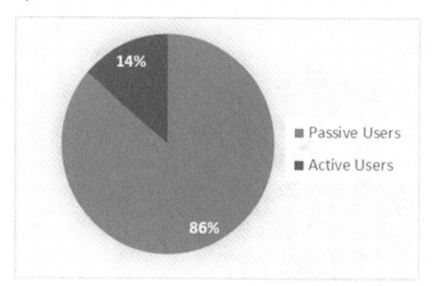

Experiment 4

The clusters formed in Experiment 3 are analyzed further as described in Experiment 2.

As described in Experiment 2, the clusters of "Active Users" and "Passive Users" formed in Experiment 3 are analyzed further in order to identify the data-level imbalance in D based on the degree of scientific contributions and technical communications.

As displayed in Figure 5, 66% of users are not taking part in any scientific contributions or communication, 12% of users are active as contributor as well as communicator, 12% users are contributor and 10% users are communicator in the cluster of "Passive Users".

In the cluster of "Active Users" as displayed in Figure 6, 67% of users are neither contributors nor communicators, 12% of users are active as both contributor and communicator, 12% users are contributor and 9% users are communicator.

It is noted that for similar portion of contributors and/or communicators in both clusters, the overall degree of participation is substantially higher (65%) in "Active Users" cluster. This experiment commends that at a great degree, the imbalance is discovered in both clusters while analyzing the scientific contributions and technical communications of RG users based on their TRI.

Experiment 5

To identify the data-level imbalance in D based upon academic position of RG users, D is divided into multiple groups. The position demographic is used to divide users.

The results depicted that based on the academic position of RG Users, six clusters: Professor, Researcher, Assistant Professor, Associate Professor, Director and Head are formed. The highest portion of sample (36%) belongs to the professor category, 22% users are assistant professors, 19% users are research scholars, 15% users are associate professors, 6% users are heads and 2% users are directors in various academic or research organizations.

Figure 5. Cluster formulation based on TRI passive users cluster

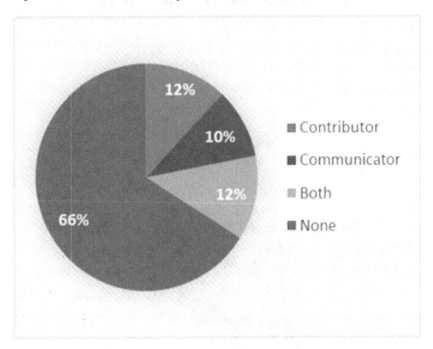

Figure 6. Cluster formulation based on TRI active users cluster

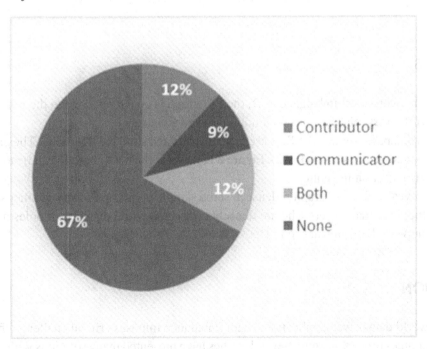

In this experiment also as displayed in Figure 7, high degree of imbalance is identified which will impact negatively on the performance in many applications such as researchers' impact calculation, reviewer/editor recommendation and research award nominee discovery.

Figure 7. Cluster formulation based on position

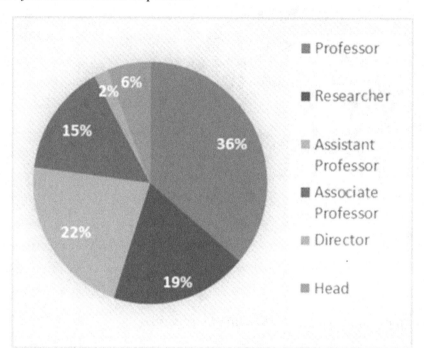

Experiment 6

To identify the network-level imbalance in D, the RG graph is constructed using the rendered data and the followings/followers relations present among targeted RG users.

Neo4j graph database (version 3.5.8) is used to construct and store the RG graph. The graph is visualized using neo4j and gephi (version 0.9.2). Figure 8 represents the neo4j based visualization and Figure 9 denotes the visualization in gephi.

The results revealed that RG graph is dense at some sample points and scatter at other sample points. In RG graph, there are many users who are densely connected while many open poles are also found. This suggests network-level imbalance in D.

CONCLUSION

In many real-world data driven applications, data imbalance imposes critical challenge that affects the application outcomes to a great extent. Several studies have presented many solutions with respect to data imbalance issue in numerous applications. In recent times, scholarly literature analytic based applications such as influence identification and ranking, recommendation system, expert finding, topical authority discovery, researchers' impact assessment etc. are seeking researchers' attention. Inspecting various

Figure 8. RG graph in Neo4j

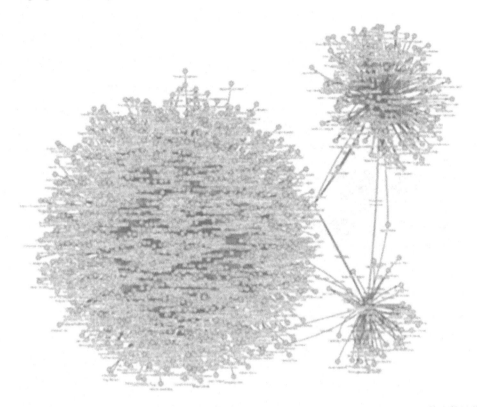

forms of data imbalance in scholarly data is still lacking in literature. This chapter aims at identifying data imbalance in scholarly data. The real scholarly data from popular scholarly platform ResearchGate is extracted. Various experiments are conducted to analyze the data-level and network-level imbalance. The results disclosed that in scholarly data, there exist an issue of data imbalance which needs the focus from researchers. Resolving the existing data imbalance in scholarly data will majorly improve the outcomes of scholarly literature analytic.

Figure 9. RG graph in Gephi

REFERENCES

Abeysinghe, C., Li, J., & He, J. (2016). A classifier hub for imbalanced financial data. In *Proceedings of the Australasian Database Conference*. Springer. 10.1007/978-3-319-46922-5_43

Desai, M., Mehta, R. G., & Rana, D. P. (2021). RGNet: The Novel Framework to Model Linked Research-Gate Information into Network Using Hicrarchical Data Rendering. In *Advances in Machine Learning and Computational Intelligence* (pp. 37–45). Springer. doi:10.1007/978-981-15-5243-4_4

Folino, G., Pisani, F. S., & Sabatino, P. (2016). An incremental ensemble evolved by using genetic programming to efficiently detect drifts in cyber security datasets. In *Proceedings of the Conference on Genetic and Evolutionary Computation Conference Companion*. ACM. 10.1145/2908961.2931682

Fu, K., Cheng, D., Tu, Y., & Zhang, L. (2016). Credit card fraud detection using convolutional neural networks. In *Proceedings of the International Conference on Neural Information Processing*. Springer. 10.1007/978-3-319-46675-0_53

Gao, Z., Zhang, L. F., Chen, M. Y., Hauptmann, A., Zhang, H., & Cai, A. N. (2014). Enhanced and hierarchical structure algorithm for data imbalance problem in semantic extraction under massive video dataset. *Multimedia Tools and Applications*, *68*(3), 641–657. doi:10.100711042-012-1071-7

Gasparyan, A. Y., Nurmashev, B., Yessirkepov, M., Endovitskiy, D. A., Voronov, A. A., & Kitas, G. D. (2017). Researcher and author profiles: Opportunities, advantages, and limitations. *Journal of Korean Medical Science, 32*(11), 1749. doi:10.3346/jkms.2017.32.11.1749 PMID:28960025

Jordan, K. (2019). From social networks to publishing platforms: A review of the history and scholarship of academic social network sites. *Frontiers in Digital Humanities, 6*, 5. doi:10.3389/fdigh.2019.00005

Kaur, H., Pannu, H. S., & Malhi, A. K. (2019). A Systematic Review on Imbalanced Data Challenges in Machine Learning: Applications and Solutions. *ACM Computing Surveys, 52*(4), 1–36.

Kaur, H., Pannu, H. S., & Malhi, A. K. (2019). A systematic review on imbalanced data challenges in machine learning: Applications and solutions. *ACM Computing Surveys, 52*(4), 1–36. doi:10.1145/3343440

Kotsiantis, S., Kanellopoulos, D., & Pintelas, P. (2006). Handling imbalanced datasets: A review. *GESTS International Transactions on Computer Science and Engineering, 30*(1), 25–36.

Krawczyk, B., Galar, M., Jeleń, Ł., & Herrera, F. (2016). Evolutionary undersampling boosting for imbalanced classification of breast cancer malignancy. *Applied Soft Computing, 38*, 714–726. doi:10.1016/j.asoc.2015.08.060

Kulkarni & Ade. (2016). Logistic regression learning model for handling concept drift with unbalanced data in credit card fraud detection system. In *Proceedings of the 2nd International Conference on Computer and Communication Technologies*. Springer.

Mahmood, A. M. (2015). Class imbalance learning in data mining–a survey. *International Journal of Communication Technology for Social Networking Services, 3*(2), 17–38. doi:10.21742/ijctsns.2015.3.2.02

Nepal, S., & Pathan, M. (Eds.). (2014). *Security, privacy and trust in cloud systems*. Springer Berlin Heidelberg. doi:10.1007/978-3-642-38586-5

Ortega, J. L. (2018). Reliability and accuracy of altmetric providers: A comparison among Altmetric. com, PlumX and Crossref Event Data. *Scientometrics, 116*(3), 2123–2138. doi:10.100711192-018-2838-z

Rapple, C. (2018). Understanding and supporting researchers' choices in sharing their publications: the launch of the FairShare Network and Shareable PDF. *Insights, 31*.

Rout, N., Mishra, D., & Mallick, M. K. (2018). Handling imbalanced data: a survey. In *International Proceedings on Advances in Soft Computing, Intelligent Systems and Applications* (pp. 431–443). Springer. doi:10.1007/978-981-10-5272-9_39

Somasundaram, A., & Reddy, U. S. (2016). Data imbalance: Effects and solutions for classification of large and highly imbalanced data. In *International Conference on Research in Engineering, Computers and Technology (ICRECT 2016)* (pp. 1-16). Academic Press.

Song, Li, Zeng, Wu, Guo, & Zou. (2014). nDNA-prot: Identification of DNA-binding proteins based on unbalanced classification. *BMC Bioinformatics, 15*(1), 298.

Wan, S., Duan, Y., & Zou, Q. (2017). HPSLPred: An ensemble multi-label classifier for human protein subcellular location prediction with imbalanced source. *Proteomics, 17*(17-18), 1700262. doi:10.1002/pmic.201700262 PMID:28776938

Yang, Zhou, Zhu, Ma, & Ji. (2016). Iterative ensemble feature selection for multiclass classification of imbalanced microarray data. *J. Biol. Res. Thessaloniki.*

Zakaryazad, A., & Duman, E. (2016). A profit-driven Artificial Neural Network (ANN) with applications to fraud detection and direct marketing. *Neurocomputing, 175*, 121–131. doi:10.1016/j.neucom.2015.10.042

Chapter 15
Gender–Based Tweet Analysis (GTA)

Dipti P. Rana
(iD) https://orcid.org/0000-0002-5058-1355
Sardar Vallabhbhai National Institute of Technology, Surat, India

Navodita Saini
Sardar Vallabhbhai National Institute of Technology, Surat, India

ABSTRACT

Each gender is having special personality and behavior characteristics that can be naturally reflected in the language used on social media to review, spread information, make relationships, etc. This information is used by different agencies for their profits. The magnified study of this information can reflect the implicit biases of their creators' gender. The ratio of gender is imbalanced across the global world, social media, discussion, etc. Twitter is used to discuss the issues caused by COVID-19 disease like its symptoms, mental health, advice, etc. This fascinating information motivated this research to propose the methodology gender-based tweet analysis (GTA) to study and magnify gender's impact on emotions of tweet data. The analysis of the experiment discovered the biases of gender on emotions of tweet data and highlighted the future real-world applications which may become more productive if gender biases are considered for the safety and benefit of society.

INTRODUCTION

The modern digital era has generated big data which are used by many researchers to discover the pattern based on content, emotions, behavior, network surfing, etc. (Gaind, Syal, Padgalwar, 2019; Kaushal & Patwardhan, 2018). These all patterns if analyzed in detail, one can observe that these patterns have an impact on gender. Each gender is having its special personality and behavior characteristics, which they are showing with the help of the language of expression when providing a review, information spreading, make friends, follow the topics/other users, etc. All this information without considering the biases of gender used by different agencies for their profits to recommend the products in terms of the

DOI: 10.4018/978-1-7998-7371-6.ch015

recommendation of items, links, movies, songs, etc. The syntactic and semantic linguistic features used by the user can reproduce the implicit biases of their creators' gender.

The ratio of both genders male and female is imbalanced across the global world. In addition, this ratio is imbalanced on social media as registered users, users' status, users per discussion, etc. The author (Top Twitter Demographics That Matter to Social Media Marketers, 2021) said that non-technical social media networks like Snapchat, Pinterest, Instagram, Facebook, etc. have more females than males, whereas the technical and scholarly social media networks like Twitter, LinkedIn, etc. have fewer females than the males. One of the most popular social network applications "twitter" shows gender discrimination in its users. The global audience of Twitter shows skewness towards the male gender with 62% over 38% female. From which only in the US, the gender division is 50 - 50 without the age information. However, among U.S. adults, the most active users are women with 65% and having more private Twitter accounts than men are. While in India, the most active users are men with 85%, which is the third country in the highest male-to-female ratio ranking. Other countries like the Brunei, Indonesia, Laos, Malaysia, Philippines, and Thailand have the highest female Twitter users.

The purpose of the usage of social media for females and males is completely different. Generally, social networking sites used by female gender is to make contacts and stay in connection with friends and family, while social networking sites used by male gender, to assimilate the data required to form influence. Social media aids in research, gather relevant contacts, and ultimately increase their status. This gender imbalance is having its impact and researchers are discussing this.

In the medical science field especially in psychology, the researchers are studying gender-based information for a long time. They identified gender-linked features using the comparison of text samples from known males and females and compared the calculated frequencies of interesting features from text like usage of the first-person singular, a positive self-presentation or other, and then interpreted the results in terms of psychological theory (Leaper & Ayres, 2007; Newman, Groom, Handelman, & Pennebaker, 2008; Fast, & Funder, 2010).

However, in the machine learning research area, gender-based research is still in its fantasy. The imbalance ratio of gender attracted the researchers to look at its impact on the emotions of text data. During the tough time like the pandemic of COVID-19, different social media platforms used by the users during the pandemic year 2019-20 to discuss the issues caused by the novel virus disease like its symptoms, mental health, health services, advice, recovery rate, hospitalization/death ratio, containment area, supply chain, etc. These period tweets involved a variety of discussions with different emotions from different categories of people like gender, profession, age, culture, etc. From all these categories of people, the author identified "gender-biased issue" as an eye-catching issue because of its applicability in a wide variety of domains.

To yield the promising knowledge outcome from the shared information by assessing the gender's impact requires gender identification. Traditionally the only way to identify the gender is through the explicit gender feature or separate gender-based questionnaire. However, in this digital world, the challenges posed to the researchers for the identification of gender due to unavailability of users' personal information hidden behind the fantasy or ambiguous name and due to the policy, the data provider is not availing the gender information.

To analyze the impact on the emotion of tweet text from the perspective of gender, this research proposed the methodology Gender based Tweet Analysis (GTA). The preprocessing of the tweet text performed to use the data for the further step. To consider the data partition based on gender, the username utilized here to identify the type of user is male, female, or organization followed by the gender detection library for fantasy name. Then the emotion analysis carried out for all the tweets together and tweets sampled by genders. The analysis of the result emphasized more biases of emotion for tweet data of the female gender over the male gender.

The flow of rest of the chapter organization is as described: The background section provides a brief introduction and the related survey. The focus of the chapter discusses the motives of the research problem. The proposed approach of Gender based Tweet Analysis introduced in the next section followed by the result discussion, future direction and conclusion.

BACKGROUND

Due to the COVID-19 pandemic, worldwide people are restricted with limited activities and worsen their health and quality of life as they locked down in their homes. Social media was the platform heavily used by people to communicate with their loved ones where people expressed themselves with different types of emotions. These emotions expressed by different gender in different ways and different qualities due to their personality differences of interactions, expressions, usage of text frequency, and psychological factors like joy, disgust, fear, anger, anticipation, trust, sadness, surprise, etc.

The identification of gender perspective knowledge for the machine learning approaches required discovering a set of content-based features and network-based features from social networking platform. The content-based features are the linguistic features and extracted from the textual content shared by the user and network-based features are the features that extracted from the network information and highlight when and how the user behaves with others on a social network.

Literature Review of Social Media Network Data

The literature review is focusing on aspects like how the gender information is extracted, how tweet sentiment or emotions are derived, and how the expression of language is differ for different genders.

The researchers are utilizing different approaches to identify the user's gender information from the Twitter data. In (HuL., & Kearney M. W., (2020)), the authors inferred the gender information from the users' first names from 84 randomly selected Twitter profiles. Other studies (McCright, A. M., (2010).), also took the tweet as the data and considered gender as well. For gender identification of the user, they used Mozdeh API that identifies the gender with 1st name of the user (http://mozdeh.wlv.ac.uk/). The study by (Garcia-Rudolph A, Laxe S, Saurí J, Bernabeu Guitart M, 2019), the author utilized Twitter user's username, profile information like name, photo, description, and tweets to review their final gender for each Twitter user.

The text content reflects the user's ability to express them with the help of language. The study of user's language helps to understand the psychology of the people and their behavior. Psychologists articulate the z.existence of personality cues in the text by discovering correlations between a range of linguistic variables and personality traits, including acoustic parameters by connecting them with the genders directly (Leaper & Ayres, 2007; Newman, Groom, Handelman, & Pennebaker, 2008; Fast, & Funder, 2010). However, from the rich and huge collection of textual and network data of social media is attempted by very few researchers. The authors attempted to predict user's personalities from the status updates by utilizing the standard Personality Recognition from Text (PRT) techniques (Golbeck, Robles & Turner, 2011). A detailed review of PRT is available in (Agarwal, 2014). In (Alm, Roth, &

Sproat, 2005), the emotion considered as a linguistic unit and its discovery as a multi-class classification problem. An approach proposed in (Go & Huang, 2009) classified automatically the sentiment of Twitter data with emoticons as either a positive or a negative with respect to a query term of products' purchase using distant supervised learning. The work (Barbosa & Feng, 2010) detected robust sentiment from Twitter from biased and noisy data by considering the two-level classifications. In the same year, (Pak & Paroubek, 2010) considered tweets with positive emoticons such as ":)", ":-)" as positive and negative emoticons such as ":(",":-(" as negative for sentiment analysis and opinion mining. The work of (Hu & Kearney, 2020; Cameron & Shaw, 2016) analyzed tweets for gender differences in the area of politics which is the issue of man and discovered that females focus the stronger sense of group awareness and desire to promote tweets. The climate change communication on Twitter was analyzed in (Holmberg & Hellsten, 2015; McCright, 2010) and showed that females are more interested in the anthropogenic impact on climate change. The influence of gender and personality from 238 undergraduate students' from the usage of online social networking websites such as MySpace, Facebook, or both examined in (Muscanell, Guadagno, 2012) and discovered individual differences in online behavior where women used for relationship maintenance while men used social networking sites for forming new relationships. In the work (Psylla, Sapiezynski, Mones &, Lehmann, 2017) classified the person's gender by evaluating the similarities and differences from the observed and behavior data of person-to-person BlueTooth interactions, metadata of calls and short text messages, GPS and wifi locations, Facebook posts and Questionnaires. The survey of (Kharde & Sonawane, 2016) discussed the characteristic attributes of human personality in terms of behavior, temperament, emotion, and intellectual. The paper (Gaind, Sya, & Padgalwar, 2019) addressed the issue of detection, classification, and quantification of emotions from tweets, using Natural Language Processing from text oriented features like emojis, Parts of Speech, degree words, negations, and other grammer analysis with classification algorithms.

In the study of (Petovska, Goldberg, Brüggemann-Klein, & Nyokabi, 2020) analyzed the concept of implicit bias in the study and based on the statistics discovered the less ratio gender i.e. female students in the computer science field department is affected by gender bias in the academic life from real student feedback data. In the work (Haferkamp, Eimler, Papadakis, Kruck, 2012) studied the multi-methodological survey of content of 106 user-profiles. They emphasized the gender differences in Internet communication and behavior where women compare themselves with others, search for information, and prefer to add portrait photos while men look at other people's profiles to find friends and prefer to add full-body shots. Using Latent Dirichlet Allocation (LDA), (Wang, Burke, & Kraut, 2013) identified topics from Facebook status updates of more than half a million and determined women have a tendency to share personal content related to family, while the male counterpart discuss more public matters like politics and sports. Moreover, women receive more feedback than men do, but "male" topics (those more often posted by men) receive more feedback, especially when posted by women. The work (Bao-Khanh & Collier, 2013) presented a novel Twitter sentiment analysis for tracking emotions in earthquakes for better managing the situations by proposing the appropriate emotions.

The work of (Park, 2016) analyzed topics by a grouping of semantically similar words automatically by using LDA from 10 million messages of 52,000 Facebook users and identified topics associated with female users as family, friends, and social life, whereas topics associated with male users as anger, swearing, discussion of objects instead of people, and the use of argumentative language. From 15,000 Facebook users, the same authors found the language used by females was interpersonally more compassionate, polite and warmer, whereas the language used by males was more hostile, impersonal, and colder. Public health research article publication data during the pandemic period from 1st January to 12th May 2020 utilized in (Bell & Fong, 2021) to classify gender based on first and corresponding authors' names and the nation of origin and discovered the exacerbated gender imbalances in scientific research submission during the pandemic period.

From the literature review found that the research work carried out on the emotions from the gender perspective is in the fantasy. The authors depicted that the research area is still open to analyze the number of a tweet posted by the male user has impact on the emotions compared to the number of tweets posted by the female user.

FOCUS OF THE CHAPTER

On March 11, 2020, the World Health Organization (WHO) declared the COVID-19 outbreak as a pandemic, as more than thirteen million people have been diagnosed with the Novel Coronavirus (COVID-19), and approximate half a million people have lost their lives due to this infectious disease. During this period, social media platforms experienced an exponential rise in the content related to the topic pandemic During a disaster, people prefer to use social media networks relatively more time than normal. When the situation unfolds, social media networks such as FaceBook, Twitter, and so on become an active news outlet because they break news more quickly than official news sources and rescue agencies. People conversed informally by expressing their safety status and by asking about the safety status of their loved ones and reporting the event scenarios. This ongoing dialogue phase on certain online forums contributes to a vast quantity of socially produced data. This process of continuous formation of conversations on such public platforms leads to accumulating a large amount of socially generated data. From this data, if properly processed in order to provide effective response to the advantages of primary responders and authorities, situational information may be derived to improve solutions that will enable more effective crisis response (Lamsal, 2020). As the different gender can represent the same content with mentioning of different topics with a variety of sentiments using the diverse language features, the objective of the chapter is to investigate the different emotions of the tweet data of COVID-19 from the gender perspective. This research will open the new study area to know that how the emotions of male and female differ during the pandemic and to help the policy makers to understand the situation.

Research Issues for Gender Perspective Research

In the psychological research (Haferkamp, Eimler, Papadakis, Kruck, 2012; Muscanell, Guadagno, 2012; Wang, Burke, & Kraut, 2013; Park, 2016), the gender information of the users is known to the authors in advance. While in the case of machine learning area, researchers are not having direct gender information most of the time and faces the issues identified from the literature review are as follows:

- The dataset used in the literature review of the publication is not having fantasy name, so require the way of identification like a dictionary-based approach where dictionary of people name or website of institutes are available. However, here the dictionary will be big that requires the novel approach of fast search to map the people's name to the gender.
- In the current era of users' privacy, the users are selecting the username, which is ambiguous among the gender or fantastic, which make it difficult for identification. So, raises the issue of gender identity from the text data shared by the user is also a challenging one.

- The female user's skewed ratio on different social media networks requires the balancing techniques for the majority and minority class of data to avoid the dominating gender biases.
- Compared to the regular pattern/events other than this year, this pandemic year showed various imbalanced issues like increase in COVID-19 disease, varieties of emotions during the lockdown period, the increased sale of items like sanitizer, disrupted supply chain, decrease in consumption of fuel, a variation of the disease, the recovery pattern of disease, etc. Thus, emphasize analyzing the emotions whether gender imbalance is having any impact or not.

There are many issues available, but this chapter is restricting up to the gender identification and emotion analysis of tweets from the gender perspective.

PROPOSED SOLUTION AND RECOMMENDATION

In this study, the tweets considered as the source for the analysis of the emotion. Even though the less length of tweet data, tweets have many possible emotions like joy, disgust, fear, anger, anticipation, trust, sadness, surprise. These emotions are in totality can be categorized as two emotions Positive and Negative. Thus, to analyze the tweet emotion from the perspective of gender, the Figure 1 shows the proposed methodology of the Gender based Tweet Analysis (GTA).

- Twitter data is collected using the twitter data extraction API on COVID-19 and similar tags. The dataset is consisting of many attributes and the tweet text will be consisting of the text with features like acronyms, emoticons, hashtags, numbers, punctuations, symbols, URLs, usernames, with a variety of attributes (Kharde & Sonawane, 2016). Therefore, here to prepare the data ready for the methodology requires the preprocessing of the tweet data.

- Tweet text contains the data expressed in different ways by different users and the raw data polarity is highly susceptible to inconsistency and redundancy. Here, considered the preprocessing of a tweet like, Remove URLs (having format: www.xyz.com), hashtags (starting with "#"), target usernames (starting with "@"), all punctuations, symbols, numbers, etc., Stop Words, Correct the spellings, sequence of repeated characters, Replace all the emoticons with their sentiment, Expand acronyms using an acronym dictionary. In addition, extracted the feature using Word2Vec.
- Gender identification is an important part of the methodology. As a first attempt, to identify the gender, available gender API (https://gender-api.com/) is utilized which takes an input of the user name of the tweet data and returns the gender category.
- To achieve the motive of analyzing the impact of gender on the tweet data, here sampling of the data performed by the gender-wise data. Thus, three types of sampling of data generated for female, male, and other than these two genders like organization, channels, etc.
- The Lexicon NRC Word-Emotion Association has 10,170 Lexical items, that have coded the basic human emotions using Plutchik (Mohammad S, Turney P. 2010) and implemented in the R syuzhet and associate one of the 10,170 Lexical items with one emotion (or more than one emotion). In the context of word and emotion X, a score (range: 0 to 1) is assumed by the NRC Word-Emotion Association Lexicon, where a score of 1 means that the word transmits the highest

Figure 1. Proposed methodology gender based tweet analysis (GTA)

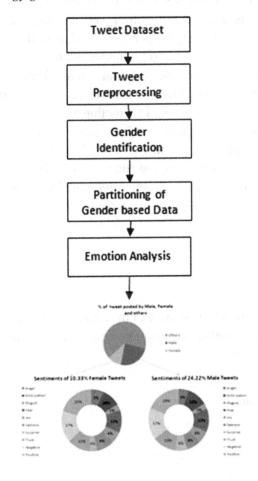

emotion X, while a score of 0 shows the lowest emotion X. The number of words which convey a positive or a negative feeling, or one (or more than one) of Plutchik's eight basic emotions, according to the NRC was then defined (via the got NRC sentiment() function).

- In this study, the emotion score is calculating for eight emotions like joy, disgust, fear, anger, anticipation, trust, sadness, surprise. These emotions if categorized in only two emotions, then it can summarize Joy, Trust, Anticipation, and Trust as positive emotions whereas joy, disgust, fear, anger, anticipation, trust, sadness, surprise as negative emotions. So, here considered total 10 emotions.

EXPERIMENT ANALYSIS

The data set covid19_tweets is collected from the (https://www.kaggle.com/gpreda/covid19-tweets) having 13 attributes and 1,79,105 instances during period of 25th July to 30th Aug 2020 with the hashtags like "corona", "#corona", "corona virus", "#coronavirus", "covid", "#covid", "covid19", "#covid19", "covid-19", "#covid-19" etc. The attributes are user_name, user_location, user_description, user_created, user_followers, user_friends, user_favourites, user_verified, date, text, hashtags, source, is_retweet.

After preprocessing of tweet text, used the gender API of R to identify the gender from the user name and found that 10.33% of tweets i.e. 18,502 instances are from the female gender, 24.21% tweets i.e. 43,373 instances are from male gender and remaining all are from the organization, news channel, etc. As to perform the calculation of emotions, two experiments performed. One experiment is without considering the equal instance as per the gender i.e. emotion analysis on the instances as found through the gender API and another one with consideration of sampling i.e. emotion analysis on the equal number of samples taken from both the genders' instances. For both the experiments, the score or polarity of each tweet calculated with the help of the emotion analyzer of R. The score or polarity of a sentence is between -1.00 to +1.00. Then, calculated the emotion-wise total score for these three categories male, female, and organization in the first experiment and for the two categories male and female in the second experiment.

RESULT DISCUSSION

The following Figure 2 represents the emotions % of the tweet which is posted by a) male user, b) female user, and c) combined genders and other organization, news channels, etc. and the very marginal variations of these three categories can be seen.

Figure 2. Percentage of emotions

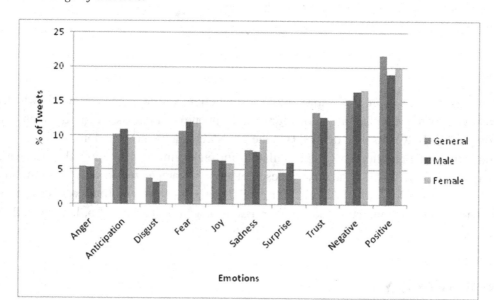

As the focus of the research is gender-wise emotion analysis, so the experiments analyzed the frequency of tweets gender-wise and the emotions of tweets. Here the instances of the female are only 10.33% tweets i.e. 18,502 instances and 24.21% tweets i.e. 43,373 instances are of the male. So, rational percentages of emotions for both genders are calculated. As the number of a female user is very less than the number of a male user so, for better analysis experiment is also performed to analyze by sampling the same number of tweets by male user and female user.

Figure 3. Categorized % of tweets and gender-wise % of emotions

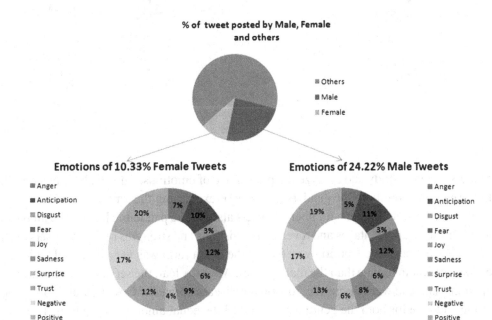

Figure 3 highlights the % ratio of male and female gender and together with that showing the emotions percentage for both the genders' users to study and analyze. There is a vast variation in the number of tweets posted by both the genders during the pandemic period. However, there is a very marginal percentage variations of all the emotions and is revealing the insights and strengths of Twitter users' gender. This figure depicted that the first negative emotion is fear and the percentage variation shows that the female can express their fear very easily, while the male gender cannot express their fear easily. After the fear, the second most negative emotion was anticipation as people were discussing to stop the disease spread of Covid-19 and to settle down in the tough time and here female gender has shown more percentage compared to the male genders, as female genders are keen to have the end of disease. The third negative emotion was sadness and which was more expressive in females compared to the male gender. The derived emotion shows that in the tough time both genders show more positive emotion than negative emotion to balance the life. The disgust and anger emotions were not much expressive in the male gender tweets, but anger was more in the female gender tweets. The female genders are more expressive in both positive and negative emotions compared to the male genders. Moreover, the female's tweets is showing more percentage of joy emotion than the male gender.

Therefore, this analysis is summarizing that as the tweet instances are less than also the emotions differences are there, which indicates there is a strong requirement of equal sampled instances of both the genders. The Figure 4 highlights the sampled approach of same number of tweets i.e. 18,502 from

Figure 4. Categorized % of emotions equal number of tweets sampled by each gender

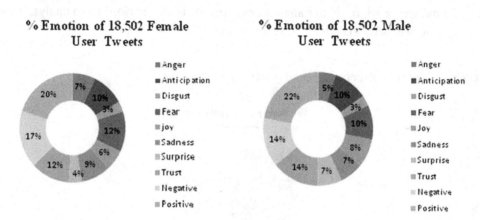

both the genders' users to study and analyze the percentage of emotions. This analysis can provide more insightful information about both the genders as a way of expressing the emotions.

Figure 4 depicted that in the same number of tweets also for the pandemic has shown all the varieties of emotions with varying percentages and revealed the insights and strengths of Twitter users during such a tough time. The first negative emotion was fear as the death ratio was very high and which reflected more percentage of fear in female than the male gender. After the fear, the second most negative emotion was anticipation as people were discussing to stop the disease spread of Covid-19 and to settle down in the tough time and here for both the genders were raised the equal amount of emotion. The third negative emotion was sadness and which was more expressive in females compared to the male gender. The derived emotion shows that in the tough time both genders show more positive emotion than negative emotion. The disgust and anger emotions were in control in the male gender, but anger was more in the female gender. The pandemic tweets have shown that female can easily express their negative emotions while male cannot. The positive emotion trust and joy are having more percentage in male than the female gender and that shows the male gender can trust easily and enjoy with ease.

Though Covid-19 pandemic is a tough situation, the people tried to maintain a positive feeling with family and thus, the raise in the emotion of trust showed in tweets. Thus, the gender based tweet analysis provided insightful knowledge that emphasizes that this gender perspective of tweets and other such gender based analysis of features could provide intuitive inputs for real-life applications.

FUTURE RESEARCH DIRECTIONS

Gender perspective analysis of social media data is a relatively new domain within machine learning research as it has many applications in a wide variety of domains. Thus, require the automatic identification of the information from a gender perspective, which lays many challenges compared to the traditional questionnaire-based gender identification tests. To break the impact of gender imbalance, it is required to ensure that the content used for analysis has no gender-biased impact. The novel scalable and efficient approach is required to prepare the gender-balanced sampling of data by identifying the gender automatically not only from the content but also together with the friend of friend information of the users' network. More profit can be achieved if, considered the gender perspective information in the real-world applications of the social media. Examples for the e-commerce are the recommendation of the item based on the review by the same gender the product belongs to, gender based sale promotion, etc. Other examples are fake news identification to avoid the havoc created due to the news if it is about particular gender or written by a particular gendered author and detection of cyber fraud where the fraudulent is hiding behind the fake gender profile, the study of a positive, a negative and a neutral emotion impact on medication, etc.

CONCLUSION

The knowledge biased by gender can offer novel quantitative and qualitative research for different applications. This research GTA analyzed tweet data from the gender's perspective and highlighted differences in expression of emotions. Thus, this area of study can help to improve real-world application effectiveness to device the novel method of gender based analysis to identify, remove the information which has the impact of gender based emotion participation in social network data and to utilize that for the effective promotion and recommendation, cyber fraud detection, improvise medication, etc.

REFERENCES

Agarwal, B. (2014). Personality detection from text: A review. *International Journal of Computer System*, *1*(1).

Alm, C. O., Roth, D., & Sproat, R. (2005) Emotions from text: machine learning for text-based emotion prediction. In *Proceedings of Human Language Technology Conference and Conference on Empirical Methods in Natural Language Processing*, (pp. 579–586). 10.3115/1220575.1220648

Bao-Khanh, H. V., & Collier, N. (2013). Twitter Emotion Analysis in Earthquake Situations. *International Journal of Computational Linguistics and Applications*, *4*(1), 159–173.

Barbosa, L., & Feng, J. (2010). Robust sentiment detection on twitter from biased and noisy data. In *Proceedings of the 23rd International Conference on Computational Linguistics: Posters*, (pp. 36–44). Academic Press.

Bell, M., & Fong, K. (2021). Gender Differences in First and Corresponding Authorship in Public Health Research Submissions during the COVID-19 Pandemic. *American Journal of Public Health*, *111*(1), 159–163. doi:10.2105/AJPH.2020.305975 PMID:33211581

Fast, L. A., & Funder, D. C. (2010). Gender Differences in the Correlates of Self-Referent Word Use: Authority, Entitlement, and Depressive Symptoms. *Journal of Personality*, *78*(1), 313–38. doi: .1467-6494.2009.00617.x doi:10.1111/j

Gaind, B., Syal, V., & Padgalwar, S. (2019). Emotion Detection and Analysis on Social Media. *Global Journal of Engineering Science and Researches*, 78-89.

Garcia-Rudolph, A., Laxe, S., Saurí, J., & Guitart, B. (2019). M Stroke Survivors on Twitter: Sentiment and Topic Analysis from a Gender Perspective. *Journal of Medical Internet Research, 21*(8), e14077. doi:10.2196/14077 PMID:31452514

Go, A., Bhayani, R., & Huang, L. (2009). Twitter Sentiment Classification using Distant Supervision. *Processing*, 1–6.

Golbeck, J., Robles, C., & Turner, K. (2011). Predicting Personality with Social Media. In *Proceedings of CHI '11 Extended Abstracts on Human Factors in Computing Systems* (pp. 253–262). Association for Computing Machinery.

Haferkamp, N., Eimler, C., Papadakis, A.-M., & Kruck, J. V. (2012). Men Are from Mars, Women Are from Venus? Examining Gender Differences in Self-Presentation on Social Networking Sites. *Cyberpsychology, Behavior, and Social Networking, 15*(2), 91–98. doi:10.1089/cyber.2011.0151 PMID:22132897

Holmberg, K., & Hellsten, I. (2015). Gender differences in the climate change communication on Twitter. *Internet Research, 25*(5), 811-828. . doi:10.1108/IntR-07-2014-0179

Hu, L., & Kearney, M. W. (2020). Gendered Tweets: Computational Text Analysis of Gender Differences in Political Discussion on Twitter. *Journal of Language and Social Psychology*.

Kaushal, V., & Patwardhan, M. (2018). Emerging Trends in Personality Identification Using Online Social Networks—A Literature Survey. *ACM Transactions on Knowledge Discovery from Data, 12*(2).

Kharde, V. A., & Sonawane, S. S. (2016). Article: Sentiment Analysis of Twitter Data: A Survey of Techniques. *International Journal of Computers and Applications, 139*(11), 5–15.

Lamsal, R. (2020). Design and analysis of a large-scale COVID-19 tweets dataset. *Applied Intelligence*.

Leaper, C., & Ayres, M. M. (2007). A meta-analytic review of gender variations in adults' language use: Talkativeness, affiliative speech, and assertive speech. *Personality and Social Psychology Review, 11*(4), 328–63. doi:10.1177/1088868307302221

McCright, A. M. (2010). The effects of gender on climate change knowledge and concern in the American public. *Population and Environment, 32*, 66–87. https://doi.org/10.1007/s11111-010-0113-1

Mohammad, S., & Turney, P. (2010). *Emotions evoked by common words and phrases: Using Mechanical Turk to create an emotion lexicon* [Paper Presentation]. NAACL-HLT Workshop on computational approaches to analysis and generation of emotion in text, California, US.

Muscanell, L. N., & Guadagno, E. R. (2012). Make new friends or keep the old: Gender and personality differences in social networking use. *Computers in Human Behavior, 28*(1).

Newman, M. L., Groom, C. J., Handelman, L. D., & Pennebaker, J. W. (2008). Gender differences in language use: An analysis of 14,000 text samples. *Discourse Processes, 45*(3), 211–236.

Pak, P., & Paroubek, A. P. (2010). *Twitter as a corpus for sentiment analysis and opinion mining*. http://www.lrec-conf.org/proceedings/lrec2010/pdf/385Paper.pdf

Park, M. (2016). Women are Warmer but No Less Assertive than Men: Gender and Language on Facebook. *PLoS One, 11*(5), 1–26.

Petovska, A., Goldberg, P., Brüggemann-Klein, A., & Nyokabi, A. (2020). Mining Gender Bias: A Preliminary Study on Implicit Biases and Gender Identity in the Department of Computer Science at the Technical University of Munich. *Proceedings of European Conference on Software Architecture Communications in Computer and Information Science, 1269.*

Psylla, I., Sapiezynski, P., Mones, E., & Lehmann, S. (2017). The role of gender in social network organization. *PLoS One, 12*(12), e0189873. https://doi.org/10.1371/journal.pone.0189873

Qrius. (2021). *Will AI prolong the gender gap in the workplace?* Available at: https://qrius.com/will-ai-prolong-the-gender-gap-in-the-workplace/

Wang, Y., Burke, M., & Kraut, R. (2013). Gender, Topic, and Audience Response: An Analysis of User-Generated Content on Facebook. In *Proceedings of the SIGCHI Conference on Human Factors in Computing Systems* (pp. 31-34). Association for Computing Machinery.

Compilation of References

Abdul-Mageed, M., & Ungar, L. (2017, July). Emonet: Fine-grained emotion detection with gated recurrent neural networks. In *Proceedings of the 55th annual meeting of the association for computational linguistics (volume 1: Long papers)* (pp. 718-728). 10.18653/v1/P17-1067

Abe, N. (2003). Sampling Approaches to Learning from Imbalanced Datasets: Active Learning, Cost Sensitive Learning and Beyond. *Proc. of the ICML-KDD'03 Workshop: Learning from Imbalanced Data Sets.*

Abeysinghe, C., Li, J., & He, J. (2016). A classifier hub for imbalanced financial data. In *Proceedings of the Australasian Database Conference.* Springer. 10.1007/978-3-319-46922-5_43

Agarwal, B. (2014). Personality detection from text: A review. *International Journal of Computer System, 1*(1).

Agrawal, R., & Srikant, R. (1994). Fast algorithms for mining association rules. *Proc. 20th int. conf. very large data bases, VLDB, 1215,* 487-499.

Agresti, A. (2014). *An Introduction to Categorical Data Analysis.* Wiley.

Agustianto, K., & Destarianto, P. (2019). Imbalance Data Handling using Neighborhood Cleaning Rule (NCL) Sampling Method for Precision Student Modeling. *2019 International Conference on Computer Science, Information Technology, and Electrical Engineering (ICOMITEE),* 86–89. 10.1109/ICOMITEE.2019.8921159

Akhtar, M. S., Gupta, D., Ekbal, A., & Bhattacharyya, P. (2017). Feature selection and ensemble construction: A two-step method for aspect-based sentiment analysis. *Knowledge-Based Systems, 125,* 116–135. doi:10.1016/j.knosys.2017.03.020

Al Masum, S. M., Prendinger, H., & Ishizuka, M. (2007, November). Emotion sensitive news agent: An approach towards user centric emotion sensing from the news. In *IEEE/WIC/ACM International Conference on Web Intelligence (WI'07)* (pp. 614-620). IEEE. 10.1109/WI.2007.124

Alcalá-Fdez, J., Fernandez, A., Luengo, J., Derrac, J., García, S., Sánchez, L., & Herrera, F. (2011). KEEL Data-Mining Software Tool: Data Set Repository, Integration of Algorithms and Experimental Analysis Framework. *Journal of Multiple-Valued Logic and Soft Computing, 17*(2-3), 255–287.

Al-Dhabyani, W., Gomaa, M., Khaled, H., & Fahmy, A. (2020). Dataset of breast ultrasound images. *Data in Brief, 28,* 104863. doi:10.1016/j.dib.2019.104863 PMID:31867417

Aleksovski, D., Kocev, D., & Dzeroski, S. (2009). Evaluation of distance measures for hierarchical multilabel classification in functional genomics. *Proceedings of the 1st workshop on learning from multi-label data (MLD) held in conjunction with ECML/PKDD,* 5–16.

Ali, A., Shamsuddin, S. M., & Ralescu, A. L. (2013). Classification with class imbalance problem. *Int. J. Advance Soft Compu. Appl, 5*(3).

Alippi, C., Boracchi, G., & Roveri, M. (2011). A just-in-time adaptive classification system based on the intersection of confidence intervals rule. *Neural Networks*, *24*(8), 791–800. doi:10.1016/j.neunet.2011.05.012 PMID:21723706

Allcott, H., & Gentzkow, M. (2017). Social Media and Fake News in the 2016 Election. *The Journal of Economic Perspectives*, *31*(2), 211–236. doi:10.1257/jep.31.2.211

Almahairi, A., Rajeshwar, S., Sordoni, A., Bachman, P., & Courville, A. (2018, July). Augmented cyclegan: Learning many-to-many mappings from unpaired data. In *International Conference on Machine Learning* (pp. 195-204). PMLR.

Alm, C. O., Roth, D., & Sproat, R. (2005) Emotions from text: machine learning for text-based emotion prediction. In *Proceedings of Human Language Technology Conference and Conference on Empirical Methods in Natural Language Processing*, (pp. 579–586). 10.3115/1220575.1220648

Amazon. (1996a). http://www.amazon.com

Amazon. (1996b). http://www.amazon.in

An, A., Cercone, N., & Huang, X. (2001, June). A case study for learning from imbalanced data sets. In *Conference of the Canadian Society for Computational Studies of Intelligence* (pp. 1–15). Springer.

Angelo, P., Resende, A., & Drummond, A. C. (2018). A Survey of Random Forest Based Methods for Intrusion Detection Systems. *ACM Comput. Surv.*, *51*(3), 48-48.

Ansari, G., Saxena, C., Ahmad, T., & Doja, M. N. (2020). Aspect term extraction using graph-based semi-supervised learning. *Procedia Computer Science*, *167*, 2080–2090. doi:10.1016/j.procs.2020.03.249

Arabmakki, E. (2016). *A reduced labeled samples (RLS) framework for classification of imbalanced concept-drifting streaming data*. University of Louisville. doi:10.18297/etd/2602

Armstrong, W. (2015). *Using Topic Models to Investigate Depression on Social Media*. University of Maryland.

Asghar, M. Z., Ullah, A., Ahmad, S., & Khan, A. (2020). Opinion spam detection framework using hybrid classification scheme. *Soft Computing*, *24*(5), 3475–3498. doi:10.100700500-019-04107-y

Ashok, S., Kishore, G., Rajesh, V., Suchitra, S., Sophia, S. G., & Pavithra, B. (2020, June). Tomato Leaf Disease Detection Using Deep Learning Techniques. In *2020 5th International Conference on Communication and Electronics Systems (ICCES)* (pp. 979-983). IEEE.

Ausawalaithong, W., Thirach, A., Marukatat, S., & Wilaiprasitporn, T. (2018). Automatic lung cancer prediction from chest X-ray images using the deep learning approach. *2018 11th Biomedical Engineering International Conference (BMEICON)*, 1–5.

Awan, R., Sirinukunwattana, K., Epstein, D., Jefferyes, S., Qidwai, U., Aftab, Z., Mujeeb, I., Snead, D., & Rajpoot, N. (2017). Glandular morphometrics for objective grading of colorectal adenocarcinoma histology images. *Scientific Reports*, *7*(1), 1–12. doi:10.103841598-017-16516-w PMID:29203775

Azuaje, F. (2003). Genomic data sampling and its effect on classification performance assessment. *BMC Bioinformatics*, *4*(1), 1–14. doi:10.1186/1471-2105-4-5 PMID:12553886

Bagheri, A., Saraee, M., & De Jong, F. (2013). Care more about customers: Unsupervised domain-independent aspect detection for sentiment analysis of customer reviews. *Knowledge-Based Systems*, *52*, 201–213. doi:10.1016/j.knosys.2013.08.011

Bagozzi, R. P., Gopinath, M., & Nyer, P. U. (1999). The role of emotions in marketing. *Journal of the Academy of Marketing Science*, *27*(2), 184–206. doi:10.1177/0092070399272005

Bahdanau, D., Cho, K., & Bengio, Y. (2014). *Neural machine translation by jointly learning to align and translate.* arXiv preprint arXiv:1409.0473.

Balabantaray, R. C., Mohammad, M., & Sharma, N. (2012). Multi-class twitter emotion classification: A new approach. *International Journal of Applied Information Systems, 4*(1), 48–53. doi:10.5120/ijais12-450651

Balahur, A., Hermida, J. M., & Montoyo, A. (2011, June). Detecting implicit expressions of sentiment in text based on commonsense knowledge. In *Proceedings of the 2nd Workshop on Computational Approaches to Subjectivity and Sentiment Analysis (WASSA 2011)* (pp. 53-60). Academic Press.

Bandhakavi, A., Wiratunga, N., Massie, S., & Padmanabhan, D. (2017). Lexicon generation for emotion detection from text. *IEEE Intelligent Systems, 32*(1), 102–108. doi:10.1109/MIS.2017.22

Bandhakavi, A., Wiratunga, N., Padmanabhan, D., & Massie, S. (2017). Lexicon based feature extraction for emotion text classification. *Pattern Recognition Letters, 93*, 133–142. doi:10.1016/j.patrec.2016.12.009

Bao-Khanh, H. V., & Collier, N. (2013). Twitter Emotion Analysis in Earthquake Situations. *International Journal of Computational Linguistics and Applications, 4*(1), 159–173.

Barandela, R., Sánchez, J. S., Garca, V., & Rangel, E. (2003). Strategies for learning in class imbalance problems. *Pattern Recognition, 36*(3), 849–851. doi:10.1016/S0031-3203(02)00257-1

Barbosa, L., & Feng, J. (2010). Robust sentiment detection on twitter from biased and noisy data. In *Proceedings of the 23rd International Conference on Computational Linguistics: Posters,* (pp. 36–44). Academic Press.

Barlow, H., Mao, S., & Khushi, M. (2019). Predicting high-risk prostate cancer using machine learning methods. *Data, 4*(3), 129. doi:10.3390/data4030129

Barua, S., Islam, M. M., & Murase, K. (2015). GOS-IL: A Generalized Over-Sampling Based Online Imbalanced Learning Framework. In *Proceedings of International Conference on Neural Information Processing* (pp. 680-687). 10.1007/978-3-319-26532-2_75

Basseville, M., & Nikiforov, V. (1993). *Detection of abrupt changes: Theory and application.* PTR Prentice-Hall.

Batista, G. E., Prati, R. C., & Monard, M. C. (2004). A study of the behavior of several methods for balancing machine lcarning training data. *SIGKDD Explorations, 6*(1), 20–29. doi:10.1145/1007730.1007735

Bell, M., & Fong, K. (2021). Gender Differences in First and Corresponding Authorship in Public Health Research Submissions during the COVID-19 Pandemic. *American Journal of Public Health, 111*(1), 159–163. doi:10.2105/AJPH.2020.305975 PMID:33211581

Berinsky, A. (2015). Rumors and Health Care Reform: Experiments in Political Misinformation. *British Journal of Political Science, 47*(2), 241–262. doi:10.1017/0007123415000186

Bessi, A., & Ferrara, E. (2016). *Social bots distort the 2016 us presidential election.* Academic Press.

Bhandary, S. (2020). Effectiveness of lockdown as COVID-19 intervention: Official and computed cases in Nepal. *Journal of Patan Academy of Health Sciences, 7*(1), 37–41. doi:10.3126/jpahs.v7i1.28861

Bhattacharya, P., Ghosh, K., Pal, A., & Ghosh, S. (2020). Hier-SPCNet: A Legal Statute Hierarchy-based Heterogeneous Network for Computing Legal Case Document Similarity. In *Proceedings of the 43rd International ACM SIGIR* (pp. 1657-1660). ACM.

Bifet, A., & Gavalda, R. (2007). Learning from Time-Changing Data with Adaptive Windowing. *Proceedings of the Seventh SIAM International Conference on Data Mining.* 10.1137/1.9781611972771.42

Bilge, L., Strufe, T., Balzarotti, D., & Kirda, E. (2009, April). All your contacts are belong to us: automated identity theft attacks on social networks. *Proceedings of the 18th international conference on World Wide Web*, 551-560. 10.1145/1526709.1526784

Bilic, P., Christ, P. F., Vorontsov, E., Chlebus, G., Chen, H., Dou, Q., . . . Hesser, J. (2019). *The liver tumor segmentation benchmark (lits)*. ArXiv Preprint ArXiv:1901.04056.

Bing, L. (2004). *Opinion Mining, Sentiment Analysis and Opinion Spam Detection*. http://www.cs.uic.edu~liub/FBS/sentiment-analysis.html

Blagus, R., & Lusa, L. (2013). SMOTE for high-dimensional class-imbalanced data. *BMC Bioinformatics*, *14*, 106. https://doi.org/10.1186/1471-2105-14-106

Blaszczynski, J., & Stefanowski, J. (2015). Neighbourhood sampling in bagging for imbalanced data. *Neurocomputing*, *150*(part B), 529-542.

Blei, D. M., Ng, A. Y., & Jordan, M. I. (2003). Latent dirichlet allocation. *The Journal of Machine Learning Research*, *3*, 993-1022.

Blei, D. M., Ng, A. Y., & Jordan, M. I. (2003). Latent dirichlet allocation. *Journal of Machine Learning Research*, *3*(Jan), 993–1022.

Blei, D. M., Ng, A. Y., & Jordan, M. I. (2003, March). Latent Dirichlet allocation. *Journal of Machine Learning Research*, *3*, 993–1022.

Bouazizi, M., & Ohtsuki, T. (2017). A pattern-based approach for multi-class sentiment analysis in Twitter. *IEEE Access: Practical Innovations, Open Solutions*, *5*, 20617–20639. doi:10.1109/ACCESS.2017.2740982

Bouma, G. (2009). Normalized (pointwise) mutual information in collocation extraction. *Proceedings of GSCL*, 31-40.

Bradley, P. S., & Fayyad, U. M. (1998, July). Refining initial points for k-means clustering. In ICML (Vol. 98, pp. 91-99). Academic Press.

Brave, S., & Nass, C. (2009). Emotion in human–computer interaction. In *Human-computer interaction fundamentals* (Vol. 20094635). CRC Press. doi:10.1201/b10368-6

Britton, T. (2010). Stochastic epidemic models: A survey. *Mathematical Biosciences*, *225*(1), 24–35. doi:10.1016/j.mbs.2010.01.006 PMID:20102724

Brown, P. F., Della Pietra, S. A., Della Pietra, V. J., & Mercer, R. L. (1993). The mathematics of statistical machine translation: Parameter estimation. *Computational Linguistics*, *19*(2), 263–311.

Brychcín, T., Konkol, M., & Steinberger, J. (2014). Uwb: Machine learning approach to aspect-based sentiment analysis. *Proceedings of the 8th International Workshop on Semantic Evaluation (SemEval 2014)*, 817-822. 10.3115/v1/S14-2145

Brzezinski, D., & Stefanowski, J. (2015). Prequential AUC for Classifier Evaluation and Drift Detection in Evolving Data Streams. In *3rd International Workshop on New Frontiers in Mining Complex Patterns* (vol. 8983, pp.87-101) 10.1007/978-3-319-17876-9_6

Bunkhumpornpat, C., Sinapiromsaran, K., & Lursinsap, C. (2009). Safe-level-smote: Safe-level-synthetic minority over-sampling technique for handling the class imbalanced problem. *Pacific-Asia Conference on Knowledge Discovery and Data Mining*, 475–482.

Cambria, E., Olsher, D., & Rajagopal, D. (2014). SenticNet 3: a common and common-sense knowledge base for cognition-driven sentiment analysis. *Proceedings of the AAAI Conference on Artificial Intelligence*, 28-35.

Cambria, E., Poria, S., Bajpai, R., & Schuller, B. (2016). SenticNet 4: A semantic resource for sentiment analysis based on conceptual primitives. *Proceedings of COLING 2016, the 26th international conference on computational linguistics: Technical papers*, 2666-2677.

Canales, L., & Martínez-Barco, P. (2014, October). Emotion detection from text: A survey. In *Proceedings of the workshop on natural language processing in the 5th information systems research working days (JISIC)* (pp. 37-43). 10.3115/v1/W14-6905

CancerStatistics. (2020). *National Cancer Institute*. doi:10.32388/VSUMBC

Cao, L., & Shen, H. (2019). Imbalanced Data Classification Using Improved Clustering Algorithm and Under-sampling Method, In *Proceedings of 20th International Conference on Parallel and Distributed Computing, Applications and Technologies*, (pp.361-366). 10.1109/PDCAT46702.2019.00071

Chandana, S., Leung, H., & Trpkov, K. (2009). Staging of prostate cancer using automatic feature selection, sampling and Dempster-Shafer fusion. *Cancer Informatics, 7*.

Chan, P. K., Fan, W., Prodromidis, A. L., & Stolfo, S. J. (1999). Distributed data mining in credit card fraud detection. *IEEE Intelligent Systems & their Applications, 14*(6), 67–74.

Charte, F., Rivera, A., del Jesus, M. J., & Herrera, F. (2013). A First Approach to Deal with Imbalance in Multi-label Datasets. HAIS 2013, LNAI 8073, 150–160.

Charte, F., Rivera, A. J., del Jesus, M. J., & Herrera, F. (2015). Addressing imbalance in multilabel classification: Measures and random resampling algorithms. *Neurocomputing, 163*, 3–16. doi:10.1016/j.neucom.2014.08.091

Chatterjee, A., Gupta, U., Chinnakotla, M. K., Srikanth, R., Galley, M., & Agrawal, P. (2019). Understanding emotions in text using deep learning and big data. *Computers in Human Behavior, 93*, 309–317. doi:10.1016/j.chb.2018.12.029

Chatziagapi, A., Paraskevopoulos, G., Sgouropoulos, D., Pantazopoulos, G., Nikandrou, M., Giannakopoulos, T., … Narayanan, S. (2019). Data Augmentation Using GANs for Speech Emotion Recognition. *Interspeech*, 171–175.

Chauhan, G. S., & Meena, Y. K. (2018). Prominent aspect term extraction in aspect based sentiment analysis. *2018 3rd International Conference and Workshops on Recent Advances and Innovations in Engineering (ICRAIE)*, 1-6. 10.1109/ICRAIE.2018.8710408

Chauhan, G. S., Meena, Y. K., Gopalani, D., & Nahta, R. (2020). A two-step hybrid unsupervised model with attention mechanism for aspect extraction. *Expert Systems with Applications, 161*, 113673. doi:10.1016/j.eswa.2020.113673

Chaumartin, F. R. (2007). UPAR7: A knowledge-based system for headline sentiment tagging. In *SemEval (ACL Workshop)* (pp. pp-422). 10.3115/1621474.1621568

Chavoshi, N., Hamooni, H., & Mueen, A. (2016, December). Debot: Twitter bot detection via warped correlation. ICDM, 817-822.

Chawla, N. V., Lazarevic, A., Hall, L. O., & Bowyer, K. W. (2003). SMOTEBoost: Improving Prediction of the Minority Class in Boosting. *European Conference on Principles of Data Mining and Knowledge Discovery, PKDD 2003: Knowledge Discovery in Databases*, 107-119.

Chawla, N. V., Bowyer, K. W., Hall, L. O., & Kegelmeyer, W. P. (2002). SMOTE: Synthetic Minority Oversampling Technique. *Journal of Artificial Intelligence Research, 16*, 321–357. doi:10.1613/jair.953

Chawla, N. V., Japkowicz, N., & Kotcz, A. (2004). Special issue on learning from imbalanced data sets. *SIGKDD Explorations, 6*(1), 1–6.

Chawla, N., Japkowicz, N., & Kolcz, A. (2003). *Learning from Imbalanced Data Sets II.* In *ICML'2003 Workshop,* Washington, DC.

Cheng, L., Silva, Y. N., & Liu, D. H. (2020). *Session based Cyberbullying Detection: Problems and Challenges.* Arizona State University. *IEEE Internet Computing.*

Chen, S., & He, H. (2009). Sera: Selectively recursive approach towards nonstationary imbalanced stream data mining. In *2009 International Joint Conference on Neural Networks* (pp. 522-529). 10.1109/IJCNN.2009.5178874

Chen, W., Li, X., Gao, L., & Shen, W. (2020). Improving Computer-Aided Cervical Cells Classification Using Transfer Learning Based Snapshot Ensemble. *Applied Sciences (Basel, Switzerland), 10*(20), 7292. doi:10.3390/app10207292

Chicco, D., & Jurman, G. (2020). The advantages of the Matthews correlation coefficient (MCC) over F1 score and accuracy in binary classification evaluation. *BMC Genomics, 21*(1), 1–13. doi:10.118612864-019-6413-7 PMID:31898477

Chifu, E. Ş., Leţia, T. Ş., & Chifu, V. R. (2015). Unsupervised aspect level sentiment analysis using Ant Clustering and Self-organizing Maps. *2015 International Conference on Speech Technology and Human-Computer Dialogue (SpeD),* 1-9. 10.1109/SPED.2015.7343075

Cho, K., Van Merriënboer, B., Gulcehre, C., Bahdanau, D., Bougares, F., Schwenk, H., & Bengio, Y. (2014). Learning phrase representations using RNN encoder-decoder for statistical machine translation. doi:10.3115/v1/D14-1179

Church, K., & Hanks, P. (1990). Word association norms, mutual information, and lexicography. *Computational Linguistics, 16,* 22–29.

Cilibrasi, R. L., & Vitanyi, P. M. (2007). The google similarity distance. *IEEE Transactions on Knowledge and Data Engineering, 19*(3), 370–383. doi:10.1109/TKDE.2007.48

cnet. (1994). http://www.cnet.com

Cohen, E. (2018, September 16). *How to predict Quora Question Pairs using Siamese Manhattan LSTM.* Medium. https://blog.mlreview.com/implementing-malstm-on-kaggles-quora-question-pairs-competition-8b31b0b16a07

Cong, Q., Feng, Z., Li, F., Xiang, Y., Rao, G., & Tao, C. (2018, December). XA-BiLSTM: A deep learning approach for depression detection in imbalanced data. In *2018 IEEE International Conference on Bioinformatics and Biomedicine (BIBM)* (pp. 1624-1627). IEEE.

Cornell. (2002). *Movie Review Data.* http://www.cs.cornell.edu/people/pabo/movie-review-data/

Cortes, C., & Vapnik, V. (1995). Support-vector networks. *Machine Learning, 20*(3), 273–297. doi:10.1007/BF00994018

Costa, A. F. J., Albuquerque, R. A. S., & Santos, E. (2018). A Drift Detection Method Based on Active Learning. *International Joint Conference on Neural Networks.* 10.1109/IJCNN.2018.8489364

COVID-19 in India. (2020). *Dataset on Novel Corona Virus Disease 2019 in India.* https://www.kaggle.com/sudalai-rajkumar/covid19-in-india

Croft, P., Altman, D. G., Deeks, J. J., Dunn, K. M., Hay, A. D., Hemingway, H., ... Petersen, S. E. (2015). The science of clinical practice: Disease diagnosis or patient prognosis? Evidence about "what is likely to happen" should shape clinical practice. *BMC Medicine, 13*(1), 1–8. doi:10.118612916-014-0265-4 PMID:25637245

Crunchbase. (2015.). *lvping.* https://www.crunchbase.com/organization/lvping

Culotta, A., & Sorensen, J. (2004). Dependency tree kernels for relation extraction. *Proceedings of the 42nd Annual Meeting of the Association for Computational Linguistics (ACL-04),* 423-429. 10.3115/1218955.1219009

Cutting, D., Kupiec, J., Pedersen, J., & Sibun, P. (1992). A practical part-of-speech tagger. *Third Conference on Applied Natural Language Processing*, 33-140.

Damani, S., Raviprakash, N., Gupta, U., Chatterjee, A., Joshi, M., Gupta, K., & Mathur, A. (2018). *Ruuh: A deep learning based conversational social agent.* arXiv preprint arXiv:1810.12097.

Daniels, Z. A., & Metaxas, D. N. (2017). Addressing Imbalance in Multi-Label Classification Using Structured Hellinger Forests. *Proceedings of the Thirty-First AAAI Conference on Artificial Intelligence (AAAI-17).*

Dao, B., Nguyen, T., Venkatesh, S., & Phung, D. (2017). Latent sentiment topic modelling and nonparametric discovery of online mental health related communities. *International Journal of Data Science and Analytics, 4*(3), 209–231. doi:10.100741060-017-0073-y

Das, A. (2020). *COVID-19 Predictions for India An Initial Attempt.* Technical Report. http://cse.iitkgp.ac.in/~abhij/COVID19/report.pdf

Dasgupta, S., & Schulman, L. (2013). *A two-round variant of em for gaussian mixtures.* arXiv preprint arXiv:1301.3850.

Dasgupta, S. (1999, October). Learning mixtures of Gaussians. In *40th Annual Symposium on Foundations of Computer Science (Cat. No. 99CB37039)* (pp. 634-644). IEEE. 10.1109/SFFCS.1999.814639

de Carvalho, A., & Freitas, A. A. (2009). A tutorial on multi-label classification techniques. In A. Abraham, A. E. Hassanien, & V. Snasel (Eds.), *Studies in Computational Intelligence 205* (pp. 177–195). Springer.

Deerwester, S., Dumais, S. T., Furnas, G. W., Landauer, T. K., & Harshman, R. (1990). Indexing by latent semantic analysis. *Journal of the American Society for Information Science, 41*(6), 391–407. doi:10.1002/(SICI)1097-4571(199009)41:6<391::AID-ASI1>3.0.CO;2-9

Dehade, S. K., & Bagade, A. M. (2015). A review on detecting automation on Twitter accounts. *European Journal of Advances in Engineering and Technology, 2*, 69–72.

Delplace, A., Hermoso, S., & Anandita, K. (2019). Cyber Attack Detection thanks to Machine Learning Algorithms, *COMS7507: Advanced Security,* 1-46.

Desai, M., Mehta, R. G., & Rana, D. P. (2021). RGNet: The Novel Framework to Model Linked ResearchGate Information into Network Using Hierarchical Data Rendering. In *Advances in Machine Learning and Computational Intelligence* (pp. 37–45). Springer. doi:10.1007/978-981-15-5243-4_4

Dey, A. (2016). Machine learning algorithms: A review. *International Journal of Computer Science and Information Technologies, 7*(3), 1174–1179.

DianPing. (2010). http://www.DianPing.com

Ding, C., & Peng, H. (2005). Minimum redundancy feature selection from microarray gene expression data. *Journal of Bioinformatics and Computational Biology, 30*(2), 185–205. doi:10.1142/S0219720005001004 PMID:15852500

Ditzler, G., & Polikar, R. (2010). An incremental learning algorithm for non-stationary environments and class imbalance. In *20th International Conference on Pattern Recognition* (pp. 2997-3000). 10.1109/ICPR.2010.734

Ditzler, G., & Polikar, R. (2011). Hellinger distance based drift detection for nonstationary environments. In *Proceedings of IEEE Symposium on Computational Intelligence in Dynamic and Uncertain Environments* (pp. 41-48). 10.1109/CIDUE.2011.5948491

Ditzler, G., & Polikar, R. (2013). Incremental Learning of Concept Drift from Streaming Imbalanced Data. *IEEE Transactions on Knowledge and Data Engineering, 25*(10), 2283–2301. doi:10.1109/TKDE.2012.136

Ditzler, G., Roveri, M., Alippi, C., & Polikar, R. (2015). Learning in nonstationary environments: A survey. *IEEE Computational Intelligence Magazine*, *10*(4), 12–25. doi:10.1109/MCI.2015.2471196

Dixon, S. R., Wickens, C. D., & Chang, D. (2005). Mission control of multiple unmanned aerial vehicles: A workload analysis. *Human Factors*, *47*(3), 479–487. doi:10.1518/0018720057748600005 PMID:16435690

Domingos, P., & Hulten, G. (2000). Mining high-speed data streams. In *Proceedings of 6th ACM SIGKDD international conference on knowledge discovery data mining* (pp. 71-80). ACM.

Do, T. N., Lenca, P., & Lallich, S. (2015). Classifying many-class high-dimensional fingerprint datasets using random forest of oblique decision trees. *Vietnam J Comput Sci*, *2*(1), 3–12. doi:10.100740595-014-0024-7

Druckman, J. N., & McDermott, R. (2008). Emotion and the framing of risky choice. *Political Behavior*, *30*(3), 297–321. doi:10.100711109-008-9056-y

Dubey, R., Zhou, J., Wang, Y., Thompson, P. M., & Ye, J. (2014). Analysis of sampling techniques for imbalanced data: An n = 648 ADNI study. *NeuroImage*, *87*(15), 220–241. doi:10.1016/j.neuroimage.2013.10.005 PMID:24176869

Dubey, R., Zhou, J., Wang, Y., Thompson, P. M., & Ye, J. (2014). Analysis of sampling techniques for imbalanced data: An n= 648 ADNI study. *NeuroImage*, *87*, 220–241.

Dunning, T. E. (1993). Accurate methods for the statistics of surprise and coincidence. *Computational Linguistics*, *19*(1), 61–74.

Durmuş, H., Güneş, E. O., & Kırcı, M. (2017, August). Disease detection on the leaves of the tomato plants by using deep learning. In *2017 6th International Conference on Agro-Geoinformatics* (pp. 1-5). IEEE. 10.1109/Agro-Geoinformatics.2017.8047016

Eirinaki, M., Pisal, S., & Singh, J. (2012). Feature-based opinion mining and ranking. *Journal of Computer and System Sciences*, *78*(4), 1175–1184. doi:10.1016/j.jcss.2011.10.007

Elkan, C. (2001). The Foundations of Cost-Sensitive Learning. In *Proceedings of intelligence joint conference on artificial intelligence* (pp.973-978). Academic Press.

Elwell, R., & Polikar, R. (2011). Incremental learning of concept drift in nonstationary environments. *IEEE Transactions on Neural Networks*, *22*(10), 1517–1531. doi:10.1109/TNN.2011.2160459 PMID:21824845

Elyan, E., Francisco, C., Garcia, M., & Jayne, C. (2020). CDSMOTE: Class Decomposition and Synthetic Minority Class Oversampling Technique for Imbalanced Data Classification. *Neural Computing & Applications*, *33*(7), 2839–2851. doi:10.100700521-020-05130-z

Emanet, N., Öz, H. R., Bayram, N., & Delen, D. (2014). A comparative analysis of machine learning methods for classification type decision problems in healthcare. *Decision Analysis*, *1*, 1–20.

Emotion. (2020, January 7). *Kaggle*. https://www.kaggle.com/icw123/emotion

Epinions. (1999). http://www.Epinions.com

Erşahin, B., Aktaş, Ö., Kılınç, D., & Akyol, C. (2017, October). Twitter fake account detection. *Proceedings of International Conference on Computer Science and Engineering (UBMK)*, 388-392.

Ertekin, S., Huang, J., Bottou, L., & Giles, L. (2007). Learning on the Border: Active Learning in Imbalanced Data Classification. *Proceedings of the sixteenth ACM Conference on information and knowledge management CIKM'07*, 1-77. 10.1145/1321440.1321461

Es, S. (2021b, April 9). *Data Augmentation in NLP: Best Practices From a Kaggle Master*. Neptune.Ai. https://neptune. ai/blog/data-augmentation-nlp

Estabrooks, A., & Japkowicz, N. (2001). A Mixture-of-Experts Framework for Learning from Imbalanced Data Sets. *Proceedings of the 2001 Advances in Intelligent Data Analysis (IDA)*, 34-43. 10.1007/3-540-44816-0_4

Estabrooks, A., Jo, T., & Japkowicz, N. (2004). A Multiple Resampling Method for Learning from Imbalanced Data Sets. *Computational Intelligence, 20*(1), 18–36. doi:10.1111/j.0824-7935.2004.t01-1-00228.x

Faber, V. (1994). Clustering and the continuous k-means algorithm. *Los Alamos Science, 22*(138144.21), 67.

Fadaee, M., Bisazza, A., & Monz, C. (2017). Data augmentation for low-resource neural machine translation. arXiv preprint arXiv:1705.00440. doi:10.18653/v1/P17-2090

Fairbanks, J., Fitch, N., Knauf, N., & Briscoe, E. (2018). Credibility assessment in the news: do we need to read? MIS2'18.

Fan, W., Stolfo, S. J., Zhang, J., & Chan, P. K. (1999). AdaCost: *Misclassification Cost-sensitive Boosting. Sixth International Conference of Machine Learning*, 97-105.

Fan, Y., Qi, L., & Tie, Y. (2020). *Classification of Cancer Subtypes Based on Imbalanced Data Sets*. EasyChair.

Fast, L. A., & Funder, D. C. (2010). Gender Differences in the Correlates of Self-Referent Word Use: Authority, Entitlement, and Depressive Symptoms. *Journal of Personality, 78*(1), 313–38. doi: .1467-6494.2009.00617.x doi:10.1111/j

Fawcett, T. (2006). An introduction to ROC analysis. *Pattern Recognition Letters, 27*(8), 861–874. doi:10.1016/j.patrec.2005.10.010

Felbo, B., Mislove, A., Søgaard, A., Rahwan, I., & Lehmann, S. (2017). Using millions of emoji occurrences to learn any-domain representations for detecting sentiment, emotion and sarcasm. arXiv preprint arXiv:1708.00524. doi:10.18653/v1/D17-1169

Fellbaum, C. (1998). A semantic network of English verbs. *WordNet: An Electronic Lexical Database, 3*, 153-178.

Fernández, A., Jesus, M. J., & Francisco, H. (2009). Hierarchical Fuzzy Rule Based Classification Systems with Genetic Rule Selection for Imbalanced Datasets. *International Journal of Approximate Reasoning, 50*(3), 561–577. doi:10.1016/j.ijar.2008.11.004

Ferrag, M. A., Maglaras, L., Ahmim, A., Derdour, M., & Janicke, H. (2020). RDTIDS: Rules and Decision Tree-Based Intrusion Detection System for Internet-of-Things Networks. *Future Internet Article*, 1-14.

Ferrara, E., Wang, W., Varol, O., Flammini, A., & Galstyan, A. (2016). Predicting online extremism, content adopters, and interaction reciprocity. *International conference on social informatics*, 22-39. 10.1007/978-3-319-47874-6_3

Ferreira, W., & Vlachos, A. (2016, June). Emergent: a novel data-set for stance classification. In *Proceedings of the 2016 conference of the North American chapter of the association for computational linguistics: Human language technologies* (pp. 1163-1168). Academic Press.

Folino, G., Pisani, F. S., & Sabatino, P. (2016). An incremental ensemble evolved by using genetic programming to efficiently detect drifts in cyber security datasets. In *Proceedings of the Conference on Genetic and Evolutionary Computation Conference Companion*. ACM. 10.1145/2908961.2931682

Fotouhi, S., Asadi, S., & Kattan, M. W. (2019). A comprehensive data level analysis for cancer diagnosis on imbalanced data. *Journal of Biomedical Informatics, 90*, 103089. doi:10.1016/j.jbi.2018.12.003 PMID:30611011

Frantzi, K., Ananiadou, S., & Mima, H. (2000). Automatic recognition of multi-word terms. the c-value/nc-value method. *International Journal on Digital Libraries*, *3*(2), 115–130. doi:10.1007007999900023

Freund, Y., Schapire, R., & Abe, N. (1999). A short introduction to boosting. *Jinkō Chinō Gakkaishi*, *14*, 771–780.

Frid-Adar, M., Diamant, I., Klang, E., Amitai, M., Goldberger, J., & Greenspan, H. (2018). GAN-based synthetic medical image augmentation for increased CNN performance in liver lesion classification. *Neurocomputing*, *321*, 321–331. doi:10.1016/j.neucom.2018.09.013

Fu, K., Cheng, D., Tu, Y., & Zhang, L. (2016). Credit card fraud detection using convolutional neural networks. In *Proceedings of the International Conference on Neural Information Processing*. Springer. 10.1007/978-3-319-46675-0_53

Fukenaga, K. (1990). Introduction to statistical pattern recognition (2nd ed.). Academic Press.

Gaind, B., Syal, V., & Padgalwar, S. (2019). Emotion Detection and Analysis on Social Media. *Global Journal of Engineering Science and Researches*, 78-89.

Galar, M., Fernandez, A., Barrenechea, E., Bustince, H., & Herrera, F. (2011). A review on ensembles for the class imbalance problem: Bagging-, boosting-, and hybrid-based approaches. *IEEE Transactions on Systems, Man and Cybernetics. Part C, Applications and Reviews*, *42*(4), 463–484.

Galar, M., Fernandez, A., Barrenechea, E., Bustince, H., & Herrera, F. (2012). A Review on Ensembles for the Class Imbalance Problem: Bagging-, Boosting-, and Hybrid-Based Approaches. *IEEE Transactions on Systems, Man and Cybernetics. Part C, Applications and Reviews*, *42*(4), 463–484. doi:10.1109/TSMCC.2011.2161285

Galvani, A. P., Lei, X., & Jewell, N. P. (2003). Severe acute respiratory syndrome: Temporal stability and geographic variation in death rates and doubling times. *Emerging Infectious Diseases*, *9*(8), 991.

Gama, J., Sebastiao, R., & Rodrigues, P. P. (2013). On evaluating stream learning algorithms. *Machine Learning*, *90*(3), 317–346. doi:10.100710994-012-5320-9

Gama, J., Zliobaite, I., Bifet, A., Pechenizkiy, M., & Bouchachia, A. (2013). A Survey on Concept Drift Adaptation. *ACM Computing Surveys*, *46*(4), 1–37. doi:10.1145/2523813

Ganganwar, V. (2012). An Overview of Classification Algorithms for Imbalanced Dataset. *International Journal of Emerging Technology and Advanced Engineering*, 42–47.

Gao, J., Ding, B., Fan, W., Han, J., & Yu, P. (2008). Classifying data streams with skewed class distributions and concept drifts. *IEEE Internet Computing*, *12*(6), 37–49. doi:10.1109/MIC.2008.119

Gao, J., Fan, W., Han, J., & Yu, P. S. (2007). A general framework for mining concept-drifting data streams with skewed distributions. *Proceedings of the Seventh SIAM International Conference on Data Mining*, 3-14. 10.1137/1.9781611972771.1

Gao, K., Khoshgoftaar, T. M., & Napolitano, A. (2015). Investigating Two Approaches for Adding Feature Ranking to Sampled Ensemble Learning for Software Quality Estimation. *International Journal of Software Engineering and Knowledge Engineering*, *25*(1), 115–146. doi:10.1142/S0218194015400069

Gao, Z., Zhang, L. F., Chen, M. Y., Hauptmann, A., Zhang, H., & Cai, A. N. (2014). Enhanced and hierarchical structure algorithm for data imbalance problem in semantic extraction under massive video dataset. *Multimedia Tools and Applications*, *68*(3), 641–657. doi:10.100711042-012-1071-7

García, V., Sánchez, J. S., Mollineda, R. A., Alejo, R. & Sotoca, J. M. (n.d.). The class imbalance problem in pattern classification and learning. *Pattern Analysis and Learning Group*, 283-291.

Garcia-Rudolph, A., Laxe, S., Saurí, J., & Guitart, B. (2019). M Stroke Survivors on Twitter: Sentiment and Topic Analysis from a Gender Perspective. *Journal of Medical Internet Research, 21*(8), e14077. doi:10.2196/14077 PMID:31452514

Gasparyan, A. Y., Nurmashev, B., Yessirkepov, M., Endovitskiy, D. A., Voronov, A. A., & Kitas, G. D. (2017). Researcher and author profiles: Opportunities, advantages, and limitations. *Journal of Korean Medical Science, 32*(11), 1749. doi:10.3346/jkms.2017.32.11.1749 PMID:28960025

Genism. (2009). *Topic Modelling for Humans.* https://radimrehurek.com/gensim/

Ghamrawi, N., & McCallum, A. (2005) Collective multi-label classification. In *CIKM '05: 14th ACM International Conference on Information and Knowledge Management.* ACM Press. 10.1145/1099554.1099591

Gharge, S., & Chavan, M. (2017, March). An integrated approach for malicious tweets detection using NLP. *Proceedings of International Conference on Inventive Communication and Computational Technologies (ICICCT)*, 435-438. 10.1109/ICICCT.2017.7975235

Ghazikhani, A., Monsefi, R., & Yazdi, H. S. (2013). Recursive least square perceptron model for non-stationary and imbalanced data stream classification. *Evolving Systems, 4*(2), 119–113. doi:10.100712530-013-9076-7

Ghazikhani, A., Monsefi, R., & Yazdi, H. S. (2014). Online neural network model for non-stationary and imbalanced data stream classification. *International Journal of Machine Learning and Cybernetics, 5*(1), 51–62. doi:10.100713042-013-0180-6

Gill, A. J., French, R. M., Gergle, D., & Oberlander, J. (2008). Identifying emotional characteristics from short blog texts. In *30th Annual Conference of the Cognitive Science Society* (pp. 2237-2242). Washington, DC: Cognitive Science Society.

Glavic, B. (2014). Big data provenance: Challenges and implications for benchmarking. In *Specifying big data benchmarks* (pp. 72–80). Springer. doi:10.1007/978-3-642-53974-9_7

GLOBOCAN Project. (2020). *International Agency for Research on Cancer.* Retrieved January 13, 2021, from https://gco.iarc.fr/today/home

Go, A., Bhayani, R., & Huang, L. (2009). Twitter Sentiment Classification using Distant Supervision. *Processing*, 1–6.

Godbole, S., & Sarawagi, S. (2004). *Discriminative methods for multi-labeled classification, Advances in Knowledge Discovery and Data Mining.* Springer.

Golbeck, J., Mauriello, M., Auxier, B., Bhanushali, K. H., Bonk, C., & Bouzaghrane, M. A. G. (2018, May). Fake news vs satire: A dataset and analysis. In *Proceedings of the 10th ACM Conference on Web Science* (pp. 17-21). Academic Press.

Golbeck, J., Robles, C., & Turner, K. (2011). Predicting Personality with Social Media. In *Proceedings of CHI '11 Extended Abstracts on Human Factors in Computing Systems* (pp. 253–262). Association for Computing Machinery.

Gortmaker, S. L. (1994). Theory and methods–applied logistic regression. *Contemporary Sociology, 23*(1), 159.

Gounaridis, D., Apostolou, A., & Sotirios, K. (2010). Land Cover of Greece, 2010: A Semi Automated Classification using Random Forests. *Journal of Maps, 12*(5), 1055–1062. doi:10.1080/17445647.2015.1123656

Grover, A., & Leskovec, J. (2016). Node2vec: Scalable feature learning for networks. In *Proceedings of the 22nd ACM SIGKDD international conference on Knowledge discovery and data mining* (pp. 855-864). 10.1145/2939672.2939754

Guo, H., Li, Y., Shang, J., Mingyun, G., Yuanyue, H., & Bing, G. (2017). Learning from class-imbalanced data: Review of methods and applications. *Expert Systems with Applications, 73*, 220–239. doi:10.1016/j.eswa.2016.12.035

Guo, H., & Viktor, H. L. (2004). Learning from imbalanced data sets with boosting and data generation: The DataBoost-IM approach. *SIGKDD Explorations*, *6*(1), 30–39. doi:10.1145/1007730.1007736

Gupta, D. K., Reddy, K. S., & Ekbal, A. (2015). Pso-asent: Feature selection using particle swarm optimization for aspect based sentiment analysis. *International conference on applications of natural language to information systems*, 220-233.

Haferkamp, N., Eimler, C., Papadakis, A.-M., & Kruck, J. V. (2012). Men Are from Mars, Women Are from Venus? Examining Gender Differences in Self-Presentation on Social Networking Sites. *Cyberpsychology, Behavior, and Social Networking*, *15*(2), 91–98. doi:10.1089/cyber.2011.0151 PMID:22132897

Hai, Z., Chang, K., & Cong, G. (2012). One seed to find them all: mining opinion features via association. *Proceedings of the 21st ACM international conference on Information and knowledge management*, 255-264. 10.1145/2396761.2396797

Halevy, A., Rajaraman, A., & Ordille, J. (2006, September). Data integration: the teenage years. In *Proceedings of the 32nd international conference on Very large data bases* (pp. 9-16). VLDB Endowment.

Hall, M., Frank, E., Holmes, G., Pfahringer, B., Reutemann, P., & Witten, I. H. (2009). The WEKA data mining software: An update. *SIGKDD Explorations*, *11*(1), 10–18. doi:10.1145/1656274.1656278

Hamad, R. A., Kimura, M., & Lundström, J. (2020). Efficacy of Imbalanced Data Handling Methods on Deep Learning for Smart Homes Environments. *SN. Computer Science*, *1*, 204.

Handl, J., Knowles, J., & Dorigo, M. (2006). Ant-based clustering and topographic mapping. *Artificial Life*, *12*(1), 35–62. doi:10.1162/106454606775186400 PMID:16393450

Han, H., Wang, W.-Y., & Mao, B.-H. (2005). Borderline-SMOTE: a new over-sampling method in imbalanced data sets learning. *International Conference on Intelligent Computing*, 878–887.

Han, J., & Kamber, M. (2012). *Data Mining: Concepts and Techniques*. The Morgan Kaufmann Series in Data Management Systems.

Han, J., Ngan, K. N., Li, M., & Zhang, H. J. (2005). Unsupervised extraction of visual attention objects in color images. *IEEE Transactions on Circuits and Systems for Video Technology*, *16*(1), 141–145. doi:10.1109/TCSVT.2005.859028

Hapfelmeier, A., & Ulm, K. (2013). A new variable selection approach using random forests. *Computational Statistics & Data Analysis*, *60*, 50–69.

Hart, P. (1968). The condensed nearest neighbor rule (corresp.). *IEEE Transactions on Information Theory*, *14*(3), 515–516.

Hasan, M., Agu, E., & Rundensteiner, E. (2014). Using hashtags as labels for supervised learning of emotions in twitter messages. ACM SIGKDD workshop on health informatics.

Hasan, M., Rundensteiner, E., & Agu, E. (2014). EMOTEX: Detecting Emotions in Twitter Messages *ASE Bigdata/Socialcom/Cybersecurity Conference*. Stanford University.

Hasan, M., Rundensteiner, E., & Agu, E. (2014). *Emotex: Detecting emotions in twitter messages*. Academic Press.

Hawkins, D. M., Qiu, P., & Kang, C. W. (2003). The change point model for statistical process control. *Journal of Quality Technology*, *35*(4), 355–366. doi:10.1080/00224065.2003.11980233

Haykin, S. (1998). Neural networks: A comprehensive foundation (2nd ed.). Prentice Hall.

He, H., Bai, Y., Garcia, E. A., & Li, S. (2008, June). ADASYN: Adaptive synthetic sampling approach for imbalanced learning. In *2008 IEEE international joint conference on neural networks (IEEE world congress on computational intelligence)* (pp. 1322-1328). IEEE.

He, H., Bai, Y., Garcia, E. A., & Li, S. (2008). ADASYN: Adaptive synthetic sampling approach for imbalanced learning. *2008 IEEE International Joint Conference on Neural Networks (IEEE World Congress on Computational Intelligence)*, (pp. 1322–1328). IEEE.

He, H., & Garcia, E. A. (2009). Learning from imbalanced data. *IEEE Transactions on Knowledge and Data Engineering, 21*(9), 1263–1283. doi:10.1109/TKDE.2008.239

He, Y. T., He, H., Zhai, J., Wang, X. J., & Wang, B. S. (2020). *Moving-average based index to timely evaluate the current epidemic situation after COVID-19 outbreak.* MedRxiv.

Hido, S., Kashima, H., & Takahashi, Y. (2009). Roughly balanced bagging for imbalanced data. *Statistical Analysis and Data Mining, 2*(5-6), 412–426. doi:10.1002am.10061

Hitchcock, D. B., Booth, J. G., & Casella, G. (2007). The effect of pre-smoothing functional data on cluster analysis. *Journal of Statistical Computation and Simulation, 77*(12), 1043–1055.

Hitchcock, D. B., Casella, G., & Booth, J. G. (2006). Improved estimation of dissimilarities by presmoothing functional data. *Journal of the American Statistical Association, 101*(473), 211–222.

Hochreiter, S., & Schmidhuber, J. (1997). Long short-term memory. *Neural Computation, 9*(8), 1735–1780. doi:10.1162/neco.1997.9.8.1735 PMID:9377276

Hoens, T. R., & Chawla, N. V. (2013). Imbalanced datasets: from sampling to classifiers. *Imbalanced learning: Foundations, algorithms, and applications*, 43-59.

Hoens, R. T., & Chawla, N. V. (2012). Learning in Nonstationary Environments with Class Imbalance. In *Proceedings of the 18th ACM SIGKDD International Conference on Knowledge Discovery and Data Mining* (pp. 168-176). ACM. 10.1145/2339530.2339558

Hoens, T. R., Chawla, N. V., & Polikar, R. (2011). Heuristic updatable weighted random subspaces for non-stationary environments. In *Proceedings of 11th International Conference on Data Mining* (pp. 241-250). 10.1109/ICDM.2011.75

Holewik, J., Schaefer, G., & Korovin, I. (2020). Imbalanced Ensemble Learning for Enhanced Pulsar Identification. In *Proceedings of International Conference ICSI 2020*, (pp.515-524). Academic Press.

Holmberg, K., & Hellsten, I. (2015). Gender differences in the climate change communication on Twitter. *Internet Research, 25*(5), 811-828. . doi:10.1108/IntR-07-2014-0179

Horne, B. D., & Adali, S. (2019, July). Nela-gt-2018: A large multi-labelled news dataset for the study of misinformation in news articles. In *Proceedings of the International AAAI Conference on Web and Social Media* (*Vol. 13*, pp. 630-638). Academic Press.

Horng, W. B., Peng, J. W., & Chen, C. Y. (2005, March). A new image-based real-time flame detection method using color analysis. In Proceedings. 2005 IEEE Networking, Sensing and Control, 2005 (pp. 100-105). IEEE.

Huang, J., Li, G.-R., Huang, Q.-M., & Wu, X.-D. (2015). Learning label specific features for multi-label classification. *Proc. IEEE Int. Conf. Data Min.*, 181–190. 10.1109/ICDM.2015.67

Hu, F., Liu, X., Dai, J., & Yu, H. (2014). A Novel Algorithm for Imbalance Data Classification Based on Neighborhood Hypergraph. *The Scientific World Journal*, 1–13.

Hu, L., & Kearney, M. W. (2020). Gendered Tweets: Computational Text Analysis of Gender Differences in Political Discussion on Twitter. *Journal of Language and Social Psychology.*

Hu, M., & Liu, B. (2004). Mining and summarizing customer reviews. *Proceedings of the tenth ACM SIGKDD international conference on Knowledge discovery and data mining*, 168-177.

I. (2019b, March 1). *NLP (data augmentation)*. Kaggle. https://www.kaggle.com/init927/nlp-data-augmentation#Introduction-to-Data-Augmentation-in-NLP

Iizuka, O., Kanavati, F., Kato, K., Rambeau, M., Arihiro, K., & Tsuneki, M. (2020). Deep learning models for histo-pathological classification of gastric and colonic epithelial tumours. *Scientific Reports*, *10*(1), 1–11.

Inaba, M., Imai, H., & Katoh, N. (1996, May). Experimental results of randomized clustering algorithm. In *Proceedings of the twelfth annual symposium on Computational geometry* (pp. 401-402). 10.1145/237218.237406

India Today. (n.d.). *19-year-old IIT Madras student, depressed over low marks, commits suicide*. https://www.indiatoday.in/india/story/19yearoldiitmadrasstudentdepressedoverlowmarkscommitssuicide161751420191110

Istanto, R. S., Mahmudy, W. F., & Bachtiar, F. A. (2020, November). Detection of online review spam: a literature review. In *Proceedings of the 5th International Conference on Sustainable Information Engineering and Technology* (pp. 57-63). 10.1145/3427423.3427434

it168. (2017). http://it168.com

Jain, C. (2019). *Detecting twitter bot data, Version 1*. Retrieved from https://www.kaggle.com/charvijain27/detecting-twitter-bot-data

Jamal, N., Xianqiao, C., & Aldabbas, H. (2019). Deep learning-based sentimental analysis for large-scale imbalanced twitter data. *Future Internet*, *11*(9), 190. doi:10.3390/fi11090190

Jansen, B. J., Zhang, M., Sobel, K., & Chowdury, A. (2009). Twitter power: Tweets as electronic word of mouth. *Journal of the American Society for Information Science and Technology*, *60*(11), 2169–2188. doi:10.1002/asi.21149

Jansen, M. J. A., Kuijf, H. J., Veldhuis, W. B., Wessels, F. J., Viergever, M. A., & Pluim, J. P. W. (2019). Automatic classification of focal liver lesions based on MRI and risk factors. *PLoS One*, *14*(5), e0217053.

Japkowicz, N. (2000). Concept-learning in the presence of between-class and within-class imbalances. In *Proceedings of the Fourteenth Conference of the Canadian Society for Computational Studies of Intelligence*, (pp. 67-77). Academic Press.

Japkowicz, N. (2000, June). The class imbalance problem: Significance and strategies. In *Proc. of the Int'l Conf. on Artificial Intelligence* (Vol. 56). Academic Press.

Japkowicz, N. (n.d.). *Learning from Imbalanced Data Sets*. Technical Report WS-00-05. The AAAI Press.

Japkowicz, N. (2001). Concept-learning in the Presence of between-class and within-class imbalances, In *Proceedings of the 14th Biennial Conference of the Canadian Society on Computational Studies of Intelligence: Advances in Artificial Intelligence*, (pp. 67-77). 10.1007/3-540-45153-6_7

Japkowicz, N., & Stephen, S. (2002). The class imbalance problem: A systematic study. *Intelligent Data Analysis*, *6*(5), 429–449. doi:10.3233/IDA-2002-6504

jd. (1998). http://www.jd.com

Jegierski H., & Saganowski, S. (2020). *An ''Outside the Box'' Solution for Imbalanced Data Classification*. Academic Press.

Jia, A. D., Li, B. Z., & Zhang, C. C. (2020). Detection of cervical cancer cells based on strong feature CNN-SVM network. *Neurocomputing*, *411*, 112–127.

Jindal, N., & Liu, B. (2008, February). Opinion spam and analysis. In *Proceedings of the 2008 international conference on web search and data mining* (pp. 219-230). Academic Press.

Jin, L., Takabi, H., & Joshi, J. B. (2011, February). Towards active detection of identity clone attacks on online social networks. *Proceedings of the first ACM conference on Data and application security and privacy*, 27-38. 10.1145/1943513.1943520

Jin, W., Ho, H. H., & Srihari, R. K. (2009). A novel lexicalized HMM-based learning framework for web opinion mining. *Proceedings of the 26th annual international conference on machine learning*, *10*, 1553374-1553435. 10.1145/1553374.1553435

Joachims, T. (1999). Transductive inference for text classification using support vector machines. ICML, 99, 200-209.

Jo, D. T., & Japkowicz, N. (2004). Class imbalances versus small disjuncts. *SIGKDD Explorations*, *6*(1), 40–49. doi:10.1145/1007730.1007737

Johnson, J. M., & Khoshgoftaar, T. M. (2019). Survey on deep learning with class imbalance. *Journal of Big Data*, *6*(1), 1–54.

Jordan, K. (2019). From social networks to publishing platforms: A review of the history and scholarship of academic social network sites. *Frontiers in Digital Humanities*, *6*, 5. doi:10.3389/fdigh.2019.00005

Joshi, M. V., Kumar, V., & Agarwal, R. (2001). Evaluating Boosting Algorithms to Classify Rare Classes: Comparison And Improvements. *Proceedings of IEEE international conference on data mining*, 257-264. 10.1109/ICDM.2001.989527

Kafle, K., Yousefhussien, M., & Kanan, C. (2017, September). Data augmentation for visual question answering. In *Proceedings of the 10th International Conference on Natural Language Generation* (pp. 198-202). 10.18653/v1/W17-3529

Kanavati, F., Ichihara, S., Rambeau, M., Iizuka, O., Arihiro, K., & Tsuneki, M. (2020). *Deep learning models for gastric signet ring cell carcinoma classification in whole slide images*. ArXiv Preprint ArXiv:2011.09247.

Kanungo, T., Mount, D. M., Netanyahu, N. S., Piatko, C. D., Silverman, R., & Wu, A. Y. (2002). An efficient k-means clustering algorithm: Analysis and implementation. *IEEE Transactions on Pattern Analysis and Machine Intelligence*, *24*(7), 881–892. doi:10.1109/TPAMI.2002.1017616

Kanwar, P., Mehta, R., & Tidke, B. (2019, November). Correlation Based Multi-Criteria Feature Weighting for Identification of Top-k Investors and Companies. In *2019 9th International Conference on Advances in Computing and Communication (ICACC)* (pp. 271-277). IEEE. 10.1109/ICACC48162.2019.8986183

Kaufman, L., & Rousseeuw, P. J. (2009). Finding groups in data: an introduction to cluster analysis. John Wiley & Sons.

Kaur, P., & Gosain, A. (2018). Issues and challenges of class imbalance problem in classification. *International Journal of Information Technology*. doi:10.100741870-018-0251-8

Kaur, H., Pannu, H. S., & Malhi, A. K. (2019). A Systematic Review on Imbalanced Data Challenges in Machine Learning: Applications and Solutions. *ACM Computing Surveys, 52*(4), 1–36.

Kaur, H., Pannu, H. S., & Malhi, A. K. (2019). A systematic review on imbalanced data challenges in machine learning: Applications and solutions. *ACM Computing Surveys*, *52*(4), 1–36. doi:10.1145/3343440

Kaushal, V., & Patwardhan, M. (2018). Emerging Trends in Personality Identification Using Online Social Networks—A Literature Survey. *ACM Transactions on Knowledge Discovery from Data*, *12*(2).

Kennedy, J., & Eberhart, R. C. (2001). *Swarm Intelligence*. Morgan Kaufmann Publishers Inc.

Kermack, W. O., & McKendrick, A. G. (1927). A contribution to the mathematical theory of epidemics. *Proceedings of the Royal Society of London. Series A, Containing Papers of a Mathematical and Physical Character, 115*(772), 700–721.

Khammasi, I., Mouchaweh, M. S., Hammami, M., & Ghedira, K. (2018). Discussion and Review on Evolving Data Streams and Concept Drift Adapting. *Evolving Systems, 9*(1), 1–23. doi:10.100712530-016-9168-2

Kharde, V. A., & Sonawane, S. S. (2016). Article: Sentiment Analysis of Twitter Data: A Survey of Techniques. *International Journal of Computers and Applications, 139*(11), 5–15.

Khirade, S. D., & Patil, A. B. (2015, February). Plant disease detection using image processing. In *2015 International conference on computing communication control and automation* (pp. 768-771). IEEE. 10.1109/ICCUBEA.2015.153

Kim, J., Jeong, J., & Shin, J. (2020). M2m: Imbalanced Classification via Major-to-minor Translation, In *Proceedings of IEEE/CVF Conference on Computer Vision and Pattern Recognition (CVPR)*, (pp.13893-13902). IEEE.

Kim, M.-J., Kang, D.-K., & Kim, H. B. (2015). Geometric mean based boosting algorithm with over-sampling to resolve data imbalance problem for bankruptcy prediction. *Expert Systems with Applications, 42*(3), 1074–1082.

Kim, Y. (2014). Convolutional Neural Networks for Sentence Classification. *Proceedings of the 2014 Conference on Empirical Methods in Natural Language Processing (EMNLP)*, 1746-1751. 10.3115/v1/D14-1181

Kiritchenko, S. (2005). *Hierarchical Text Categorization and its Application to Bioinformatics* (PhD thesis). Queen's University, Kingston, Canada.

Kleinberg, J. M. (1999). Authoritative sources in a hyperlinked environment. *Journal of the Association for Computing Machinery, 46*(5), 604–632. doi:10.1145/324133.324140

Kobayashi, S. (2018). Contextual augmentation: Data augmentation by words with paradigmatic relations. arXiv preprint arXiv:1805.06201. doi:10.18653/v1/N18-2072

Kobayashi, N., Inui, K., & Matsumoto, Y. (2007). Extracting aspect-evaluation and aspect-of relations in opinion mining. *Proceedings of the 2007 Joint Conference on Empirical Methods in Natural Language Processing and Computational Natural Language Learning (EMNLP-CoNLL)*, 1065-1074.

Kochkina, E., Liakata, M., & Zubiaga, A. (2018). *All-in-one: Multi-task learning for rumour verification.* arXiv preprint arXiv:1806.03713.

Kohonen, T. (2012). Self-organizing maps. Science & Business Media, Springer.

Koltcov, S., Koltsova, O., & Nikolenko, S. (2014). Latent Dirichlet Allocation: Stability and Applications to Studies of UserGenerated Content. In *Proceedings of the 2014 ACM Conference on Web Science*, (pp. 161–165). doi:10.1145/2615569.2615680

Kong, J., Kowalczyk, W., Menzel, S., & Bäck, T. (2020) Improving Imbalanced Classification by Anomaly Detection. Proceedings of Parallel Problem Solving from Nature – PPSN XVI. doi:10.1007/978-3-030-58112-1_35

Konkol, M. (2014). Brainy: A machine learning library. *International Conference on Artificial Intelligence and Soft Computing*, 490-499. 10.1007/978-3-319-07176-3_43

Kontaxis, G., Polakis, I., Ioannidis, S., & Markatos, E. P. (2011, March). *Detecting social network profile cloning. In 2011 IEEE international conference on pervasive computing and communications workshops (PERCOM Workshops), (pp. 295-300).* IEEE.

Köper, M., Kim, E., & Klinger, R. (2017, September). IMS at EmoInt-2017: Emotion intensity prediction with affective norms, automatically extended resources and deep learning. In *Proceedings of the 8th Workshop on Computational Approaches to Subjectivity, Sentiment and Social Media Analysis* (pp. 50-57). 10.18653/v1/W17-5206

Korycki, L., Cano, A., & Krawczyk, B. (2019). Active learning with abstaining classifiers for imbalanced drifting data streams. In *Proceedings of 2019 IEEE International Conference on Big Data* (pp. 2334-2343). Los Angeles, CA: IEEE. 10.1109/BigData47090.2019.9006453

Kothiya, Y. (2020, July 17). *How I handled imbalanced text data - Towards Data Science*. Medium. https://towardsdatascience.com/how-i-handled-imbalanced-text-data-ba9b757ab1d8

Kotsiantis, S., Kanellopoulos, D., & Pintelas, P. (2005). Handling imbalanced datasets: A review. *GESTS International Transactions on Computer Science and Engineering, 30*, 1–13.

Koziarski, M. (2020). *Two-Stage Resampling for Convolutional Neural Network Training in the Imbalanced Colorectal Cancer Image Classification.* ArXiv Preprint ArXiv:2004.03332.

Krawczyk. (2016). Learning from imbalanced data: Open challenges and future directions. *Prog. Artif. Intell.*

Krawczyk, B. (2016). Learning from Imbalanced Data: Open Challenges and Future Directions. *Artificial Intelligence*, 221–232.

Krawczyk, B. (2016). Learning from imbalanced data: Open challenges and future directions. *Progress in Artificial Intelligence, 5*(4), 221–232.

Krawczyk, B., Galar, M., Jeleń, Ł., & Herrera, F. (2016). Evolutionary undersampling boosting for imbalanced classification of breast cancer malignancy. *Applied Soft Computing, 38*, 714–726. doi:10.1016/j.asoc.2015.08.060

Kubat, M., & Matwin, S. (1997). Addressing the curse of imbalanced training sets: One-sided selection. *ICML, 97*, 179–186.

Kudugunta, S., & Ferrara, E. (2018). Deep neural networks for bot detection. *Information Sciences, 467*, 312–322. doi:10.1016/j.ins.2018.08.019

Kulkarni & Ade. (2016). Logistic regression learning model for handling concept drift with unbalanced data in credit card fraud detection system. In *Proceedings of the 2nd International Conference on Computer and Communication Technologies*. Springer.

Kumar, S., Reddy, P. K., Reddy, V. B., & Singh, A. (2011). Similarity analysis of legal judgments. In *Proceedings of the Fourth Annual ACM Bangalore Conference* (pp. 1-4). ACM.

Kumar, S., Reddy, P. K., Reddy, V. B., & Suri, M. (2013). Finding similar legal judgements under common law system. In *Proceedings of International workshop on databases in networked information systems* (pp. 103-116). Springer. 10.1007/978-3-642-37134-9_9

Lafferty, J., McCallum, A., & Pereira, F. C. (2001). Conditional random fields: Probabilistic models for segmenting and labeling sequence data. *Proceedings of the 18th International Conference on Machine Learning 2001 (ICML 2001)*, 282-289.

Lakshmipadmaja, D., & Vishnuvardhan, B. (2018). Classification Performance Improvement using Random Subset Feature Selection Algorithm for Data Mining. *Big Data Research*, 1-12.

Lamsal, R. (2020). Design and analysis of a large-scale COVID-19 tweets dataset. *Applied Intelligence*.

Langville, A. N., & Meyer, C. D. (2008). Google's PageRank and beyond: The science of search engine rankings. *The Mathematical Intelligencer, 30*(1), 68–68. doi:10.1007/BF02985759

Lars, W., Jochumsen, J., Ostergaard, S., Jensen, H., Clemente, C., & Morten, O. (2016). Pedersen A Recursive Kinematic Random Forest and Alpha Beta Filter Classifier for 2d Radar Tracks. *EURASIP Journal on Advances in Signal Processing, 82*, 1–12.

Lau, R. Y., Liao, S. Y., Kwok, R. C. W., Xu, K., Xia, Y., & Li, Y. (2015). Text mining and probabilistic modeling for online review spam detection. *ACM Transactions on Management Information Systems, 2*(4), 1–30. doi:10.1145/2070710.2070716

Leaper, C., & Ayres, M. M. (2007). A meta-analytic review of gender variations in adults' language use: Talkativeness, affiliative speech, and assertive speech. *Personality and Social Psychology Review, 11*(4), 328–63. doi:10.1177/1088868307302221

LeCun, Y., Bengio, Y., & Hinton, G. (2015). Deep learning. *Nature, 521*(7553), 436-444.

Lee, S. Y. M., Chen, Y., & Huang, C. R. (2010, June). A text-driven rule-based system for emotion cause detection. In *Proceedings of the NAACL HLT 2010 Workshop on Computational Approaches to Analysis and Generation of Emotion in Text* (pp. 45-53). Academic Press.

Lee, H., & Cho, S. (2006).). The Novelty Detection Approach for Different Degrees of Class Imbalance. *Lecture Notes in Computer Science, 4233*.

Leevy, J. L., Khoshgoftaar, T. M., Bauder, R. A., & Seliya, N. (2018). A survey on addressing high-class imbalance in big data. *Journal of Big Data, 5*(1), 1–30.

Lemaitre, G., Martí, R., Rastgoo, M., & Mériaudeau, F. (2017). Computer-aided detection for prostate cancer detection based on multi-parametric magnetic resonance imaging. *2017 39th Annual International Conference of the IEEE Engineering in Medicine and Biology Society (EMBC)*, 3138–3141.

Le, Q., & Mikolov, T. (2014). Distributed representations of sentences and documents. In *Proceedings of International conference on machine learning* (pp. 1188-1196). PMLR.

Lerman, R. I., & Yitzhaki, S. (1984). A note on the calculation and interpretation of the Gini index. *Economics Letters, 15*(3), 363–368. doi:10.1016/0165-1765(84)90126-5

Lessmann, S. (2014). Solving Imbalanced Classification Problems with Support Vector Machines. *Inst. of Business Information Systems*, 1-8.

Liar, Liar, Pants on Fire? Psychophysiological Deception Detection Unraveled. (2017). *Psychophysiology, 54*, S12-S13. doi:10.1111/psyp.12928

Li, C., & Lee, C. (1993). Minimum cross entropy thresholding. *Pattern Recognition, 26*(4), 617–625. doi:10.1016/0031-3203(93)90115-D

Lichtenwalter, R. N., & Chawla, N. V. (2010). Adaptive methods for classification in arbitrarily imbalanced and drifting data streams. In New Frontiers in Applied Data Mining, Lecture Notes in Computer Science (vol. 5669, pp. 53-75). doi:10.1007/978-3-642-14640-4_5

Li, F., Han, C., Huang, M., Zhu, X., Xia, Y., Zhang, S., & Yu, H. (2010). Structure-aware review mining and summarization. *Proceedings of the 23rd International Conference on Computational Linguistics (Coling 2010)*, 653-661.

Li, M., & Ghosal, S. (2014). Bayesian multiscale smoothing of Gaussian noised images. *Bayesian Analysis, 9*(3), 733–758.

Li, S., Wang, R., & Zhou, G. (2012). Opinion target extraction using a shallow semantic parsing framework. *Proceedings of the AAAI Conference on Artificial Intelligence, 26*(1).

Litjens, G., Kooi, T., Bejnordi, B. E., Setio, A. A. A., Ciompi, F., Ghafoorian, M., ... Sánchez, C. I. (2017). A survey on deep learning in medical image analysis. *Medical Image Analysis, 42*, 60–88.

Liu, B. (2012). Sentiment analysis and opinion mining. *Synthesis Lectures on Human Language Technologies, 5*(1), 1-167.

Liu, B. (2011). Opinion mining and sentiment analysis. In *Web Data Mining* (pp. 459–526). Springer. doi:10.1007/978-3-642-19460-3_11

Liu, B., & Tsoumakas, G. (2018). *Making Classifier Chains Resilient to Class Imbalance.* ACML.

Liu, G. R., Zhang, J., Lam, K. Y., Li, H., Xu, G., Zhong, Z. H., ... Han, X. (2008). A gradient smoothing method (GSM) with directional correction for solid mechanics problems. *Computational Mechanics, 41*(3), 457–472.

Liu, K., Xu, L., & Zhao, J. (2013). Syntactic patterns versus word alignment: Extracting opinion targets from online reviews. *Proceedings of the 51st Annual Meeting of the Association for Computational Linguistics, 1*, 1754-1763.

Liu, X., Wu, J., & Zhou, Z. (2009). Exploratory undersampling for class imbalance learning. *IEEE Transactions on Systems, Man, and Cybernetics. Part B, Cybernetics, 39*(2), 539–550. doi:10.1109/TSMCB.2008.2007853 PMID:19095540

Liu, X., & Zhou, Z. (2006). The Influence of Class Imbalance on Cost-Sensitive Learning: An Empirical Study. In *Sixth International Conference on Data Mining (ICDM'06)* (pp. 970-974). 10.1109/ICDM.2006.158

Liu, Y. (2011). Random Forest Algorithm in Big Data Environment. *Computer Modeling and New Technologies, 18*, 147–151.

Li, W., & Xu, H. (2014). Text-based emotion classification using emotion cause extraction. *Expert Systems with Applications, 41*(4), 1742–1749. doi:10.1016/j.eswa.2013.08.073

Li, Y., Qin, Z., Xu, W., & Guo, J. (2015). A holistic model of mining product aspects and associated sentiments from online reviews. *Multimedia Tools and Applications, 74*(23), 10177–10194. doi:10.100711042-014-2158-0

Loey, M., Jasim, M. W., El-Bakry, H. M., Taha, M. H. N., & Khalifa, N. E. M. (2020). Breast and colon cancer classification from gene expression profiles using data mining techniques. *Symmetry, 12*(3), 408.

Loezer, L., Enembreck, F., Barddal, J. P., & Britto, A. D. S. (2020). Cost sensitive learning for imbalanced data streams. In *Proceedings of SAC '20: Proceedings of the 35th Annual ACM Symposium on Applied Computing* (pp. 498-504). 10.1145/3341105.3373949

López, V., Fernández, A., García, S., Palade, V., & Herrera, F. (2013). An insight into classification with imbalanced data: Empirical results and current trends on using data intrinsic characteristics. *Information Sciences, 250*, 113–141.

López, V., Río, S., Benítez, J. M., & Herrera, F. (2015). Cost-sensitive linguistic fuzzy rule based classification systems under the MapReduce framework for imbalanced big data. *Fuzzy Sets and Systems, 258*, 5–38. doi:10.1016/j.fss.2014.01.015

Lowen, R. (1977). On fuzzy complements. *1977 IEEE Conference on Decision and Control including the 16th Symposium on Adaptive Processes and A Special Symposium on Fuzzy Set Theory and Applications*, 1338-1342. doi: 10.1109/CDC.1977.271511

Lukasz, K., & Krawczyk, B. (2020). Online Oversampling for Sparsely Labeled Imbalanced and Non-Stationary Data Streams. In *International Joint Conference on Neural Networks* (pp. 1-8). Academic Press.

Lu, L., & Daigle, B. J. Jr. (2020). Prognostic analysis of histopathological images using pre-trained convolutional neural networks: Application to hepatocellular carcinoma. *PeerJ, 8*, e8668.

Lurie, M. N., Silva, J., Yorlets, R. R., Tao, J., & Chan, P. A. (2020). Coronavirus disease 2019 epidemic doubling time in the United States before and during stay-at-home restrictions. *The Journal of Infectious Diseases, 222*(10), 1601–1606.

Lu, Y., Cheung, Y., & Tang, Y. Y. (2019). Adaptive Chunk-Based Dynamic Weighted Majority for Imbalanced Data Streams with Concept Drift. *IEEE Transactions on Neural Networks and Learning Systems*, *31*(8), 2764–2788. doi:10.1109/TNNLS.2019.2951814 PMID:31825880

Lu, Y., Cheung, Y., & Tan, Y. Y. (2017). Dynamic Weighted Majority for Incremental Learning of Imbalanced Data Streams with Concept Drift. In *Proceedings of the Twenty-Sixth International Joint Conference on Artificial Intelligence* (pp. 2393-2399). 10.24963/ijcai.2017/333

Ma, J., Gao, W., Mitra, P., Kwon, S., Jansen, B. J., Wong, K. F., & Cha, M. (2016). *Detecting rumors from microblogs with recurrent neural networks*. Academic Press.

Ma, B., Zhang, D., Yan, Z., & Kim, T. (2013). An LDA and synonym lexicon based approach to product feature extraction from online consumer product reviews. *Journal of Electronic Commerce Research*, *14*(4), 304.

Ma, C., Prendinger, H., & Ishizuka, M. (2005, October). Emotion estimation and reasoning based on affective textual interaction. In *International conference on affective computing and intelligent interaction* (pp. 622-628). Springer. 10.1007/11573548_80

Madjarov, G., Kocev, D., Gjorgjevikj, D., & Džeroski, S. (2012). An extensive experimental comparison of methods for multi-label learning. *Pattern Recognition*, *45*(9), 3084–3104. doi:10.1016/j.patcog.2012.03.004

Ma, H., Yang, H., Lyu, M. R., & King, I. (2008, October). Mining social networks using heat diffusion processes for marketing candidates selection. In *Proceedings of the 17th ACM conference on Information and knowledge management* (pp. 233-242). 10.1145/1458082.1458115

Maheshwari, S., Jain, R. C., & Jadon, R. S. (2017). A review on class imbalance problem: Analysis and potential solutions. *International Journal of Computer Science Issues*, *14*(6), 43–51.

Mahmood, A. M. (2015). Class imbalance learning in data mining–a survey. *International Journal of Communication Technology for Social Networking Services*, *3*(2), 17–38. doi:10.21742/ijctsns.2015.3.2.02

Mandal, A., Chaki, R., Saha, S., Ghosh, K., Pal, A., & Ghosh, S. (2017). Measuring similarity among legal court case documents. In *Proceedings of the 10th annual ACM Indiacompute conference* (pp. 1-9). 10.1145/3140107.3140119

Manek, A. S., Shenoy, P. D., Mohan, M. C., & Venugopal, K. R. (2017). Aspect term extraction for sentiment analysis in large movie reviews using Gini Index feature selection method and SVM classifier. *World Wide Web (Bussum)*, *20*(2), 135–154. doi:10.100711280-015-0381-x

Mao, Z., Liu, G. R., & Huang, Y. (2019). A local Lagrangian gradient smoothing method for fluids and fluid-like solids: A novel particle-like method. *Engineering Analysis with Boundary Elements*, *107*, 96–114.

Marrese-Taylor, E., Velásquez, J. D., & Bravo-Marquez, F. (2014). A novel deterministic approach for aspect-based media (SocialNLP). *Expert Systems with Applications*, *41*(17), 7764–7775. doi:10.1016/j.eswa.2014.05.045

Matsuki, T., Yokoya, N., & Iwasaki, A. (2015). Hyperspectral Tree Species Classification of Japanese Complex Mixed Forest With the Aid of Lidar Data. *IEEE Journal of Selected Topics in Applied Earth Observations and Remote Sensing*, *8*(5), 2177–2187. doi:10.1109/JSTARS.2015.2417859

Maupomés, D., & Meurs, M. (2018, September). Using topic extraction on social media content for the early detection of depression. In *Proceedings of CLEF (Working Notes)*, (vol. 2125). Available: https://CEURWS.org

Ma, Y., Peng, H., & Cambria, E. (2018). Targeted aspect-based sentiment analysis via embedding commonsense knowledge into an attentive LSTM. *Proceedings of the AAAI Conference on Artificial Intelligence*, *32*(1).

Mazurowskia, M. A., Habasa, P. A., Zuradaa, J. M., Lob, J. Y., Bakerb, J. A., & Tourassib, G. D. (2008). Training Neural Network Classifiers for Medical Decision Making: The Effects of Imbalanced Datasets on Classification Performance. *Neural Network PMC*, 427–436.

McCright, A. M. (2010). The effects of gender on climate change knowledge and concern in the American public. *Population and Environment*, 32, 66–87. https://doi.org/10.1007/s11111-010-0113-1

Meda, C., Ragusa, E., Gianoglio, C., Zunino, R., Ottaviano, A., Scillia, E., & Surlinelli, R. (2016, August). Spam detection of Twitter traffic: A framework based on random forests and non-uniform feature sampling. In *2016 IEEE/ACM International Conference on Advances in Social Networks Analysis and Mining (ASONAM)*, (pp. 811-817). IEEE. 10.1109/ASONAM.2016.7752331

Mena, L. J., & Gonzalez, J. A. (2006). Machine Learning for Imbalanced Datasets: Application in Medical Diagnostic. *Flairs Conference*, 574–579.

Mental Health and Substance Use: Suicide data. (n.d.). Available: https://www.who.int/teams/mentalhealthandsubstanceuse/suicidedata

Mihaylov, T., Mihaylova, T., Nakov, P., Màrquez, L., Georgiev, G., & Koychev, I. (2018). The dark side of news community forums: Opinion manipulation trolls. *Internet Research*, 28(5), 1292–1312. doi:10.1108/intr-03-2017-0118

Mikolov, T., Chen, K., Corrado, G., & Dean, J. (2013a). *Efficient estimation of word representations in vector space.* ArXiv Preprint arXiv:1301.3781.

Mikolov, T., Sutskever, I., Chen, K., Corrado, G., & Dean, J. (2013). *Distributed representations of words and phrases and their compositionality.* arXiv preprint arXiv:1310.4546.

Mikolov, T., Sutskever, I., Chen, K., Corrado, G. S., & Dean, J. (2013b). Distributed representations of words and phrases and their compositionality. *Advances in Neural Information Processing Systems*, 3111–3119.

Minku, L. L., White, A., & Yao, X. (2010). The impact of diversity on online ensemble learning in the presence of concept drift. *IEEE Transactions on Knowledge and Data Engineering*, 22(5), 731–742. doi:10.1109/TKDE.2009.156

Minku, L. L., & Yao, X. (2012). DDD: A New Ensemble Approach For Dealing With Concept Drift. *IEEE Transactions on Knowledge and Data Engineering*, 24(4), 619–633. doi:10.1109/TKDE.2011.58

Mishra, S., Agarwal, S., Guo, J., Phelps, K., Picco, J., & Diesner, J. (2014). Enthusiasm and Support: Alternative Sentiment Classification for Social Movements on Social Media. In *Proceedings of the 2014 ACM conference on Web science* (pp. 261–262). ACM.

Mitre. (1958). https://www.mitre.org/publications/

Moghaddam, S., & Ester, M. (2010). Opinion digger: an unsupervised opinion miner from unstructured product reviews. *Proceedings of the 19th ACM international conference on Information and knowledge management*, 1825-1828. 10.1145/1871437.1871739

Mohammad, S., & Turney, P. (2010). *Emotions evoked by common words and phrases: Using Mechanical Turk to create an emotion lexicon* [Paper Presentation]. NAACL-HLT Workshop on computational approaches to analysis and generation of emotion in text, California, US.

Mohammadrezaei, M., Shiri, M. E., & Rahmani, A. M. (2018). Identifying fake accounts on social networks based on graph analysis and classification algorithms. *Security and Communication Networks*, 2018, 1–8. doi:10.1155/2018/5923156

Mohri, M., Rostamizadeh, A., & Talwalkar, A. (2012). *Foundations of machine learning.* Academic Press.

Moon, T. K. (1996). The expectation-maximization algorithm. *IEEE Signal Processing Magazine, 13*(6), 47–60. doi:10.1109/79.543975

Moraes, R., Valiati, J. F., & Neto, W. P. G. (2018). *Unbalanced sentiment classification: an assessment of ANN in the context of sampling the majority class*. PeerJ Preprints.

More, A. S., & Rana, D. P. (2017). Review of Random Forest Classification Techniques to Resolve Data Imbalance. In *Proceedings of IEEE 1st International Conference on Intelligent Systems and Information Management (ICISIM)*, (pp.72-78). 10.1109/ICISIM.2017.8122151

More, A. S., & Rana, D. P. (2020). An Experimental Assessment of Random Forest Classification Performance Improvisation with Sampling and Stage Wise Success Rate Calculation. Elsevier *procedia. Computer Science, 167*, 1711–1721.

More, A. S., Rana, D. P., & Agarwal, I. (2018). Random Forest Classifier Approach for Imbalanced Big Data Classification for Smart City Application Domains. *International Journal of Computational Intelligence & IoT, 1*(2), 261–266.

More, S, A., P Rana, D., & Agarwal, I. (2018). Random forest classifier approach for imbalanced big data classification for smart city application domains. *International Journal of Computational Intelligence & IoT, 1*(2).

Morik, K., Brockhausen, P., & Joachims, T. (1999). Combining Statistical Learning with a Knowledge-Based Approach - A Case Study in Intensive Care Monitoring. In *Proceedings of the 16th International Conference on Machine Learning ICML* (pp. 268-277). Academic Press.

Mukherjee, S., & Weikum, G. (2015, October). Leveraging joint interactions for credibility analysis in news communities. In *Proceedings of the 24th ACM International on Conference on Information and Knowledge Management* (pp. 353-362). ACM.

Mullen, T., & Collier, N. (2004). Sentiment analysis using support vector machines with diverse information sources. *Proceedings of the 2004 conference on empirical methods in natural language processing*, 412-418.

Multi-Class Emotion Classification for Short Texts. (2018, March 17). *Github*. https://tlkh.github.io/text-emotion-classification/

Mundra, S., Sen, A., Sinha, M., Mannarswamy, S., Dandapat, S., & Roy, S. (2017, May). Fine-grained emotion detection in contact center chat utterances. In *Pacific-Asia Conference on Knowledge Discovery and Data Mining* (pp. 337-349). Springer. 10.1007/978-3-319-57529-2_27

Muscanell, L. N., & Guadagno, E. R. (2012). Make new friends or keep the old: Gender and personality differences in social networking use. *Computers in Human Behavior, 28*(1).

Nakagawa, H., & Mori, T. (2003). Automatic term recognition based on statistics of compound nouns and their components. *Terminology. International Journal of Theoretical and Applied Issues in Specialized Communication, 9*(2), 201–219.

Napierala, K., & Stefanowski, J. (2016). Types of minority class examples and their influence on learning classifiers from imbalanced data. *Journal of Intelligent Information Systems, 46*(3), 563–597.

Na, S., Xumin, L., & Yong, G. (2010, April). Research on k-means clustering algorithm: An improved k-means clustering algorithm. In *2010 Third International Symposium on intelligent information technology and security informatics* (pp. 63-67). IEEE. 10.1109/IITSI.2010.74

Nemati, A., & Kumar, M. (2014, June). Modeling and control of a single axis tilting quadcopter. In *2014 American Control Conference* (pp. 3077-3082). IEEE. doi:10.1109/ICECA.2017.8212855

Nepal, S., & Pathan, M. (Eds.). (2014). *Security, privacy and trust in cloud systems.* Springer Berlin Heidelberg. doi:10.1007/978-3-642-38586-5

Neviarouskaya, A., Prendinger, H., & Ishizuka, M. (2010, August). Recognition of affect, judgment, and appreciation in text. In *Proceedings of the 23rd International Conference on Computational Linguistics (Coling 2010)* (pp. 806-814). Academic Press.

Newman, M. L., Groom, C. J., Handelman, L. D., & Pennebaker, J. W. (2008). Gender differences in language use: An analysis of 14,000 text samples. *Discourse Processes, 45*(3), 211–236.

Nigam, K., Lafferty, J., & McCallum, A. (1999). Using maximum entropy for text classification. IJCAI-99 workshop on machine learning for information filtering, 1(1), 61-67.

Nishida, K., & Yamauchi, K. (2007). Detecting concept drift using statistical testing. In *Proceedings of tenth international conference on discovery science* (pp. 264-269). 10.1007/978-3-540-75488-6_27

Nltk. (2002). *Natural Language Toolkit.* https://www.nltk.org/

Noble, W. S. (2006). What is a support vector machine? *Nature Biotechnology, 24*(12), 1565–1567.

Orhan, U., Hekim, M., & Ozer, M. (2011). EEG signals classification using the K-means clustering and a multilayer perceptron neural network model. *Expert Systems with Applications, 38*(10), 13475–13481.

Ortega, J. L. (2018). Reliability and accuracy of altmetric providers: A comparison among Altmetric. com, PlumX and Crossref Event Data. *Scientometrics, 116*(3), 2123–2138. doi:10.100711192-018-2838-z

Ortony, A., Clore, G. L., & Collins, A. (1988). *The cognitive structure of emotions.* Cambridge University Press.

Padmaja, TM., Dhulipalla, N., Radha Krishna, P., Bapi, R.S., & Arjith, L. (2007). An Unbalanced Data Classification Model Using Hybrid Sampling Technique for Fraud Detection. *Pattern Recognition and Machine Intelligence*, 341-348.

Padmaja, T. M., Dhulipalla, N., Bapi, R. S., & Krishna, P. R. (2007, December). Unbalanced data classification using extreme outlier elimination and sampling techniques for fraud detection. In *15th International Conference on Advanced Computing and Communications (ADCOM 2007)* (pp. 511-516). IEEE.

Padol, P. B., & Yadav, A. A. (2016, June). SVM classifier based grape leaf disease detection. In *2016 Conference on advances in signal processing (CASP)* (pp. 175-179). IEEE. 10.1109/CASP.2016.7746160

Paing, M. P., & Choomchuay, S. (2018). Improved random forest (RF) classifier for imbalanced classification of lung nodules. *2018 International Conference on Engineering, Applied Sciences, and Technology (ICEAST)*, 1–4.

Pak, P., & Paroubek, A. P. (2010). *Twitter as a corpus for sentiment analysis and opinion mining.* http://www.lrec-conf.org/proceedings/lrec2010/pdf/385Paper.pdf

Park, M. (2016). Women are Warmer but No Less Assertive than Men: Gender and Language on Facebook. *PLoS One, 11*(5), 1–26.

Patel, S. & Patel, P. (2020). Doubling Time and its Interpretation for COVID 19 Cases. *National Journal of Community Medicine, 11*(3).

Patist, J. P. (2007). Optimal window change detection. In *Proceedings of Seventh IEEE international conference on data mining workshops* (pp. 557-562). 10.1109/ICDMW.2007.9

Pei, J., Han, J., Mortazavi-Asl, B., Wang, J., Pinto, H., Chen, Q., ... Hsu, M. C. (2004). Mining sequential patterns by pattern-growth: The prefixspan approach. *IEEE Transactions on Knowledge and Data Engineering, 16*(11), 1424–1440. doi:10.1109/TKDE.2004.77

Pellis, L., Scarabel, F., Stage, H. B., Overton, C. E., Chappell, L. H. K., Lythgoe, K. A., Fearon, E., Bennett, E., Curran-Sebastian, J., Das, R., Fyles, M., Lewkowicz, H., Pang, X., Vekaria, B., Webb, L., House, T. A., & Hall, I. (2020). Challenges in control of Covid-19: short doubling time and long delay to effect of interventions. *medRxiv*. doi:10.1101/2020.04.12.20059972

Peng-fei, J., Chunkai, Z., & Zhen-yu, H. (2014). A new sampling approach for classification of imbalanced data sets with high density. *Proceedings of 2014 International Conference on Big Data and Smart Computing (BIGCOMP)*, 217-222. 10.1109/BIGCOMP.2014.6741439

Pennebaker, J. W., Booth, R. J., Boyd, R. L., & Francis, M. E. (2015). *Linguistic Inquiry and Word Count: LIWC2015*. Pennebaker Conglomerates. Available www.LIWC.net

Pennington, J., Socher, R., & Manning, C. D. (2014, October). Glove: Global vectors for word representation. In *Proceedings of the 2014 conference on empirical methods in natural language processing (EMNLP)* (pp. 1532-1543). 10.3115/v1/D14-1162

Pesquita, C., Faria, D., Bastos, H., Falcao, A. O., & Couto, F. M. (2007). Evaluating GO-based Semantic Similarity Measures. *The 10th Annual Bio-Ontologies Meeting, ISMB/ECCB*.

Petovska, A., Goldberg, P., Brüggemann-Klein, A., & Nyokabi, A. (2020). Mining Gender Bias: A Preliminary Study on Implicit Biases and Gender Identity in the Department of Computer Science at the Technical University of Munich. *Proceedings of European Conference on Software Architecture Communications in Computer and Information Science, 1269*.

Phua, C., Alahakoon, D., & Lee, V. (2004). Minority report in fraud detection: Classification of skewed data. *SIGKDD Explorations, 6*(1), 50–59.

Phua, C., Alahakoon, D., & Lee, V. C. S. (2004). Minority Report in Fraud Detection: Classification of Skewed Data. *SIGKDD Explorations, 6*(1), 50–59. doi:10.1145/1007730.1007738

Picard, R. W. (2000). *Affective computing*. MIT Press. doi:10.7551/mitpress/1140.001.0001

Polikar, R. (2006). Ensemble based systems in decision making. *IEEE Circuits and Systems Magazine, 6*(3), 21–45.

Poria, S., Cambria, E., Ku, L. W., Gui, C., & Gelbukh, A. (2014). A rule-based approach to aspect extraction from product reviews. *Proceedings of the second workshop on natural language processing for social media (SocialNLP)*, 28-37. 10.3115/v1/W14-5905

Pozzolo, A. D., Johnson, R. A., Caelen, O., Waterschoot, S., Chawla, N. V., & Bontempi, G. (2014). HDDT to avoid instances propagation in unbalanced and evolving data streams. In *IEEE International Joint Conference on Neural Networks IJCNN*. 10.1109/IJCNN.2014.6889638

Prati, R. C., Batista, G. E. A. P. A., & Monard, M. C. (2004). Class Imbalances *versus* Class Overlapping: An Analysis of a Learning System Behavior. In *Mexican International Conference on Artificial Intelligence* (vol 2972, pp. 312-321). 10.1007/978-3-540-24694-7_32

Protas, E., Bratti, J. D., Gaya, J. F., Drews, P., & Botelho, S. S. (2018). Visualization methods for image transformation convolutional neural networks. *IEEE Transactions on Neural Networks and Learning Systems, 30*(7), 2231–2243. doi:10.1109/TNNLS.2018.2881194 PMID:30561353

Psylla, I., Sapiezynski, P., Mones, E., & Lehmann, S. (2017). The role of gender in social network organization. *PLoS One*, *12*(12), e0189873. https://doi.org/10.1371/journal.pone.0189873

Pugoy, R. A. D., & Mariano, V. Y. (2011, July). Automated rice leaf disease detection using color image analysis. In *Third international conference on digital image processing (ICDIP 2011)* (Vol. 8009, p. 80090F). International Society for Optics and Photonics.

PyDictionary. (2020, July 9). *PyPI*. https://pypi.org/project/PyDictionary/

Qian, Q. (2020). *A Deep Learning Pipeline for Lung Cancer Classification on Imbalanced Data Set*. Academic Press.

Qian, Y., Dong, J., Wang, W., & Tan, T. (2016, September). Learning and transferring representations for image steganalysis using convolutional neural network. In 2016 IEEE international conference on image processing (ICIP) (pp. 2752-2756). IEEE. doi:10.1109/ICIP.2016.7532860

Qian, Y., Liang, Y., Li, M., Feng, G., & Shi, X. (2014). A resampling ensemble algorithm for classification of imbalance problems. *Neurocomputing*, *143*, 57–67.

Qiu, G., Liu, B., Bu, J., & Chen, C. (2009). Expanding domain sentiment lexicon through double propagation. *IJCAI (United States)*, *9*, 1199–1204.

Qrius. (2021). *Will AI prolong the gender gap in the workplace?* Available at: https://qrius.com/will-ai-prolong-the-gender-gap-in-the-workplace/

Quan, & Ren, F. (2014). Unsupervised product feature extraction for feature-oriented opinion determination. *Information Sciences, 272*, 16-28.

Raghav, K., Reddy, P. K., & Reddy, V. B. (2016). Analyzing the extraction of relevant legal judgments using paragraph-level and citation information. In Proceedings of AI4JC Artificial Intelligence for Justice (pp. 1-8). Academic Press.

Raghav, K., Reddy, P. B., Reddy, V. B., & Reddy, P. K. (2015). Text and citations based cluster analysis of legal judgments. In *Proceedings of International conference on mining intelligence and knowledge exploration* (pp. 449-459). Springer. 10.1007/978-3-319-26832-3_42

Raju, S., Pingali, P., & Varma, V. (2009). An unsupervised approach to product attribute extraction. *European Conference on Information Retrieval*, 796-800. 10.1007/978-3-642-00958-7_88

Ramchoun, H., Idrissi, M. A. J., Ghanou, Y., & Ettaouil, M. (2016). Multilayer perceptron: Architecture optimization and training. *International Journal of Interactive Multimedia and Artificial Intelligence*, *4*(1), 26–30. doi:10.9781/ijimai.2016.415

Rana, T. A., & Cheah, Y. N. (2015). Hybrid rule-based approach for aspect extraction and categorization from customer reviews. *2015 9th International Conference on IT in Asia (CITA)*, 1-5. 10.1109/CITA.2015.7349820

Rana, T. A., & Cheah, Y. N. (2017). A two-fold rule-based model for aspect extraction. *Expert Systems with Applications*, *89*, 273–285. doi:10.1016/j.eswa.2017.07.047

Rao, R. B., Krishnan, S., & Niculescu, R. S. (2006). Data mining for improved cardiac care. *SIGKDD Explorations*, *8*(1), 3–10.

Rapple, C. (2018). Understanding and supporting researchers' choices in sharing their publications: the launch of the FairShare Network and Shareable PDF. *Insights*, 31.

Rastogi, A., Arora, R., & Sharma, S. (2015, February). Leaf disease detection and grading using computer vision technology & fuzzy logic. In *2015 2nd international conference on signal processing and integrated networks (SPIN)* (pp. 500-505). IEEE. 10.1109/SPIN.2015.7095350

Ray, P., & Chakrabarti, A. (2020). A mixed approach of deep learning method and rule-based method to improve aspect level sentiment analysis. *Applied Computing and Informatics*, 1-9.

Read, J., & Peter, R. (2012). *MEKA: A multi-label extension to WEKA*. http://meka.sourceforge.net

Read, J., Pfahringer, B., Holmes, G., & Frank, E. (2009). Classifier chains for multi-label classification. In *Proc. of European Conf. on Machine Learning and Knowledge Discovery in Databases: Part II. ECML PKDD '09*. Springer-Verlag. 10.1007/978-3-642-04174-7_17

Read, J. (2008). Multi-label classification using ensembles of pruned sets. *Proc. of 8th IEEE Int. Conf. on Data Mining*, 995-1000. 10.1109/ICDM.2008.74

Read, J. (2010). *Scalable Multi-label Classification*. The University of Waikato.

Rehman, A., Ali, N., Taj, I., Sajid, M., & Karimov, K. S. (2020). An Automatic Mass Screening System for Cervical Cancer Detection Based on Convolutional Neural Network. *Mathematical Problems in Engineering*.

Reza, M. S., & Ma, J. (2018). Imbalanced histopathological breast cancer image classification with convolutional neural network. *2018 14th IEEE International Conference on Signal Processing (ICSP)*, 619–624.

Richhariya, P., & Singh, K, P. (2014). Evaluating and Emerging Payment Card Fraud Challenges and Resolution. *International Journal of Computers and Applications*, *107*(14), 5–10. doi:10.5120/18817-0215

Roberts, K., Roach, M. A., Johnson, J., Guthrie, J., & Harabagiu, S. M. (2012, May). EmpaTweet: Annotating and Detecting Emotions on Twitter. In Lrec (Vol. 12, pp. 3806-3813). Academic Press.

Rout, J. K., Singh, S., Jena, S. K., & Bakshi, S. (2017). Deceptive review detection using labeled and unlabeled data. *Multimedia Tools and Applications*, *76*(3), 3187–3211. doi:10.100711042-016-3819-y

Rout, N., Mishra, D., & Mallick, M. K. (2018). Handling imbalanced data: a survey. In *International Proceedings on Advances in Soft Computing, Intelligent Systems and Applications* (pp. 431–443). Springer. doi:10.1007/978-981-10-5272-9_39

Saini, M., & Susan, S. (2020). Deep transfer with minority data augmentation for imbalanced breast cancer dataset. *Applied Soft Computing*, *97*, 106759.

Salton, G., & Buckley, C. (1988). Term-weighting approaches in automatic text retrieval. *Information Processing & Management*, *24*(5), 513–523. doi:10.1016/0306-4573(88)90021-0

Sane, S. S., & Tidake, V. S. (2020). Efficient Multi-label Classification using Attribute and Instance Selection. *Biosc. Biotech. Res. Comm. Special Issue*, *13*(14), 221–226. doi:10.21786/bbrc/13.14/52

Sarangdhar, A. A., & Pawar, V. R. (2017, April). Machine learning regression technique for cotton leaf disease detection and controlling using IoT. In *2017 International conference of Electronics, Communication and Aerospace Technology (ICECA)* (Vol. 2, pp. 449-454). IEEE.

Sardogan, M., Tuncer, A., & Ozen, Y. (2018, September). Plant leaf disease detection and classification based on CNN with LVQ algorithm. In *2018 3rd International Conference on Computer Science and Engineering (UBMK)* (pp. 382-385). IEEE. 10.1109/UBMK.2018.8566635

Sarkar, D. (2020). *Doubling times of COVID-19 cases*. https://deepayan.github.io/covid-19/doubling

Sasahara, K. (2014). Quantifying Collective Mood by Emoticon Networks. In *WebSci '14: Proceedings of the 2014 ACM conference on Web science*, (pp. 253–254). 10.1145/2615569.2615658

Schuster, M., & Paliwal, K. K. (1997). Bidirectional recurrent neural networks. *IEEE Transactions on Signal Processing*, *45*(11), 2673–2681. doi:10.1109/78.650093

Scott, L. B., & Scott, L. R. (1989). Efficient methods for data smoothing. *SIAM Journal on Numerical Analysis*, *26*(3), 681–692.

Seiffert, C., Khoshgoftaar, T. M., Hulse, J. V., & Napolitano, A. (2010). RUSBoost: A Hybrid Approach to Alleviating Class Imbalance. *IEEE Transactions on Systems, Man, and Cybernetics. Part A, Systems and Humans*, *40*(1), 185–197. doi:10.1109/TSMCA.2009.2029559

Seiffert, C., Khoshgoftaar, T. M., Van Hulse, J., & Napolitano, A. (2008, December). A comparative study of data sampling and cost sensitive learning. In *2008 IEEE International Conference on Data Mining Workshops* (pp. 46-52). IEEE.

SemEval. (2014). https://alt.qcri.org/semeval2014/task-4/

Seol, Y. S., Kim, D. J., & Kim, H. W. (2008, July). Emotion recognition from text using knowledge-based ANN. In *ITC-CSCC: International Technical Conference on Circuits Systems, Computers and Communications* (pp. 1569-1572). Academic Press.

Shaikh, S., Daudpota, S. M., Imran, A. S., & Kastrati, Z. (2021). Towards Improved Classification Accuracy on Highly Imbalanced Text Dataset Using Deep Neural Language Models. *Applied Sciences (Basel, Switzerland)*, *11*(2), 869. doi:10.3390/app11020869

Shapcott, M., Hewitt, K. J., & Rajpoot, N. (2019). Deep learning with sampling in colon cancer histology. *Frontiers in Bioengineering and Biotechnology*, *7*, 52.

Sharma, K., & Lin, K. I. (2013) Review spam detector with rating consistency check. In *Proceedings of the 51st ACM Southeast conference*. ACM. 10.1145/2498328.2500083

Shujian, Yu., Wang, X., & Principe, J. C. (2018). Request-and Reverify: hierarchical hypothesis testing for concept drift detection with expensive labels. In *Proceedings of the Twenty-Seventh International Joint Conference on Artificial Intelligence* (pp. 3033-3039). Academic Press.

Shujian, Yu., Abraham, Z., Wang, H., Shah, M., Wei, Y., & Principe, J. C. (2019). Concept Drift Detection and adaptation with Hierarchical Hypothesis Testing. *Journal of the Franklin Institute*, *356*(5), 3187–3215. doi:10.1016/j.jfranklin.2019.01.043

Silverman, C., & Strapagiel, L. (2016). Hyperpartisan Facebook pages are publishing false and misleading information at an alarming rate. Buzzfeed News 20.

Singh, A., Kumar, P., Pachauri, K., & Singh, K. (2020*).* Drone Ambulance. In *2nd International Conference on Advances in Computing, Communication Control and Networking (ICACCCN)*. IEEE. 10.1109/ICACCCN51052.2020.9362879

Smith, J. R., & Chang, S. F. (1995, October). Single color extraction and image query. *Proceedings - International Conference on Image Processing*, *3*, 528–531.

Somasundaram, A., & Reddy, U. S. (2016). Data Imbalance: Effects and Solutions for Classification of Large and Highly Imbalanced Data, In *Proceedings of International Conference on Research in Engineering, Computers and Technology*, (pp. 28–34). Academic Press.

Somasundaram, A., & Reddy, U. S. (2016). Data imbalance: Effects and solutions for classification of large and highly imbalanced data. In *International Conference on Research in Engineering, Computers and Technology (ICRECT 2016)* (pp. 1-16). Academic Press.

Song, Li, Zeng, Wu, Guo, & Zou. (2014). nDNA-prot: Identification of DNA-binding proteins based on unbalanced classification. *BMC Bioinformatics, 15*(1), 298.

Sotto, L. F., Coelho, R. C., & de Melo, V. V. (2016, July). Classification of cardiac arrhythmia by random forests with features constructed by kaizen programming with linear genetic programming. In *Proceedings of the Genetic and Evolutionary Computation Conference 2016* (pp. 813-820). Academic Press.

Spacy. (2015.). Industrial-Strength Natural Language Processing. https://spacy.io/

Spyromitros-Xioufis, E. (2011). *Dealing with Concept Drift and Class Imbalance in Multi-label Stream Classification.* Thesis.

Spyromitros-Xioufis, E., Tsoumakas, G., & Vlahavas, I. (2008). An empirical study of lazy multi-label classification algorithms. *Proc. 5th Hellenic Conf. Artif. Intell.*, 401–406.

Srivastava, N., Hinton, G., Krizhevsky, A., Sutskever, I., & Salakhutdinov, R. (2014). Dropout: A simple way to prevent neural networks from overfitting. *Journal of Machine Learning Research, 15*(1), 1929–1958.

Stanford. (2008). http://nlp.stanford.edu:8080/parser/

Stefanowski, J., & Wilk, S. (2008). Selective pre-processing of imbalanced data for improving classification performance. *International Conference on Data Warehousing and Knowledge Discovery*, 283–292.

Strapparava, C., & Mihalcea, R. (2008, March). Learning to identify emotions in text. In *Proceedings of the 2008 ACM symposium on Applied computing* (pp. 1556-1560). 10.1145/1363686.1364052

Subramanian, D. (2020b, January 7). *Emotion analysis in text mining | Towards AI.* Medium. https://pub.towardsai.net/emoticon-and-emoji-in-text-mining-7392c49f596a

Sudre, C. H., Li, W., Vercauteren, T., Ourselin, S., & Cardoso, M. J. (2017). Generalised dice overlap as a deep learning loss function for highly unbalanced segmentations. In *Deep learning in medical image analysis and multimodal learning for clinical decision support* (pp. 240–248). Springer.

Sugathadasa, K., Ayesha, B., de Silva, N., Perera, A. S., Jayawardana, V., Lakmal, D., & Perera, M. (2018, July). Legal document retrieval using document vector embeddings and deep learning. In *Proceedings of Science and information conference* (pp. 160-175). Springer.

Suicide: Statistics, Warning Signs and Prevention. (n.d.). Available: https://www.livescience.com/44615suicidehelp.html

Sun, Y., Kamel, M. S., & Wang, Y. (2006). Boosting for learning multiple classes with imbalanced class distribution. In *Proceedings of Sixth IEEE Int. Conf. Data Mining*, (pp. 592–602). 10.1109/ICDM.2006.29

Sun, Y., Kamel, M. S., Wong, A. K. C., & Wang, Y. (2007). Cost-sensitive boosting for classification of imbalanced data. *Pattern Recognition, 40*(12), 3358–3378. doi:10.1016/j.patcog.2007.04.009

Sun, Y., Wong, A., & Kamel, M. S. (2009). Classification of imbalanced data: A review. *International Journal of Pattern Recognition and Artificial Intelligence, 23*(4), 687–719. doi:10.1142/S0218001409007326

Susan, S., & Kumar, A. (2020). The balancing trick: Optimized sampling of imbalanced datasets—A brief survey of the recent State of the Art. *Engineering Reports*, e12298.

Suttles, J., & Ide, N. (2013, March). Distant supervision for emotion classification with discrete binary values. In *International Conference on Intelligent Text Processing and Computational Linguistics* (pp. 121-136). Springer. 10.1007/978-3-642-37256-8_11

Sutton, C., & McCallum, A. (2006). An introduction to conditional random fields for relational learning. *Introduction to Statistical Relational Learning, 2*, 93-128.

Sutton, R. S., McAllester, D. A., Singh, S. P., & Mansour, Y. (1999, November). Policy gradient methods for reinforcement learning with function approximation. NIPs, 99, 1057-1063.

Swain, P. H., & Hauska, H. (1977). The decision tree classifier: Design and potential. *IEEE Transactions on Geoscience Electronics, 15*(3), 142–147.

Sykora, M. D., Jackson, T., O'Brien, A., & Elayan, S. (2013). Emotive ontology: Extracting fine-grained emotions from terse, informal messages. *IADIS Int. J. Comput. Sci. Inf. Syst, 2013*, 19–26.

T. (2018a, November 16). *Using Word Embeddings for Data Augmentation.* Kaggle. https://www.kaggle.com/theoviel/using-word-embeddings-for-data-augmentation

T. (2020a, September 7). *Using Google Translate for NLP Augmentation.* Kaggle. https://www.kaggle.com/tuckerarrants/using-google-translate-for-nlp-augmentation

Tacchini, E., Ballarin, G., Della Vedova, M. L., Moret, S., & de Alfaro, L. (2017). *Some like it hoax: Automated fake news detection in social networks.* arXiv preprint arXiv:1704.07506.

Tadesse, M. M., Lin, H., Xu, B., & Yang, L. (2019). Detection of Depression Related Posts in Reddit Social Media Forum. In *IEEE Access* (vol. 7, pp. 44883-44893). doi: 10.1109/ACCESS.2019.2909180

Tajbakhsh, N., Shin, J. Y., Gurudu, S. R., Hurst, R. T., Kendall, C. B., Gotway, M. B., & Liang, J. (2016). Convolutional neural networks for medical image analysis: Full training or fine tuning? *IEEE Transactions on Medical Imaging, 35*(5), 1299–1312.

Tammy & Wimpee. (2017, Dec 9). *Convolutional Neural Networks (CNNs) Explained* [Video post]. Deeplizard. https://deeplizard.com/learn/video/YRhxdVk_sIs

Tang, Y., & Wang, S. (2020). Mathematic modeling of COVID-19 in the United States. *Emerging Microbes & Infections, 9*(1), 827–829.

Tavallaee, M., Bagheri, E., Lu, W., & Ali, A. G. (2009). A Detailed Analysis of the KDD CUP 99 Data Set. In *Proceedings of the IEEE Symposium on Computational Intelligence on Security and Defense Applications,* (pp. 1-6). 10.1109/CISDA.2009.5356528

Tegjyoth, S. S., & Kantardzic, M. (2017). On the reliable detection of concept drift from streaming unlabeled data. *Expert Systems with Applications: An International Journal, 82*(C), 77–99.

Tharwat, A., & Schenck, W. (2020). Balancing Exploration and Exploitation: A novel active learner for imbalanced data. *Knowledge-Based Systems, 210*, 106500. doi:10.1016/j.knosys.2020.106500

Tidake, V. S., & Sane, S. S. (2018). Multi-label Classification: A Survey. *International Journal of Engineering and Technology, 7*(4.19), 1045-1054.

Tidake, V. S., & Sane, S. S. (2021). Effect of Distance Metrics on Multi-label Classification. In *Proceeding of First Doctoral Symposium on Natural Computing Research, Lecture Notes in Networks and Systems 169.* Springer Nature Singapore Pte Ltd.

Tidake, V. S., & Sane, S. S. (2016). Multi-label learning with MEKA. *CSI Communications, 2016*(August issue), 33–37.

Tomokiyo, T., & Hurst, M. (2003). A language model approach to keyphrase extraction. *Proceedings of the ACL 2003 workshop on Multiword expressions: analysis, acquisition and treatment*, 33-40. 10.3115/1119282.1119287

Trattner, C., & Kappe, F. (2013). Social stream marketing on Facebook: A case study. *International Journal of Social and Humanistic Computing, 2*(1-2), 86–103. doi:10.1504/IJSHC.2013.053268

Tripadvisor. (2000). http://www.tripadvisor,in

Trivedi, A., Trivedi, A., Varshney, S., Joshipura, V., Mehta, R., & Dhanani, J. (2020). Extracted Summary Based Recommendation System for Indian Legal Documents. In *Proceedings of 2020 11th International Conference on Computing, Communication and Networking Technologies (ICCCNT)* (pp. 1-6). IEEE.

Trohidis, K. (2008). Multi-Label Classification of Music into Emotions. *ISMIR, 8.*

Tsoumakas, G., & Katakis, I. (2008). Effective and efficient multi-label classification in domains with large number of labels. *Proc. Work. Notes ECML PKDD Workshop MMD.*

Tsoumakas, G., Zhang, M. L., & Zhou, Z. H. (2009). *Tutorial on learning from multi-label data, in ECML PKDD.* Available: http://www.ecmlpkdd2009.net/wpcontent/uploads/2009/08/learning-from-multi-label-data.pdf

Tsoumakas, G. (2010). *Mining multi-label data.* In O. Maimon & L. Rokach (Eds.), *Data Mining and Knowledge Discovery Handbook* (pp. 667–686). Springer.

Tsoumakas, G., & Katakis, I. (2007). Multi-label classification: An overview. *International Journal of Data Warehousing and Mining, 3*(3), 1–13. doi:10.4018/jdwm.2007070101

Tsoumakas, G., Katakis, I., & Vlahavas, I. (2011). Random k-Labelsets for Multi-Label Classification. *IEEE Transactions on Knowledge and Data Engineering, 23*(7), 1079–1089. doi:10.1109/TKDE.2010.164

Tsoumakas, G., Spyromitros-Xioufis, E., Vilcek, J., & Vlahavas, I. (2011). MULAN: A Java library for multi-label learning. *Journal of Machine Learning Research, 12*, 2411–2414.

Tweepy. (2009). https://www.tweepy.org/

Uniyal, N., Eskandari, H., Abolmaesumi, P., Sojoudi, S., Gordon, P., & Warren, L. M. (2014). Ultrasound RF time series for classification of breast lesions. *IEEE Transactions on Medical Imaging, 34*(2), 652–661.

Valentino, N. A., Brader, T., Groenendyk, E. W., Gregorowicz, K., & Hutchings, V. L. (2011). Election night's alright for fighting: The role of emotions in political participation. *The Journal of Politics, 73*(1), 156–170. doi:10.1017/S0022381610000939

Van der Zanden, R., Curie, K., Van Londen, M., Kramer, J., Steen, G., & Cuijpers, P. (2014). Keshia Curie, Monique Van Londen, Jeannet Kramer, Gerard Steen, and Pim Cuijpers. Web-based depression treatment: Associations of clients' word use with adherence and outcome. *Journal of Affective Disorders, 160*, 10–13. doi:10.1016/j.jad.2014.01.005 PMID:24709016

Varol, O., Ferrara, E., Davis, C. A., Menczer, F., & Flammini, A. (2017). *Online human-bot interactions: Detection, estimation, and characterization.* arXiv preprint arXiv:1703.03107.

Veloso, A., Meira, W. Jr, Goncalves, M., & Zaki, M. (2007). Multi-label lazy associative classification. In *PKDD '07: 11th European Conference on Principles and Practice of Knowledge Discovery in Databases.* Springer

Vosoughi, S., Roy, D., & Aral, S. (2018). The spread of true and false news online. *Science, 359*(6380), 1146–1151. doi:10.1126cience.aap9559

Wagh, R. S., & Anand, D. (2020). Legal document similarity: A multi-criteria decision-making perspective. *PeerJ. Computer Science, 6*, 1–20. doi:10.7717/peerj-cs.262 PMID:33816914

Walls, A. C., Park, Y. J., Tortorici, M. A., Wall, A., McGuire, A. T., & Veesler, D. (2020). Structure, function, and antigenicity of the SARS-CoV-2 spike glycoprotein. *Cell, 181*(2), 281–292.

Wang, B., & Liu, M. (2015). Deep learning for aspect-based sentiment analysis. Stanford University report

Wang, J., Sun, C., Li, S., Wang, J., Si, L., Zhang, M., . . . Zhou, G. (2019). Human-like decision making: Document-level aspect sentiment classification via hierarchical reinforcement learning. arXiv preprint arXiv:1910.09260. doi:10.18653/v1/D19-1560

Wang, W. Y. (2017). *"Liar, liar pants on fire": A new benchmark dataset for fake news detection.* arXiv preprint arXiv:1705.00648.

Wang, W., Chen, L., Thirunarayan, K., & Sheth, A. P. (2012, September). Harnessing twitter" big data" for automatic emotion identification. In *2012 International Conference on Privacy, Security, Risk and Trust and 2012 International Conference on Social Computing* (pp. 587-592). IEEE.

Wang, A. H. (2010). Detecting spam bots in online social networking sites: a machine learning approach. In *Proceedings of IFIP Annual Conference on Data and Applications Security and Privacy*, (pp. 335-342). Springer. 10.1007/978-3-642-13739-6_25

Wang, B., & Wang, H. (2008). Bootstrapping both product features and opinion words from chinese customer reviews with cross-inducing. *Proceedings of the Third International Joint Conference on Natural Language Processing*.

Wang, H., & Abraham, Z. (2015). Concept Drift Detection for Streaming Data. *International Joint Conference of Neural Networks*.

Wang, J., Zhang, J., Luo, C., & Chen, F. (2012). Joint Head Pose and Facial Landmark Regression from Depth Images. *Computational Visual Media, 3*(3), 229–241. doi:10.100741095-017-0082-8

Wang, S., Ding, Y., Zhao, W., Huang, Y., Perkins, R., Zou, W., & Chen, J. J. (2016). Text mining for identifying topics in the literature about adolescent substance use and depression. *BMC Public Health, 16*, 279.

Wang, S., Minku, L. L., Ghezzi, D., Caltabiano, D., Tino, P., & Yao, X. (2013). Concept drift detection for online class imbalance learning. In *International Joint Conference on Neural Networks (IJCNN)* (1-10). 10.1109/IJCNN.2013.6706768

Wang, S., Minku, L. L., & Yao, M. (2015). Resampling-Based Ensemble Methods for Online Class Imbalance Learning. *IEEE Transactions on Knowledge and Data Engineering, 27*(5), 1356–1368. doi:10.1109/TKDE.2014.2345380

Wang, S., Minku, L. L., & Yao, X. (2013). Online Class Imbalance Learning and Its Applications in Fault Detection. *Special Issue of International Journal of Computational Intelligence and Applications, 12*(4), 1–19. doi:10.1142/S1469026813400014

Wang, S., Minku, L. L., & Yao, X. (2018). A Systematic Study of Online Class Imbalance Learning with Concept Drift. *IEEE Transactions on Neural Networks and Learning Systems, 29*(10), 4802–4821. doi:10.1109/TNNLS.2017.2771290 PMID:29993955

Wang, S., & Yao, X. (2009). Diversity analysis on imbalanced data sets by using ensemble models. In *IEEE Symposium on Computational Intelligence and Data Mining* (pp. 324-331). 10.1109/CIDM.2009.4938667

Wang, S., & Yao, X. (2012). Multiclass imbalance problems: Analysis and potential solutions. *IEEE Transactions on Systems, Man, and Cybernetics. Part B, Cybernetics*, *42*(4), 1119–1130.

Wang, S., & Yao, X. (2012). Multiclass Imbalance Problems: Analysis and Potential Solutions. *IEEE Transactions on Systems, Man, and Cybernetics. Part B, Cybernetics*, *42*(4), 1119–1130. doi:10.1109/tsmcb.2012.2187280

Wang, T., Zhou, J., Hu, Q. V., & He, L. (2019). Aspect-level sentiment classification with reinforcement learning. In *2019 International Joint Conference on Neural Networks (IJCNN)*, 1-8.

Wang, W. Y., & Yang, D. (2015, September). That's so annoying!!!: A lexical and frame-semantic embedding based data augmentation approach to automatic categorization of annoying behaviors using# petpeeve tweets. In *Proceedings of the 2015 Conference on Empirical Methods in Natural Language Processing* (pp. 2557-2563). 10.18653/v1/D15-1306

Wang, X., & Zheng, Q. (2013, March). Text emotion classification research based on improved latent semantic analysis algorithm. In *Proceedings of the 2nd International Conference on Computer Science and Electronics Engineering* (pp. 210-213). Atlantis Press. 10.2991/iccsee.2013.55

Wang, Y., Burke, M., & Kraut, R. (2013). Gender, Topic, and Audience Response: An Analysis of User-Generated Content on Facebook. In *Proceedings of the SIGCHI Conference on Human Factors in Computing Systems* (pp. 31-34). Association for Computing Machinery.

Wan, S., Duan, Y., & Zou, Q. (2017). HPSLPred: An ensemble multi-label classifier for human protein subcellular location prediction with imbalanced source. *Proteomics*, *17*(17-18), 1700262. doi:10.1002/pmic.201700262 PMID:28776938

Ward, M. P., Maftei, D., Apostu, C., & Suru, A. (2009). Estimation of the basic reproductive number (R0) for epidemic, highly pathogenic avian influenza subtype H5N1 spread. *Epidemiology and Infection*, *137*(2), 219–226.

Wasikowski, M., & Chen, X. (2010). Combating the Small Sample Class Imbalance Problem Using Feature Selection. *IEEE Transactions on Knowledge and Data Engineering*, *22*(10), 1388–1400. doi:10.1109/tkde.2009.187

Webb, G. I. (2010). Naïve Bayes. Encyclopedia of Machine Learning, 15, 713-714.

Weiss, G. M., & Provost, F. (2003). Learning when training data are costly: The effect of class distribution on tree induction. *Journal of Artificial Intelligence Research*, *19*, 315–354.

Wei, W., Li, J., Cao, L., Ou, Y., & Chen, J. (2013). Effective detection of sophisticated online banking fraud on extremely imbalanced data. *World Wide Web (Bussum)*, *16*(4), 449–475.

Wen, L., Li, X., & Gao, L. (2019). A transfer convolutional neural network for fault diagnosis based on ResNet-50. *Neural Computing & Applications*, 1–14.

Wiebe, J., Bruce, R., & O'Hara, T. P. (1999). Development and use of a gold-standard data set for subjectivity classifications. *Proceedings of the 37th annual meeting of the Association for Computational Linguistics*, 246-253. 10.3115/1034678.1034721

Willemink, M. J., Koszek, W. A., Hardell, C., Wu, J., Fleischmann, D., Harvey, H., ... Lungren, M. P. (2020). Preparing medical imaging data for machine learning. *Radiology*, *295*(1), 4–15.

Willett, P. (2006). *The Porter stemming algorithm: then and now*. Academic Press.

Wold, S., Esbensen, K., & Geladi, P. (1987). Principal component analysis. *Chemometrics and Intelligent Laboratory Systems*, *2*(1), 37–52. doi:10.1016/0169-7439(87)80084-9

Wright, R. E. (1995). *Logistic regression*. Springer.

Wu, C., Wu, F., Wu, S., Yuan, Z., & Huang, Y. (2018). A hybrid unsupervised method for aspect term and opinion target extraction. *Knowledge-Based Systems, 148*, 66–73. doi:10.1016/j.knosys.2018.01.019

Wu, E., Wu, K., Cox, D., & Lotter, W. (2018). Conditional infilling GANs for data augmentation in mammogram classification. In *Image analysis for moving organ, breast, and thoracic images* (pp. 98–106). Springer.

Wu, G., & Chang, E. Y. (2003). Class-boundary alignment for imbalanced dataset learning. *ICML 2003 Workshop on Learning from Imbalanced Data Sets*.

Wu, T., Wen, S., Xiang, Y., & Zhou, W. (2018). Twitter spam detection: Survey of new approaches and comparative study. *Computers & Security, 76*, 265–284. doi:10.1016/j.cose.2017.11.013

Wu, W., Li, H., Wang, H., & Zhu, K. Q. (2012). Probase: A probabilistic taxonomy for text understanding. *Proceedings of the 2012 ACM SIGMOD International Conference on Management of Data*, 81-492. 10.1145/2213836.2213891

Wu, Y., Zhang, Q., Huang, X. J., & Wu, L. (2009). Phrase dependency parsing for opinion mining. *Proceedings of the 2009 conference on empirical methods in natural language processing*, 1533-1541.

Xiao, H. (2018). *Multi-sourced information trustworthiness analysis: Applications and theory*. Retrieved from https://search.proquest.com/openview/f40c14b131693f2a1ce8cb198041ed99/1?pq-origsite=gscholar&cbl=18750&diss=y

Xie, J., Wang, G., Lin, S., & Philip, S. (2012). Review spam detection via time series pattern discovery. *ACM Proceedings of the 21st international conference companion on World Wide Web*, 635-636.

Xu, B., Ye, Y., & Nie, L. (2012, June). An improved random forest classifier for image classification. In *Proceedings of IEEE International Conference Information Automation* (pp. 795–800). 10.1109/ICInfA.2012.6246927

Xu, L., Liu, K., Lai, S., Chen, Y., & Zhao, J. (2013). Walk and learn: a two-stage approach for opinion words and opinion targets co-extraction. *Proceedings of the 22nd International Conference on World Wide Web*, 95-96. 10.1145/2487788.2487831

Xu, R., & Wunsch, D. (2008). *Clustering* (Vol. 10). John Wiley & Sons. doi:10.1002/9780470382776

Yang, Zhou, Zhu, Ma, & Ji. (2016). Iterative ensemble feature selection for multiclass classification of imbalanced microarray data. *J. Biol. Res. Thessaloniki.*

Yan, Z., Xing, M., Zhang, D., & Ma, B. (2015). EXPRS: An extended pagerank method for product feature extraction from online consumer reviews. *Information & Management, 52*(7), 850–858. doi:10.1016/j.im.2015.02.002

Yen, S.-J., & Lee, Y.-S. (2006). Under-sampling approaches for improving prediction of the minority class in an imbalanced dataset. In *Intelligent Control and Automation* (pp. 731–740). Springer.

Yoo, S., Gujrathi, I., Haider, M. A., & Khalvati, F. (2019). Prostate cancer detection using deep convolutional neural networks. *Scientific Reports, 9*(1), 1–10.

You, Z., Qian, T., Zhang, B., & Ying, S. (2016). Identifying Implicit Enterprise Users from the Imbalanced Social Data. In *International Conference on Web Information Systems Engineering* (pp. 94-101). Springer International Publishing. 10.1007/978-3-319-48743-4_8

Yu, J., Zha, Z. J., Wang, M., & Chua, T. S. (2011). Aspect ranking: identifying important product aspects from online consumer reviews. *Proceedings of the 49th annual meeting of the association for computational linguistics: human language technologies*, 496-1505.

Zahiri, S. M., & Choi, J. D. (2017). *Emotion detection on tv show transcripts with sequence-based convolutional neural networks*. arXiv preprint arXiv:1708.04299.

Zakaryazad, A., & Duman, E. (2016). A profit-driven Artificial Neural Network (ANN) with applications to fraud detection and direct marketing. *Neurocomputing*, *175*, 121–131. doi:10.1016/j.neucom.2015.10.042

Zar, J. H. (2005). Spearman rank correlation. Encyclopedia of Biostatistics, 7.

Zeng, M., Zou, B., Wei, F., Liu, X., & Wang, L. (2016). Effective prediction of three common diseases by combining SMOTE with Tomek links technique for imbalanced medical data. *2016 IEEE International Conference of Online Analysis and Computing Science (ICOACS)*, 225–228.

Zhang, C. (2019). *Medical image classification under class imbalance*. Academic Press.

Zhang, S., Liu, L., Zhu, X., & Zhang, C. (2008). A strategy for attributes selection in cost-sensitive decision trees induction. *2008 IEEE 8th International Conference on Computer and Information Technology Workshops*, 8–13.

Zhang, X., Zhao, J., & LeCun, Y. (2015). *Character-level convolutional networks for text classification*. arXiv preprint arXiv:1509.01626.

Zhang, H., Liu, W., Shan, J., & Liu, Q. (2018). Online Active Learning Paired Ensemble for Concept Drift and Class imbalance. *IEEE Access: Practical Innovations, Open Solutions*, *99*, 1–1. doi:10.1109/ACCESS.2018.2882872

Zhang, J., Chen, L., & Abid, F. (2019). Prediction of Breast Cancer from Imbalance Respect Using Cluster-Based Undersampling Method. *Journal of Healthcare Engineering*.

Zhang, L., Liu, B., Lim, S. H., & O'Brien-Strain, E. (2010). Extracting and ranking product features in opinion documents. In *Coling 2010* (pp. 1462–1470). Posters.

Zhang, L., Lu, L., Nogues, I., Summers, R. M., Liu, S., & Yao, J. (2017). DeepPap: Deep convolutional networks for cervical cell classification. *IEEE Journal of Biomedical and Health Informatics*, *21*(6), 1633–1643.

Zhang, M. L., Li, Y.-K., Liu, X.-Y., & Geng, X. (2018). Binary relevance for multi-label learning: An overview. *Frontiers of Computer Science*, *12*(2), 191–202. doi:10.100711704-017-7031-7

Zhang, M. L., Li, Y.-K., Yang, H., & Liu, X.-Y. (2020). Towards Class-Imbalance Aware Multi-Label Learning. *IEEE Transactions on Cybernetics*, *2020*, 1–13. doi:10.1109/TCYB.2020.3027509 PMID:33206614

Zhang, M. L., & Zhou, Z. H. (2005). A k-nearest neighbor based algorithm for multi-label classification. *IEEE International Conference on Granular Computing*, 718-721. 10.1109/GRC.2005.1547385

Zhang, M. L., & Zhou, Z. H. (2007). ML-KNN: A lazy learning approach to multi-label learning. *Pattern Recognition*, *40*(7), 2038–2048. doi:10.1016/j.patcog.2006.12.019

Zhang, M. L., & Zhou, Z. H. (2014). A Review on Multi-Label Learning Algorithms. Knowledge and Data Engineering. *IEEE Transactions on.*, *26*(8), 1819–1837. doi:10.1109/TKDE.2013.39

Zhang, Q., Lipani, A., Liang, S., & Yilmaz, E. (2019). Reply-Aided Detection of Misinformation via Bayesian Deep Learning. In *The Web Conference 2019*. ACM Press.

Zhang, X., Yang, T., & Srinivasan, P. (2016).4 Online Asymmetric Active Learning with Imbalanced Data. In *Proceedings of the 22nd ACM SIGKDD International Conference on Knowledge Discovery and Data Mining* (pp. 2055-2064). 10.1145/2939672.2939854

Zhao, C., Xin, Y., Li, X., Yang, Y., & Chen, Y. (2020). A heterogeneous ensemble learning framework for spam detection in social networks with imbalanced data. *Applied Sciences (Basel, Switzerland)*, *10*(3), 936. doi:10.3390/app10030936

Zhao, P., & Hoi, S. C. H. (2013). Cost-Sensitive Online Active Learning with application to malicious URL detection. In *Proceedings of the 19th ACM SIGKDD International Conference on Knowledge Discovery and Data Mining* (pp. 919-927). 10.1145/2487575.2487647

Zhao, Y., Wong, Z. S.-Y., & Tsui, K. L. (2018). A framework of rebalancing imbalanced healthcare data for rare events' classification: A case of look-alike sound-alike mix-up incident detection. *Journal of Healthcare Engineering*.

Zhen, S., Cheng, M., Tao, Y., Wang, Y., Juengpanich, S., Jiang, Z., ... Lue, J. (2020). Deep learning for accurate diagnosis of liver tumor based on magnetic resonance imaging and clinical data. *Frontiers in Oncology*, *10*, 680.

Zhou, D., Bousquet, O., Lal, T. N., Weston, J., & Schölkopf, B. (2004). Learning with local and global consistency. *Advances in Neural Information Processing Systems*, *16*(16), 321–328.

Zhou, L., Liu, J. M., Dong, X. P., McGoogan, J. M., & Wu, Z. Y. (2020). COVID-19 seeding time and doubling time model: An early epidemic risk assessment tool. *Infectious Diseases of Poverty*, *9*(1), 1–9.

Zhou, Z.-H., & Liu, X.-Y. (2006). Training cost-sensitive neural networks with methods addressing the class imbalance problem. *IEEE Transactions on Knowledge and Data Engineering*, *18*(1), 63–77. doi:10.1109/tkde.2006.17

Zhu, S., Ji, X., Xu, W., & Gong, Y. (2005). Multi-labelled classification using maximum entropy method. *SIGIR: '05: 27th Annual ACM Conference on Research and Development in Information Retrieval*, 274-281.

Zhu, J., Wang, H., Zhu, M., Tsou, B. K., & Ma, M. (2011). Aspect-based opinion polling from customer reviews. *IEEE Transactions on Affective Computing*, *2*(1), 37–49. doi:10.1109/T-AFFC.2011.2

Zliobaite, I., Bifet, A., Pfahringer, A., & Holmes, G. (2014). Active learning with drifting streaming data. *IEEE Transactions on Neural Networks and Learning Systems*, *25*(1), 27–39. doi:10.1109/TNNLS.2012.2236570 PMID:24806642

zol. (2010). https://www.zol.com/

Zubiaga, A., Aker, A., Bontcheva, K., Liakata, M., & Procter, R. (2018). Detection and resolution of rumours in social media: A survey. *ACM Computing Surveys*, *51*(2), 32. doi:10.1145/3161603

About the Contributors

Dipti P. Rana is working as Assistant Professor in the Computer Engineering Department, Sardar Vallabhbhai National Institute of Technology (SVNIT), Surat, India. She completed her Ph.D. in from SVNIT, Surat. She has 21+ years of experience in teaching. She delivers expert talks at national and research organizations. She supervised 15+ M. Tech. theses and currently supervising 5+ Ph.D. students. She published many papers in reputed conferences and international journals and served as reviewer in international conferences and peer reviewed journals. She published a book on "Temporal Association Rule Based Models for Weather Prediction". Her current area of research includes Big Data Mining especially in the field of imbalanced data, health data, social network and legal data, machine learning, artificial intelligence and high performance computing.

Rupa G. Mehta is working as Associate Professor in the Computer Engineering Department, Sardar Vallabhbhai National Institute of Technology (SVNIT), Surat, India. She completed her Ph.D. in from SVNIT, Surat. She has 25+ years of experience in teaching. She delivers expert talks at national and research organizations. She supervised 15+ M. Tech. theses and currently supervising 5+ Ph.D. students. She published many papers in reputed conferences and international journals and served as reviewer in international conferences and peer reviewed journals. She published books "A Novel Approach for High Dimensional Data Clustering" and "Decision Tree Algorithms for Concept Drifted Data Stream". Her current area of research includes Big Data Analytics, social network mining and legal data mining, machine learning and artificial intelligence.

* * *

Isha Agarwal received her ME in Computer Engineering from the GTU in 2015. In 2015 she was hired as Assistant Professor by Uka Tarsadia University. She is currently pursuing Ph.D. from SVNIT. She has published several papers in national and international journals.

Amogh Agrawal pursued his B.Tech in Computer Engineering from Sardar Vallabhbhai National Institute of Technology, Surat. He is currently working as a member technical in Quality and Test engineering in De Shaw. His research interests include Machine learning.

Debapriya Banik is pursuing PhD under CSIR-SRF direct scheme in the Department of Computer Science and Engineering, Jadavpur University, Kolkata, India. He received his M.Tech degree in Computer Science and Engineering from Tripura University (A central university), India in 2015 with gold medal and B.Tech degree from NIT Agartala, India in 2011. He visited Medical University of Vienna, Austria as a visiting research scholar. His current research interests include Image processing, Deep learning, and Medical image analysis.

Debotosh Bhattacharjee is working as a full professor in the Department of Computer Science and Engineering, Jadavpur University with fourteen years of post-PhD experience. His research interests pertain to the applications of machine learning techniques for Face Recognition, Gait Analysis, Hand Geometry Recognition, and Diagnostic Image Analysis. He has authored or coauthored more than 250 journals, conference publications, including several book chapters in the areas of Biometrics and Medical Image Processing. Two US patents have been granted on his works. Prof. Bhattacharjee has been granted sponsored projects by the Govt. of India with a total amount of around INR 2 Crore.

Tushar Biswas is pursuing B.Tech. in Electronics and Instrumentation Engineering from Galgotias College of Engineering and Technology, Greater Noida. His area of interest is Image Processing, Machine Learning and Artificial Intelligence, Embedded System.He has already published a research paper in IEEE with title ,"Autonomous Robot to Perform Touchless Assistance for Doctors" and one Patent in IPR (Intellectual Property Rights), India.

Karan Chevli received the B.Tech. in Computer Engineering from Sardar Vallabhbhai National Institute of Technology, Surat. His research interests include Machine Learning, Natural Language Processing, and Big Data analytics. Currently, he is working as a Software Development Engineer at Mastercard.

Mitali Desai received her M.E. degree in Computer Engineering from Sarvajanik College of Engineering and Technology, Surat. She is pursuing her Ph.D. in Computer Engineering at Sardar Vallabhbhai National Institute of Technology (SVNIT), Surat. Her research areas are Data Mining, Web Mining, Social Network Analysis and Big Data Analytics.

Jenish Dhanani obtained his B.Tech and M.E degree in Computer Engineering from Sardar Vallabhbhai National Institute of Technology, Surat and Sarvajanik College of Engineering & Technology, Surat, India respectively. He is currently pursuing a PhD from Sardar Vallabhbhai National Institute of Technology, Surat, India. He published many papers in reputed international journals and conferences. His research interests comprise Big data mining, Stream Data Analytics, Machine Learning and Natural Language Processing.

Preeti Dhiman is working as Assistant Professor in Electronics and Instrumentation Department, Galgotias College of Engineering and Technology. Her area of research includes Image Processing, Machine Learning, Artificial Intelligence and IoT and Embedded System.

D. Himaja is pursuing her Ph.D. at Vignan's Foundation for Science, Technology and Research (Deemed to be University), Vadlamudi, Guntur, India. She worked as Junior Research Fellow for Defense Research and Development Organization (DRDO) sanctioned project where Center for Artificial Intelligence and Robotics (CAIR, Bangalore) acted as reviewing lab. Her research interests include Machine Learning and Data Mining.

Rahul Lad obtained his B.Tech degree in Computer Engineering from Sardar Vallabhbhai National Institute of Technology, Surat, India respectively. His research interests comprise Machine Learning, Data Science and Natural Language Processing. He is currently working as Associate Software Engineer at Tekion, Bangalore, India.

Praveen Kumar Maduri is Dean Academics and HoD (Electronics and Instrumentation Department), Galgotias College of Engineering and Technology. He did his PhD from Leicester University, Leicestershire, England. His area of research includes Signal Processing, Biomedical Instrumentation, Machine Learning, Artificial Intelligence and IoT.

Soumen Maji is an Assistant Professor in the Department of Civil Engineering, Central Institute of Technology (CIT) Kokrajhar. He completed his M.Tech and Ph. D. degree from the Indian Institute of Technology (IIT) Kharagpur in 2013 and 2018 respectively. He has total of six years of experience in teaching and research. He has published many research papers in reputed journals and also attended many international conferences. His general areas of research interests are sediment transport, applied hydrodynamics, turbulence, and other recent trends. Presently, he is engaged in studying various hydrodynamics related problems and study on covid-19 infection spreading using theoretical models.

Arunendu Mondal completed his Ph.D. in Science from Indian Association for the Cultivation of Science, Kolkata, India on the year 1998. From 1998 to 2004 he worked as postdoctoral researcher at different Universities like N.S.Y.S.U., Taiwan; University of South Florida, USA; University of Oklahoma, USA and Syracuse University, USA. On the year 2005, he joined as Assistant Professor and head at the Department of Engineering Sciences and Humanities at Siliguri Institute of Technology. Currently he is serving as Associate Professor and head at the Department of Chemistry, Central Institute of Technology, Kokrajhar, Assam, India. Till date he published 28 research papers in reputed international journals. His field of research covers a broad range of material chemistry and study on covid-19 infection spreading using theoretical models.

Anjali S. More is Assistant Professor in Department of Computer Engineering, Suman Ramesh Tulsiani Technical Campus Faculty of Engineering Pune and PhD Research Scholar at National Institute of Technology (SVNIT), Surat, India. She completed her ME (Computer Science Engineering) from Walchand Institute of Technology Solapur. She has several years of experience in teaching and research, also published many papers in reputed international journals and conferences. Her area of research includes Big Data Mining, Imbalanced Data Mining, intrusion Detection, etc. She is guiding several UG Students at SRTTC FoE.

P. Radha Krishna is currently a Professor at NIT Warangal, Telangana, India. Prior to this he was a Principal Research Scientist at Infosys Labs, Infosys Limited, Hyderabad, India. Prior to joining Infosys, he was a faculty at the Institute for Development and Research in Banking Technology (IDRBT) and a Scientist at the National Informatics Centre, India. His research interests include datawarehousing, data mining, and electronic contracts and services.

T. Maruthi Padmaja received the Ph.D. degree in computer Science and Engineering from University of Hyderabad (HCU), Hyderabad, India. Prior to that she received MTech degree from Tezpur

University, India. Her research interests include Data Mining and Machine Learning. She is currently a Faculty Member of the Department of Information Technology, Vardhaman College of Engineering, Shamshabad Rd, Kacharam, Hyderabad, Telangana, India.

Shreyas Kishorkumar Patel received the B.Tech. in Computer Engineering from Sardar Vallabhbhai National Institute of Technology, Surat. His research interests include Machine Learning, Natural Language Processing, and Data Mining. Currently, he is working as a Software Engineer at Samsung R&D Institute India-Delhi (SRI-D).

Jashwanth Reddy completed his B.Tech in Computer Engineering from Sardar Vallabhbhai National Institute of Technology. He is interested in the fields of Computer Vision, Internet of Things and Machine Learning.

Navodita Saini is a post-graduate student of Master of Technology in Computer Science and Engineering Department, Sardar Vallabhbhai National Institute of Technology, Surat, India.

Shirish Sane obtained his Bachelors Degree in Computer Engineering from PICT, Pune (1987), M. Tech (CSE) from IIT Bombay (1995) and Ph D (Computer Engineering) from COEP, Pune (2009). He is currently working as Chairman BOS in Computer Applications and member BOS in Comp Engineering, SPPU, Pune. He is a fellow of IE(I) and IETE, Life member of CSI and ISTE. He has worked as Regional Vice President for CSI Region VI (Maharashtra & Goa). He has authored text books on Data structures and Theory of Computations and published more than 80 research papers in national and International journals and Conferences. In all five research scholars have completed their Ph D program under his supervision.

Apurbalal Senapati serves as an Assistant Professor for the last six years at Central Institute of Technology Kokrajhar, India. He received his MTech and Ph.D. degrees from Indian Statistical Institute, Kolkata, India. He has also industry experience of four years as a Software Engineer in Anshin Software (P) Ltd., Kolkata India. He received a Postdoctoral Fellowship from CIMAT, Mexico. He has numerous publications, including several book chapters, International Journals, and Conferences. Dr. Senapati attended many national and international conferences in India and abroad (Bulgaria, Mexico, Singapore, Malaysia, Vietnam, Nepal, etc.). His current research area is Natural Language Processing, Machine Learning, Data Science, etc.

Kushagra Singh has done B.Tech. in Electronics and Instrumentation Engineering from Galgotias College of Engineering and Technology, Greater Noida, affiliated to AKTU. His area of interest is Image Processing, Machine Learning, Artificial Intelligence, and Embedded systems with expertise in Renewable energy and Agricultural technologies. He has published more than 10 research papers in IEEE and 3 in IOP science. He has also published over 15 Indian patents and 2 Australian patents.

Apurva Soni has done B.Tech. in Electronics and Instrumentation Engineering from Galgotias College of Engineering and Technology, Greater Noida, affiliated to AKTU. Her area of interest is Image Processing, Artificial Intelligence, and Embedded systems with expertise in Renewable energy and

Agricultural technologies. She has published 2 research papers in IEEE and 3 in IOP science. she has also published over 6 Indian patents and 1 Australian patents.

Vaishali S. Tidake obtained her Bachelors Degree in Computer Engineering from KKWCOE, Nashik in 1999, M. E. (CSE-IT) from VIT, Pune in 2008 and Ph. D. (Computer Engineering) from MCERC, Nashik, SPPU in (2021). She is currently working as Associate Professor in Dept. of Computer Engineering, MVPS's KBT College of Engineering Nashik. She has published several research papers in national and international journals and conferences.

Bharat Tidke is currently working as an Assistant Professor at Vellore Institute of Technology and did his MTech and PhD from Sardar Vallabhbhai National Institute of Technology, Surat. His areas of interest include Data Analytics, Big data, and Social network analysis.

Shivani Vora is Assistant Professor in Department of Computer Engineering, Chhotubhai Gopalbhai Patel Institute of Technology (CGPIT), UTU, Bardoli and PhD Research Scholar at National Institute of Technology (SVNIT), Surat, India. She completed her M.Tech (Research) in Computer Engineering from Sardar Vallabhbhai National Institute of Technology, Surat. She has several years of experience in teaching and research, also published many papers in reputed international journals and conferences. Her area of research includes Data Mining, Machine Learning, Natural Language Processing, Artificial Intelligence, etc. She is guiding several UG and PG Students at CGPIT, UTU, Bardoli.

Index

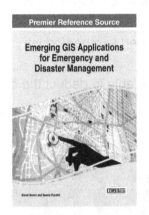
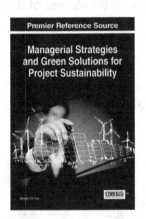

www.igi-global.com

IGI Global's Transformative Open Access (OA) Model:
How to Turn Your University Library's Database Acquisitions Into a Source of OA Funding

Well in advance of Plan S, IGI Global unveiled their OA Fee Waiver (Read & Publish) Initiative. Under this initiative, librarians who invest in IGI Global's InfoSci-Books and/or InfoSci-Journals databases will be able to subsidize their patrons' OA article processing charges (APCs) when their work is submitted and accepted (after the peer review process) into an IGI Global journal.

How Does it Work?

Step 1: **Library Invests in the InfoSci-Databases:** A library perpetually purchases or subscribes to the InfoSci-Books, InfoSci-Journals, or discipline/subject databases.

Step 2: **IGI Global Matches the Library Investment with OA Subsidies Fund:** IGI Global provides a fund to go towards subsidizing the OA APCs for the library's patrons.

Step 3: **Patron of the Library is Accepted into IGI Global Journal (After Peer Review):** When a patron's paper is accepted into an IGI Global journal, they option to have their paper published under a traditional publishing model or as OA.

Step 4: **IGI Global Will Deduct APC Cost from OA Subsidies Fund:** If the author decides to publish under OA, the OA APC fee will be deducted from the OA subsidies fund.

Step 5: **Author's Work Becomes Freely Available:** The patron's work will be freely available under CC BY copyright license, enabling them to share it freely with the academic community.

Note: *This fund will be offered on an annual basis and will renew as the subscription is renewed for each year thereafter. IGI Global will manage the fund and award the APC waivers unless the librarian has a preference as to how the funds should be managed.*

Hear From the Experts on This Initiative:

"I'm very happy to have been able to make one of my recent research contributions *freely available* along with having access to the *valuable resources* found within IGI Global's InfoSci-Journals database."

– **Prof. Stuart Palmer,**
Deakin University, Australia

"Receiving the support from IGI Global's OA Fee Waiver Initiative *encourages me to continue my research work without any hesitation.*"

– **Prof. Wenlong Liu,** College of Economics and Management at Nanjing University of Aeronautics & Astronautics, China

Printed in the United States
by Baker & Taylor Publisher Services